of the Dawn

3

Story & Art by

Mizuho Kusanagi

Yona of the Dawn

Volume 3

CONTENTS

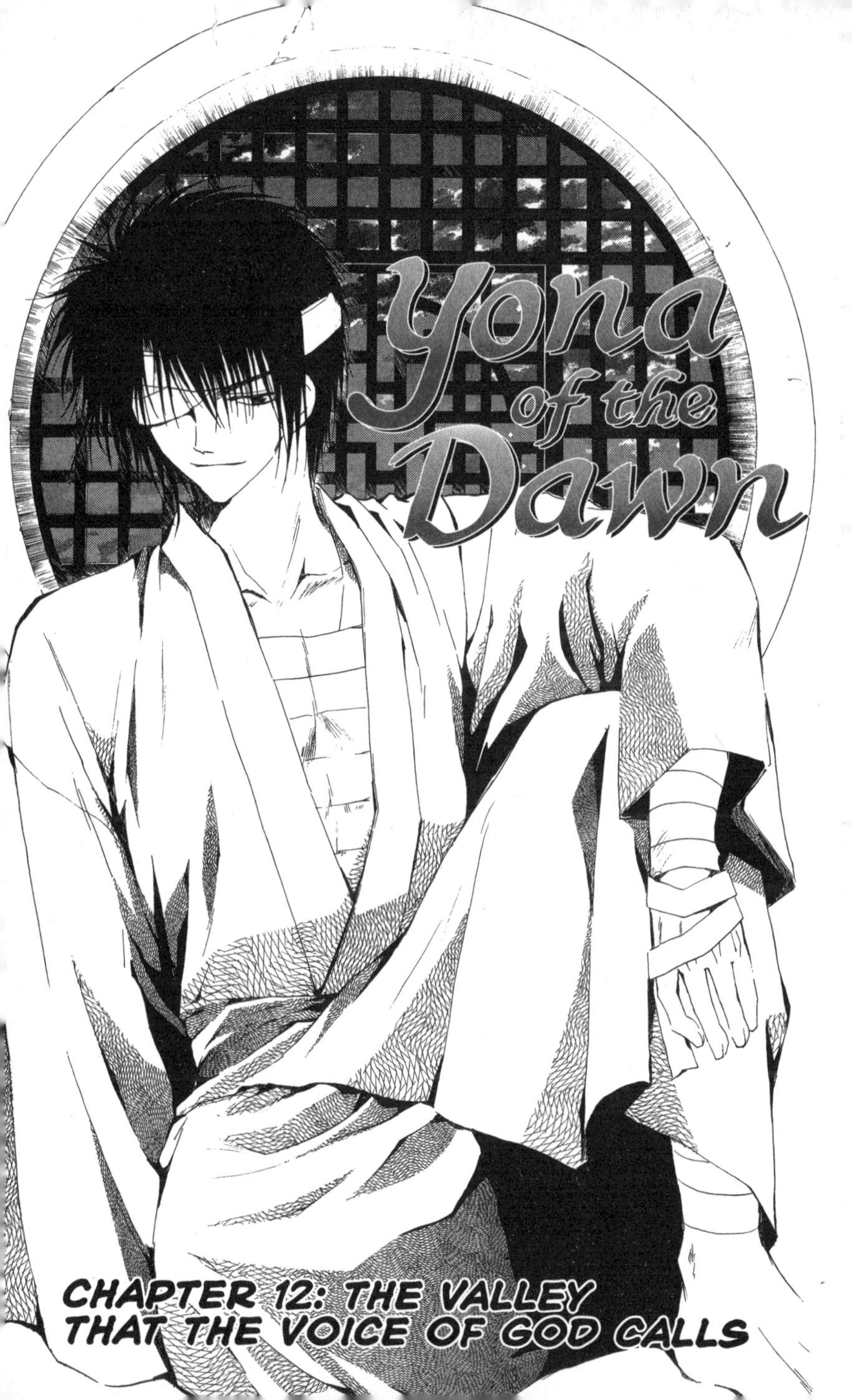
Yona of the Dawn
CHAPTER 12: THE VALLEY THAT THE VOICE OF GOD CALLS

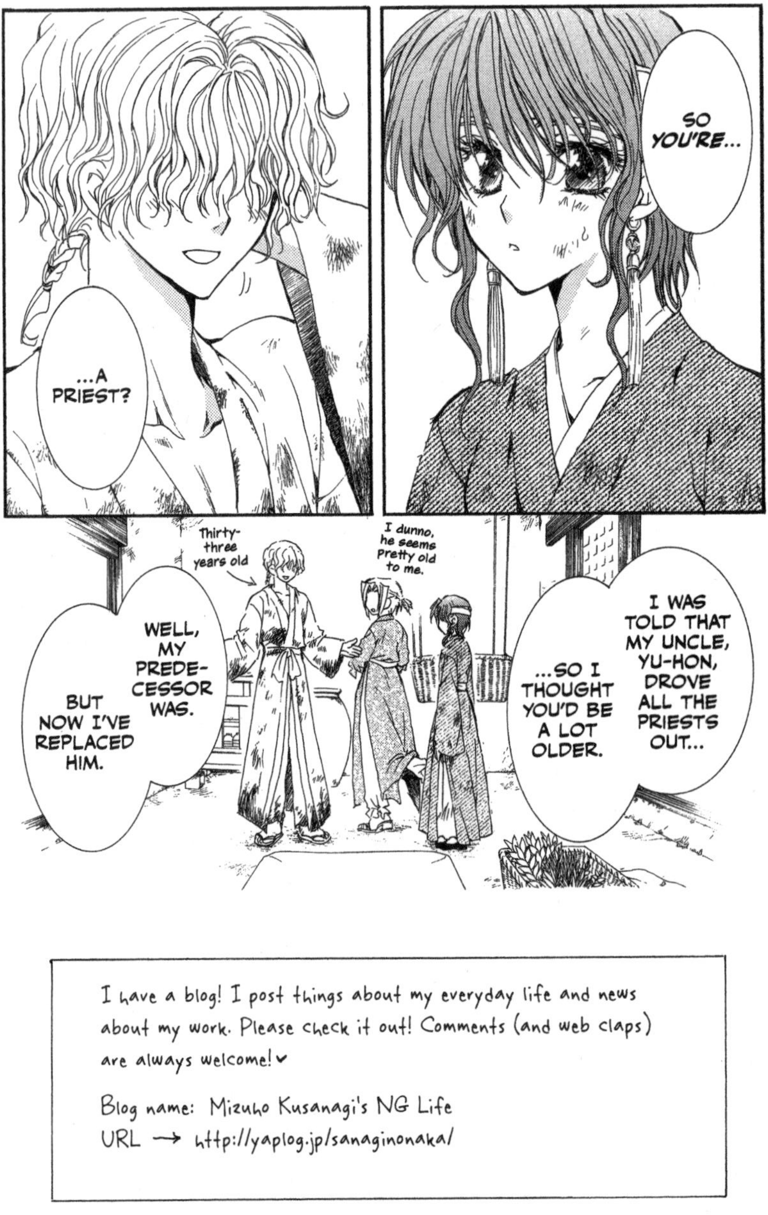
SO YOU'RE...
...A PRIEST?
I WAS TOLD THAT MY UNCLE, YU-HON, DROVE ALL THE PRIESTS OUT...
...SO I THOUGHT YOU'D BE A LOT OLDER.
I dunno, he seems pretty old to me.
Thirty-three years old
WELL, MY PREDE-CESSOR WAS.
BUT NOW I'VE REPLACED HIM.

I have a blog! I post things about my everyday life and news about my work. Please check it out! Comments (and web claps) are always welcome! ✔

Blog name: Mizuho Kusanagi's NG Life
URL → http://yaplog.jp/sanaginonaka/

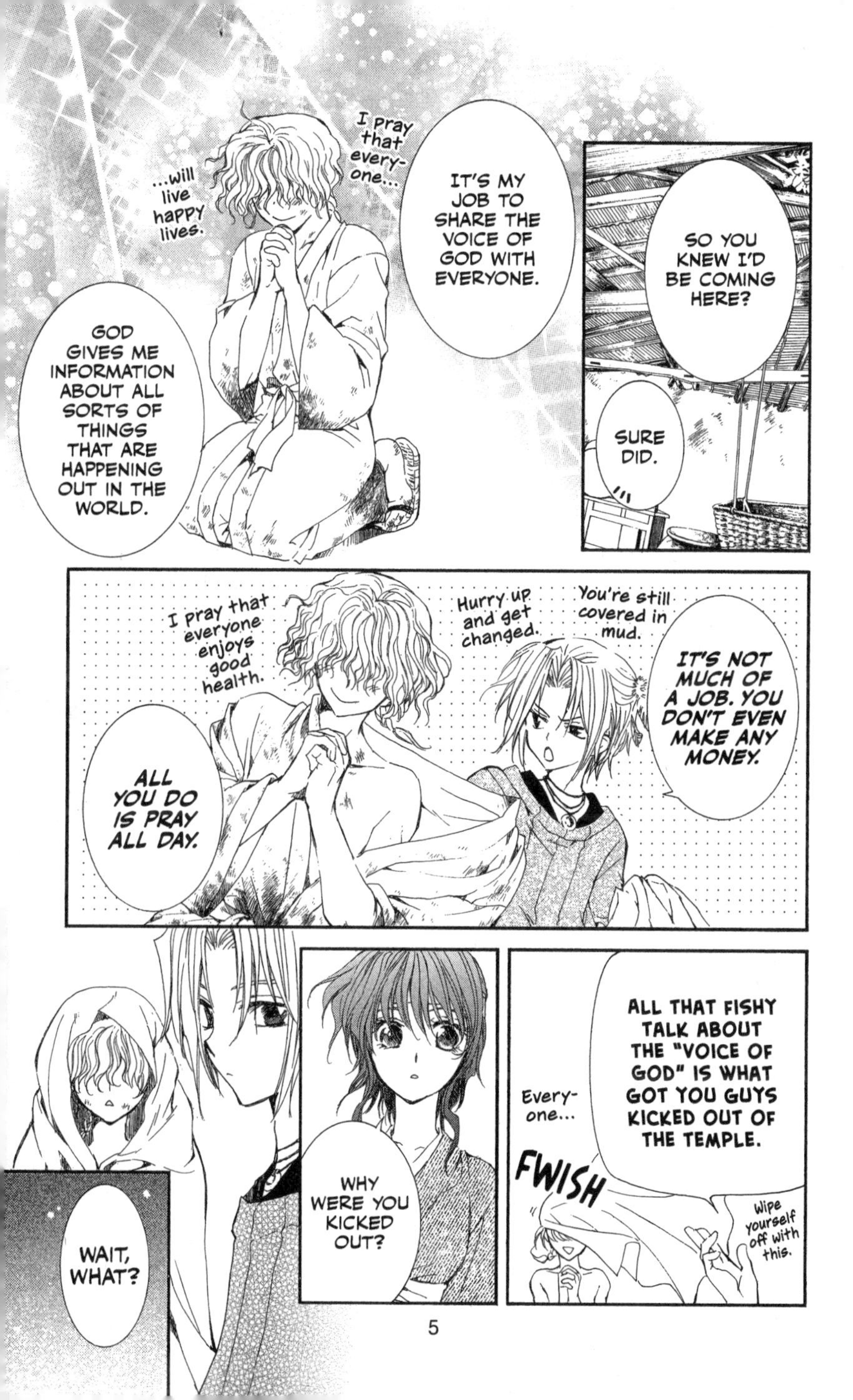
SO YOU KNEW I'D BE COMING HERE?
SURE DID.
IT'S MY JOB TO SHARE THE VOICE OF GOD WITH EVERYONE.
I pray that every-one...
...will live happy lives.
GOD GIVES ME INFORMATION ABOUT ALL SORTS OF THINGS THAT ARE HAPPENING OUT IN THE WORLD.
You're still covered in mud.
IT'S NOT MUCH OF A JOB. YOU DON'T EVEN MAKE ANY MONEY.
Hurry up and get changed.
I pray that everyone enjoys good health.
ALL YOU DO IS PRAY ALL DAY.
ALL THAT FISHY TALK ABOUT THE "VOICE OF GOD" IS WHAT GOT YOU GUYS KICKED OUT OF THE TEMPLE.
Every-one...
FWISH
Wipe yourself off with this.
WHY WERE YOU KICKED OUT?
WAIT, WHAT?

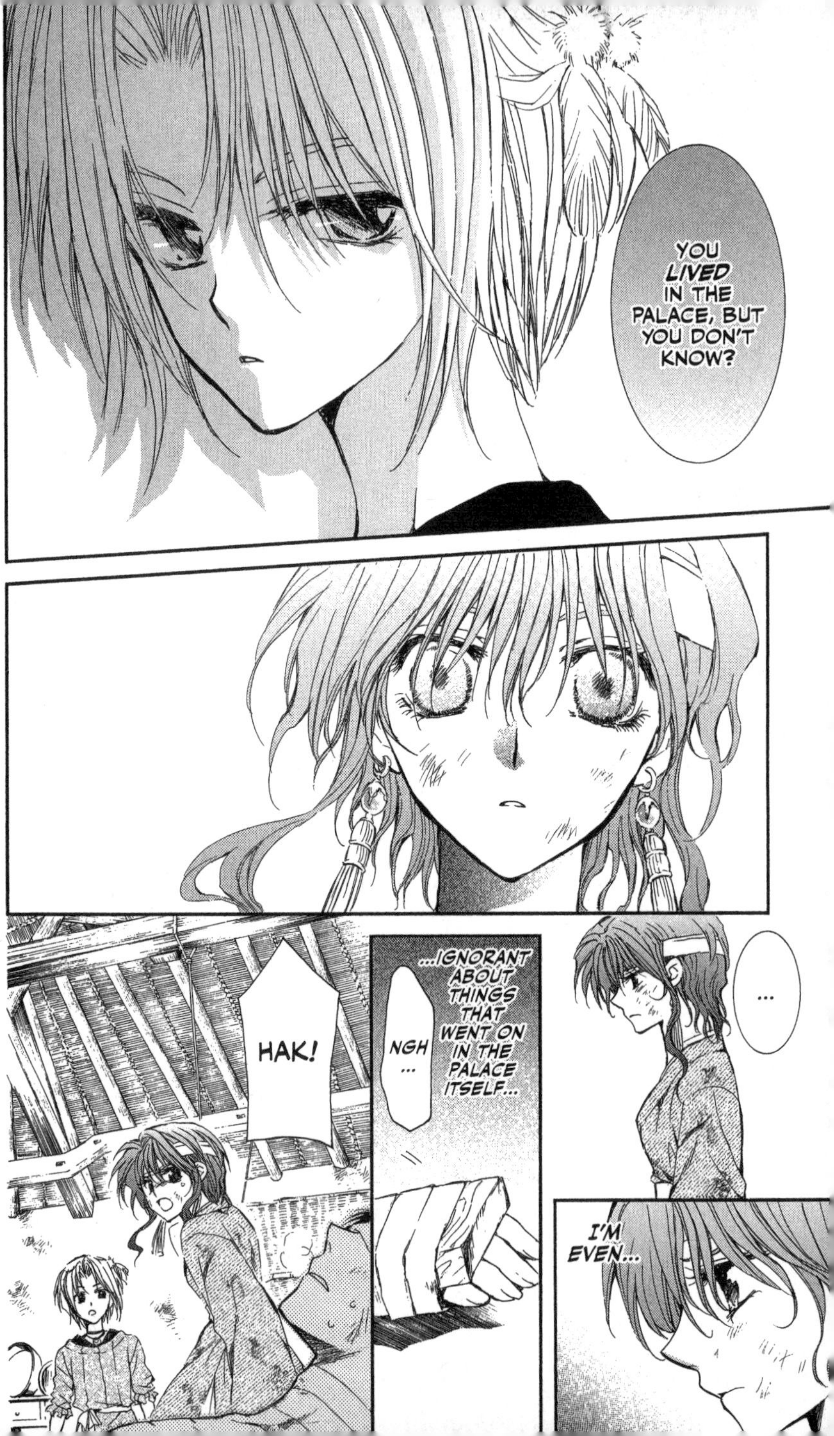
YOU *LIVED* IN THE PALACE, BUT YOU DON'T KNOW?
...
I'M EVEN...
...IGNORANT ABOUT THINGS THAT WENT ON IN THE PALACE ITSELF...
NGH...
HAK!

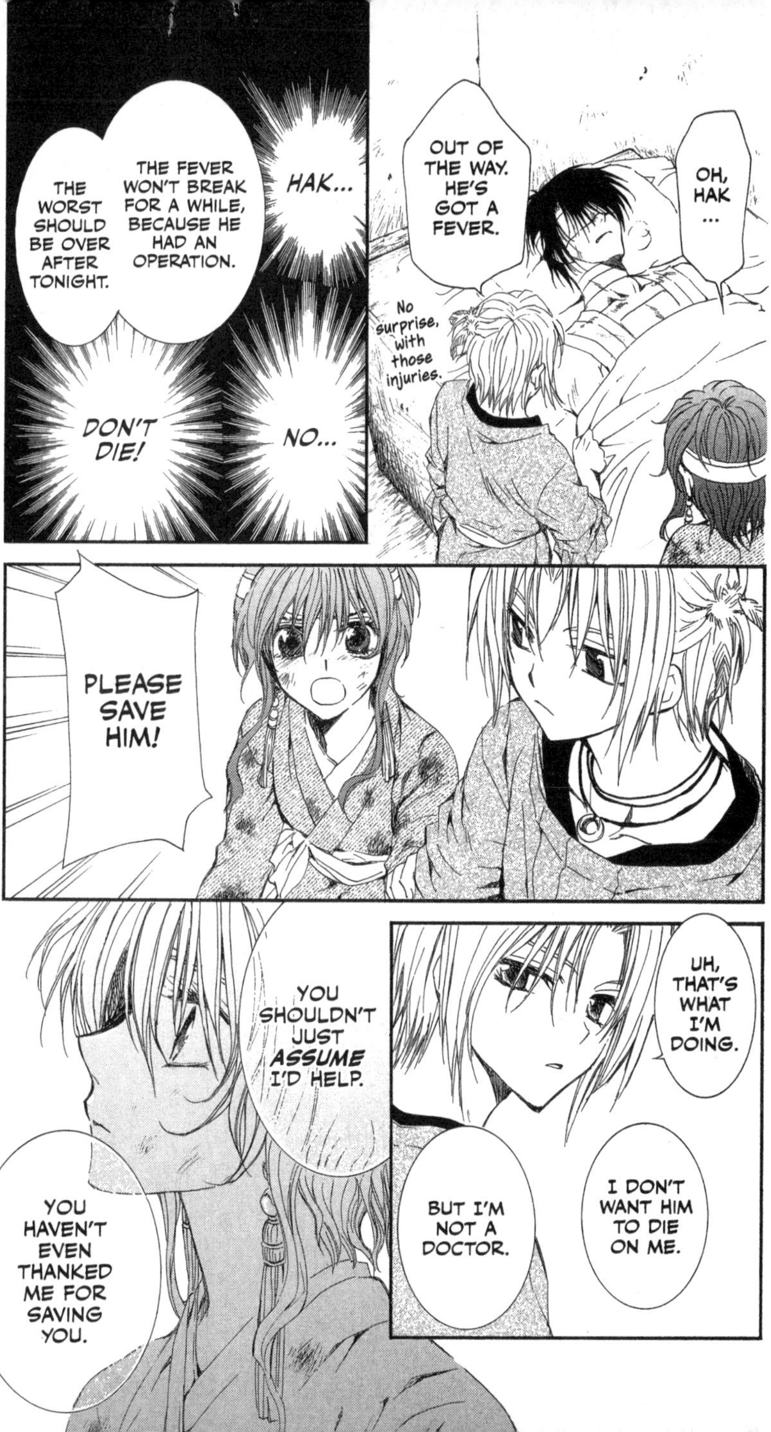
OH, HAK ...
OUT OF THE WAY. HE'S GOT A FEVER.
No surprise, with those injuries.
HAK...
THE FEVER WON'T BREAK FOR A WHILE, BECAUSE HE HAD AN OPERATION.
THE WORST SHOULD BE OVER AFTER TONIGHT.
NO...
DON'T DIE!
PLEASE SAVE HIM!
UH, THAT'S WHAT I'M DOING.
I DON'T WANT HIM TO DIE ON ME.
BUT I'M NOT A DOCTOR.
YOU SHOULDN'T JUST *ASSUME* I'D HELP.
YOU HAVEN'T EVEN THANKED ME FOR SAVING YOU.

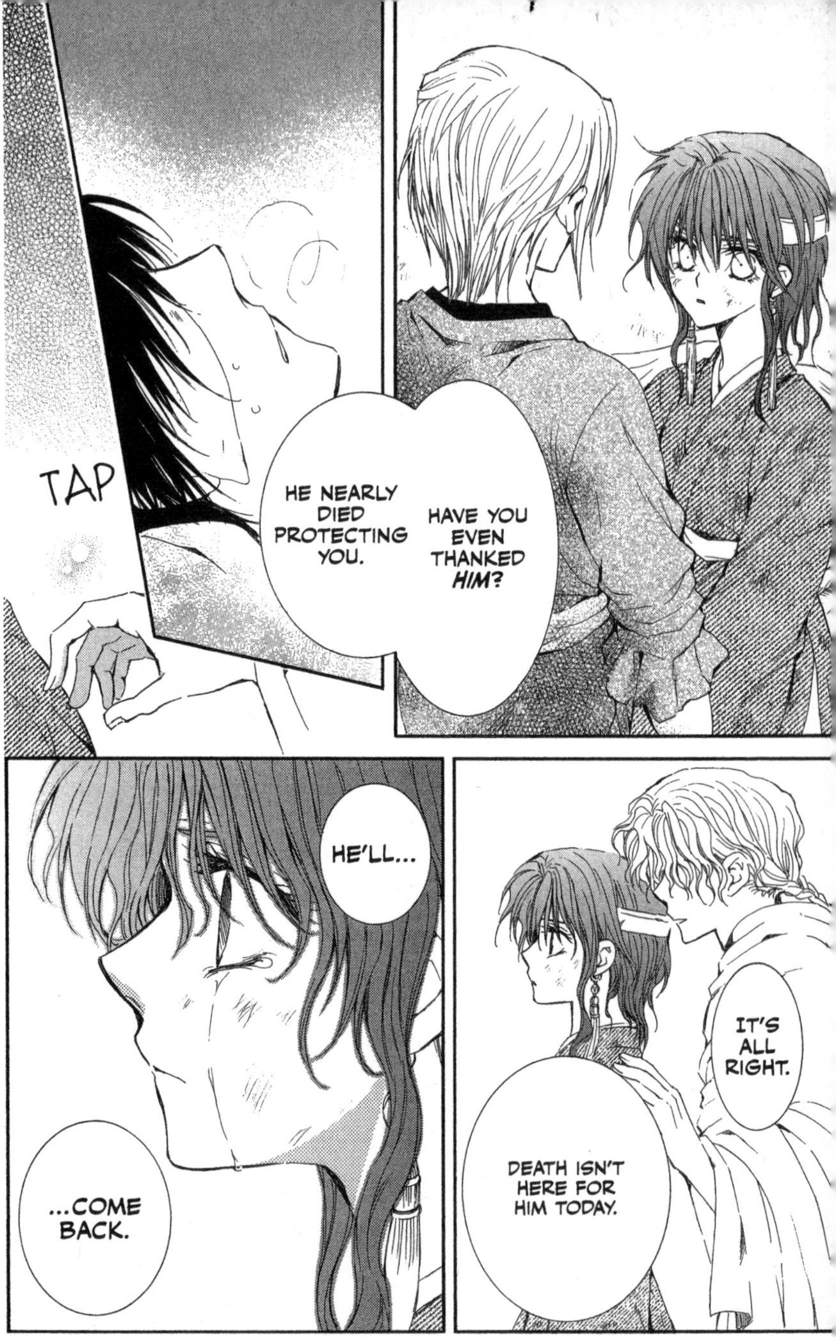
HE NEARLY DIED PROTECTING YOU.
HAVE YOU EVEN THANKED *HIM*?
TAP
IT'S ALL RIGHT.
DEATH ISN'T HERE FOR HIM TODAY.
HE'LL...
...COME BACK.

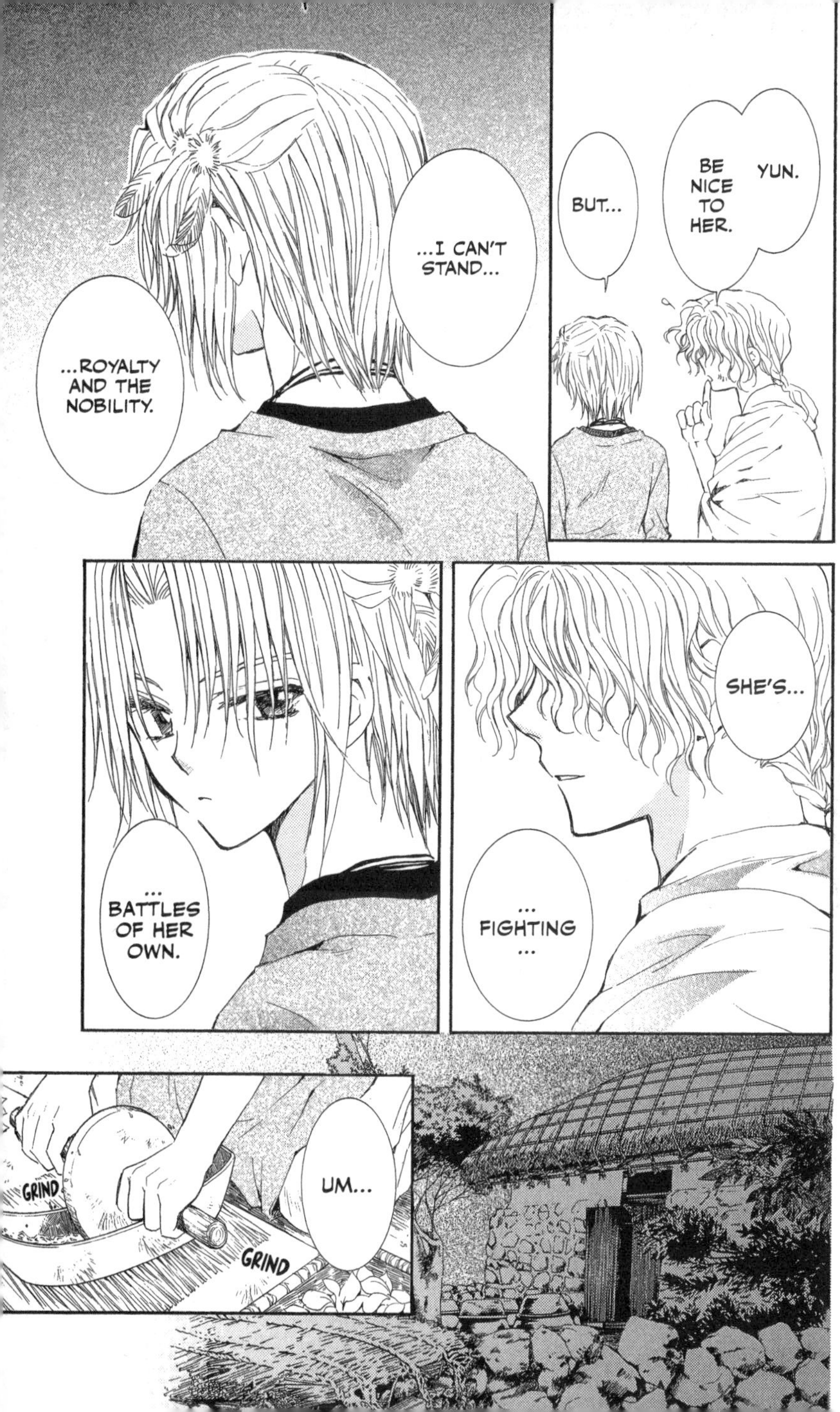
YUN. BE NICE TO HER.
BUT...
...I CAN'T STAND...
...ROYALTY AND THE NOBILITY.
SHE'S...
...FIGHTING...
...BATTLES OF HER OWN.
UM...
GRIND
GRIND

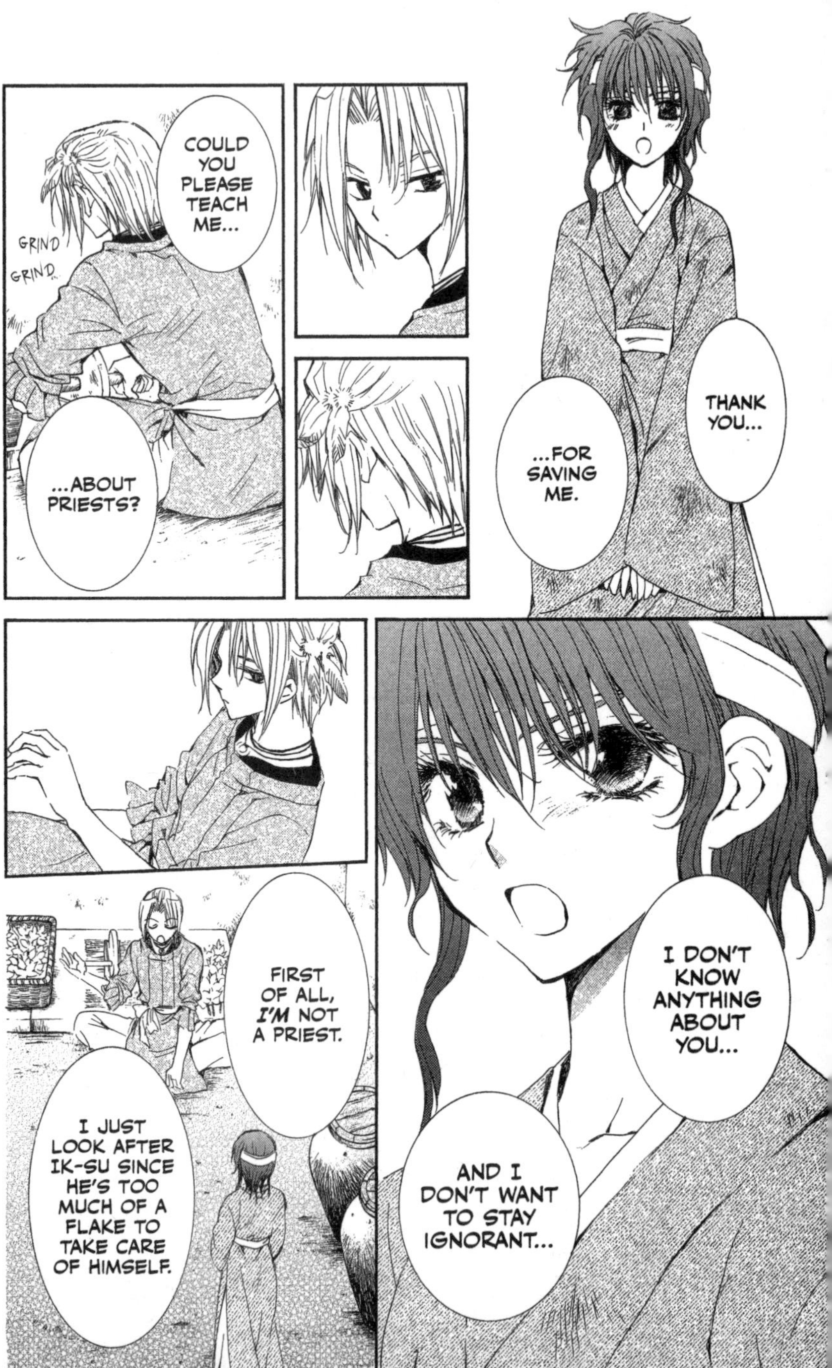
THANK YOU...
...FOR SAVING ME.
COULD YOU PLEASE TEACH ME...
GRIND GRIND
...ABOUT PRIESTS?
I DON'T KNOW ANYTHING ABOUT YOU...
AND I DON'T WANT TO STAY IGNORANT...
FIRST OF ALL, *I'M* NOT A PRIEST.
I JUST LOOK AFTER IK-SU SINCE HE'S TOO MUCH OF A FLAKE TO TAKE CARE OF HIMSELF.

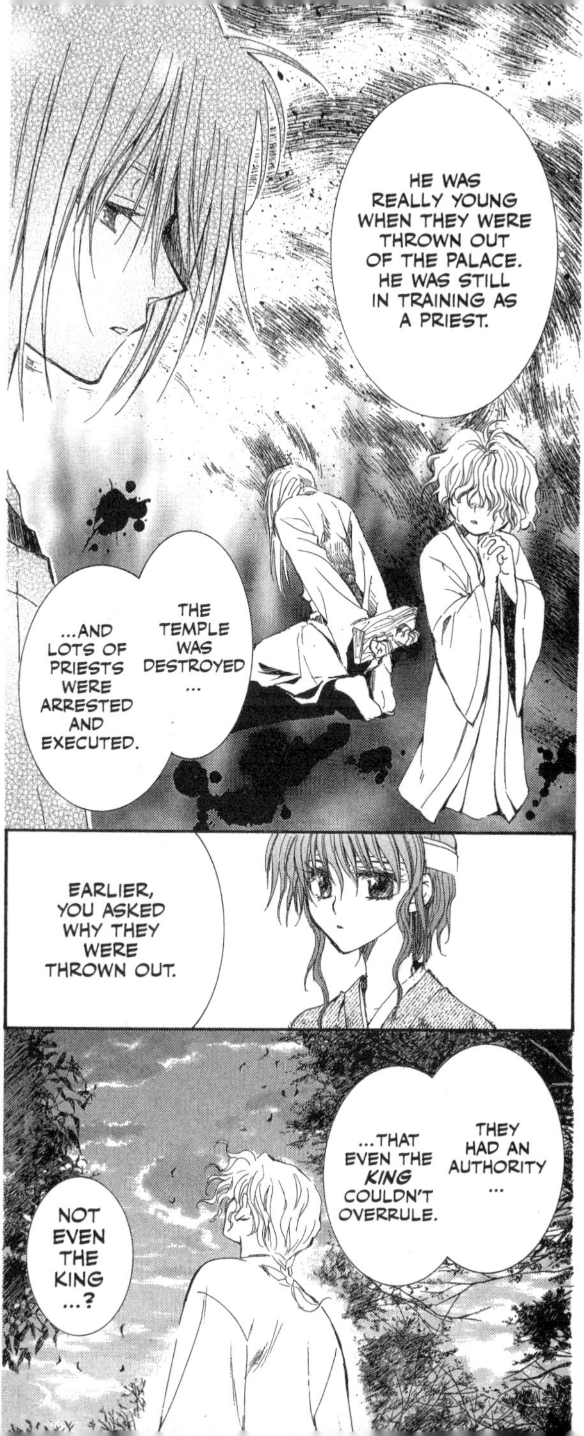
HE WAS REALLY YOUNG WHEN THEY WERE THROWN OUT OF THE PALACE. HE WAS STILL IN TRAINING AS A PRIEST.
THE TEMPLE WAS DESTROYED...
...AND LOTS OF PRIESTS WERE ARRESTED AND EXECUTED.
EARLIER, YOU ASKED WHY THEY WERE THROWN OUT.
THEY HAD AN AUTHORITY...
...THAT EVEN THE *KING* COULDN'T OVERRULE.
NOT EVEN THE KING...?

Hello! I'm Mizuho Kusanagi, and this is volume 3 of *Yona of the Dawn*!

Thank you for picking this book up. We've finally reached the third volume! I'd like to thank those tenacious readers who have been following the series since the very first chapter. (*Smile*)

There's a new development (?) unfolding in *Yona*! I hope you'll keep reading! Yona cut her hair off. It was a popular move with most readers. I like it when girls have bobbed or short hair.♡ I always notice when celebrities or girls in hair magazines wear their hair short. Yona feels good about having cut hers.

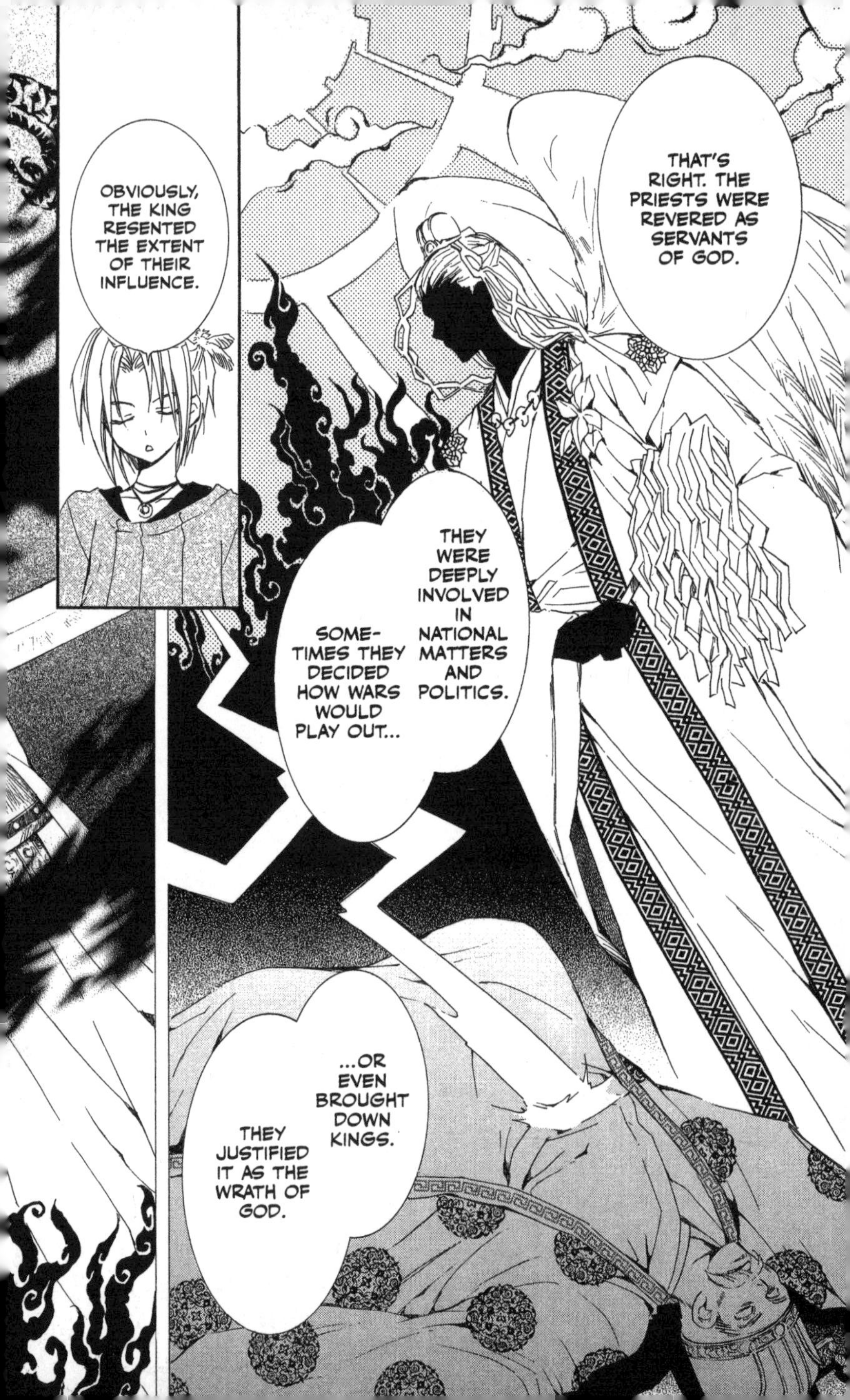
THAT'S RIGHT. THE PRIESTS WERE REVERED AS SERVANTS OF GOD.
THEY WERE DEEPLY INVOLVED IN NATIONAL MATTERS AND POLITICS.
SOME-TIMES THEY DECIDED HOW WARS WOULD PLAY OUT...
...OR EVEN BROUGHT DOWN KINGS.
THEY JUSTIFIED IT AS THE WRATH OF GOD.
OBVIOUSLY, THE KING RESENTED THE EXTENT OF THEIR INFLUENCE.

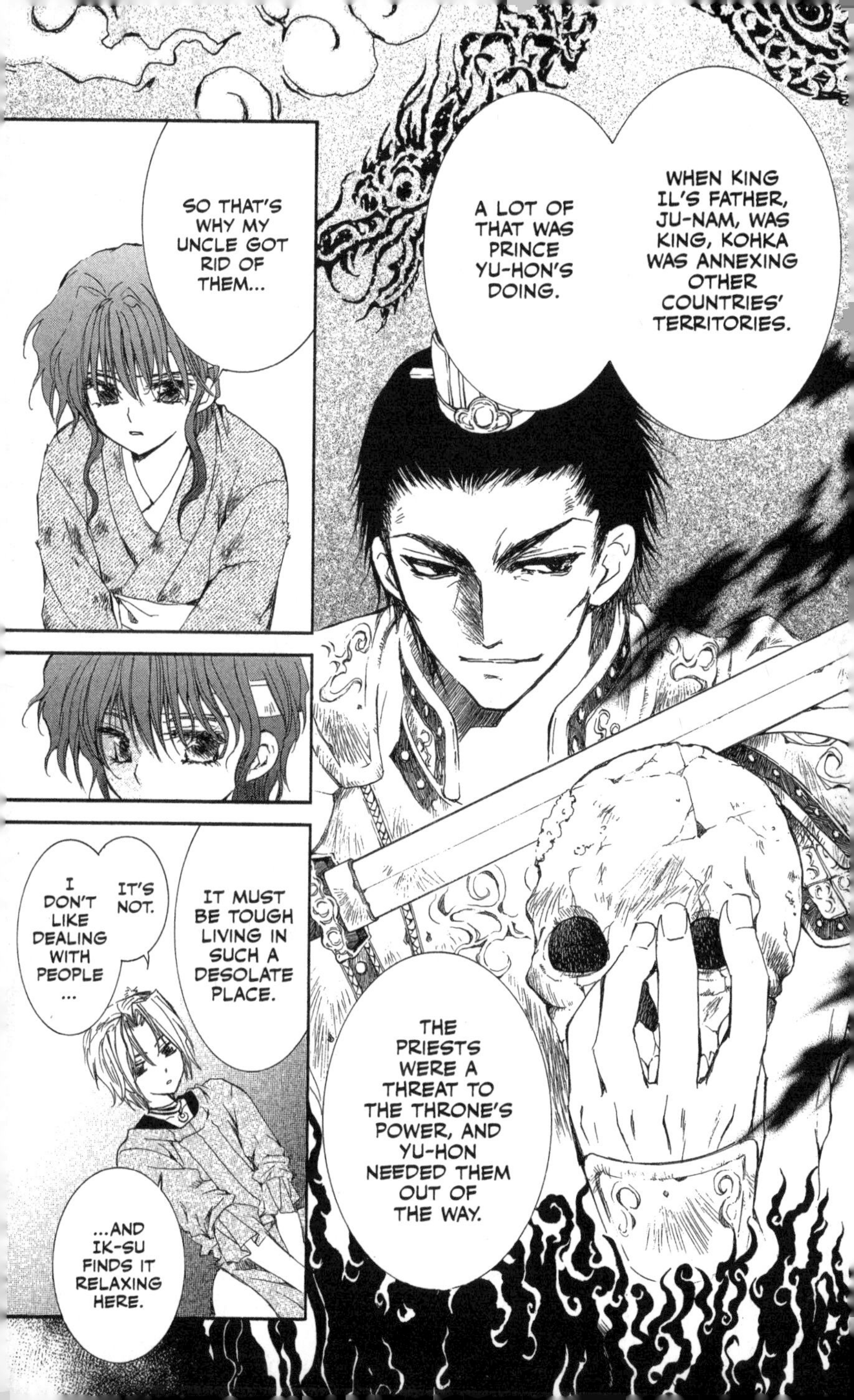
WHEN KING IL'S FATHER, JU-NAM, WAS KING, KOHKA WAS ANNEXING OTHER COUNTRIES' TERRITORIES.
A LOT OF THAT WAS PRINCE YU-HON'S DOING.
THE PRIESTS WERE A THREAT TO THE THRONE'S POWER, AND YU-HON NEEDED THEM OUT OF THE WAY.
SO THAT'S WHY MY UNCLE GOT RID OF THEM...
IT MUST BE TOUGH LIVING IN SUCH A DESOLATE PLACE.
IT'S NOT.
I DON'T LIKE DEALING WITH PEOPLE ...
...AND IK-SU FINDS IT RELAXING HERE.

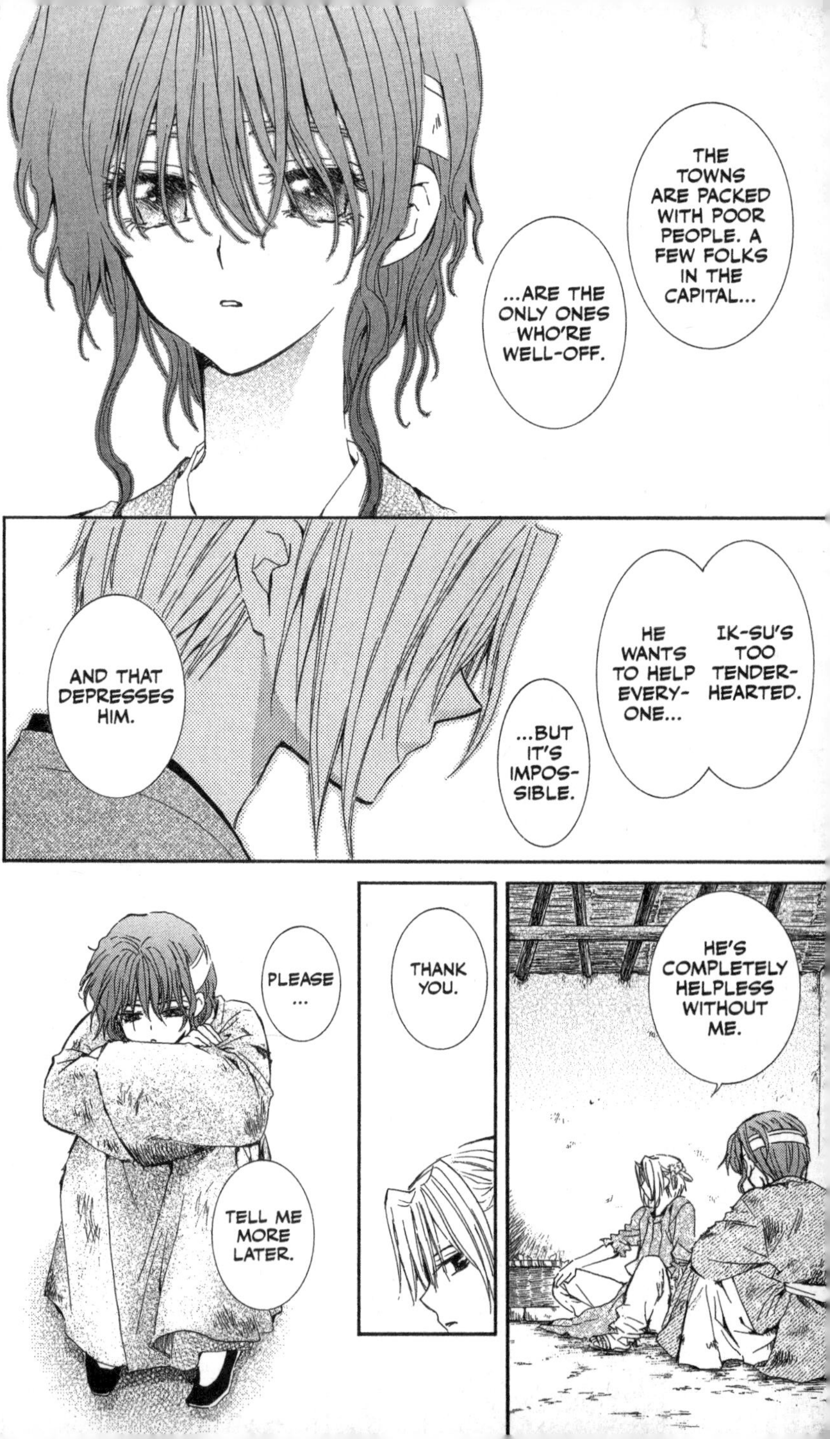
THE TOWNS ARE PACKED WITH POOR PEOPLE. A FEW FOLKS IN THE CAPITAL...
...ARE THE ONLY ONES WHO'RE WELL-OFF.
IK-SU'S TOO TENDER-HEARTED.
HE WANTS TO HELP EVERY-ONE...
...BUT IT'S IMPOS-SIBLE.
AND THAT DEPRESSES HIM.
HE'S COMPLETELY HELPLESS WITHOUT ME.
THANK YOU.
PLEASE...
TELL ME MORE LATER.

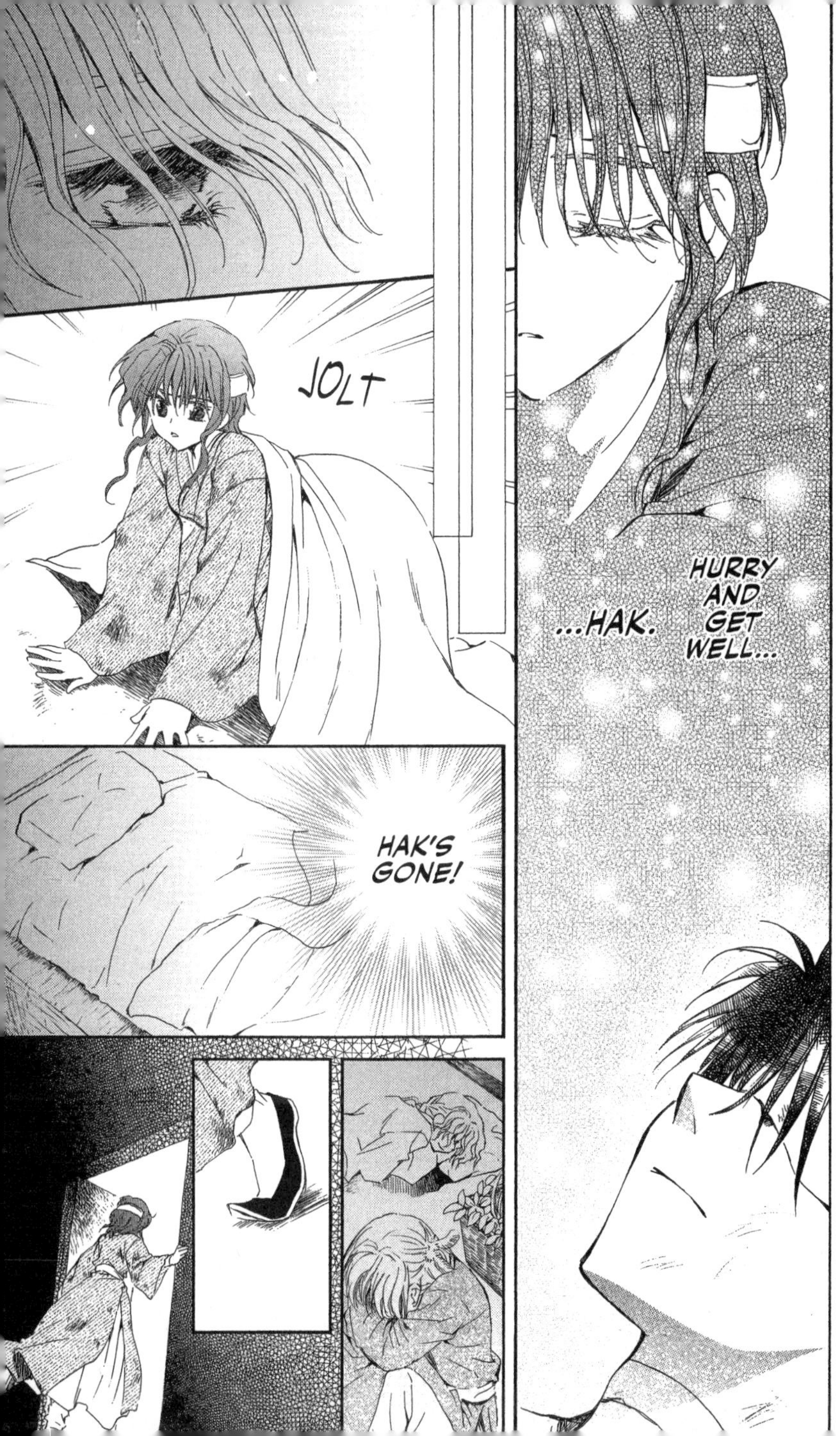
HURRY AND GET WELL...
...HAK.
JOLT
HAK'S GONE!

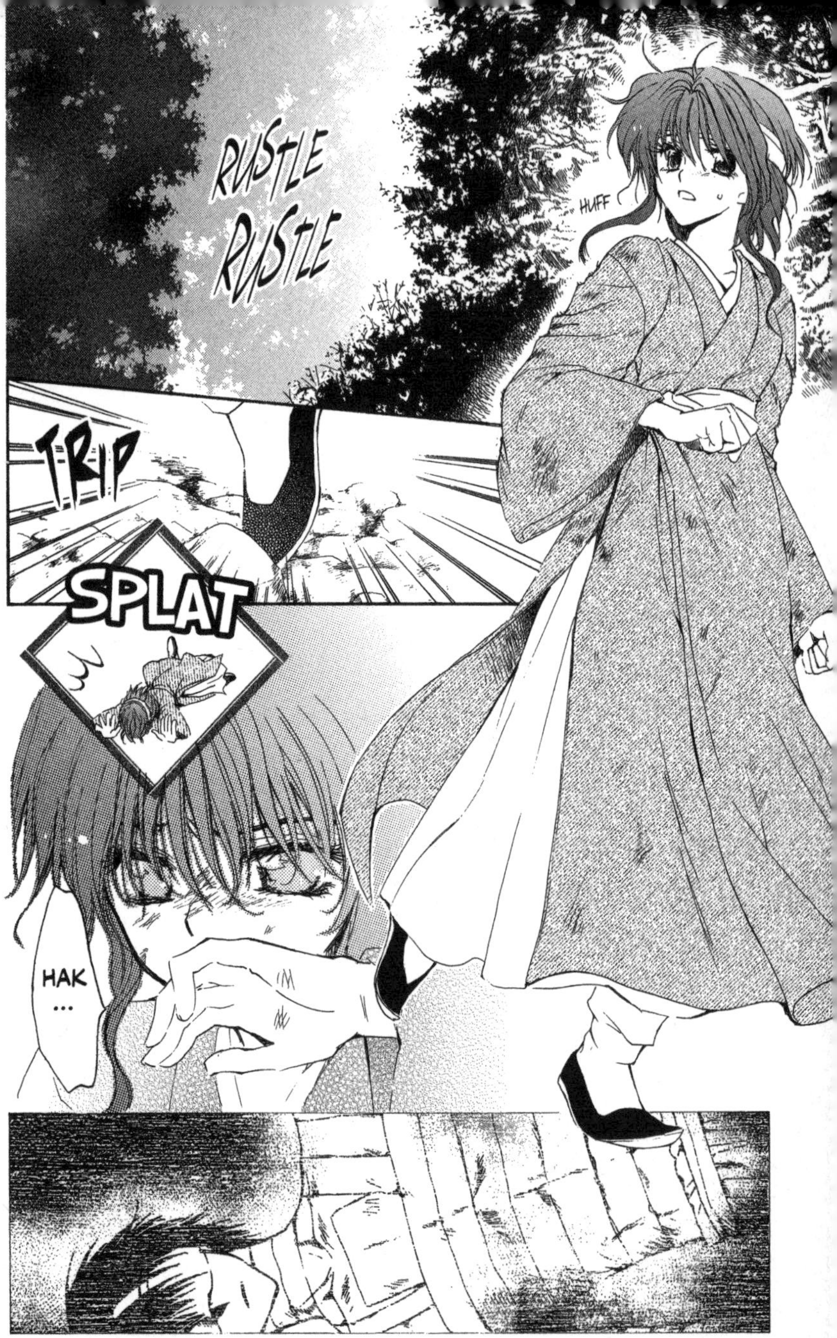
HUFF
RUSTLE RUSTLE
TRIP
SPLAT
HAK...

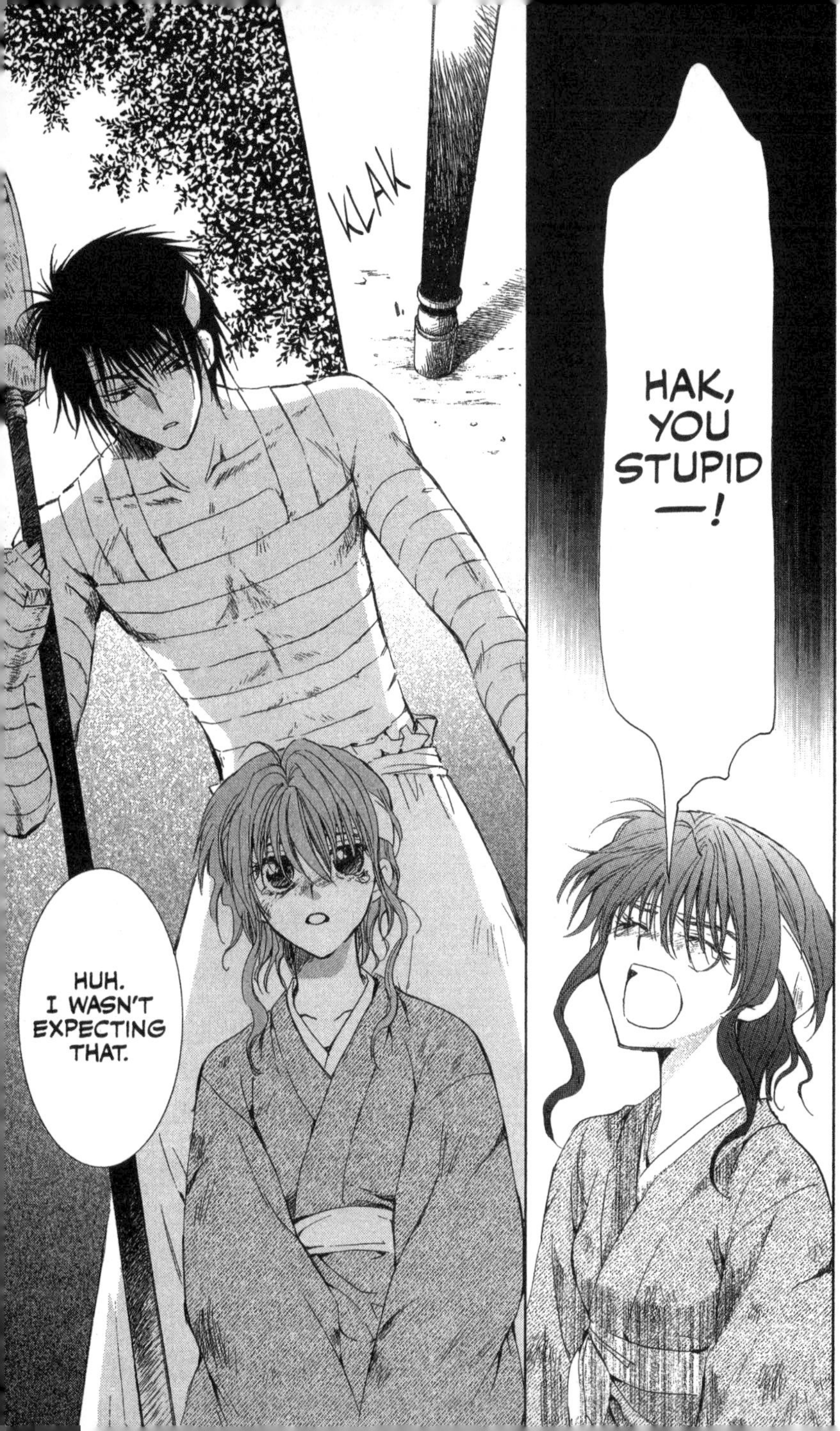
HAK, YOU STUPID —!
KLAK
HUH. I WASN'T EXPECTING THAT.

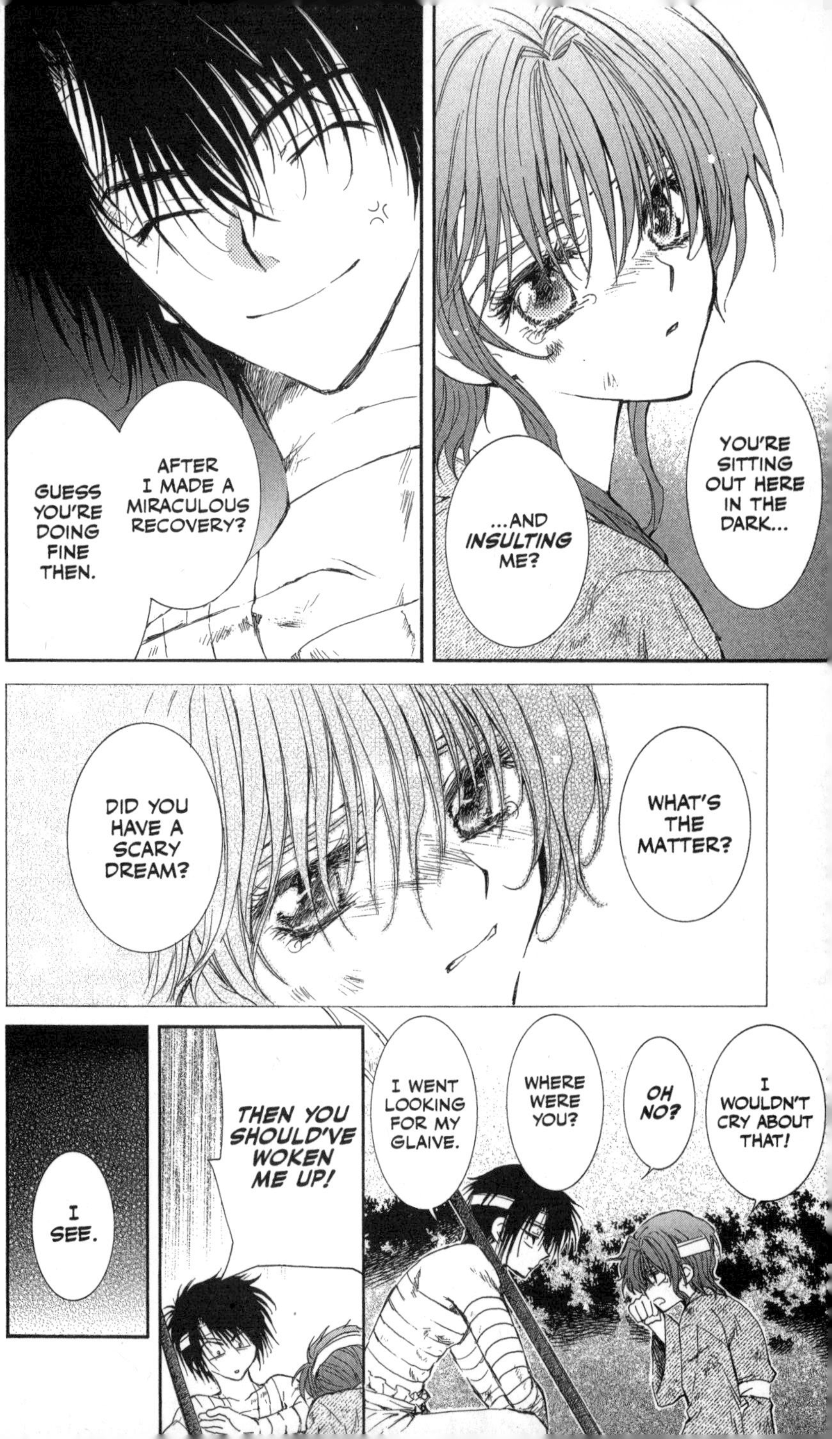
YOU'RE SITTING OUT HERE IN THE DARK...
...AND *INSULTING* ME?
AFTER I MADE A MIRACULOUS RECOVERY?
GUESS YOU'RE DOING FINE THEN.
WHAT'S THE MATTER?
DID YOU HAVE A SCARY DREAM?
I WOULDN'T CRY ABOUT THAT!
OH NO?
WHERE WERE YOU?
I WENT LOOKING FOR MY GLAIVE.
THEN YOU SHOULD'VE WOKEN ME UP!
I SEE.

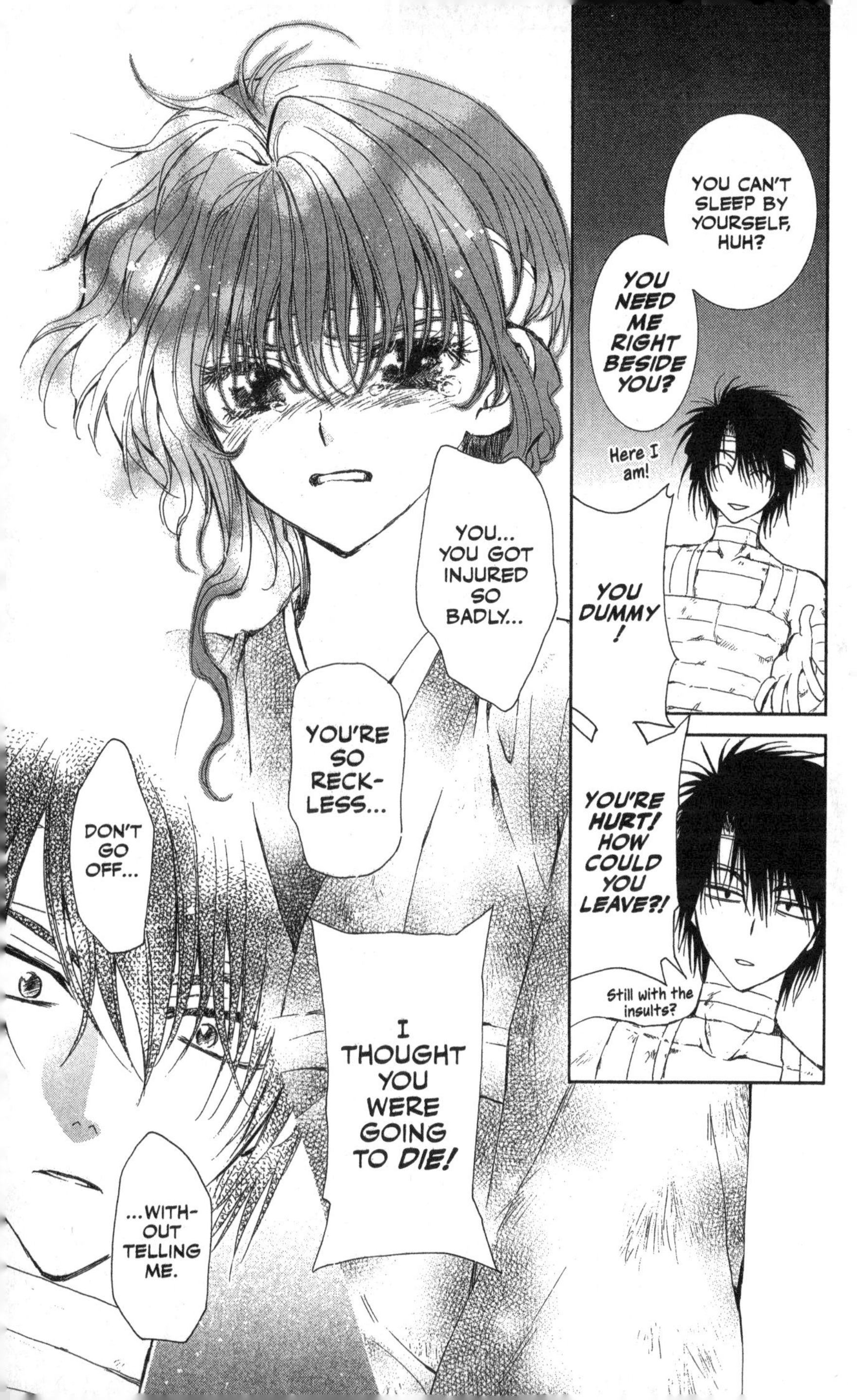
YOU CAN'T SLEEP BY YOURSELF, HUH?
YOU NEED ME RIGHT BESIDE YOU?
Here I am!
YOU DUMMY!
YOU'RE HURT! HOW COULD YOU LEAVE?!
Still with the insults?
YOU... YOU GOT INJURED SO BADLY...
YOU'RE SO RECK-LESS...
I THOUGHT YOU WERE GOING TO DIE!
DON'T GO OFF...
...WITH-OUT TELLING ME.

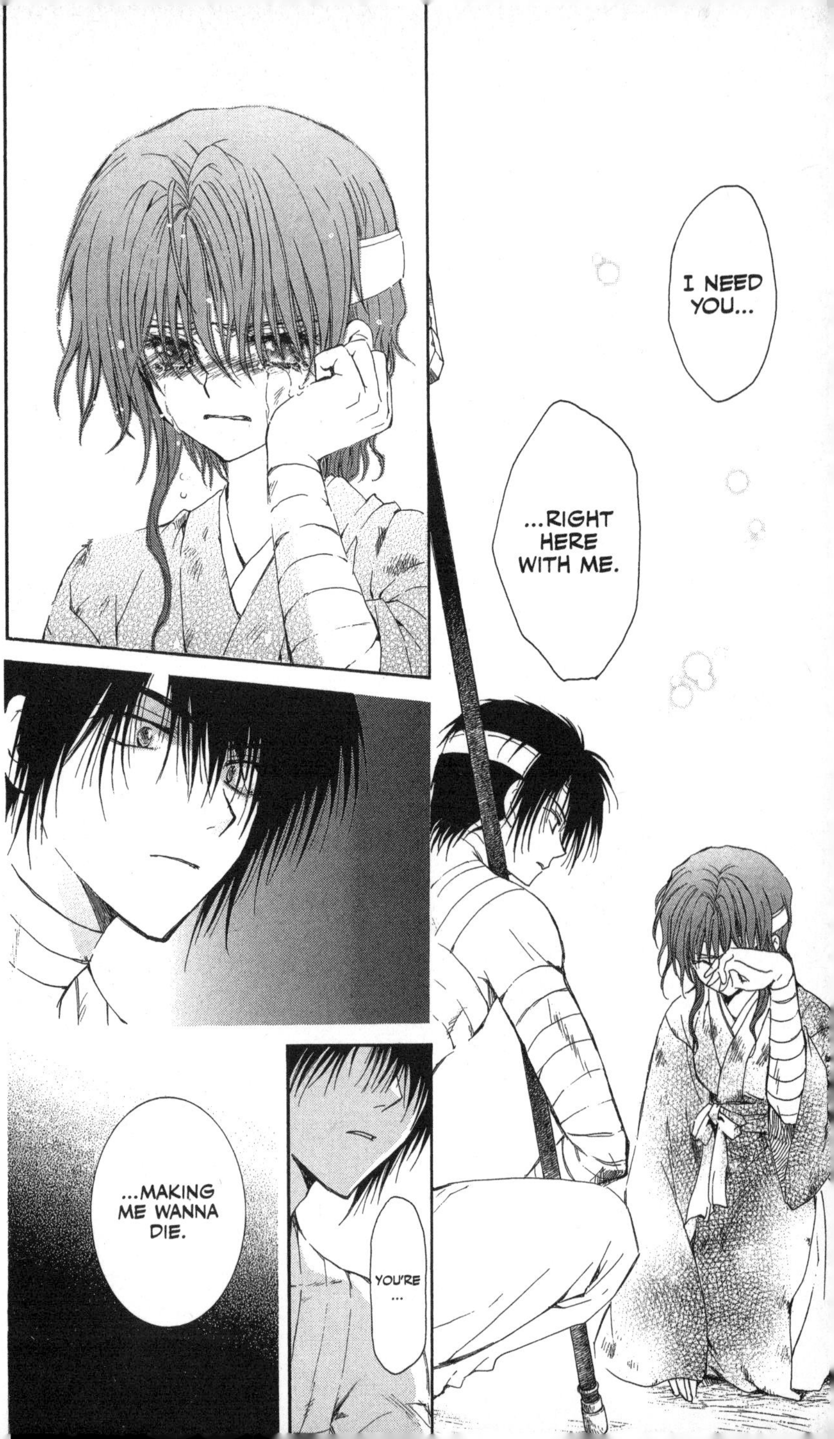
I NEED YOU...
...RIGHT HERE WITH ME.
YOU'RE ...
...MAKING ME WANNA DIE.

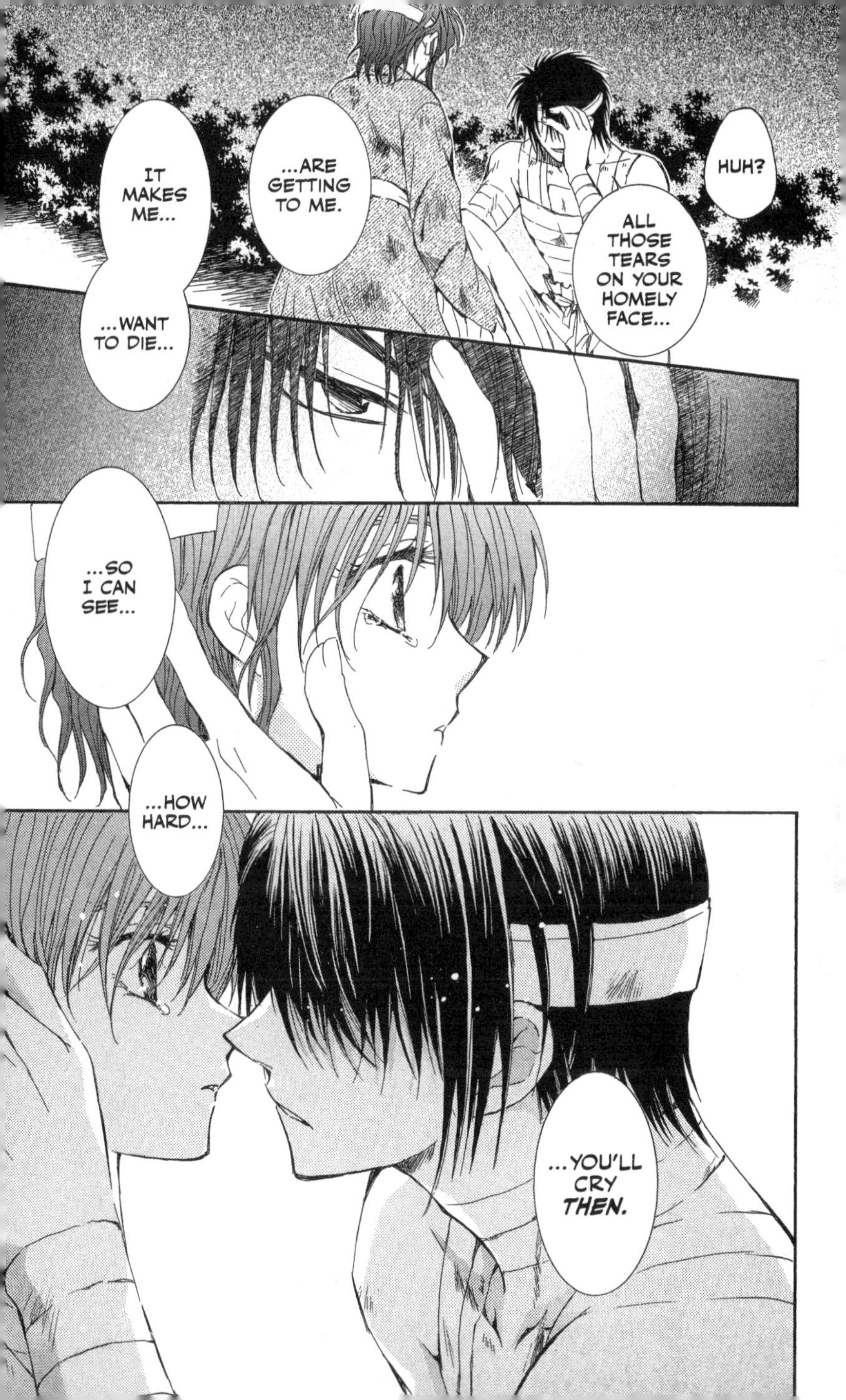
HUH?
ALL THOSE TEARS ON YOUR HOMELY FACE...
...ARE GETTING TO ME.
IT MAKES ME...
...WANT TO DIE...
...SO I CAN SEE...
...HOW HARD...
...YOU'LL CRY *THEN.*

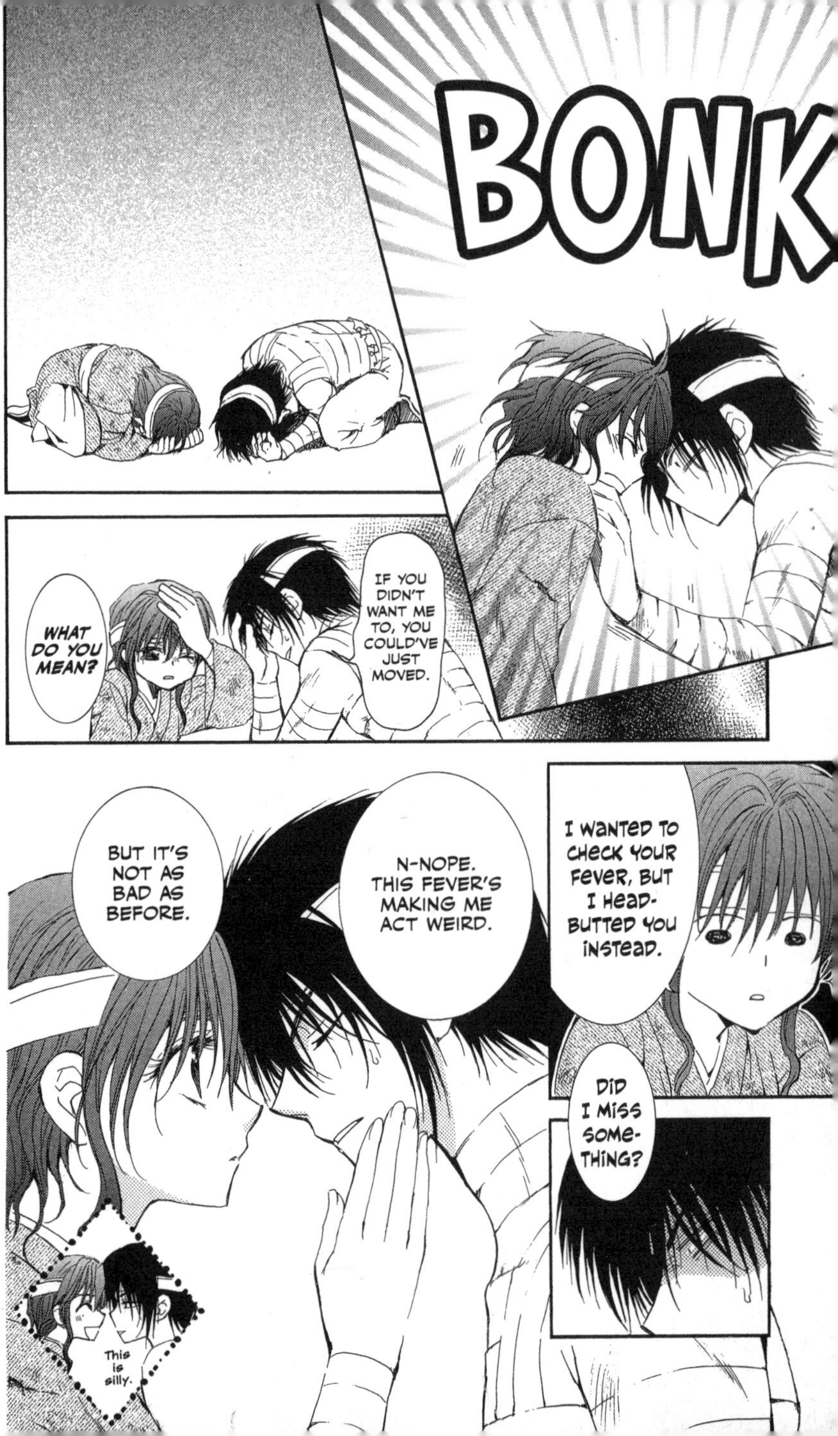
BONK
IF YOU DIDN'T WANT ME TO, YOU COULD'VE JUST MOVED.
WHAT DO YOU MEAN?
I WANTED TO CHECK YOUR FEVER, BUT I HEAD-BUTTED YOU INSTEAD.
DID I MISS SOME-THING?
N-NOPE. THIS FEVER'S MAKING ME ACT WEIRD.
BUT IT'S NOT AS BAD AS BEFORE.
This is silly.

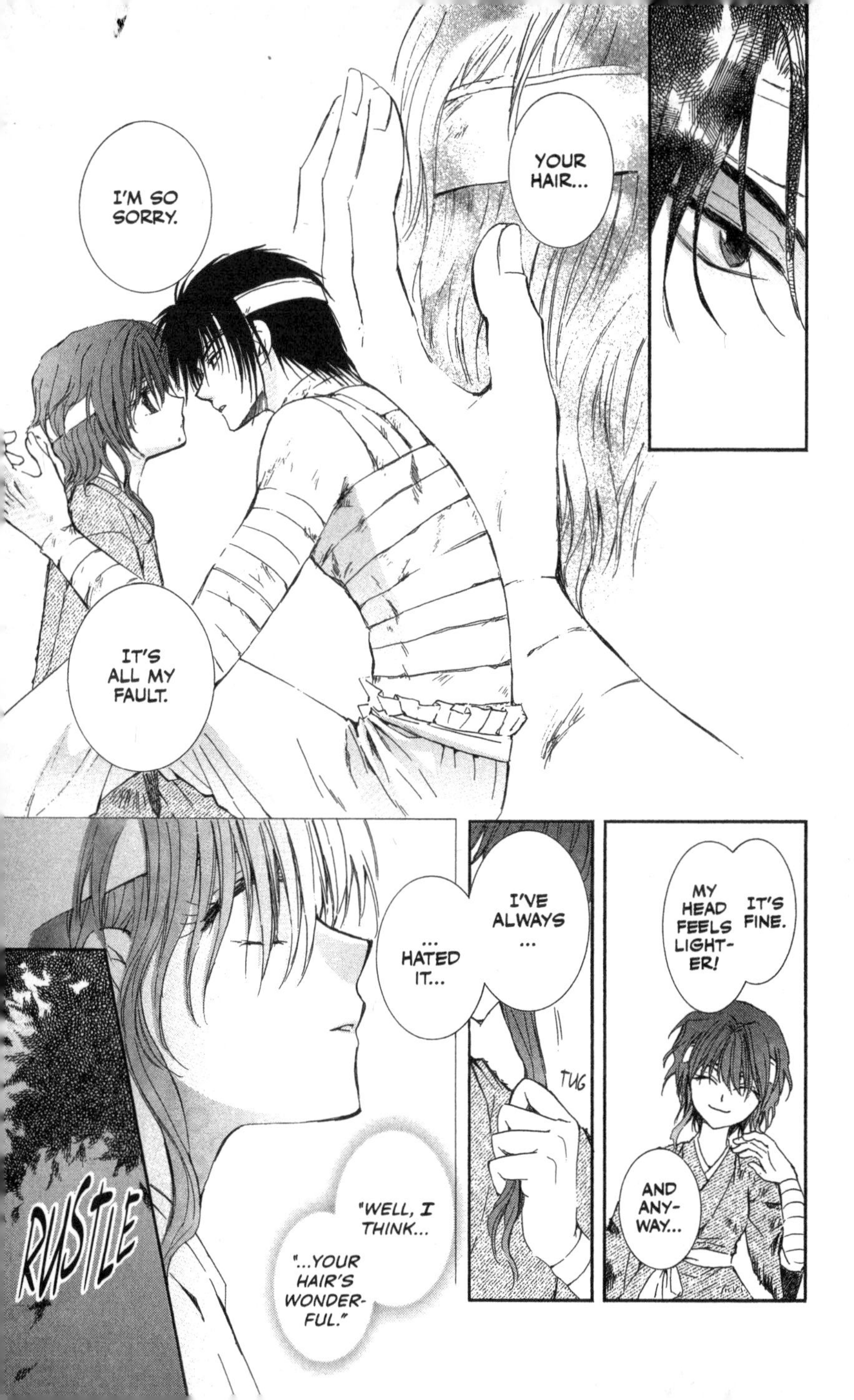
YOUR HAIR...
I'M SO SORRY.
IT'S ALL MY FAULT.
IT'S FINE.
MY HEAD FEELS LIGHTER!
AND ANYWAY...
I'VE ALWAYS...
...HATED IT...
TUG
"WELL, I THINK...
"...YOUR HAIR'S WONDERFUL."
RUSTLE

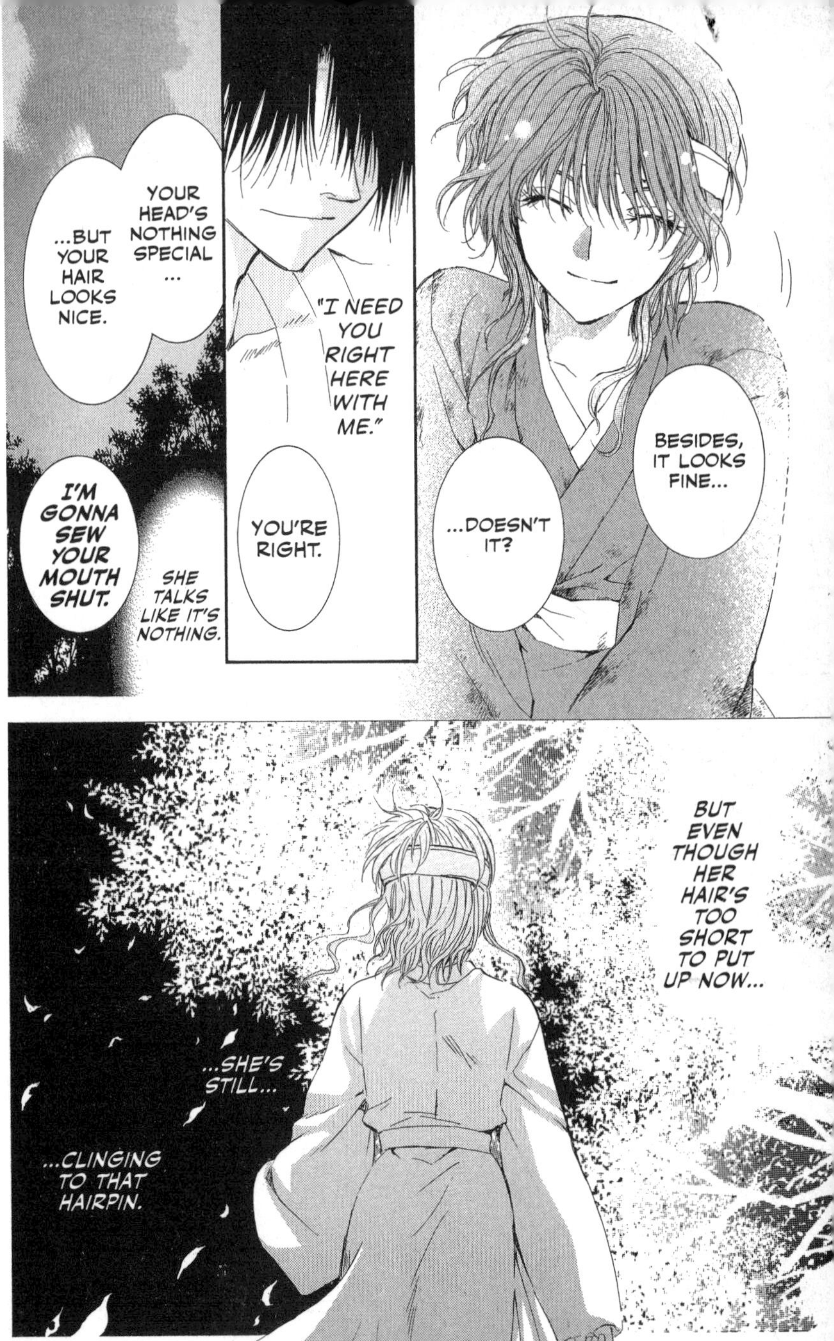
BESIDES, IT LOOKS FINE...
...DOESN'T IT?
"I NEED YOU RIGHT HERE WITH ME."
YOU'RE RIGHT.
YOUR HEAD'S NOTHING SPECIAL...
...BUT YOUR HAIR LOOKS NICE.
SHE TALKS LIKE IT'S NOTHING.
I'M GONNA SEW YOUR MOUTH SHUT.
BUT EVEN THOUGH HER HAIR'S TOO SHORT TO PUT UP NOW...
...SHE'S STILL...
...CLINGING TO THAT HAIRPIN.

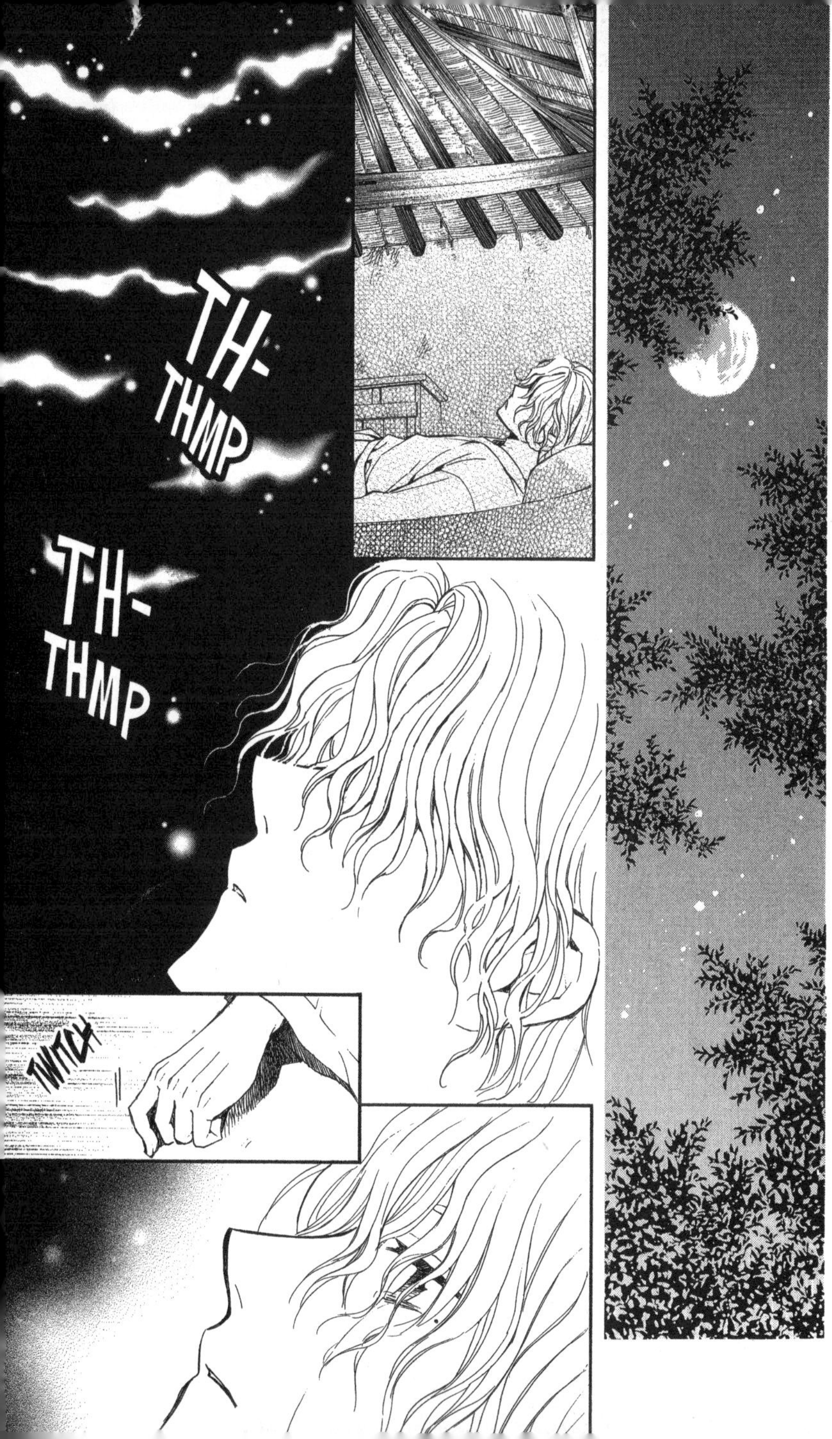
TH-THMP
TH-THMP
TWITCH

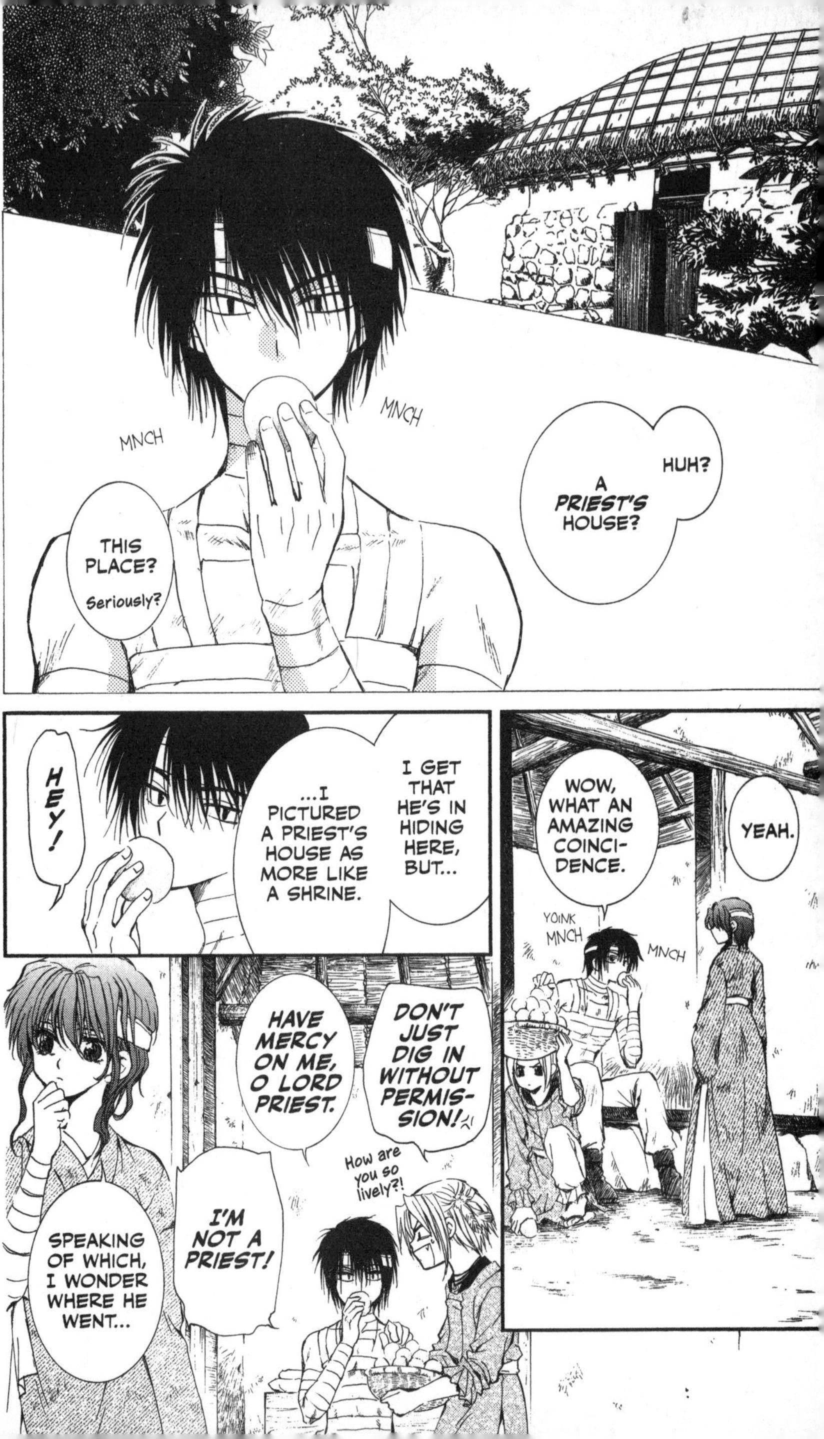
HUH? A PRIEST'S HOUSE?
MNCH
MNCH
THIS PLACE? Seriously?
YEAH.
WOW, WHAT AN AMAZING COINCIDENCE.
YOINK
MNCH
MNCH
I GET THAT HE'S IN HIDING HERE, BUT...
...I PICTURED A PRIEST'S HOUSE AS MORE LIKE A SHRINE.
HEY!
DON'T JUST DIG IN WITHOUT PERMISSION!
HAVE MERCY ON ME, O LORD PRIEST.
How are you so lively?!
I'M NOT A PRIEST!
SPEAKING OF WHICH, I WONDER WHERE HE WENT...

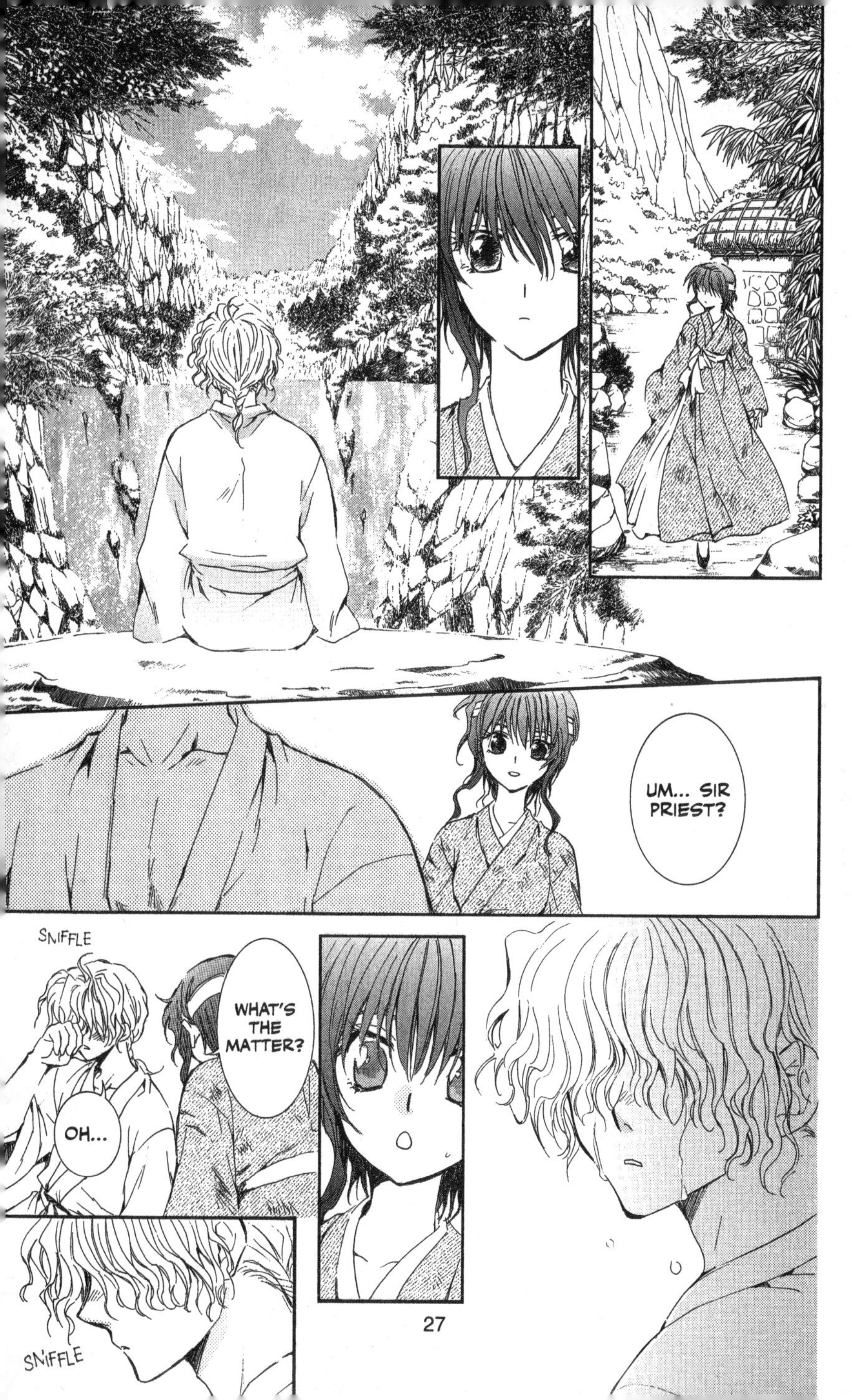
UM... SIR PRIEST?
WHAT'S THE MATTER?
SNIFFLE
OH...
SNIFFLE

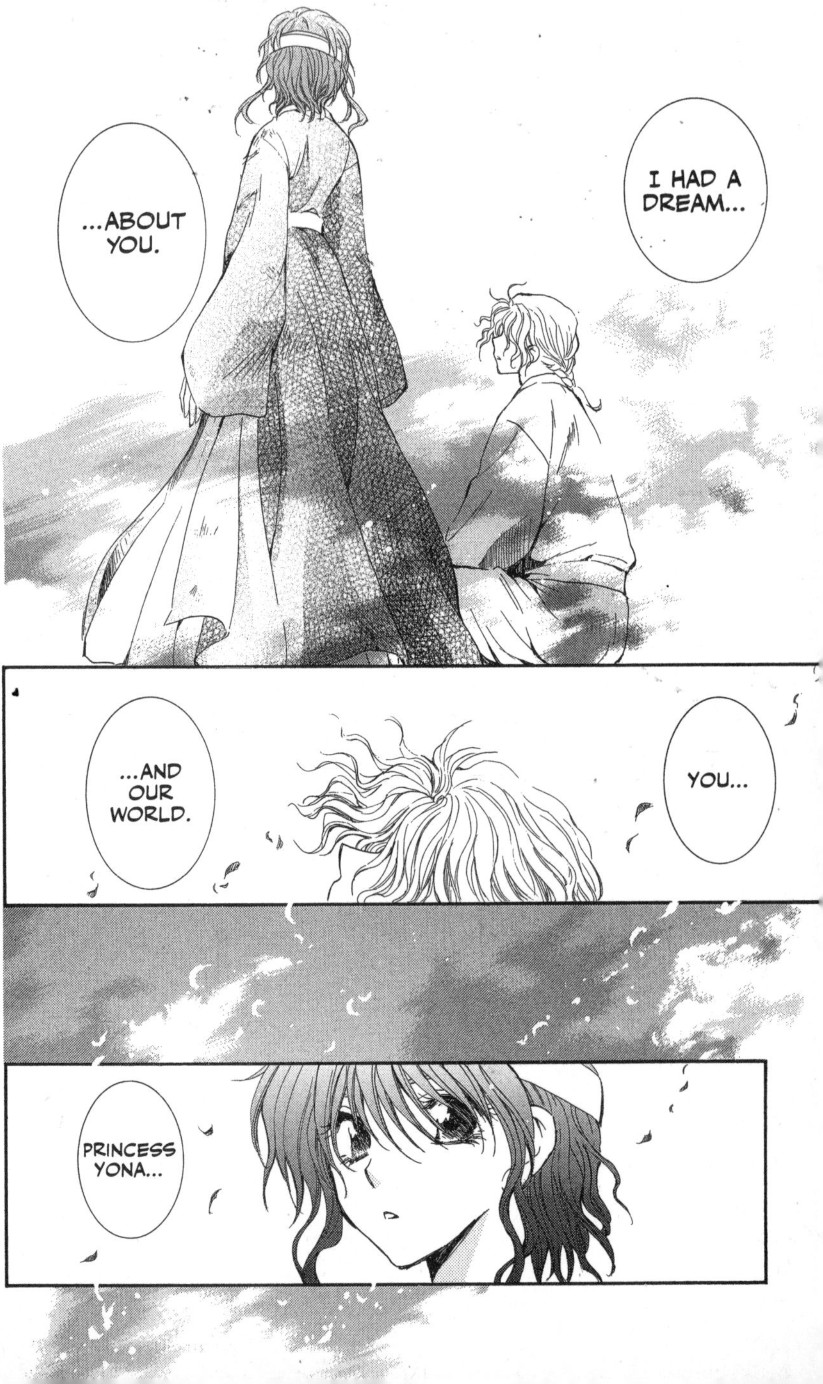
I HAD A DREAM...
...ABOUT YOU.
YOU...
...AND OUR WORLD.
PRINCESS YONA...

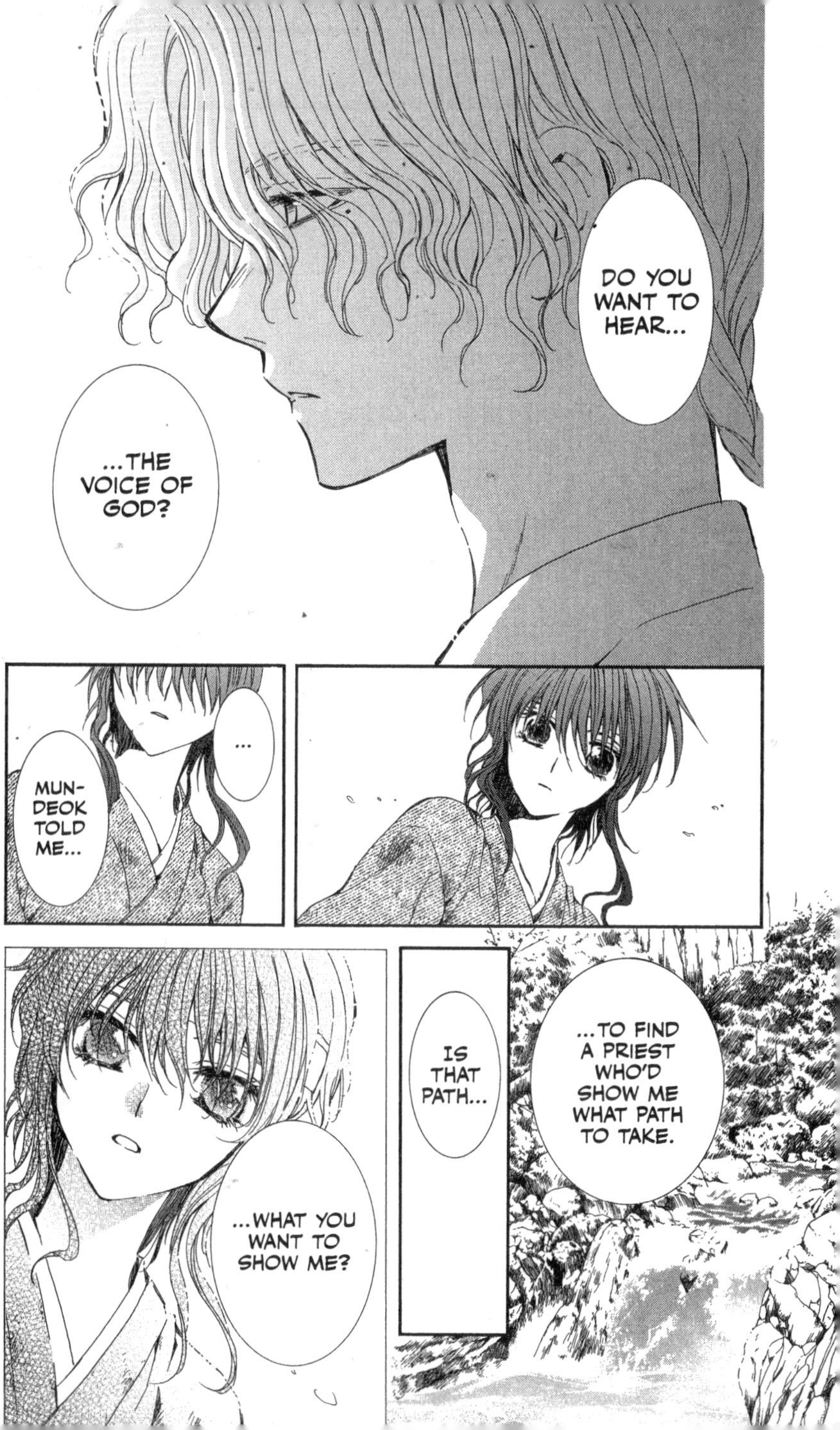
DO YOU WANT TO HEAR...
...THE VOICE OF GOD?
...
MUN-DEOK TOLD ME...
...TO FIND A PRIEST WHO'D SHOW ME WHAT PATH TO TAKE.
IS THAT PATH...
...WHAT YOU WANT TO SHOW ME?

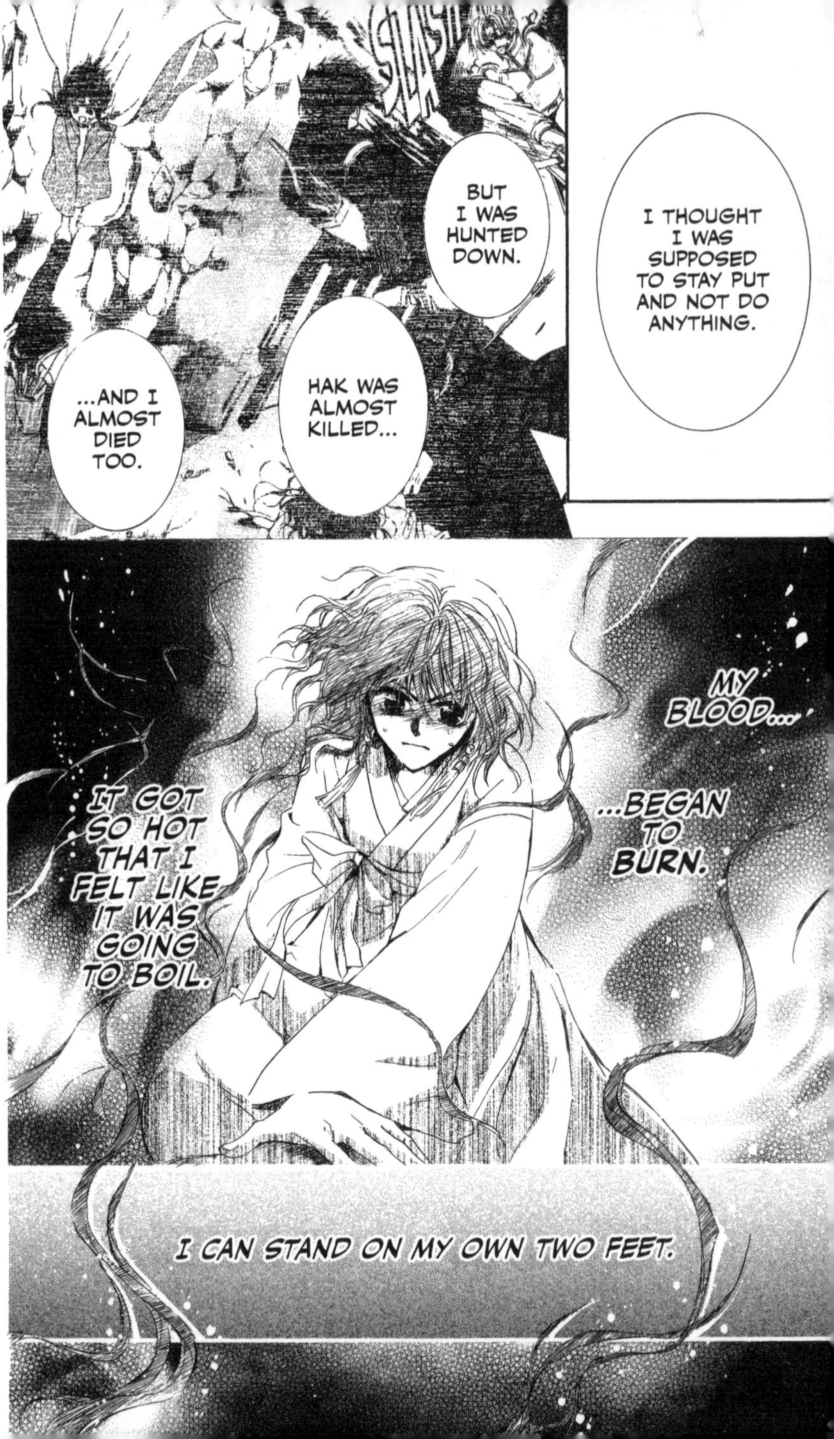
I THOUGHT I WAS SUPPOSED TO STAY PUT AND NOT DO ANYTHING.
BUT I WAS HUNTED DOWN.
HAK WAS ALMOST KILLED...
...AND I ALMOST DIED TOO.
MY BLOOD...
...BEGAN TO BURN.
IT GOT SO HOT THAT I FELT LIKE IT WAS GOING TO BOIL.
I CAN STAND ON MY OWN TWO FEET.

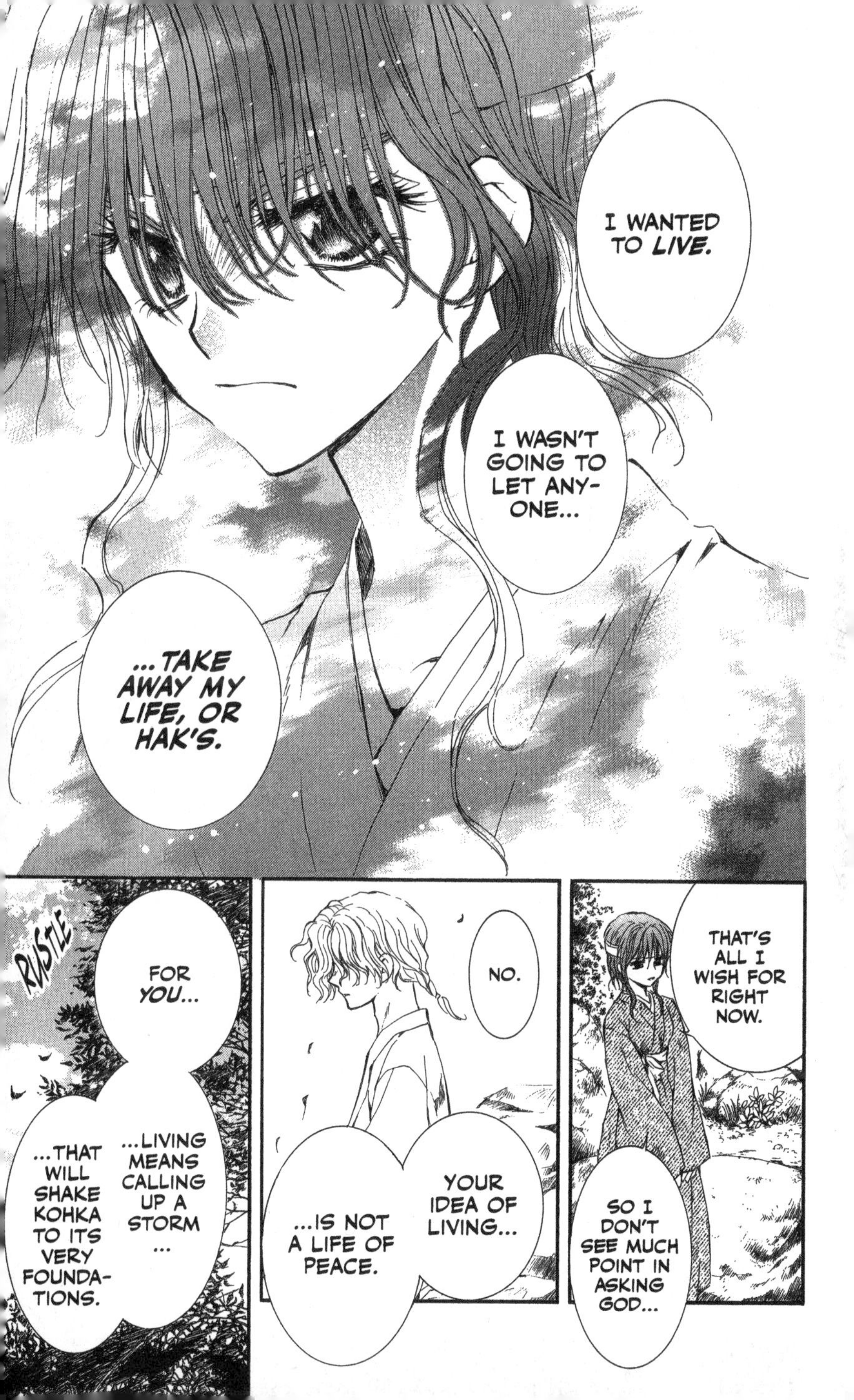

I WANTED TO *LIVE.*
I WASN'T GOING TO LET ANY-ONE...
...TAKE AWAY MY LIFE, OR HAK'S.
THAT'S ALL I WISH FOR RIGHT NOW.
SO I DON'T SEE MUCH POINT IN ASKING GOD...
NO.
YOUR IDEA OF LIVING...
...IS NOT A LIFE OF PEACE.
RUSTLE
FOR *YOU*...
...LIVING MEANS CALLING UP A STORM...
...THAT WILL SHAKE KOHKA TO ITS VERY FOUNDA-TIONS.

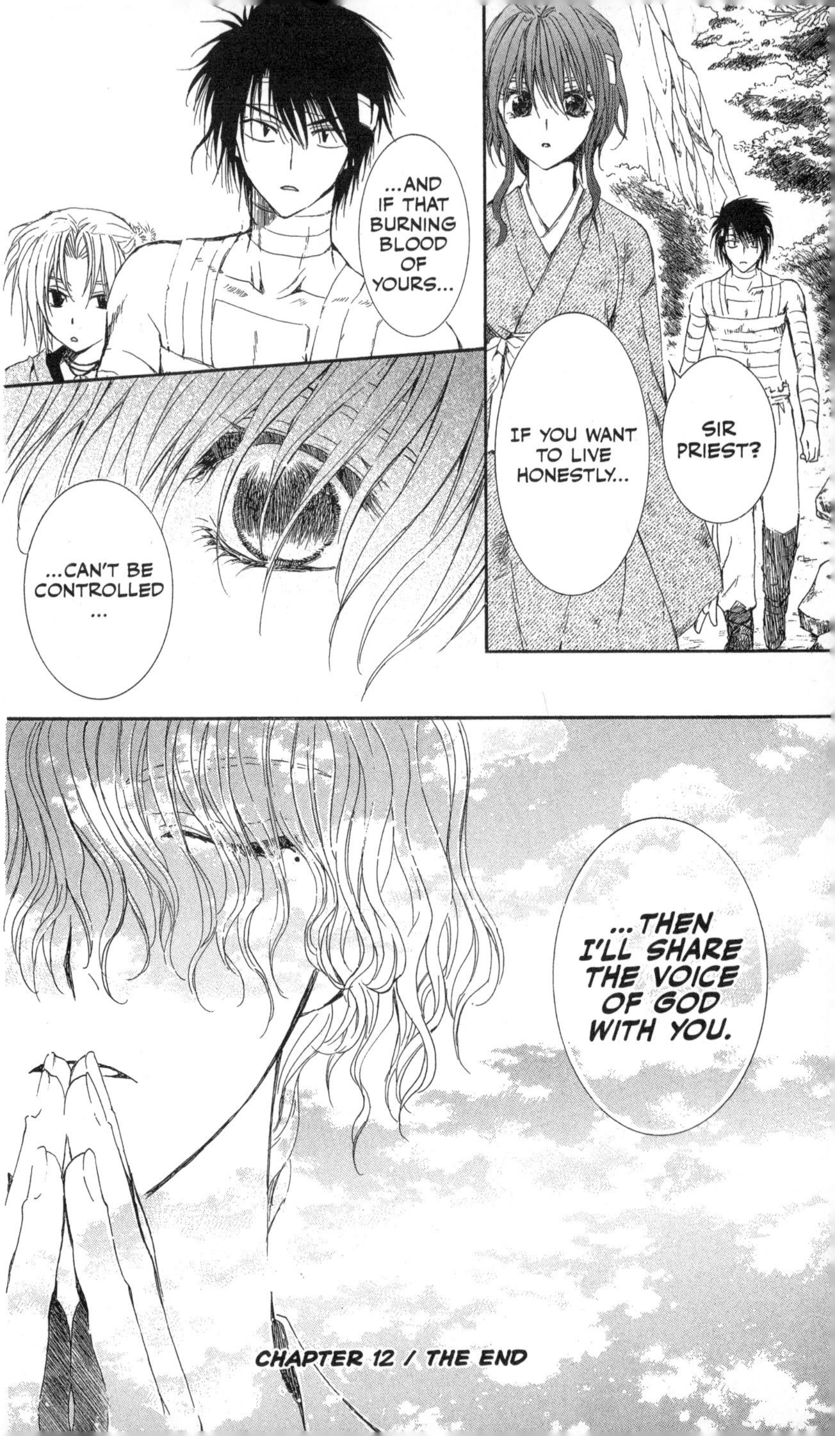
SIR PRIEST?
IF YOU WANT TO LIVE HONESTLY...
...AND IF THAT BURNING BLOOD OF YOURS...
...CAN'T BE CONTROLLED ...
...THEN I'LL SHARE THE VOICE OF GOD WITH YOU.
CHAPTER 12 / THE END

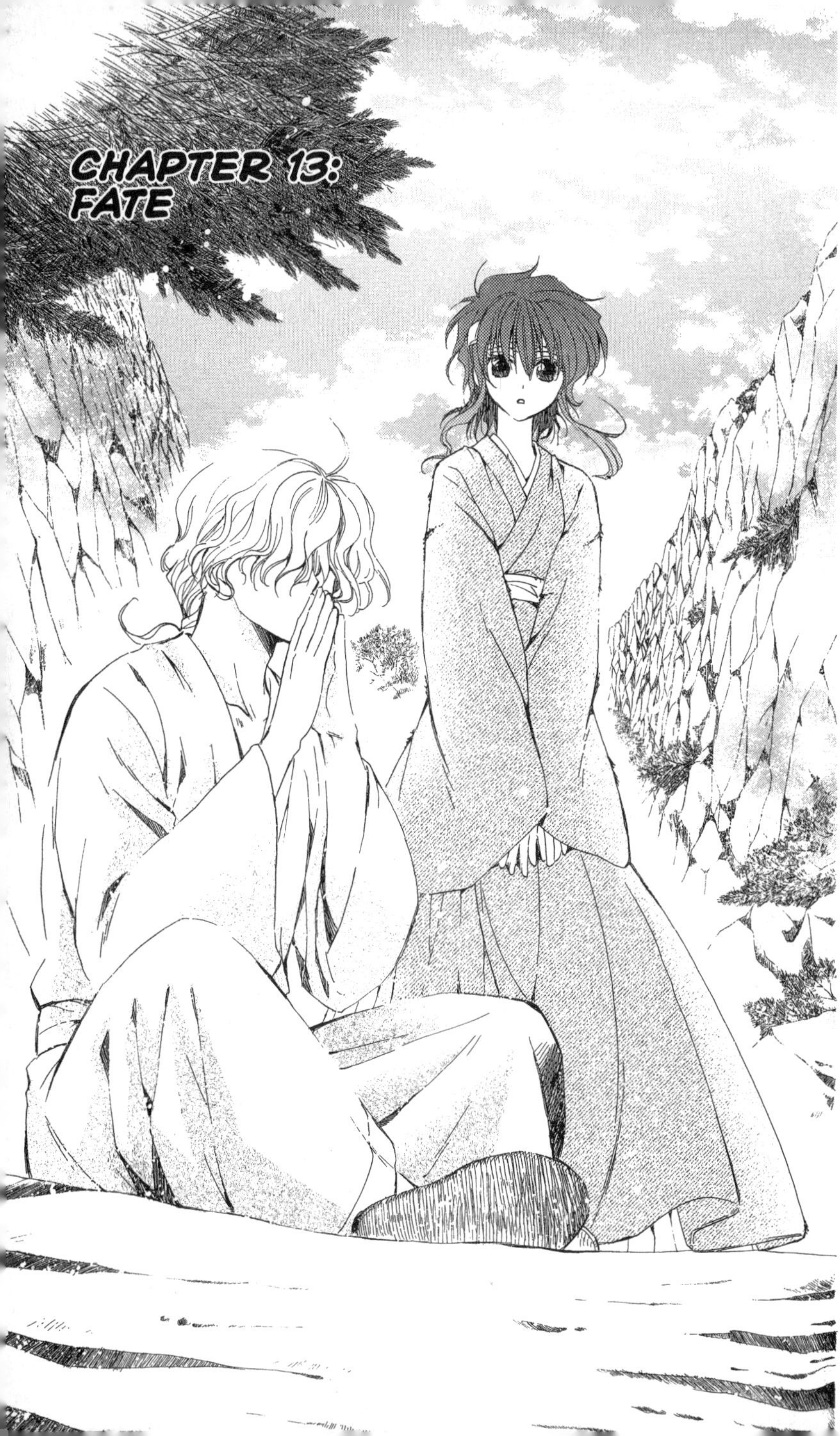
CHAPTER 13:
FATE

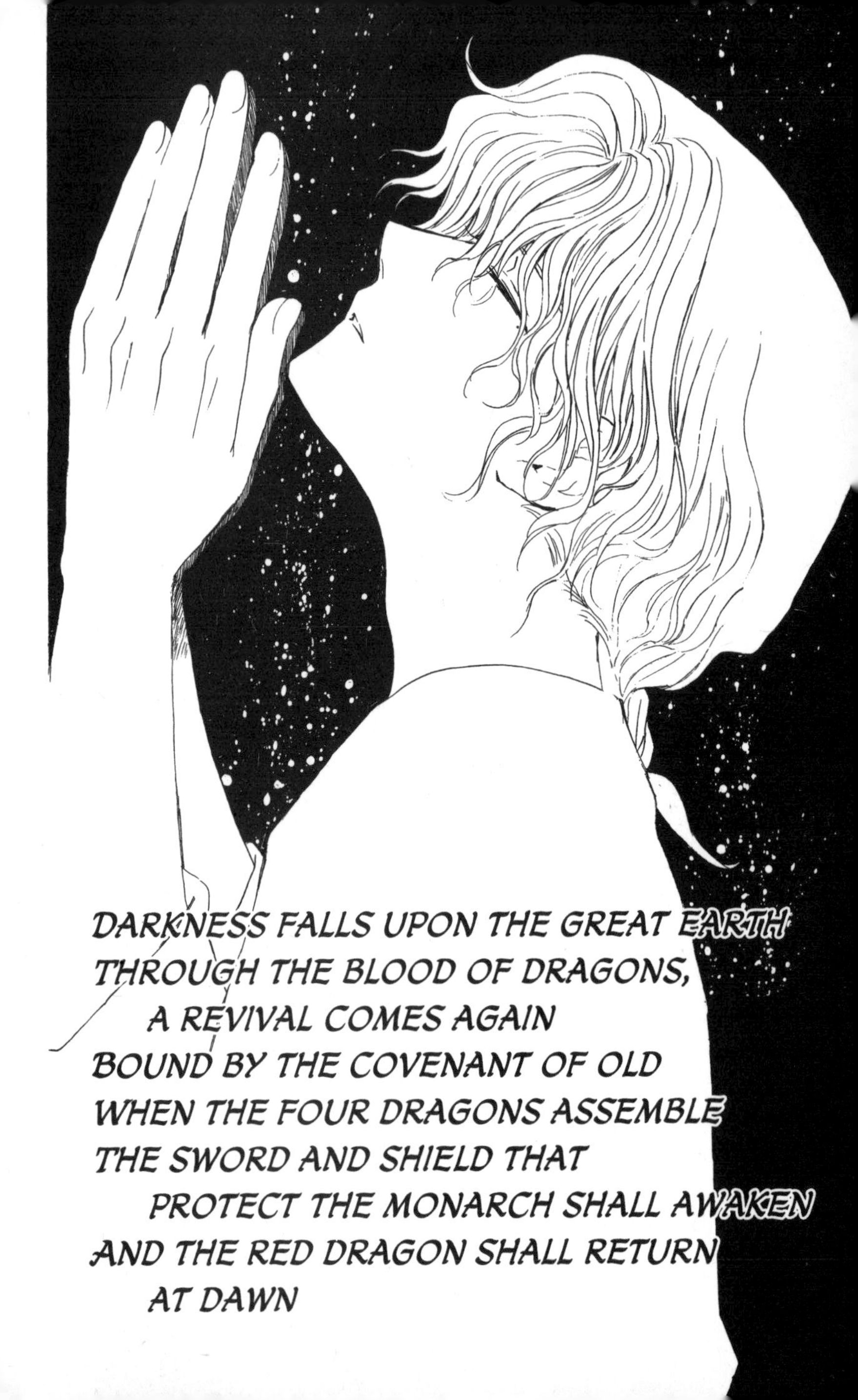
DARKNESS FALLS UPON THE GREAT EARTH
THROUGH THE BLOOD OF DRAGONS,
A REVIVAL COMES AGAIN
BOUND BY THE COVENANT OF OLD
WHEN THE FOUR DRAGONS ASSEMBLE
THE SWORD AND SHIELD THAT
PROTECT THE MONARCH SHALL AWAKEN
AND THE RED DRAGON SHALL RETURN
AT DAWN

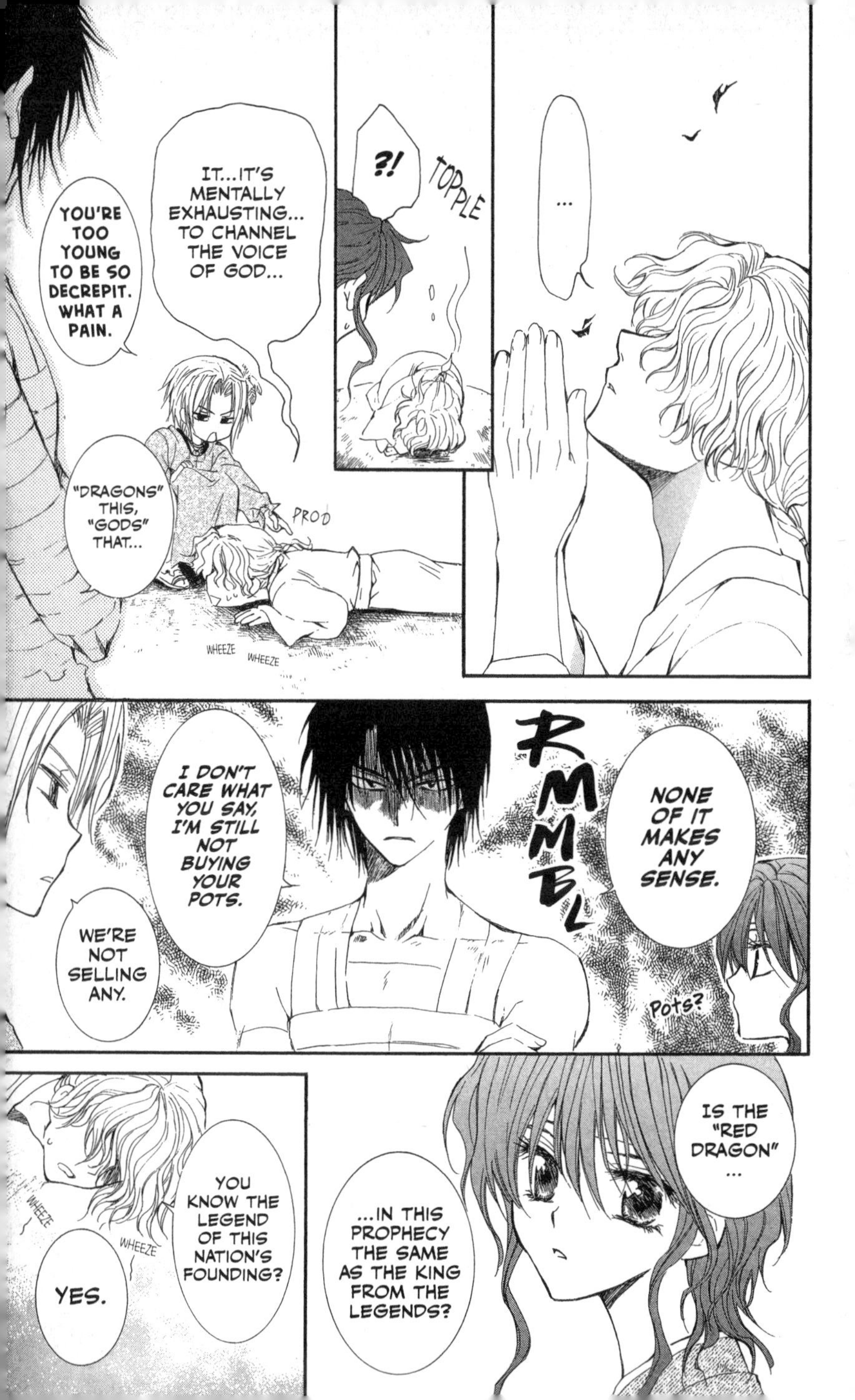
...
?!
TOPPLE
IT...IT'S MENTALLY EXHAUSTING... TO CHANNEL THE VOICE OF GOD...
YOU'RE TOO YOUNG TO BE SO DECREPIT. WHAT A PAIN.
PROD
"DRAGONS" THIS, "GODS" THAT...
WHEEZE WHEEZE
NONE OF IT MAKES ANY SENSE.
RMMBL
Pots?
I DON'T CARE WHAT YOU SAY, I'M STILL NOT BUYING YOUR POTS.
WE'RE NOT SELLING ANY.
IS THE "RED DRAGON"...
...IN THIS PROPHECY THE SAME AS THE KING FROM THE LEGENDS?
YOU KNOW THE LEGEND OF THIS NATION'S FOUNDING?
WHEEZE
YES.
WHEEZE

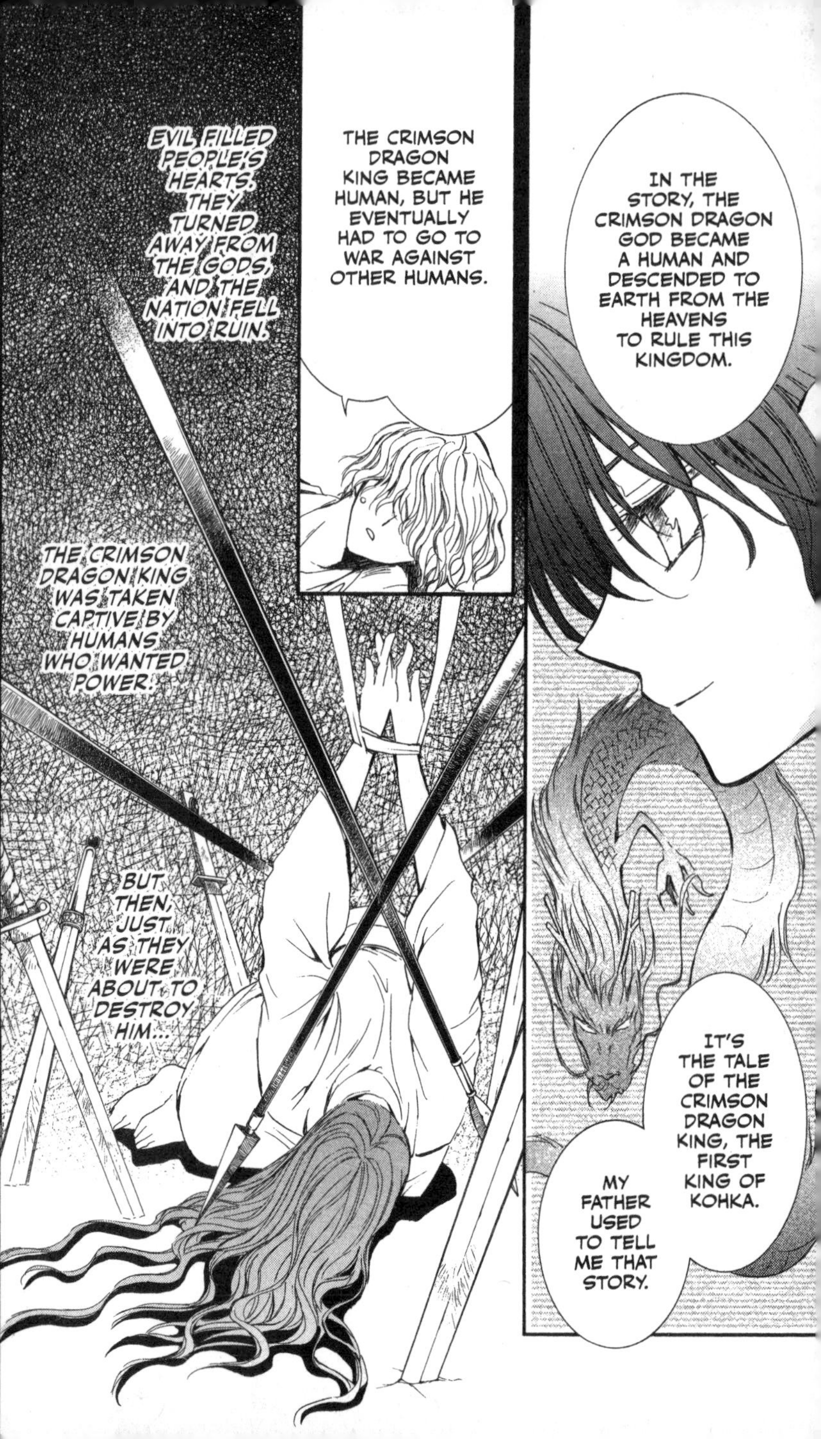
IN THE STORY, THE CRIMSON DRAGON GOD BECAME A HUMAN AND DESCENDED TO EARTH FROM THE HEAVENS TO RULE THIS KINGDOM.
IT'S THE TALE OF THE CRIMSON DRAGON KING, THE FIRST KING OF KOHKA.
MY FATHER USED TO TELL ME THAT STORY.
THE CRIMSON DRAGON KING BECAME HUMAN, BUT HE EVENTUALLY HAD TO GO TO WAR AGAINST OTHER HUMANS.
EVIL FILLED PEOPLE'S HEARTS. THEY TURNED AWAY FROM THE GODS, AND THE NATION FELL INTO RUIN.
THE CRIMSON DRAGON KING WAS TAKEN CAPTIVE BY HUMANS WHO WANTED POWER.
BUT THEN, JUST AS THEY WERE ABOUT TO DESTROY HIM...

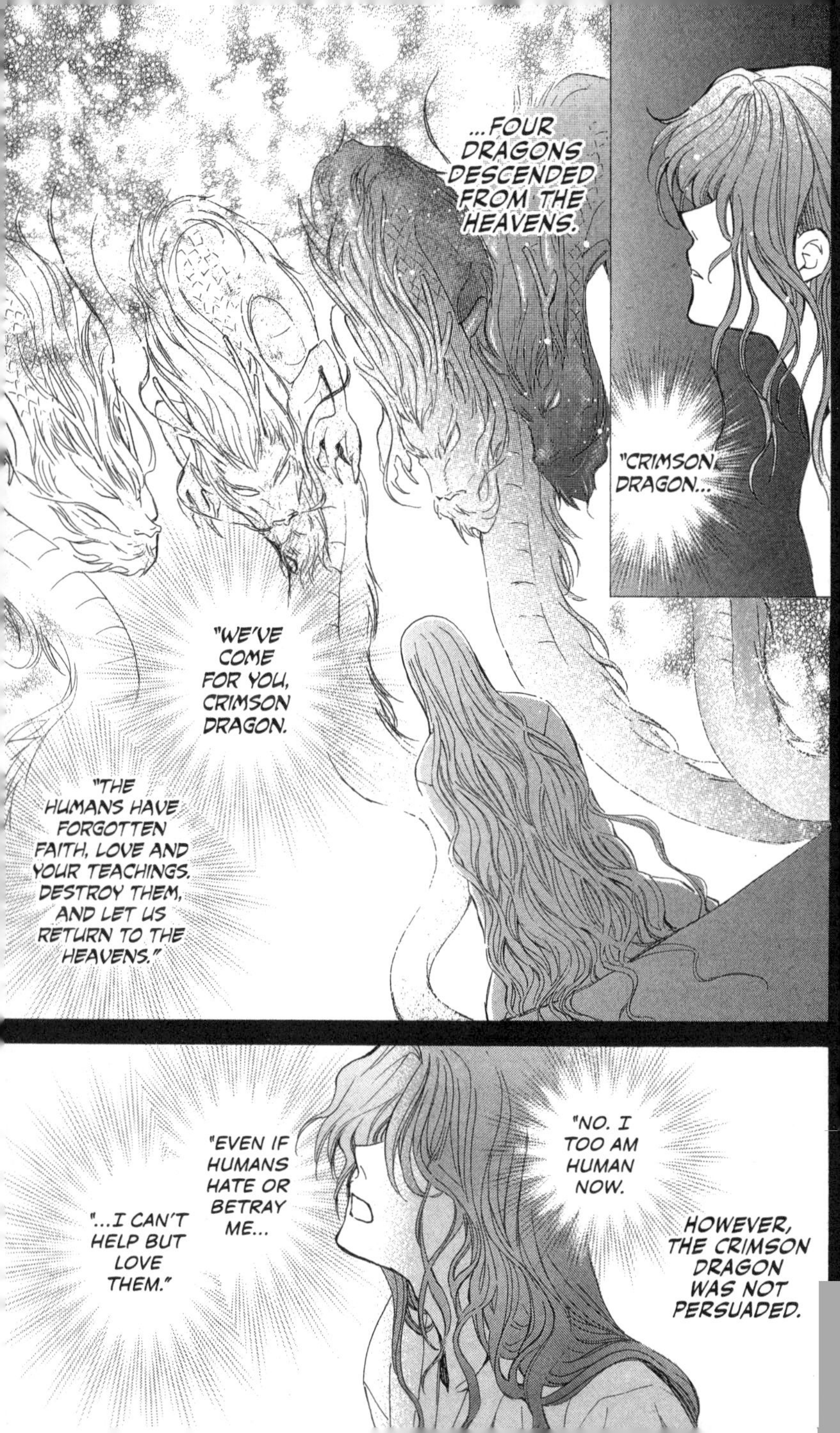
...FOUR DRAGONS DESCENDED FROM THE HEAVENS.
"CRIMSON DRAGON...
"WE'VE COME FOR YOU, CRIMSON DRAGON.
"THE HUMANS HAVE FORGOTTEN FAITH, LOVE AND YOUR TEACHINGS. DESTROY THEM, AND LET US RETURN TO THE HEAVENS."
HOWEVER, THE CRIMSON DRAGON WAS NOT PERSUADED.
"NO. I TOO AM HUMAN NOW.
"EVEN IF HUMANS HATE OR BETRAY ME...
"...I CAN'T HELP BUT LOVE THEM."

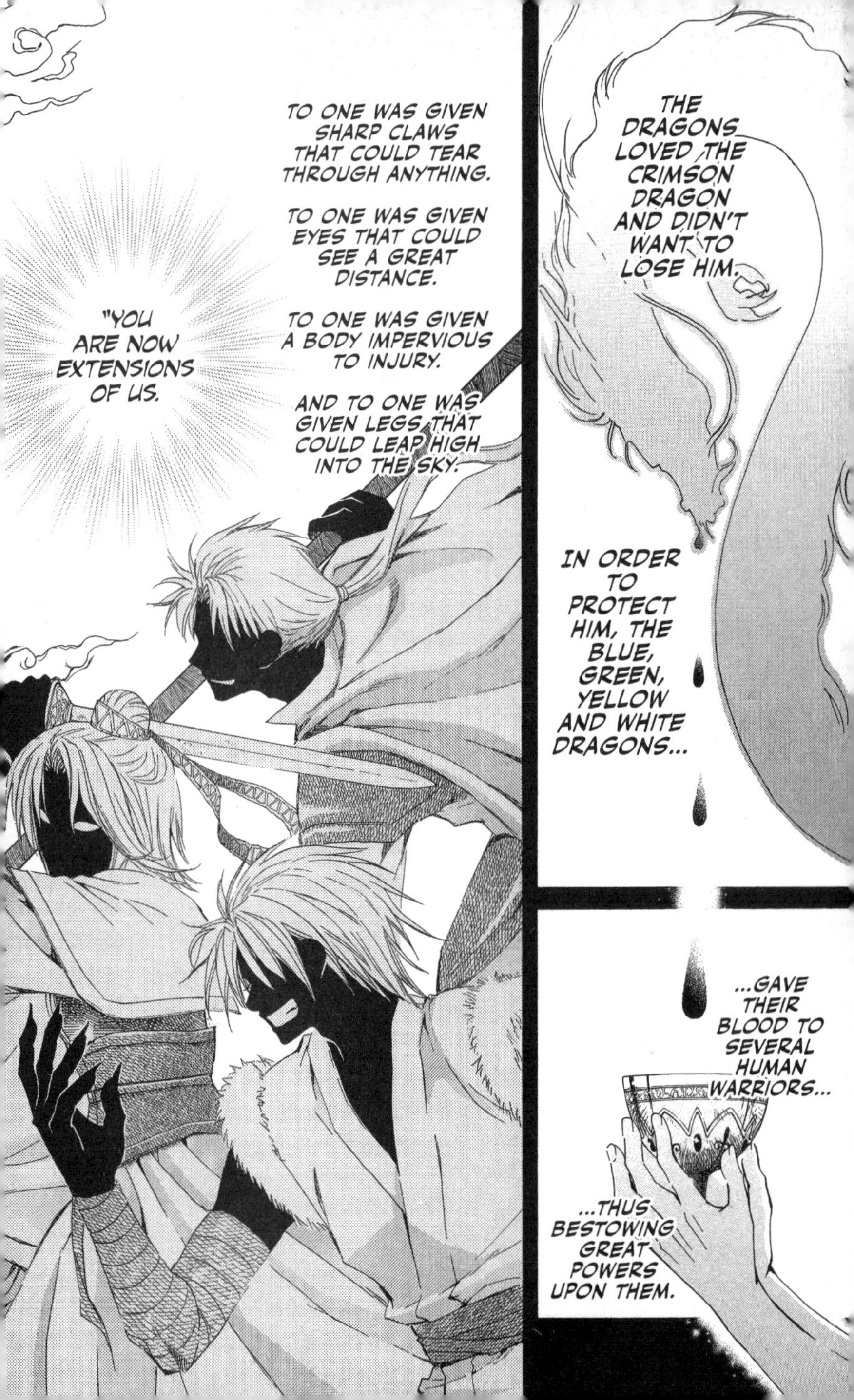
THE DRAGONS LOVED THE CRIMSON DRAGON AND DIDN'T WANT TO LOSE HIM.
IN ORDER TO PROTECT HIM, THE BLUE, GREEN, YELLOW AND WHITE DRAGONS...
...GAVE THEIR BLOOD TO SEVERAL HUMAN WARRIORS...
...THUS BESTOWING GREAT POWERS UPON THEM.
TO ONE WAS GIVEN SHARP CLAWS THAT COULD TEAR THROUGH ANYTHING.
TO ONE WAS GIVEN EYES THAT COULD SEE A GREAT DISTANCE.
TO ONE WAS GIVEN A BODY IMPERVIOUS TO INJURY.
AND TO ONE WAS GIVEN LEGS THAT COULD LEAP HIGH INTO THE SKY.
"YOU ARE NOW EXTENSIONS OF US.

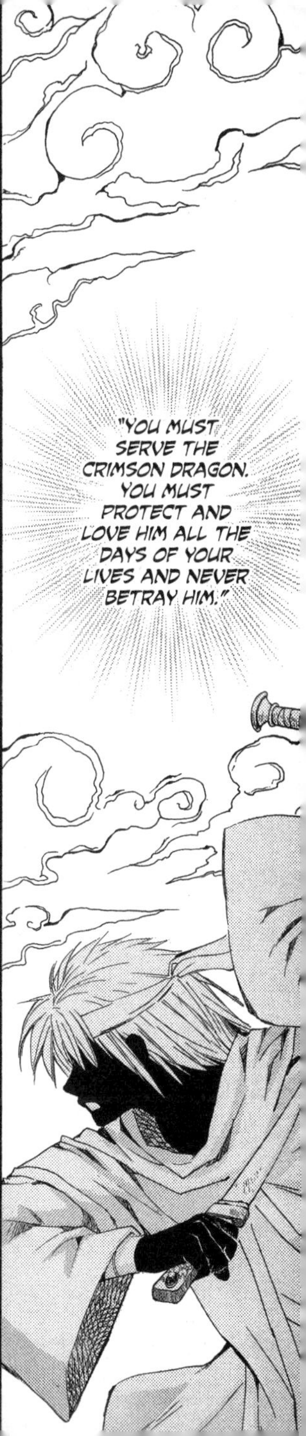
"YOU MUST SERVE THE CRIMSON DRAGON. YOU MUST PROTECT AND LOVE HIM ALL THE DAYS OF YOUR LIVES AND NEVER BETRAY HIM."

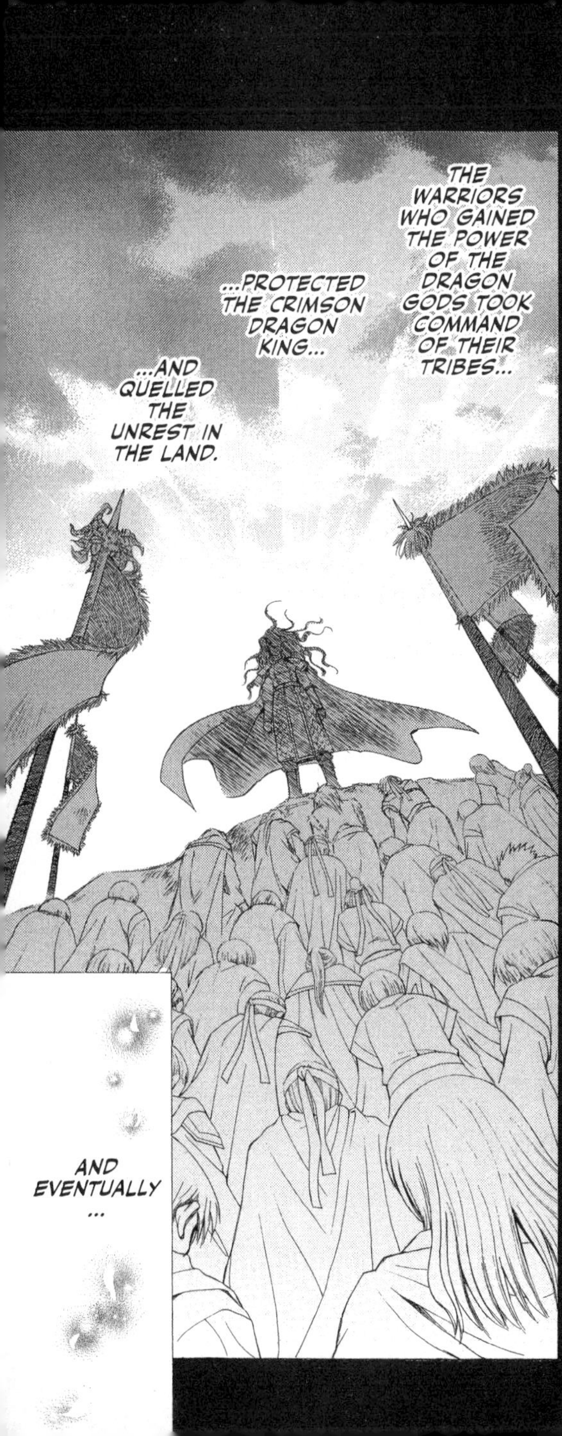
THE WARRIORS WHO GAINED THE POWER OF THE DRAGON GODS TOOK COMMAND OF THEIR TRIBES...
...PROTECTED THE CRIMSON DRAGON KING...
...AND QUELLED THE UNREST IN THE LAND.
AND EVENTUALLY ...

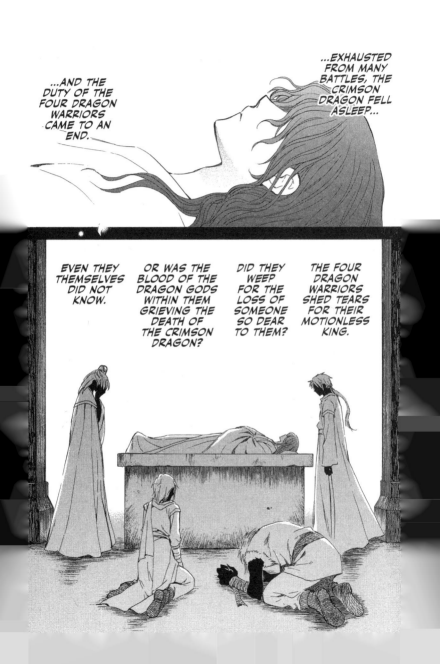

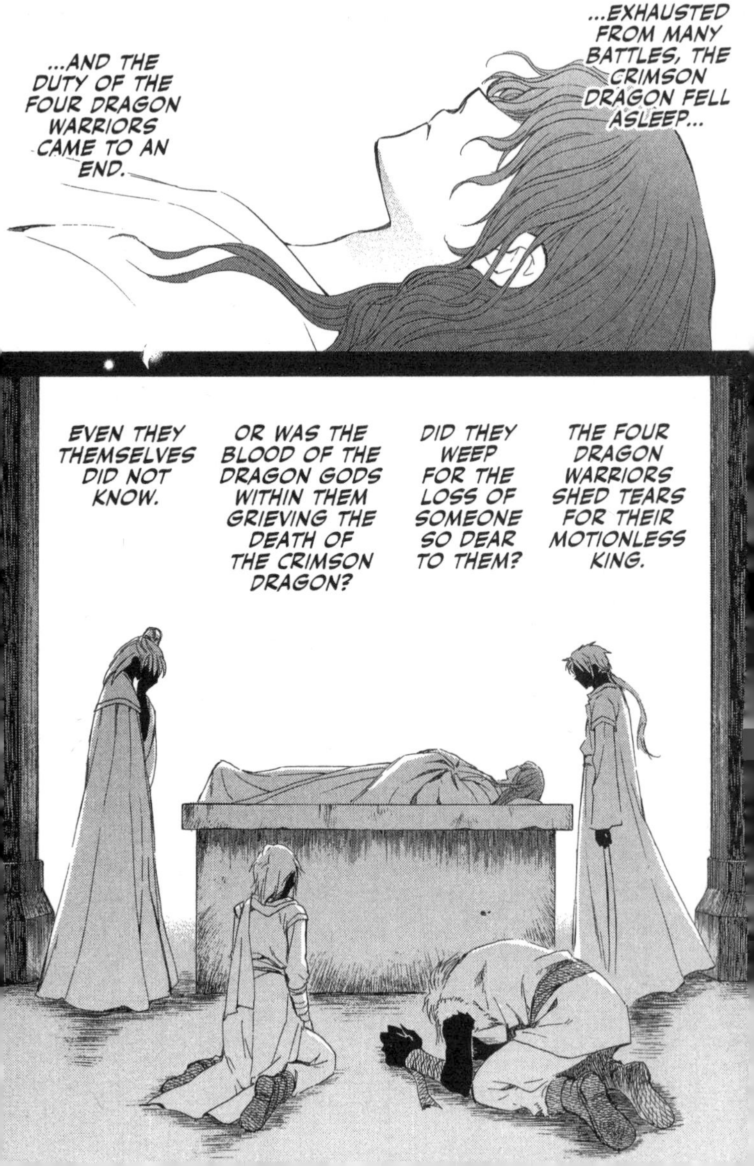
...EXHAUSTED FROM MANY BATTLES, THE CRIMSON DRAGON FELL ASLEEP...
...AND THE DUTY OF THE FOUR DRAGON WARRIORS CAME TO AN END.
THE FOUR DRAGON WARRIORS SHED TEARS FOR THEIR MOTIONLESS KING.
DID THEY WEEP FOR THE LOSS OF SOMEONE SO DEAR TO THEM?
OR WAS THE BLOOD OF THE DRAGON GODS WITHIN THEM GRIEVING THE DEATH OF THE CRIMSON DRAGON?
EVEN THEY THEMSELVES DID NOT KNOW.

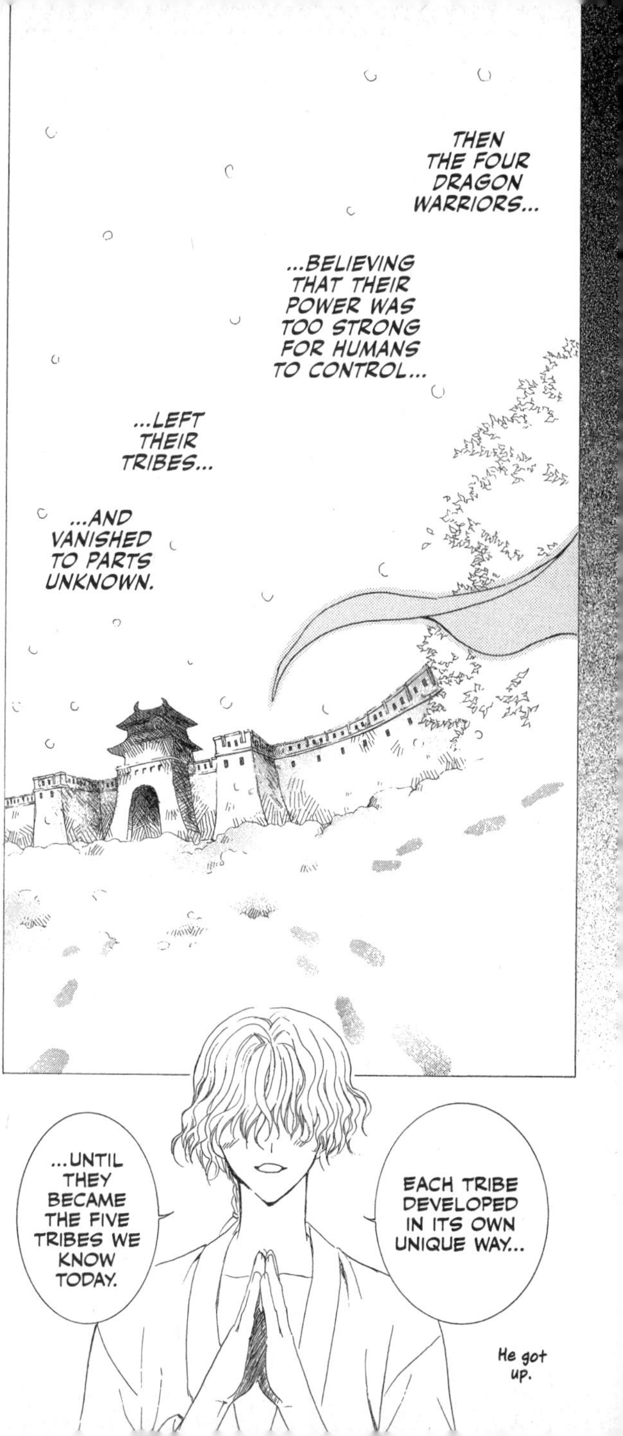
THEN THE FOUR DRAGON WARRIORS...
...BELIEVING THAT THEIR POWER WAS TOO STRONG FOR HUMANS TO CONTROL...
...LEFT THEIR TRIBES...
...AND VANISHED TO PARTS UNKNOWN.
EACH TRIBE DEVELOPED IN ITS OWN UNIQUE WAY...
...UNTIL THEY BECAME THE FIVE TRIBES WE KNOW TODAY.
He got up.

It's a lot of fun to draw Yun and Ik-su. And their hair is easy to draw since it's white. (*Laughs*)

In my previous series, *NG Life*, I used tone to color the hero's hair...and it was just awful. I told myself I'd never, ever use tone to color my protagonist's hair again! It was a good theory, but in order to get the "redness" I wanted for my heroine's hair, I had to use tone. And to make things worse, it's frizzy hair, which is tricky to apply tone to. It reduces my assistants to tears. Sorry...

I thought it would be a little easier after she cut her hair, but that was a delusional hope.

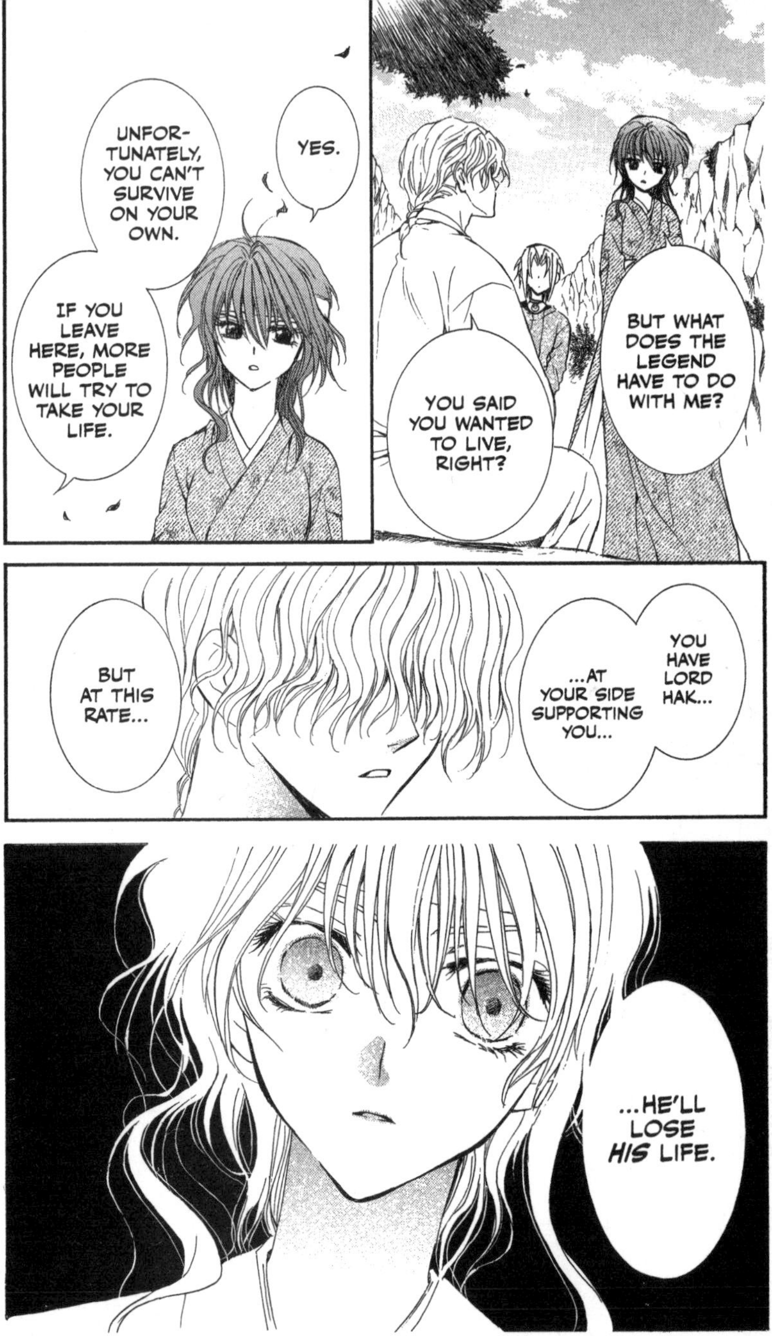
BUT WHAT DOES THE LEGEND HAVE TO DO WITH ME?
YOU SAID YOU WANTED TO LIVE, RIGHT?
YES.
UNFORTUNATELY, YOU CAN'T SURVIVE ON YOUR OWN.
IF YOU LEAVE HERE, MORE PEOPLE WILL TRY TO TAKE YOUR LIFE.
YOU HAVE LORD HAK...
...AT YOUR SIDE SUPPORTING YOU...
BUT AT THIS RATE...
...HE'LL LOSE *HIS* LIFE.

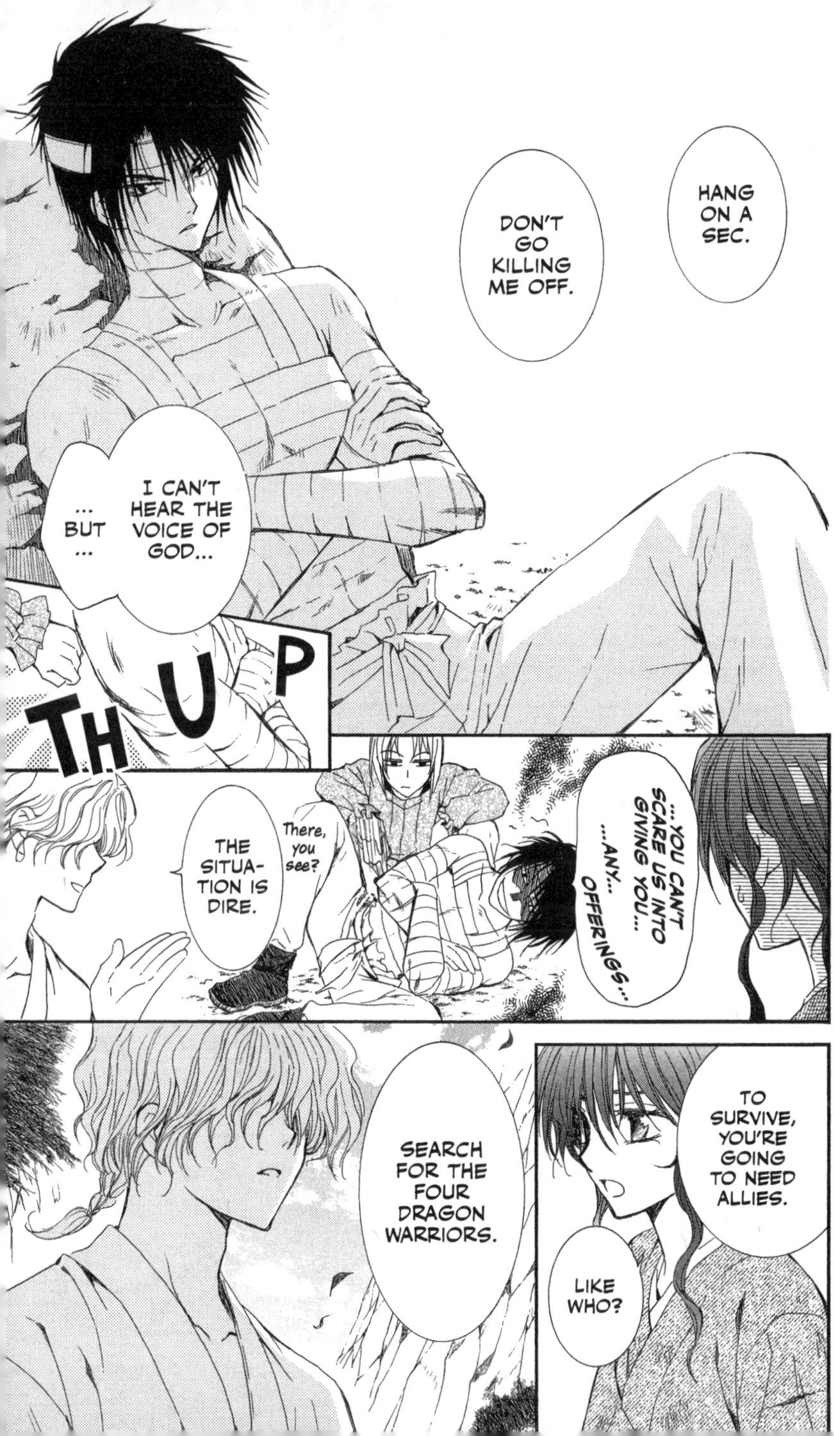
HANG ON A SEC.
DON'T GO KILLING ME OFF.
I CAN'T HEAR THE VOICE OF GOD...
... BUT ...
THUP
...YOU CAN'T SCARE US INTO GIVING YOU... ...ANY... OFFERINGS...
There, you see?
THE SITUATION IS DIRE.
TO SURVIVE, YOU'RE GOING TO NEED ALLIES.
LIKE WHO?
SEARCH FOR THE FOUR DRAGON WARRIORS.

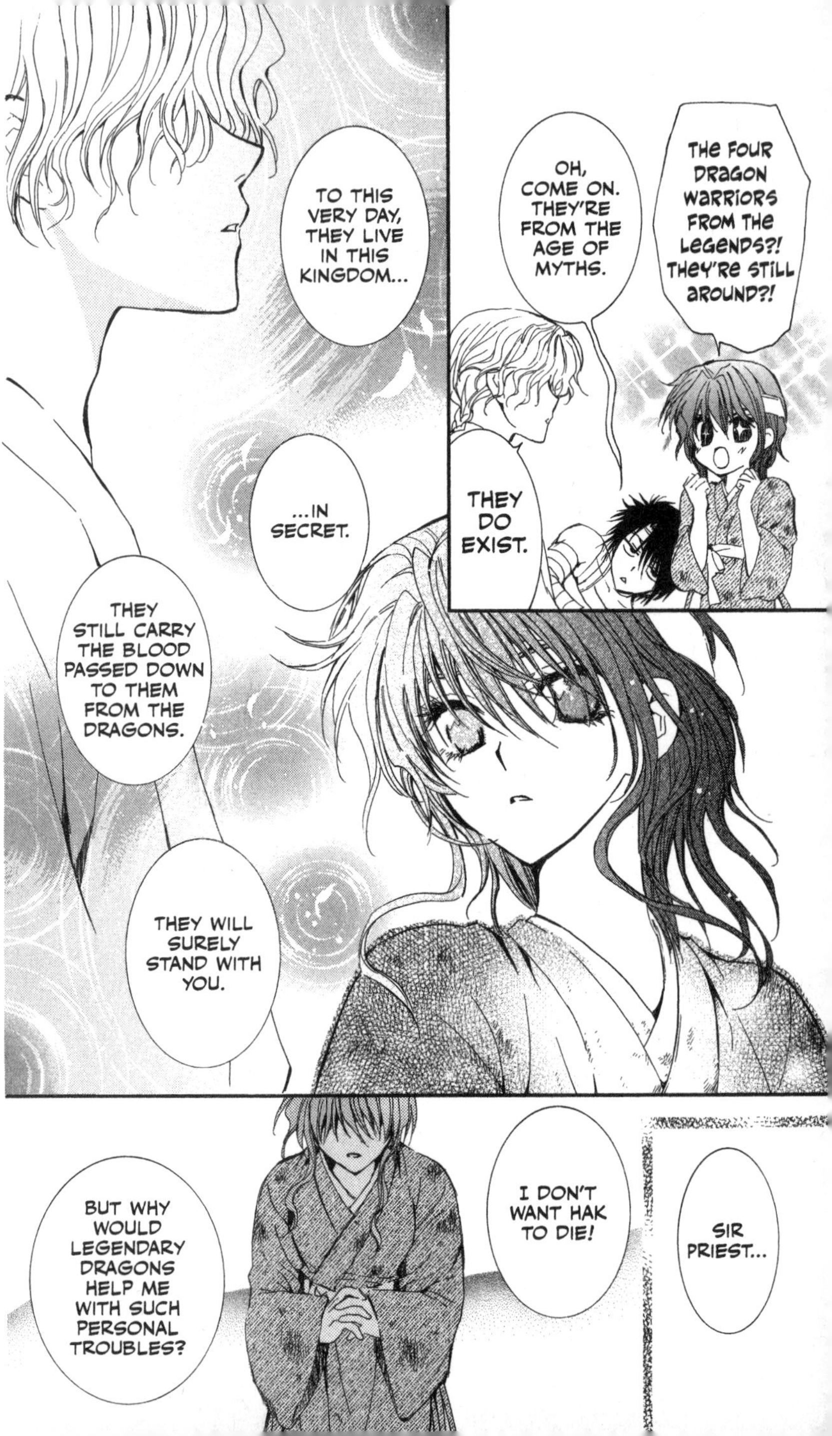
THE FOUR DRAGON WARRIORS FROM THE LEGENDS?! THEY'RE STILL AROUND?!
OH, COME ON. THEY'RE FROM THE AGE OF MYTHS.
THEY DO EXIST.
TO THIS VERY DAY, THEY LIVE IN THIS KINGDOM...
...IN SECRET.
THEY STILL CARRY THE BLOOD PASSED DOWN TO THEM FROM THE DRAGONS.
THEY WILL SURELY STAND WITH YOU.
SIR PRIEST...
I DON'T WANT HAK TO DIE!
BUT WHY WOULD LEGENDARY DRAGONS HELP ME WITH SUCH PERSONAL TROUBLES?

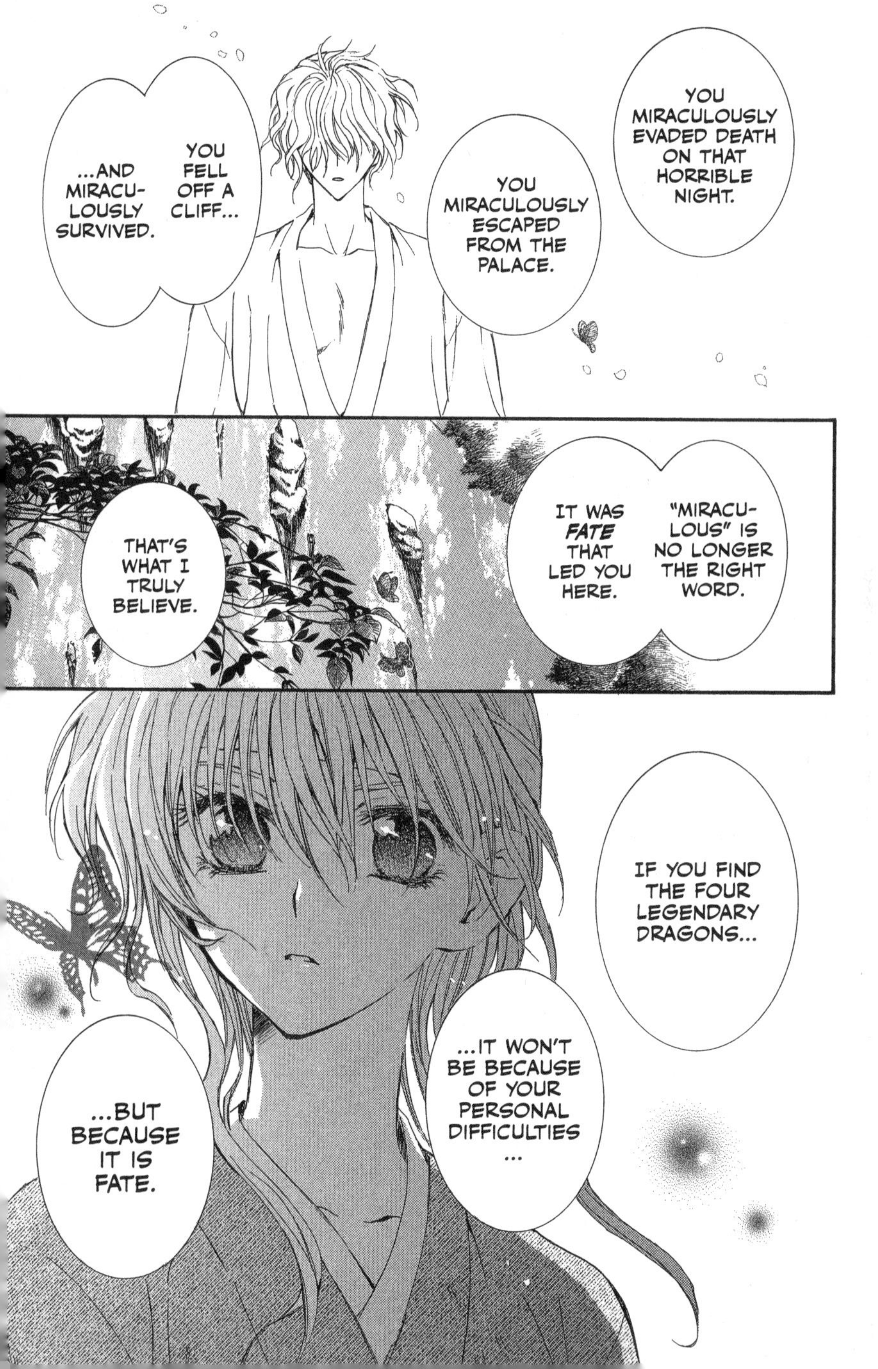
YOU MIRACULOUSLY EVADED DEATH ON THAT HORRIBLE NIGHT.
YOU MIRACULOUSLY ESCAPED FROM THE PALACE.
YOU FELL OFF A CLIFF...
...AND MIRACU-LOUSLY SURVIVED.
"MIRACU-LOUS" IS NO LONGER THE RIGHT WORD.
IT WAS *FATE* THAT LED YOU HERE.
THAT'S WHAT I TRULY BELIEVE.
IF YOU FIND THE FOUR LEGENDARY DRAGONS...
...IT WON'T BE BECAUSE OF YOUR PERSONAL DIFFICULTIES...
...BUT BECAUSE IT IS FATE.

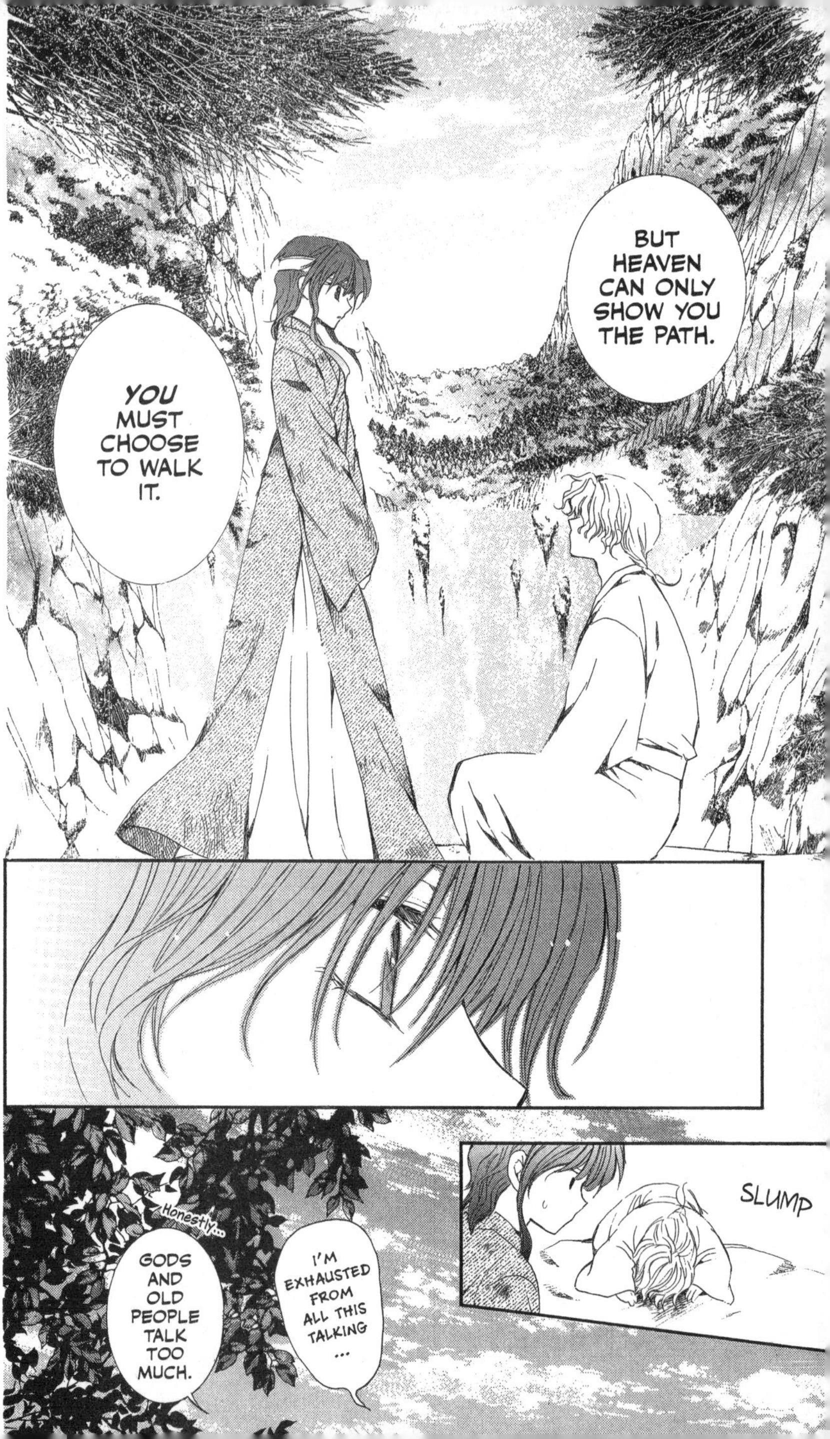

BUT HEAVEN CAN ONLY SHOW YOU THE PATH.
YOU MUST CHOOSE TO WALK IT.
SLUMP
I'M EXHAUSTED FROM ALL THIS TALKING ...
Honestly...
GODS AND OLD PEOPLE TALK TOO MUCH.

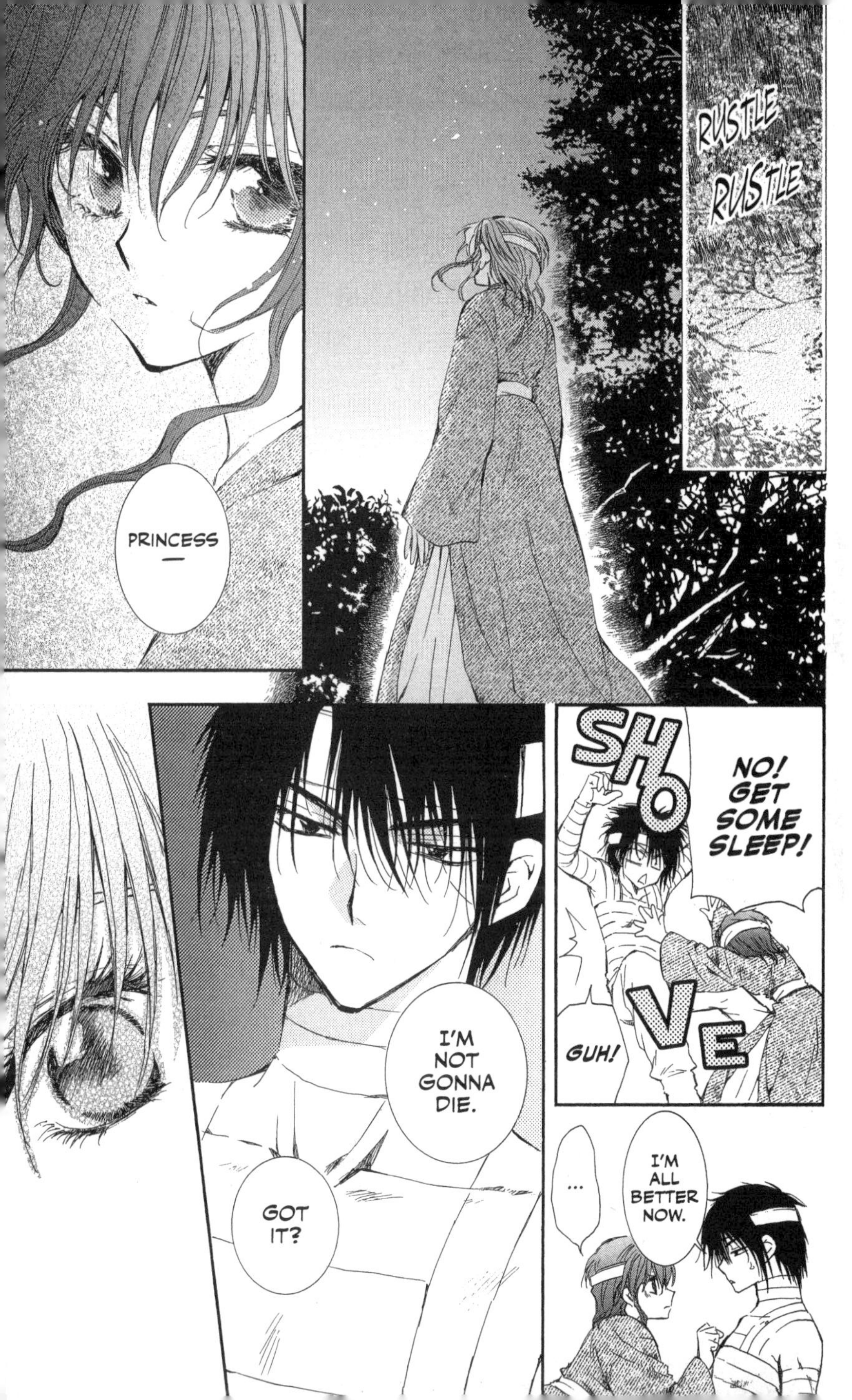
RUSTLE
RUSTLE
PRINCESS —
NO! GET SOME SLEEP!
SHOVE
GUH!
I'M ALL BETTER NOW.
...
I'M NOT GONNA DIE.
GOT IT?

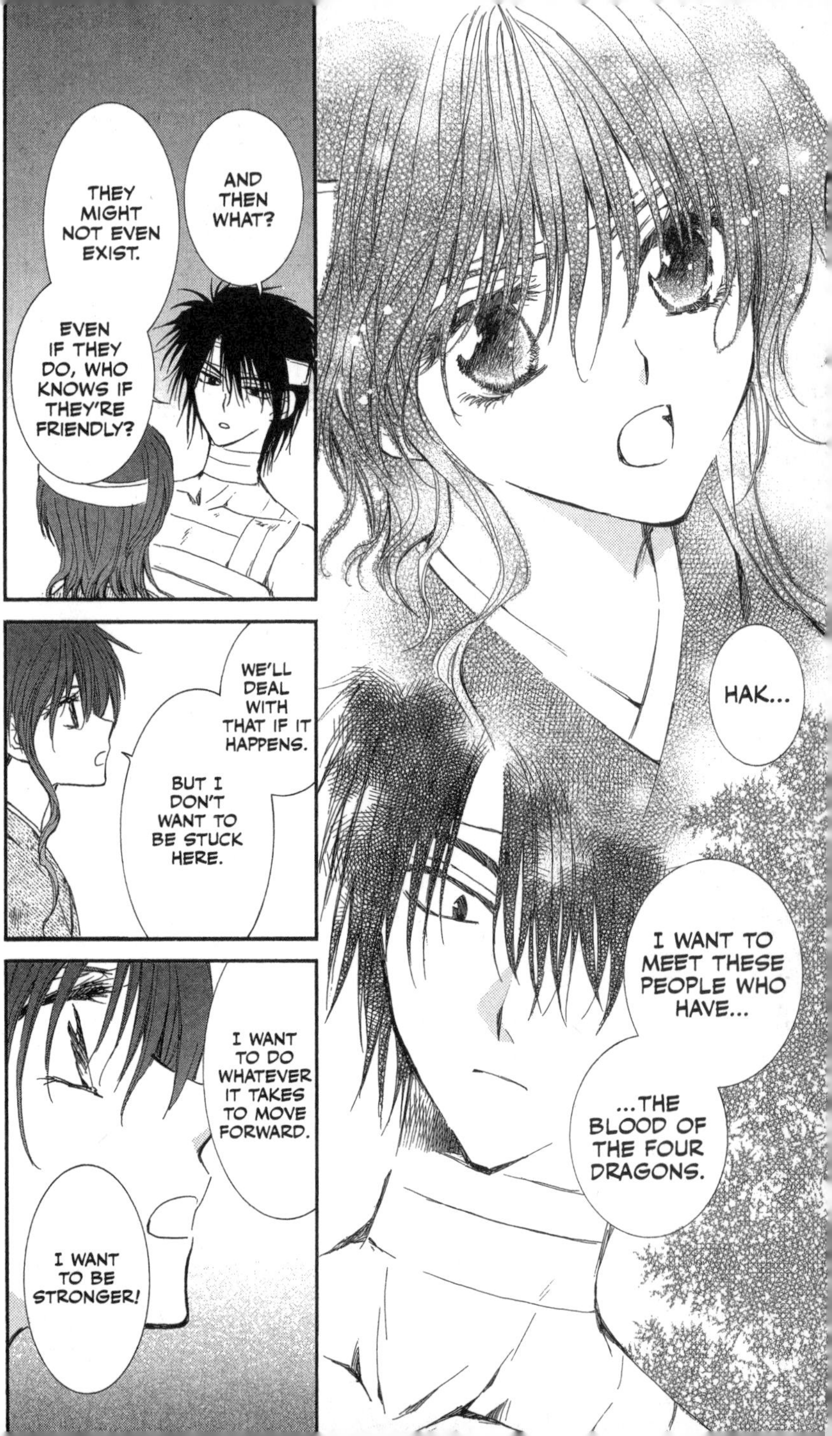
HAK...
I WANT TO MEET THESE PEOPLE WHO HAVE...
...THE BLOOD OF THE FOUR DRAGONS.
AND THEN WHAT?
THEY MIGHT NOT EVEN EXIST.
EVEN IF THEY DO, WHO KNOWS IF THEY'RE FRIENDLY?
WE'LL DEAL WITH THAT IF IT HAPPENS.
BUT I DON'T WANT TO BE STUCK HERE.
I WANT TO DO WHATEVER IT TAKES TO MOVE FORWARD.
I WANT TO BE STRONGER!

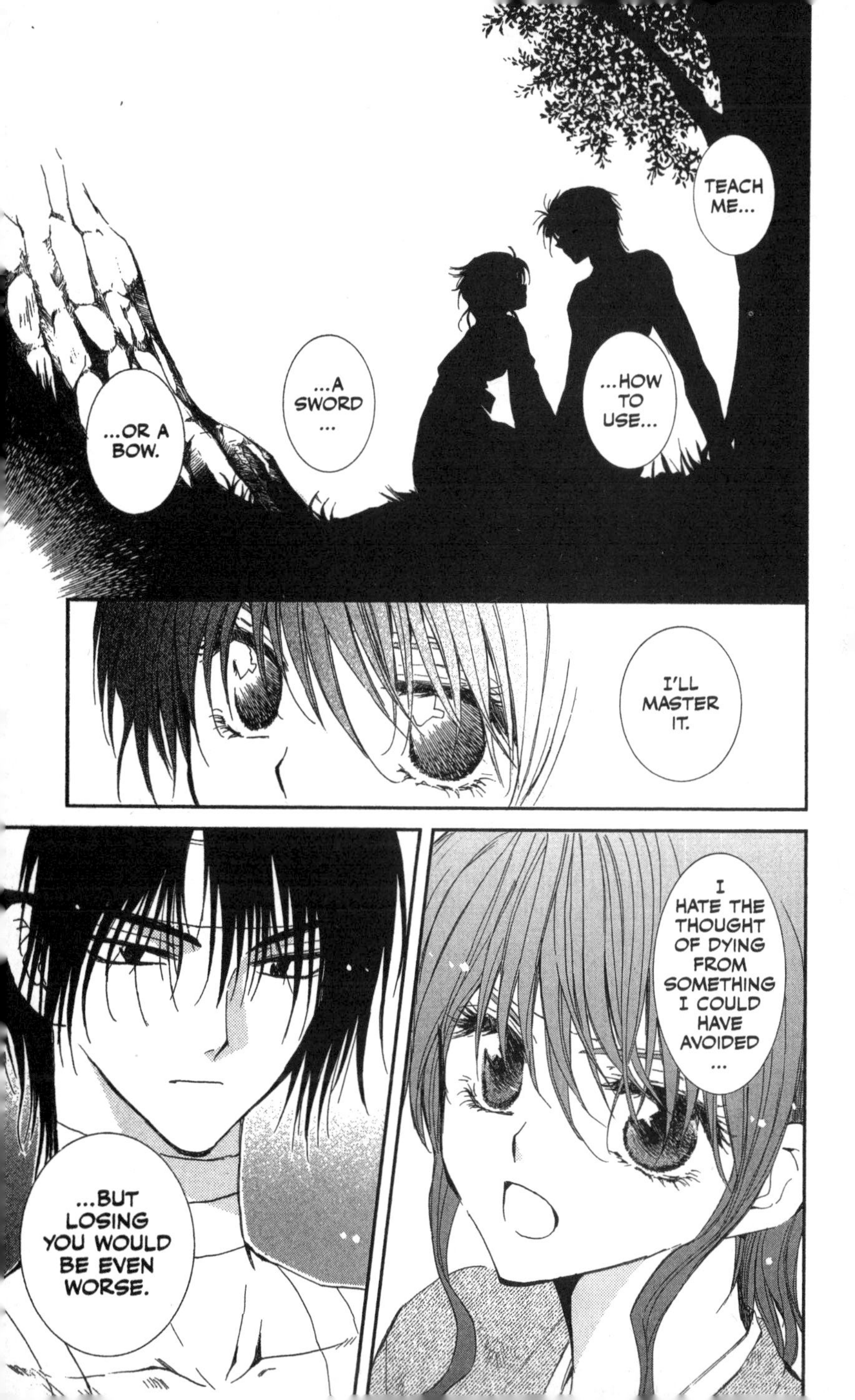
TEACH ME...
...HOW TO USE...
...A SWORD...
...OR A BOW.
I'LL MASTER IT.
I HATE THE THOUGHT OF DYING FROM SOMETHING I COULD HAVE AVOIDED...
...BUT LOSING YOU WOULD BE EVEN WORSE.

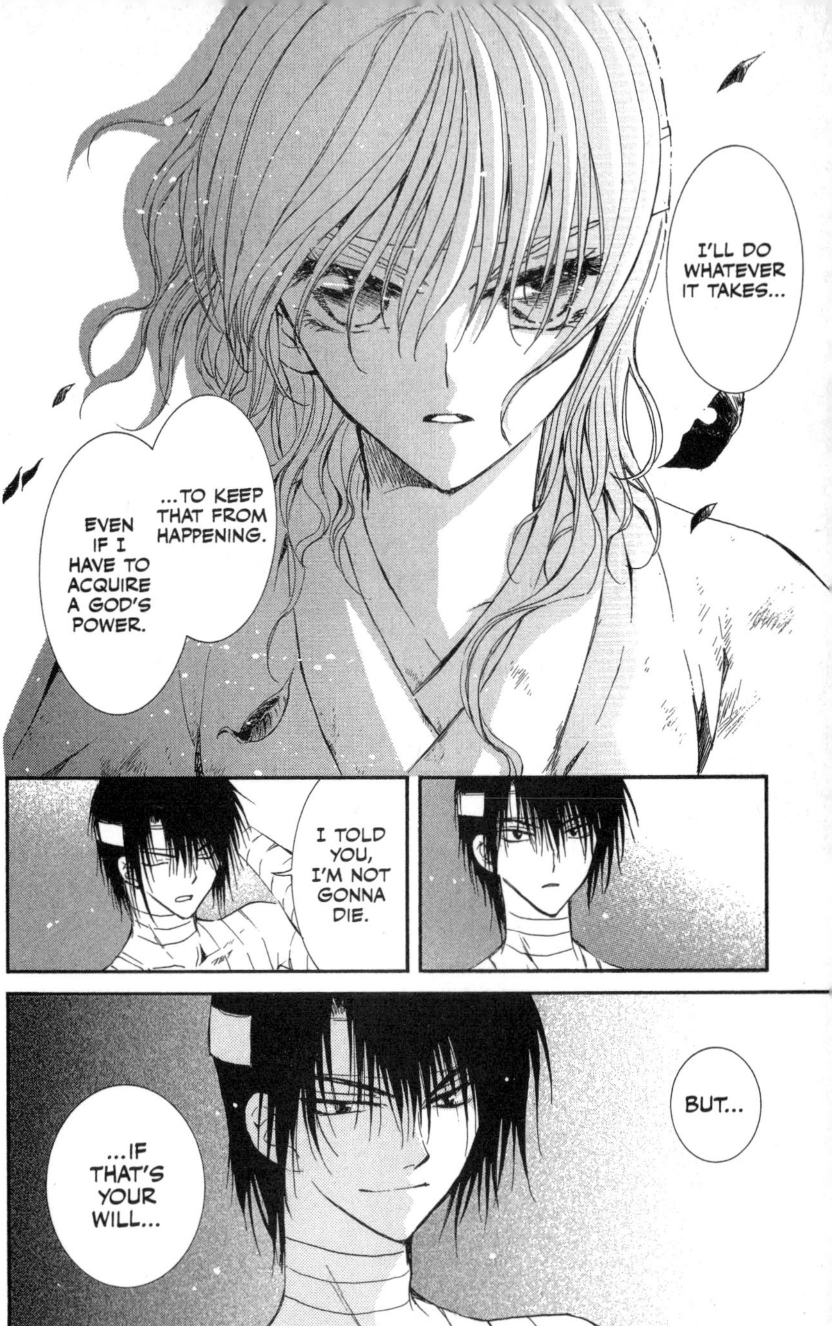
I'LL DO WHATEVER IT TAKES...
...TO KEEP THAT FROM HAPPENING.
EVEN IF I HAVE TO ACQUIRE A GOD'S POWER.
I TOLD YOU, I'M NOT GONNA DIE.
BUT...
...IF THAT'S YOUR WILL...

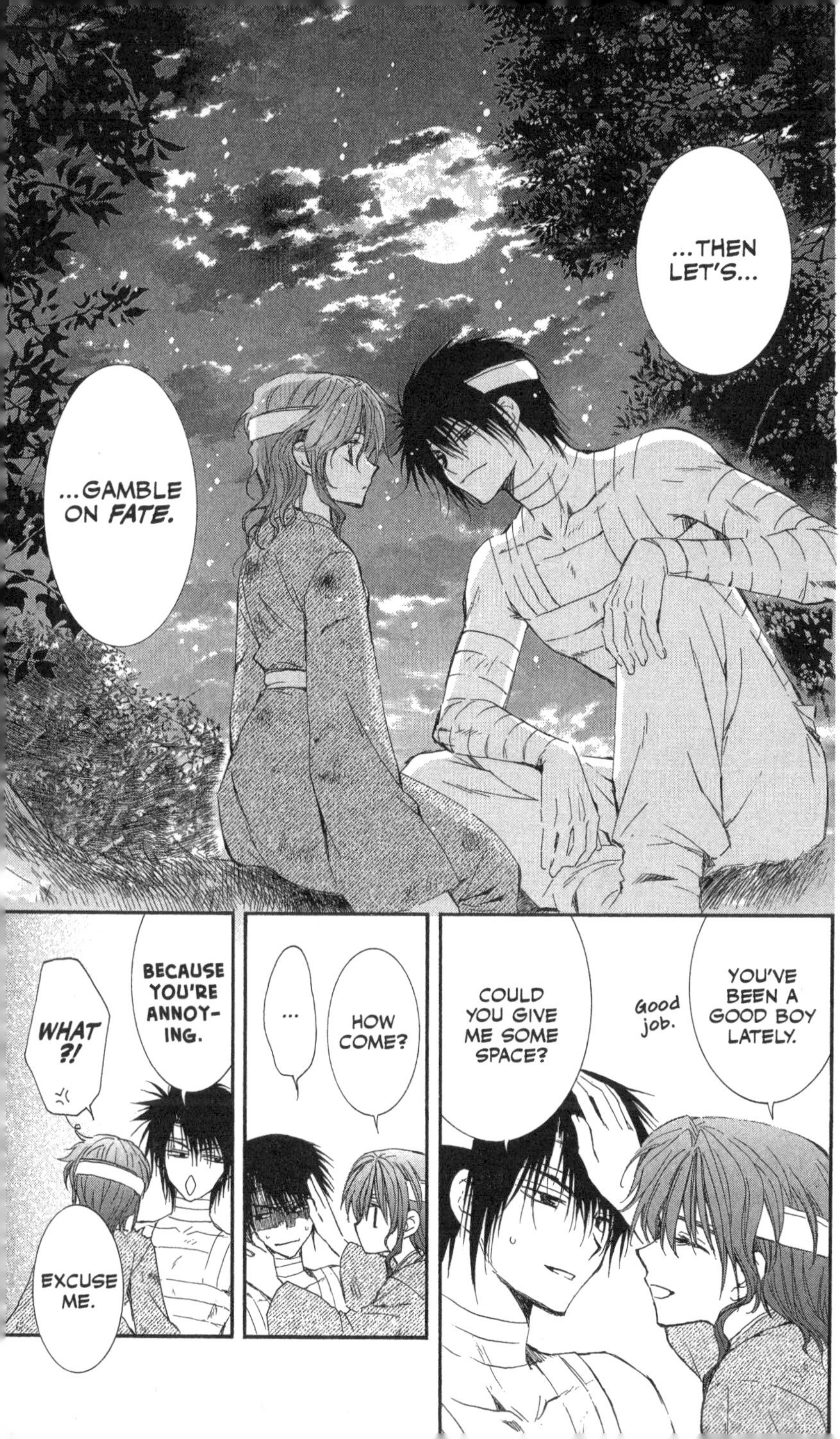
...THEN LET'S...
...GAMBLE ON *FATE.*
YOU'VE BEEN A GOOD BOY LATELY.
Good job.
COULD YOU GIVE ME SOME SPACE?
HOW COME?
...
BECAUSE YOU'RE ANNOY-ING.
WHAT ?!
EXCUSE ME.

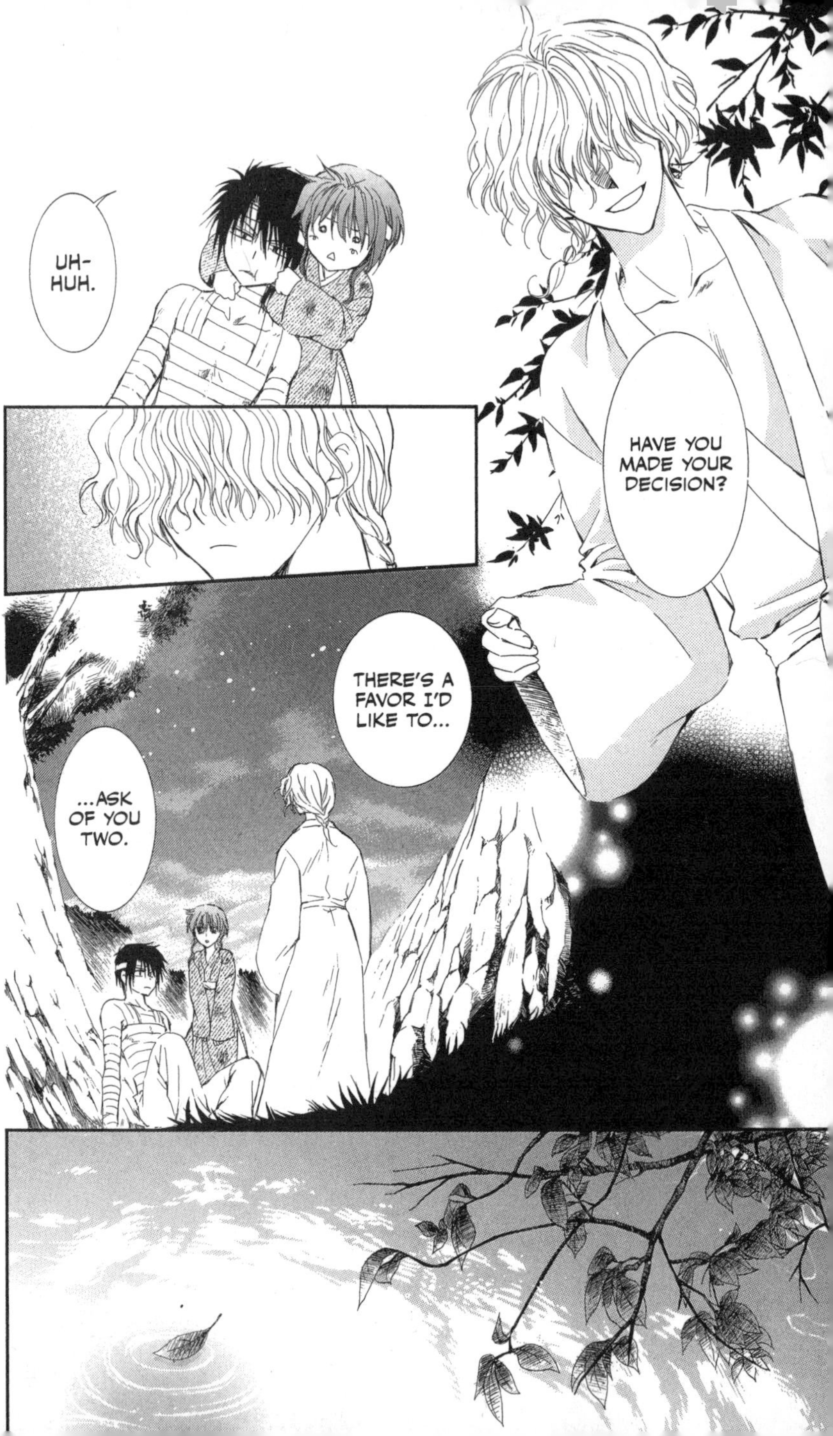
HAVE YOU MADE YOUR DECISION?
UH-HUH.
THERE'S A FAVOR I'D LIKE TO...
...ASK OF YOU TWO.

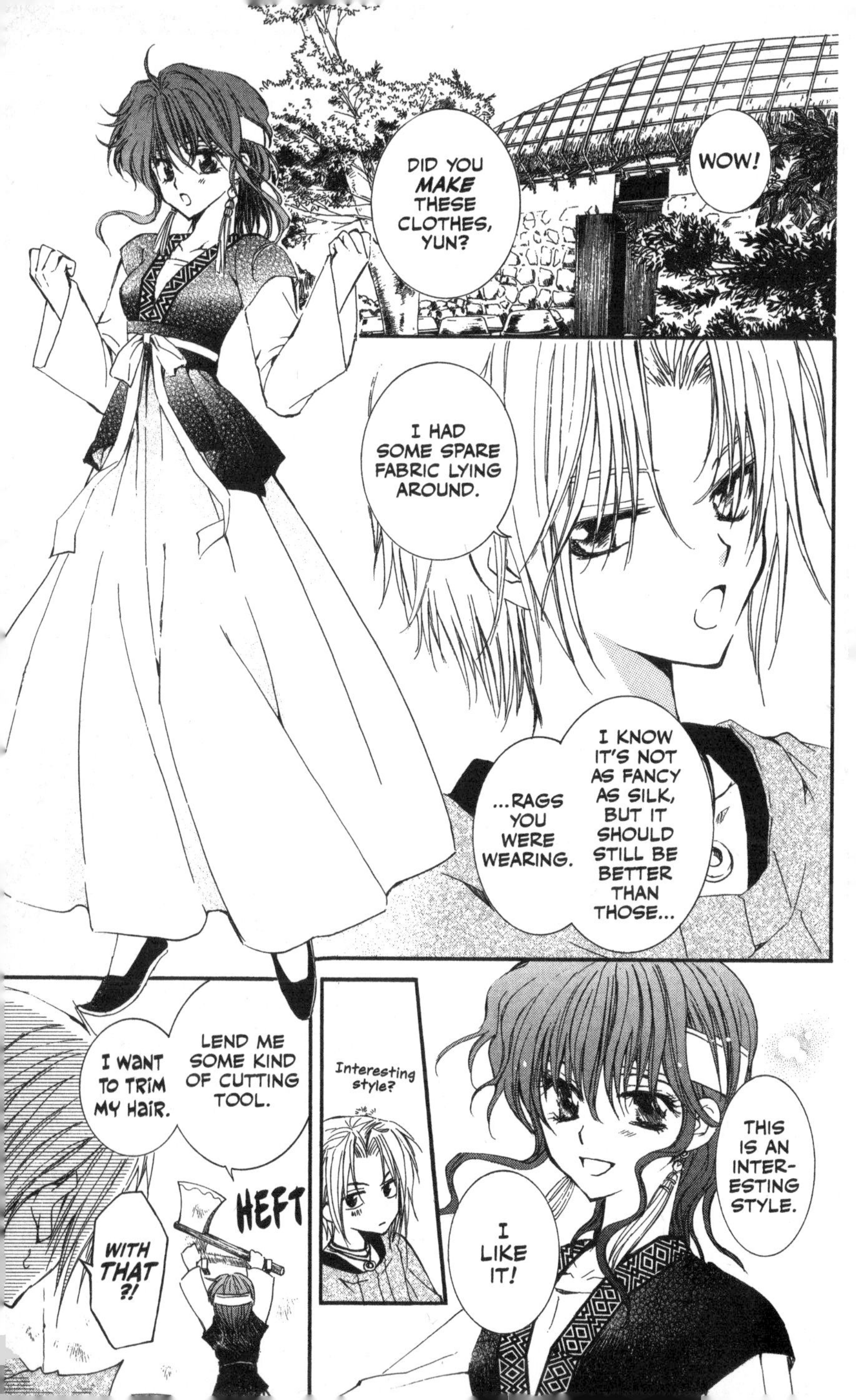
WOW!
DID YOU MAKE THESE CLOTHES, YUN?
I HAD SOME SPARE FABRIC LYING AROUND.
I KNOW IT'S NOT AS FANCY AS SILK, BUT IT SHOULD STILL BE BETTER THAN THOSE...
...RAGS YOU WERE WEARING.
THIS IS AN INTER-ESTING STYLE.
I LIKE IT!
Interesting style?
LEND ME SOME KIND OF CUTTING TOOL.
I WANT TO TRIM MY HAIR.
HEFT
WITH THAT?!

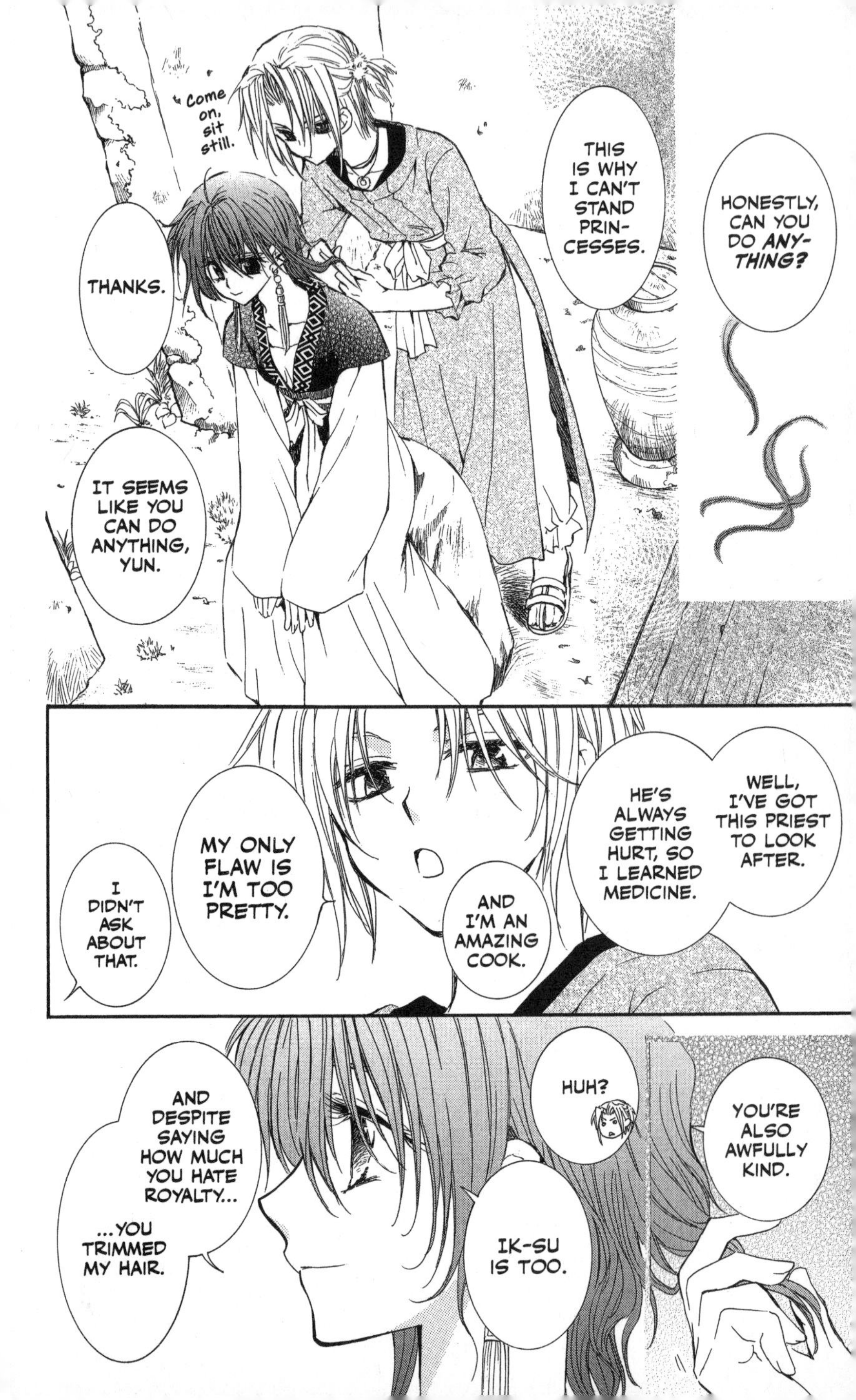
HONESTLY, CAN YOU DO *ANYTHING?*
THIS IS WHY I CAN'T STAND PRIN-CESSES.
Come on, sit still.
THANKS.
IT SEEMS LIKE YOU CAN DO ANYTHING, YUN.
WELL, I'VE GOT THIS PRIEST TO LOOK AFTER.
HE'S ALWAYS GETTING HURT, SO I LEARNED MEDICINE.
AND I'M AN AMAZING COOK.
MY ONLY FLAW IS I'M TOO PRETTY.
I DIDN'T ASK ABOUT THAT.
YOU'RE ALSO AWFULLY KIND.
HUH?
IK-SU IS TOO.
AND DESPITE SAYING HOW MUCH YOU HATE ROYALTY...
...YOU TRIMMED MY HAIR.

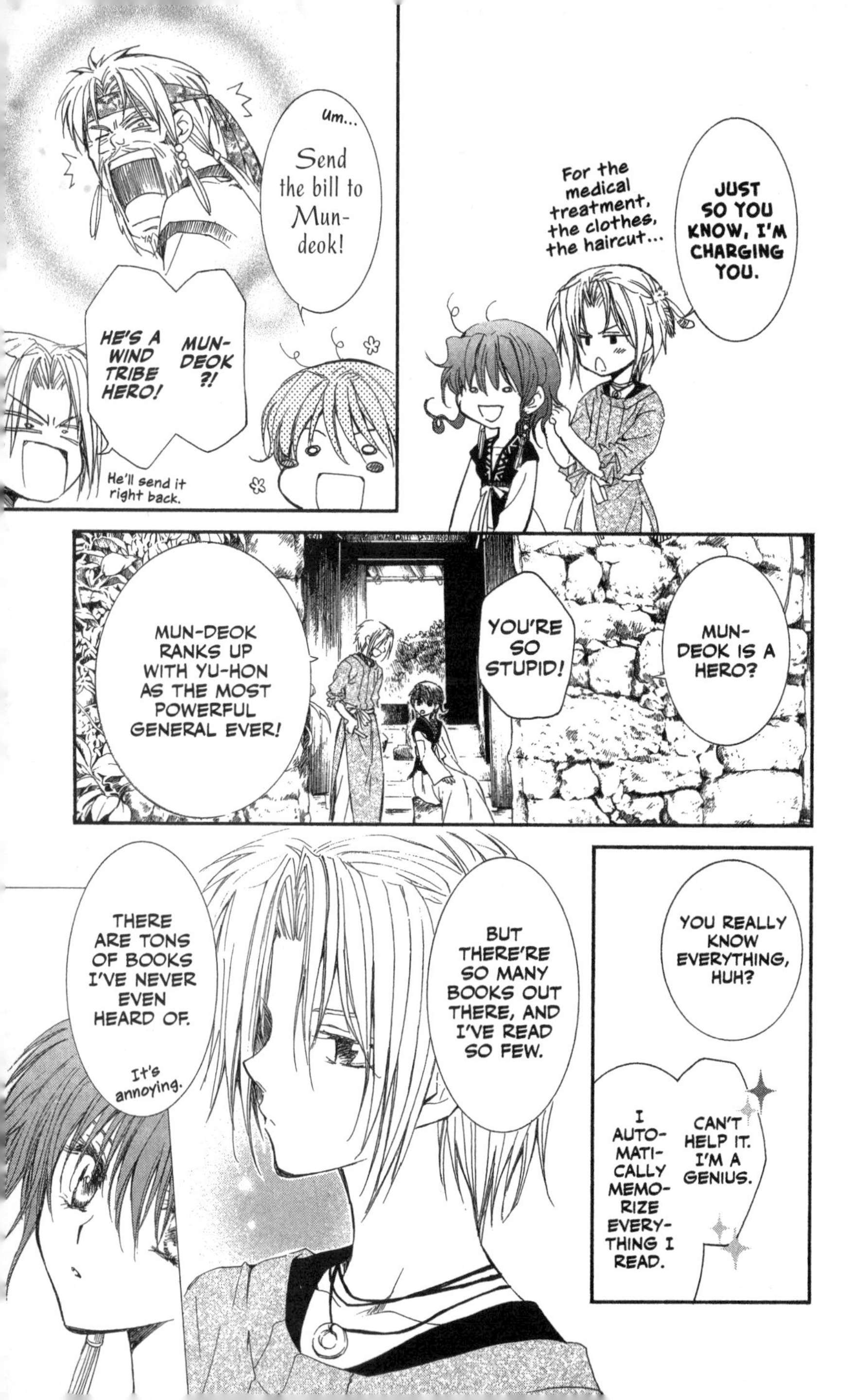
For the medical treatment, the clothes, the haircut...
JUST SO YOU KNOW, I'M CHARGING YOU.
Um...
Send the bill to Mun-deok!
MUN-DEOK?!
HE'S A WIND TRIBE HERO!
He'll send it right back.
MUN-DEOK IS A HERO?
YOU'RE SO STUPID!
MUN-DEOK RANKS UP WITH YU-HON AS THE MOST POWERFUL GENERAL EVER!
YOU REALLY KNOW EVERYTHING, HUH?
CAN'T HELP IT. I'M A GENIUS.
I AUTOMATICALLY MEMORIZE EVERYTHING I READ.
BUT THERE'RE SO MANY BOOKS OUT THERE, AND I'VE READ SO FEW.
THERE ARE TONS OF BOOKS I'VE NEVER EVEN HEARD OF.
It's annoying.

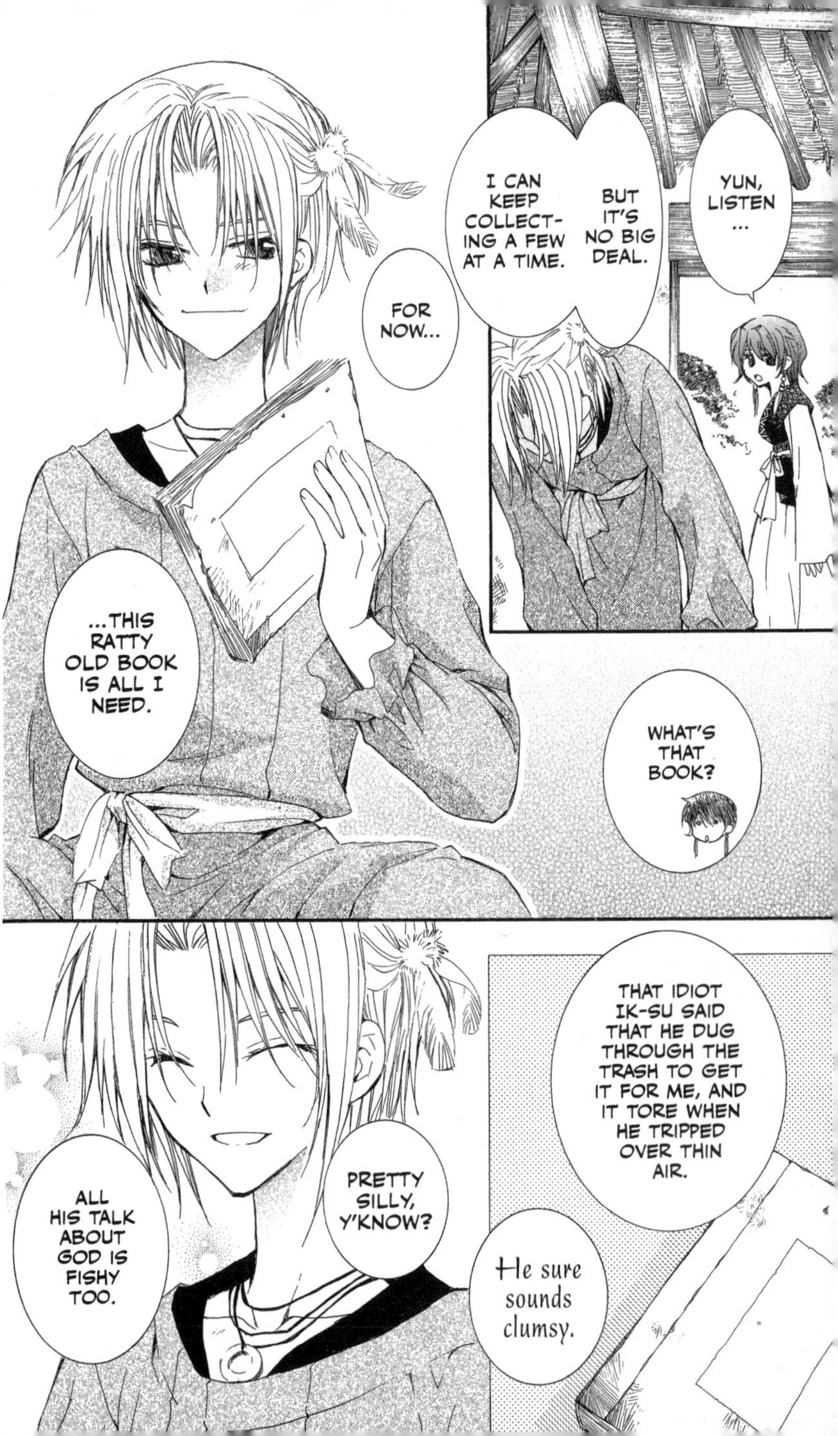
YUN, LISTEN ...
BUT IT'S NO BIG DEAL.
I CAN KEEP COLLECT-ING A FEW AT A TIME.
FOR NOW...
...THIS RATTY OLD BOOK IS ALL I NEED.
WHAT'S THAT BOOK?
THAT IDIOT IK-SU SAID THAT HE DUG THROUGH THE TRASH TO GET IT FOR ME, AND IT TORE WHEN HE TRIPPED OVER THIN AIR.
He sure sounds clumsy.
PRETTY SILLY, Y'KNOW?
ALL HIS TALK ABOUT GOD IS FISHY TOO.

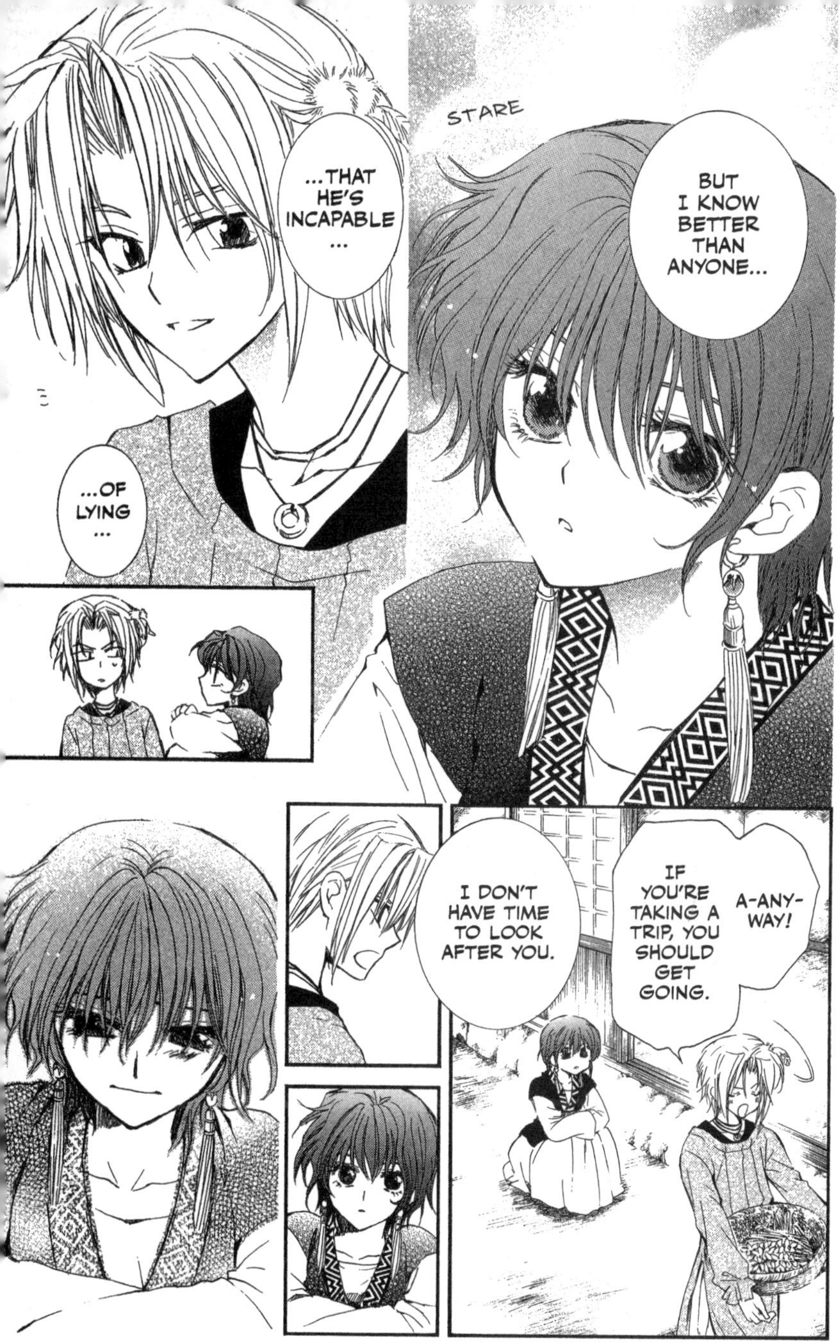
STARE
BUT I KNOW BETTER THAN ANYONE...
...THAT HE'S INCAPABLE ...
...OF LYING ...
A-ANY-WAY!
IF YOU'RE TAKING A TRIP, YOU SHOULD GET GOING.
I DON'T HAVE TIME TO LOOK AFTER YOU.

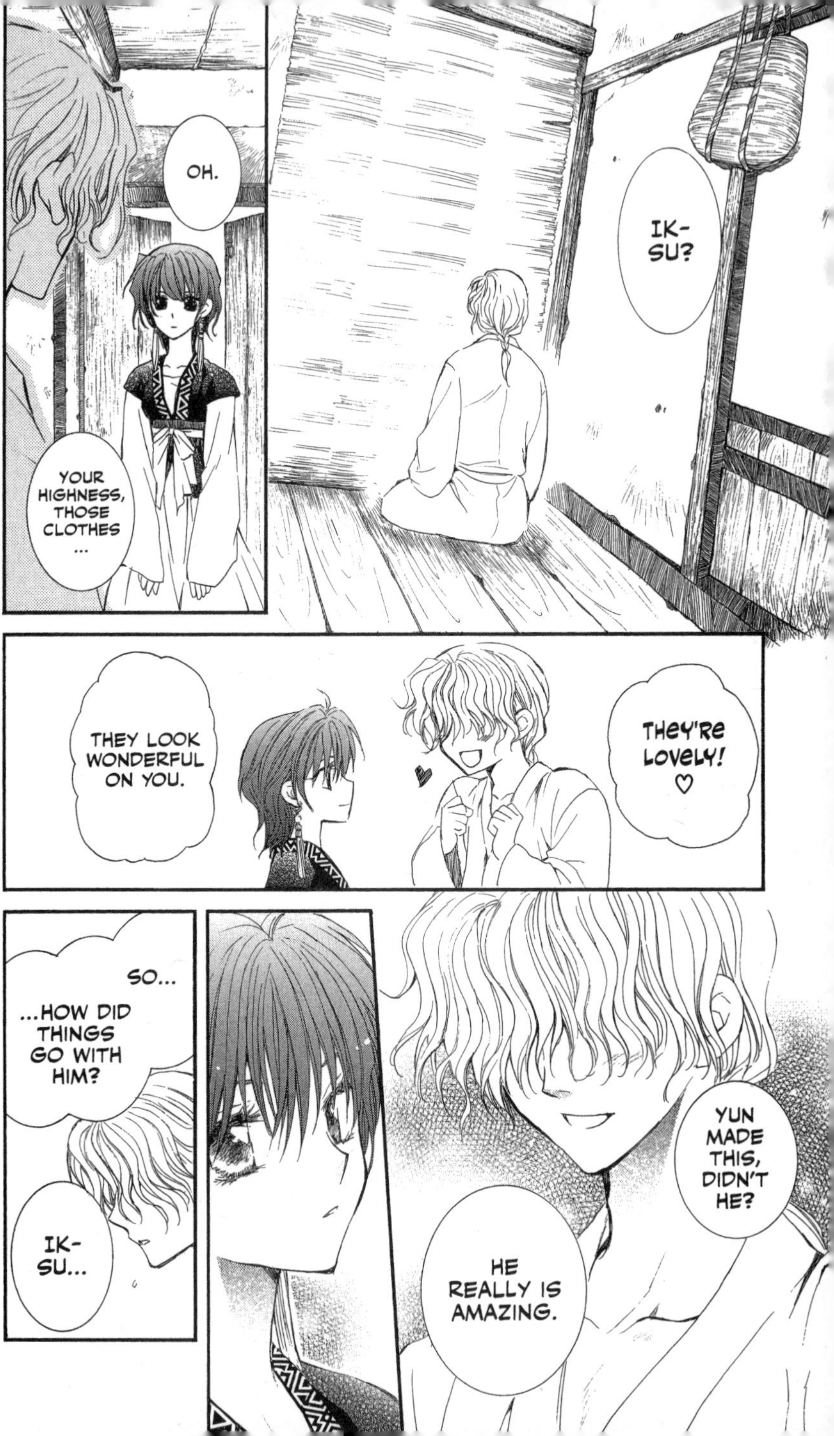
IK-SU?
OH.
YOUR HIGHNESS, THOSE CLOTHES ...
THEY'RE LOVELY! ♡
THEY LOOK WONDERFUL ON YOU.
YUN MADE THIS, DIDN'T HE?
HE REALLY IS AMAZING.
SO...
...HOW DID THINGS GO WITH HIM?
IK-SU...

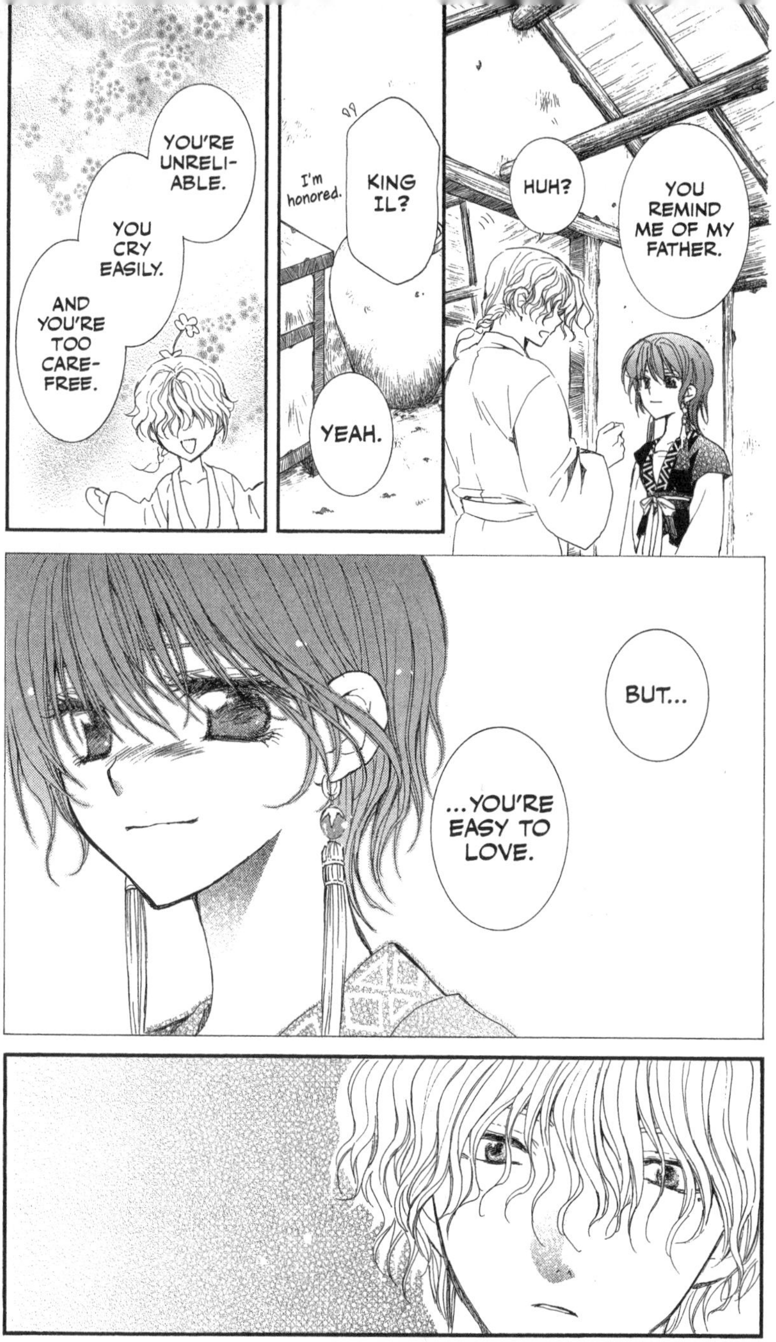
YOU REMIND ME OF MY FATHER.
HUH?
KING IL?
I'm honored.
YEAH.
YOU'RE UNRELI-ABLE.
YOU CRY EASILY.
AND YOU'RE TOO CARE-FREE.
BUT...
...YOU'RE EASY TO LOVE.

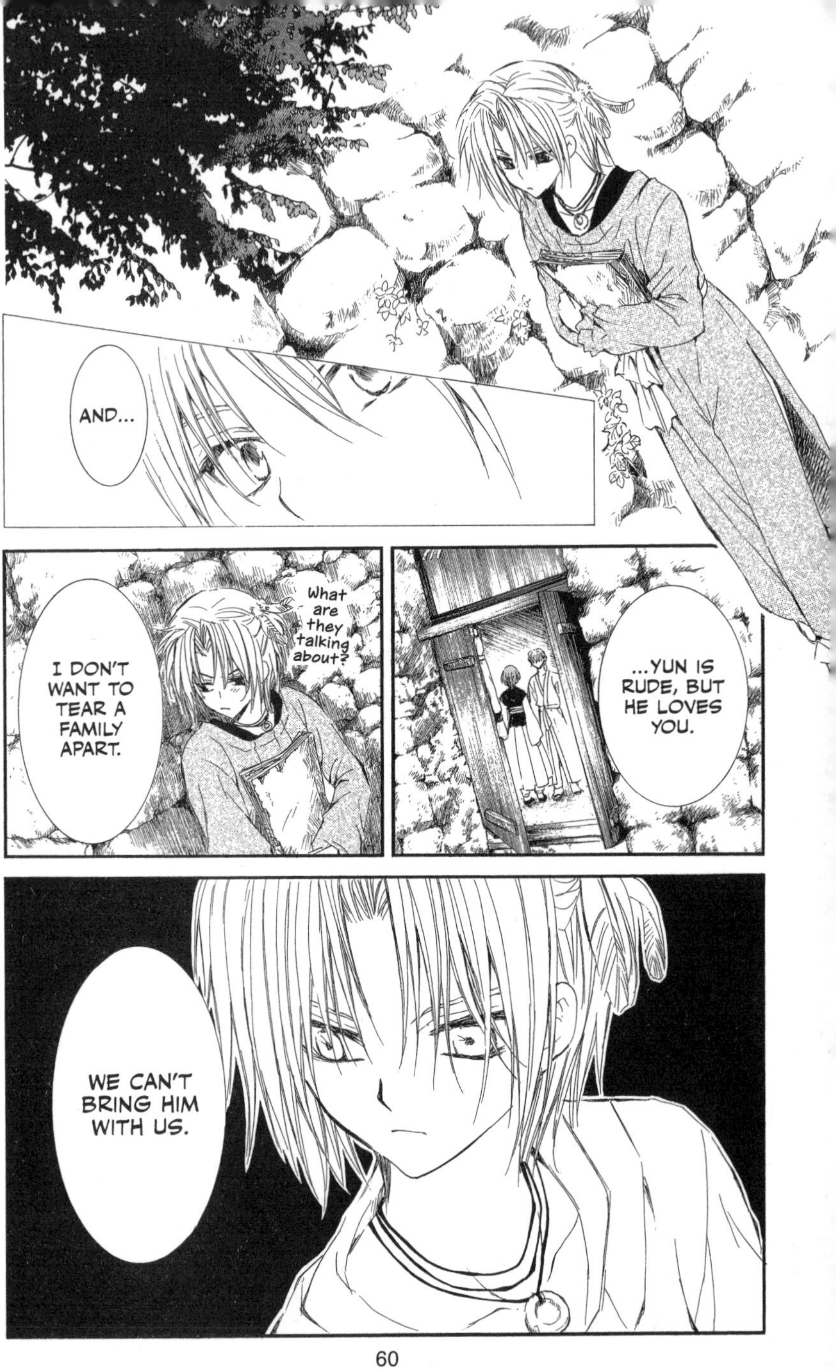
AND...
...YUN IS RUDE, BUT HE LOVES YOU.
What are they talking about?
I DON'T WANT TO TEAR A FAMILY APART.
WE CAN'T BRING HIM WITH US.

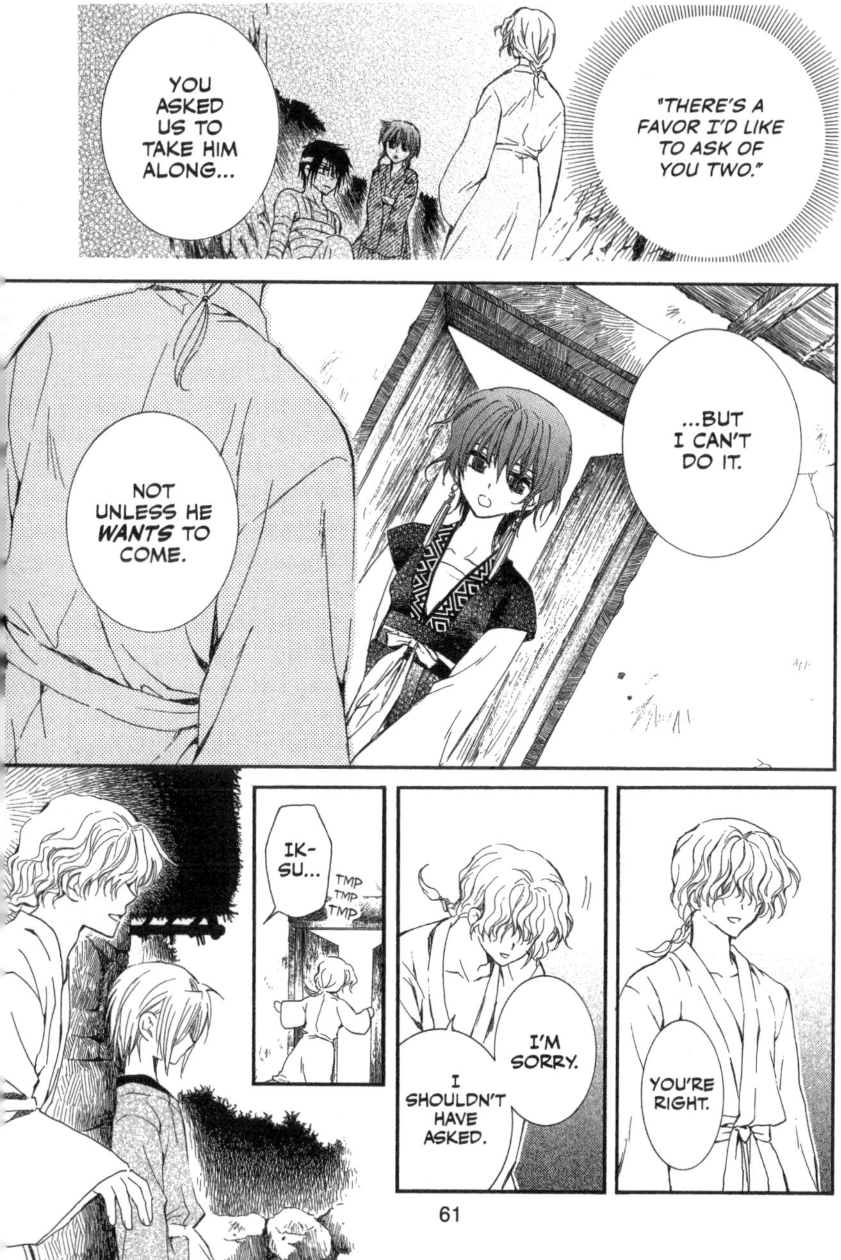
"THERE'S A FAVOR I'D LIKE TO ASK OF YOU TWO."
YOU ASKED US TO TAKE HIM ALONG...
...BUT I CAN'T DO IT.
NOT UNLESS HE *WANTS* TO COME.
YOU'RE RIGHT.
I'M SORRY.
I SHOULDN'T HAVE ASKED.
IK-SU...
TMP TMP TMP

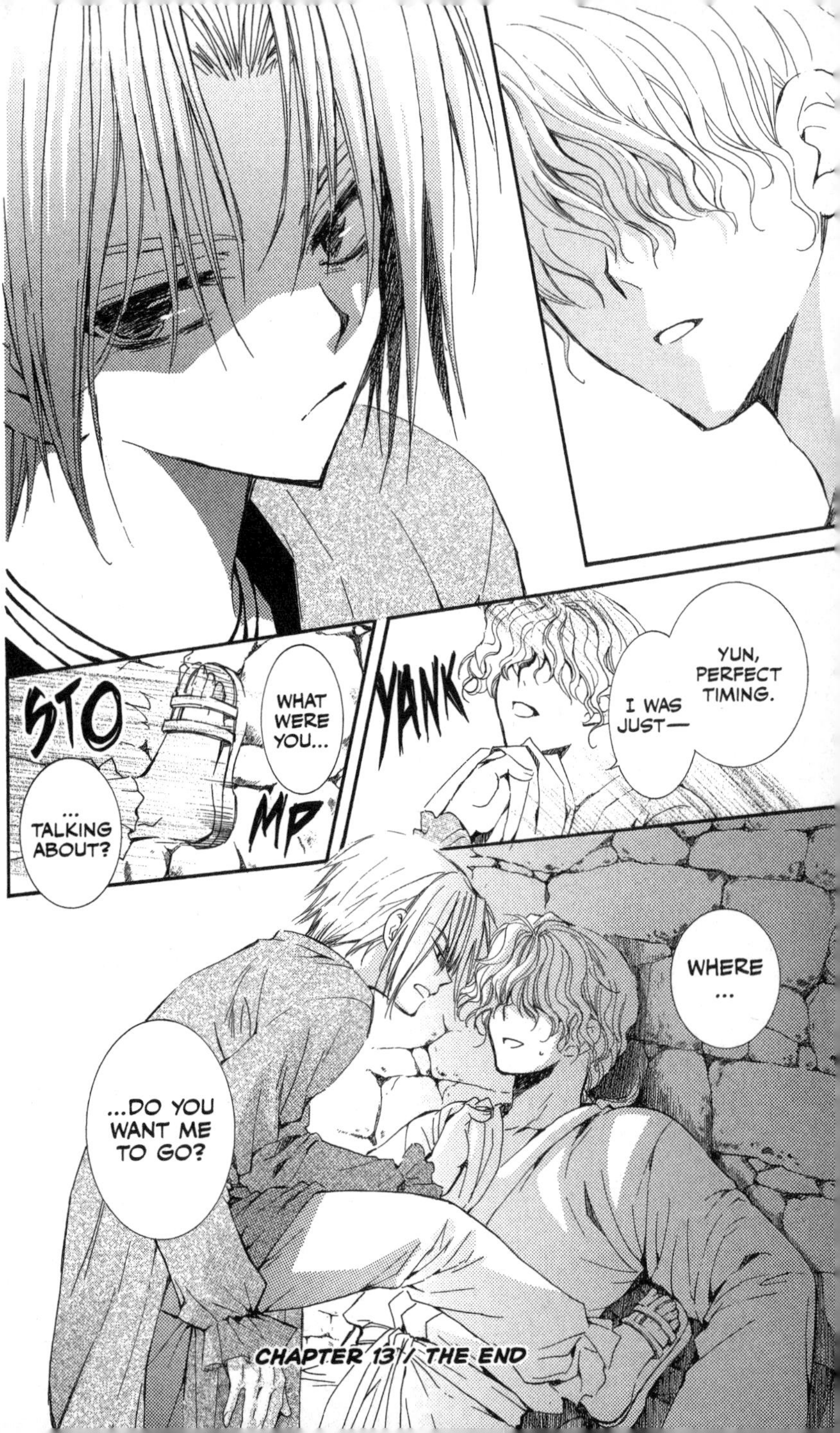
YUN, PERFECT TIMING.
I WAS JUST—
YANK
WHAT WERE YOU...
STO
MP
...TALKING ABOUT?
WHERE ...
...DO YOU WANT ME TO GO?
CHAPTER 13 / THE END

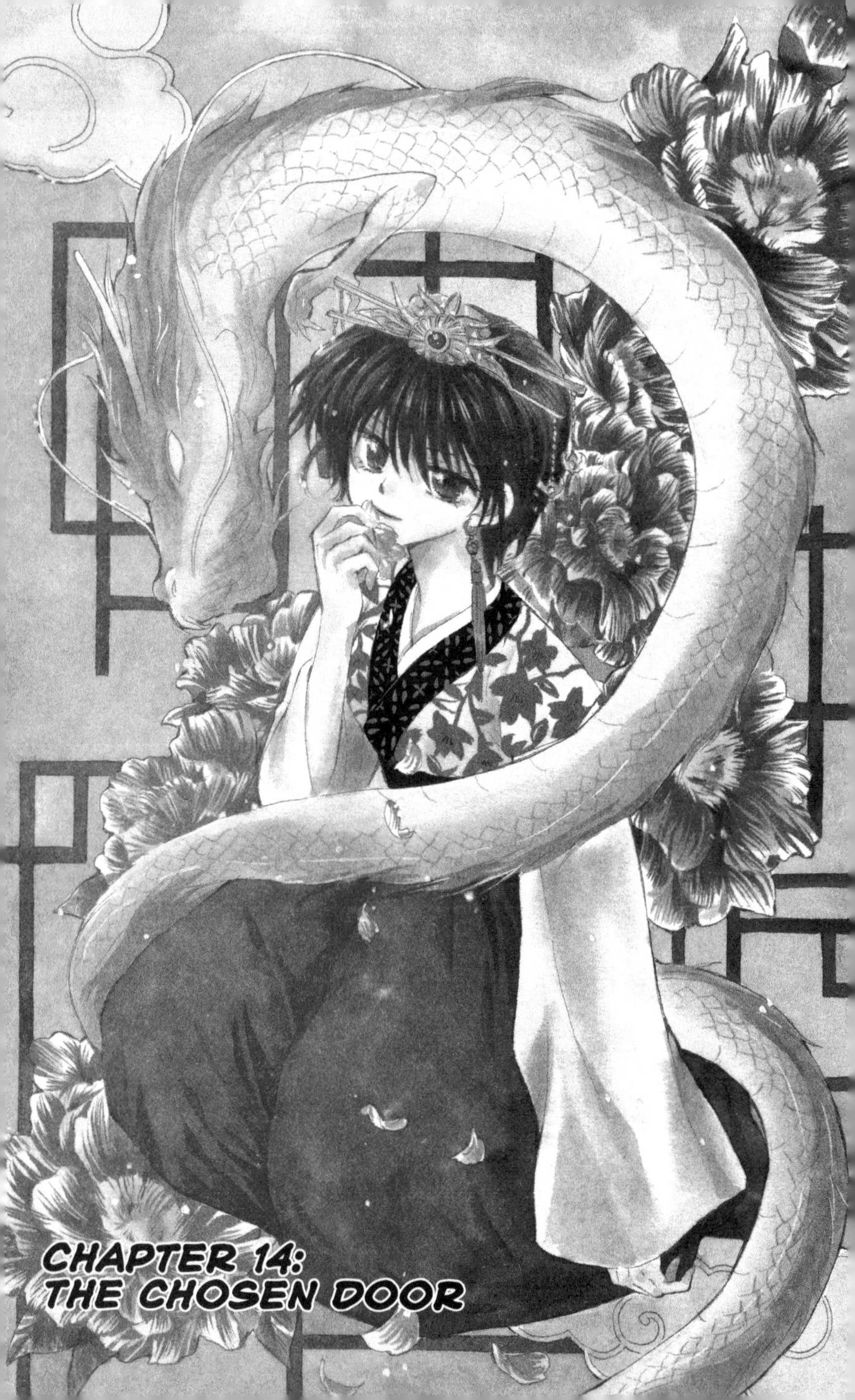
CHAPTER 14:
THE CHOSEN DOOR

Yona
of the
Dawn

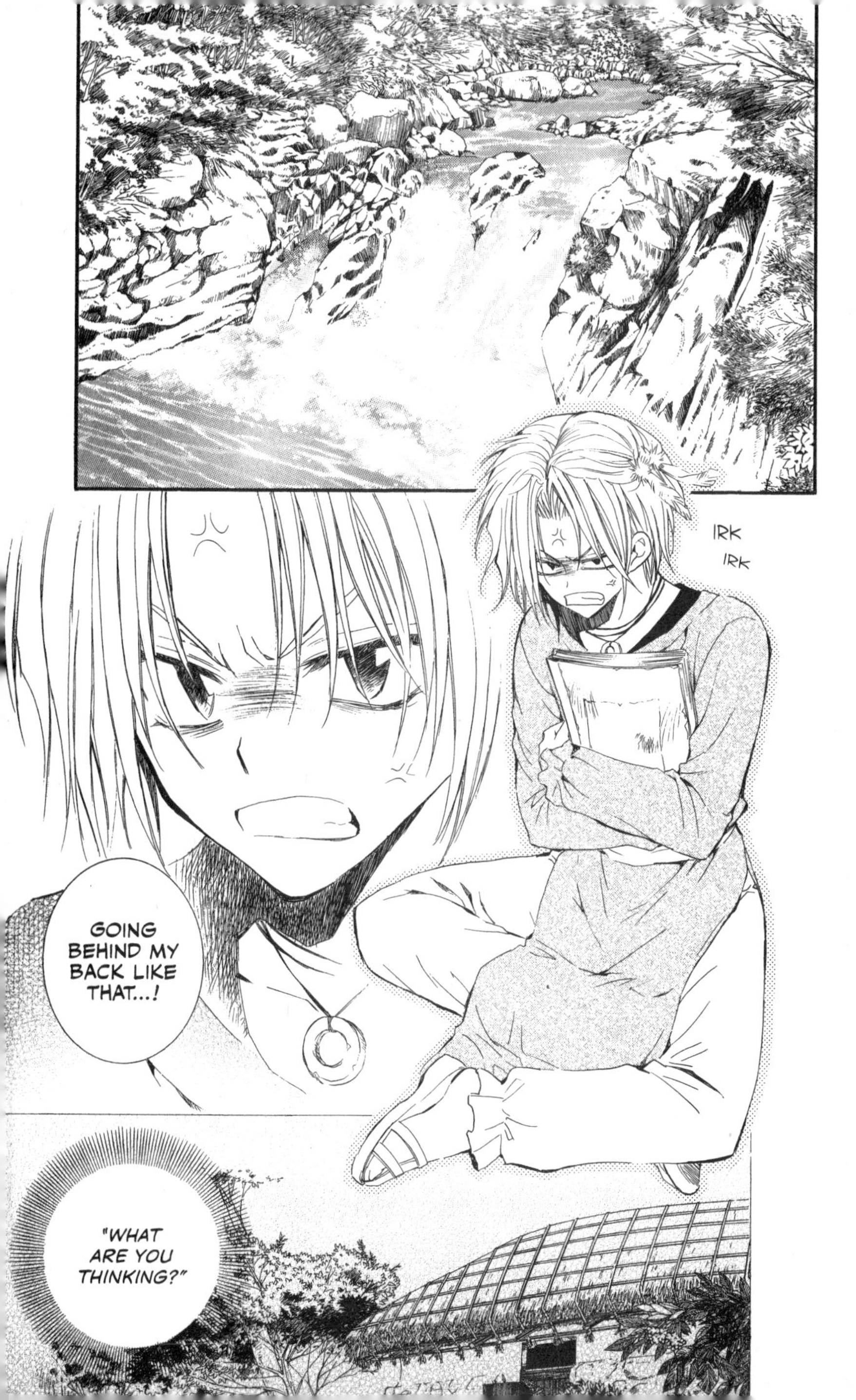
IRK
IRK
GOING BEHIND MY BACK LIKE THAT...!
"WHAT ARE YOU THINKING?"

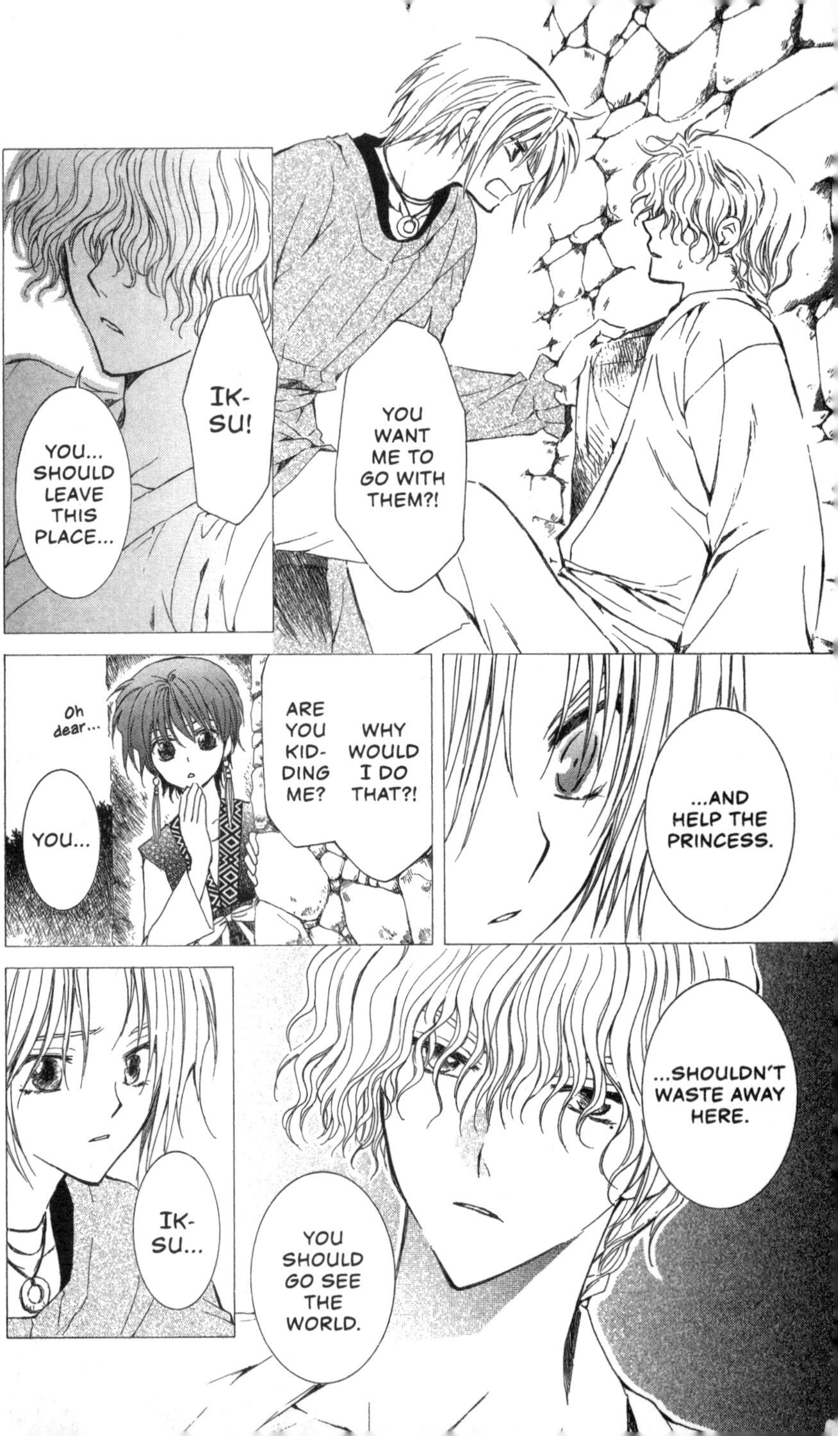
YOU WANT ME TO GO WITH THEM?!
IK-SU!
YOU... SHOULD LEAVE THIS PLACE...
...AND HELP THE PRINCESS.
ARE YOU KID-DING ME? WHY WOULD I DO THAT?!
Oh dear...
YOU...
...SHOULDN'T WASTE AWAY HERE.
YOU SHOULD GO SEE THE WORLD.
IK-SU...

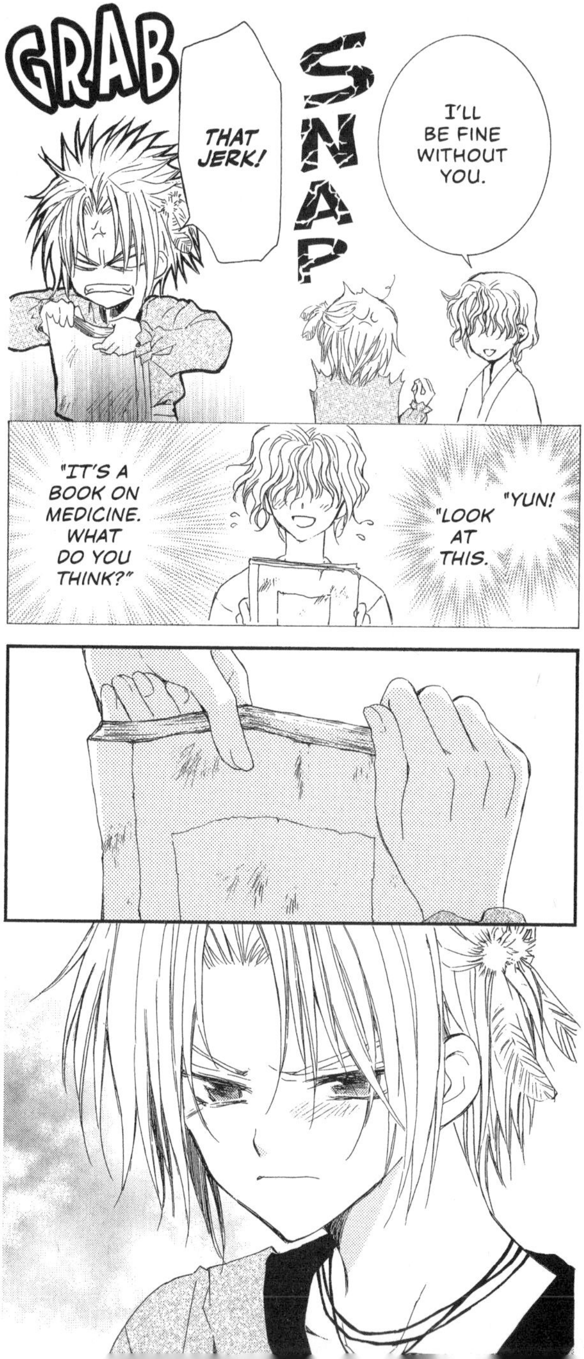
I'LL BE FINE WITHOUT YOU.
SNAP
THAT JERK!
GRAB
"YUN!
"LOOK AT THIS.
"IT'S A BOOK ON MEDICINE. WHAT DO YOU THINK?"

The *Hana to Yume* editorial office has a mobile classroom on how to create manga. Artists answer questions about drawing and give live demonstrations. I don't have much experience, but I got to be an instructor!

That was right around when I was working on the storyboard for this chapter. I was hoping to finish it before I had to go, but it didn't occur to me that I wouldn't finish that day. And then the ink in my kit of art supplies spilled all over the manga I took with me!

That day the class was in Osaka, so I finished my storyboard in a café at the airport on my way home. This chapter was a struggle. (Laugh)

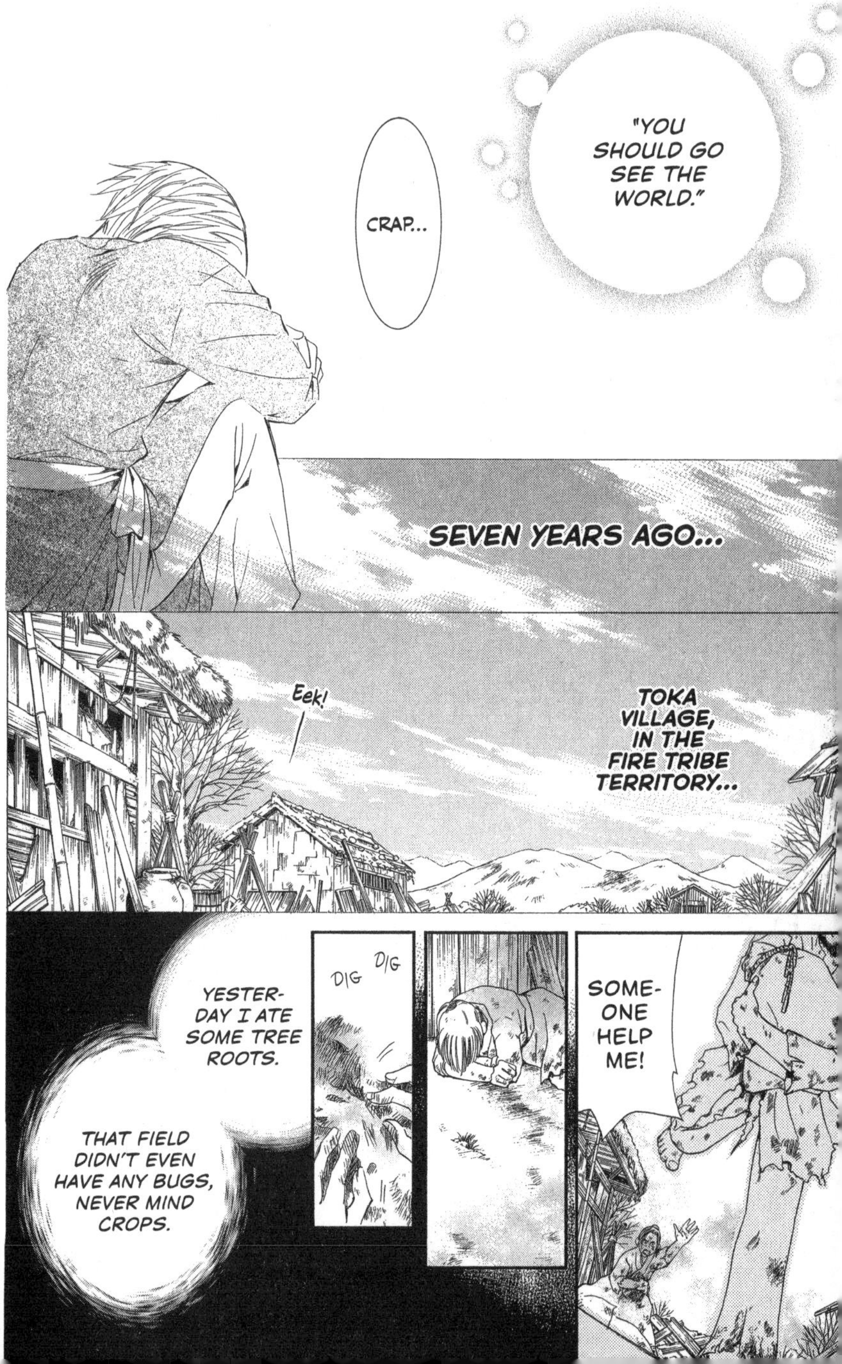
"YOU SHOULD GO SEE THE WORLD."
CRAP...
SEVEN YEARS AGO...
TOKA VILLAGE, IN THE FIRE TRIBE TERRITORY...
Eek!
SOME-ONE HELP ME!
DIG
DIG
YESTER-DAY I ATE SOME TREE ROOTS.
THAT FIELD DIDN'T EVEN HAVE ANY BUGS, NEVER MIND CROPS.

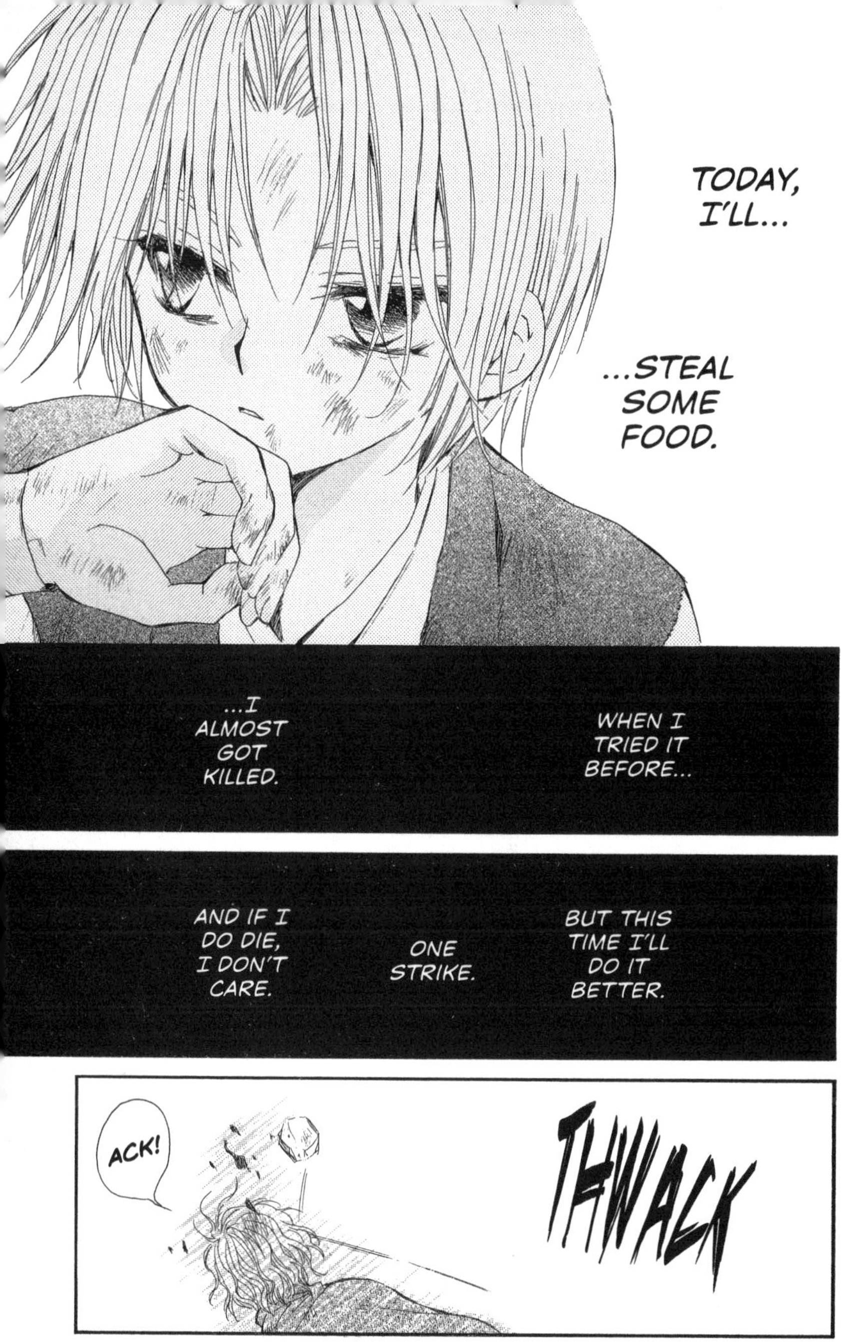
TODAY, I'LL...
...STEAL SOME FOOD.
WHEN I TRIED IT BEFORE...
...I ALMOST GOT KILLED.
BUT THIS TIME I'LL DO IT BETTER.
ONE STRIKE.
AND IF I DO DIE, I DON'T CARE.
THWACK
ACK!

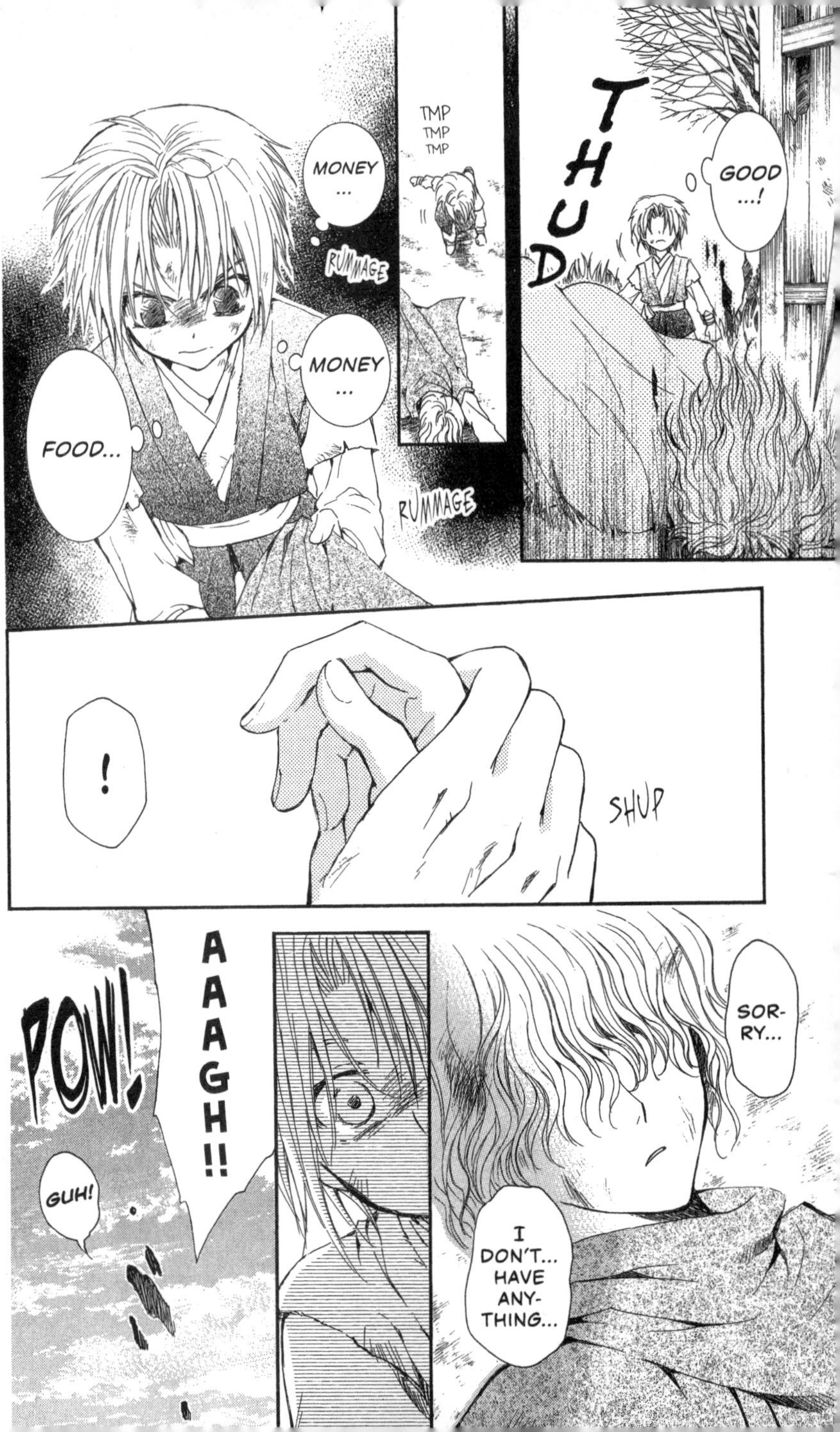
THUD
GOOD...!
TMP TMP TMP
MONEY...
RUMMAGE
MONEY...
FOOD...
RUMMAGE
SHUP
!
SORRY...
I DON'T... HAVE ANYTHING...
AAAAGH!!
POW!
GUH!

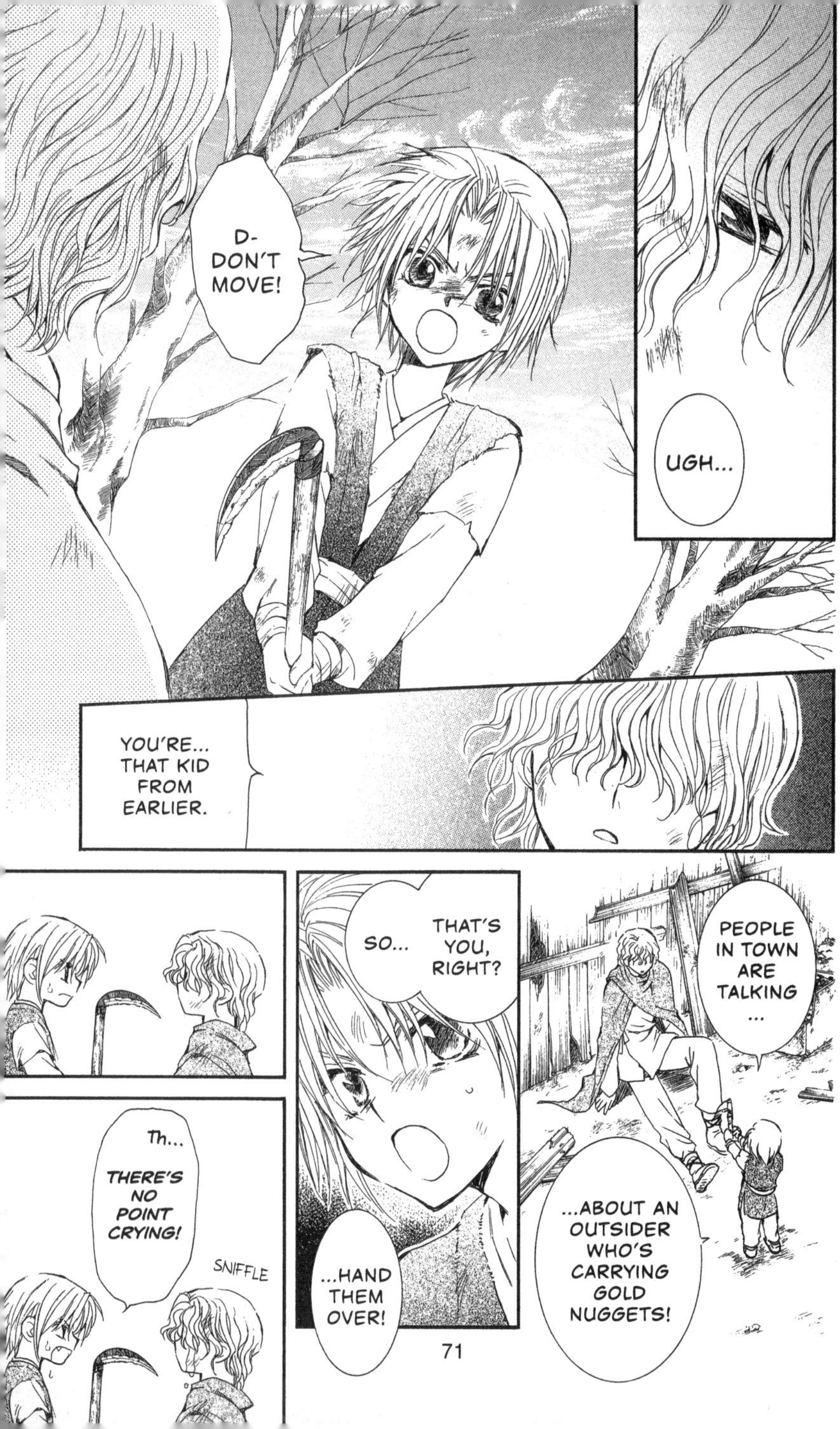
UGH...
D-DON'T MOVE!
YOU'RE... THAT KID FROM EARLIER.
PEOPLE IN TOWN ARE TALKING ...
...ABOUT AN OUTSIDER WHO'S CARRYING GOLD NUGGETS!
SO... THAT'S YOU, RIGHT?
...HAND THEM OVER!
Th... THERE'S NO POINT CRYING!
SNIFFLE

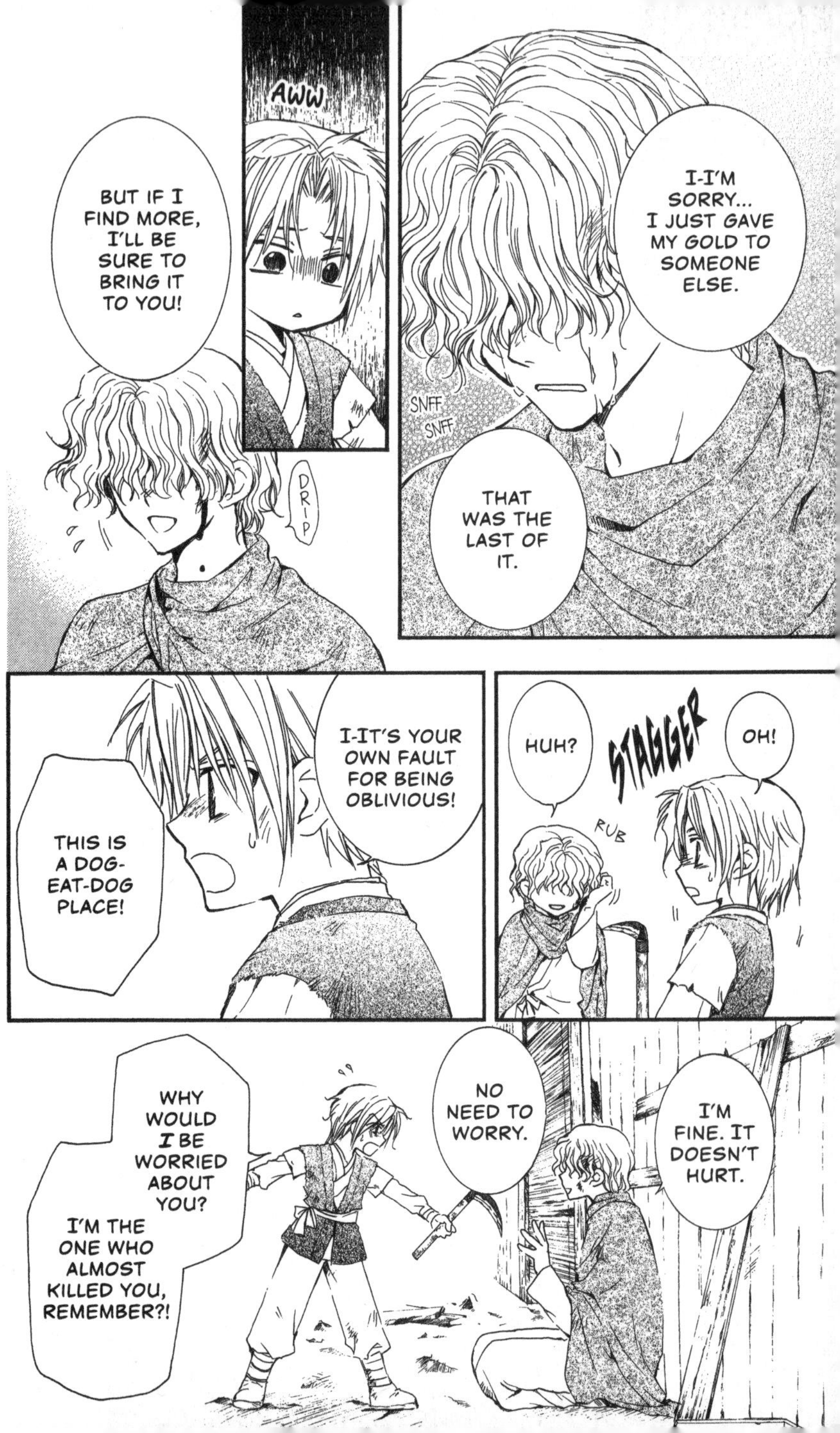

I-I'M SORRY... I JUST GAVE MY GOLD TO SOMEONE ELSE.
SNFF SNFF
THAT WAS THE LAST OF IT.
AWW
BUT IF I FIND MORE, I'LL BE SURE TO BRING IT TO YOU!
DRIP
OH!
STAGGER
HUH?
RUB
I-IT'S YOUR OWN FAULT FOR BEING OBLIVIOUS!
THIS IS A DOG-EAT-DOG PLACE!
I'M FINE. IT DOESN'T HURT.
NO NEED TO WORRY.
WHY WOULD I BE WORRIED ABOUT YOU?
I'M THE ONE WHO ALMOST KILLED YOU, REMEMBER?!

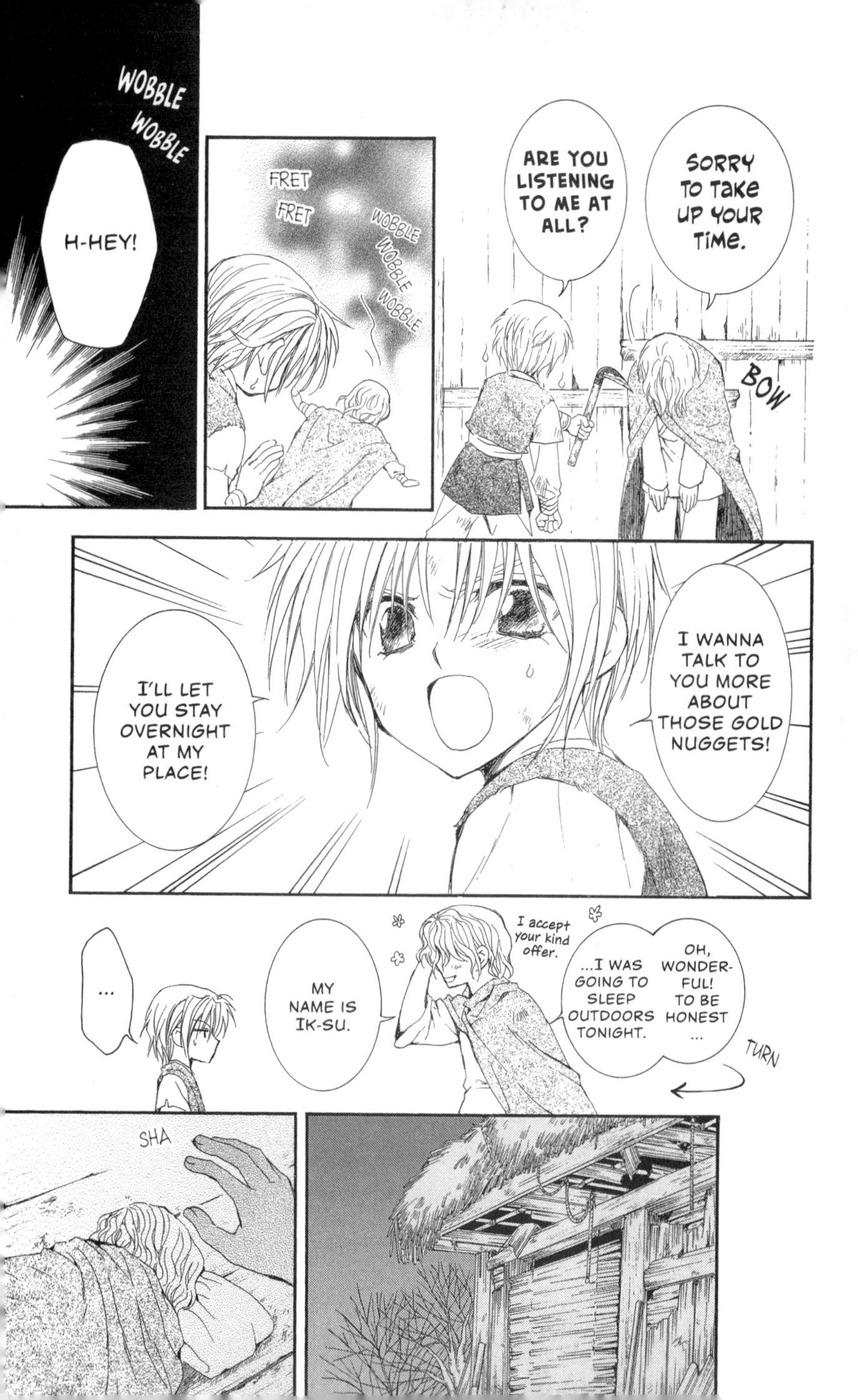
SORRY TO TAKE UP YOUR TIME.
BOW
ARE YOU LISTENING TO ME AT ALL?
FRET FRET
WOBBLE WOBBLE WOBBLE
WOBBLE WOBBLE
H-HEY!
I WANNA TALK TO YOU MORE ABOUT THOSE GOLD NUGGETS!
I'LL LET YOU STAY OVERNIGHT AT MY PLACE!
OH, WONDERFUL! TO BE HONEST...
...I WAS GOING TO SLEEP OUTDOORS TONIGHT.
I accept your kind offer.
TURN
MY NAME IS IK-SU.
...
SHA

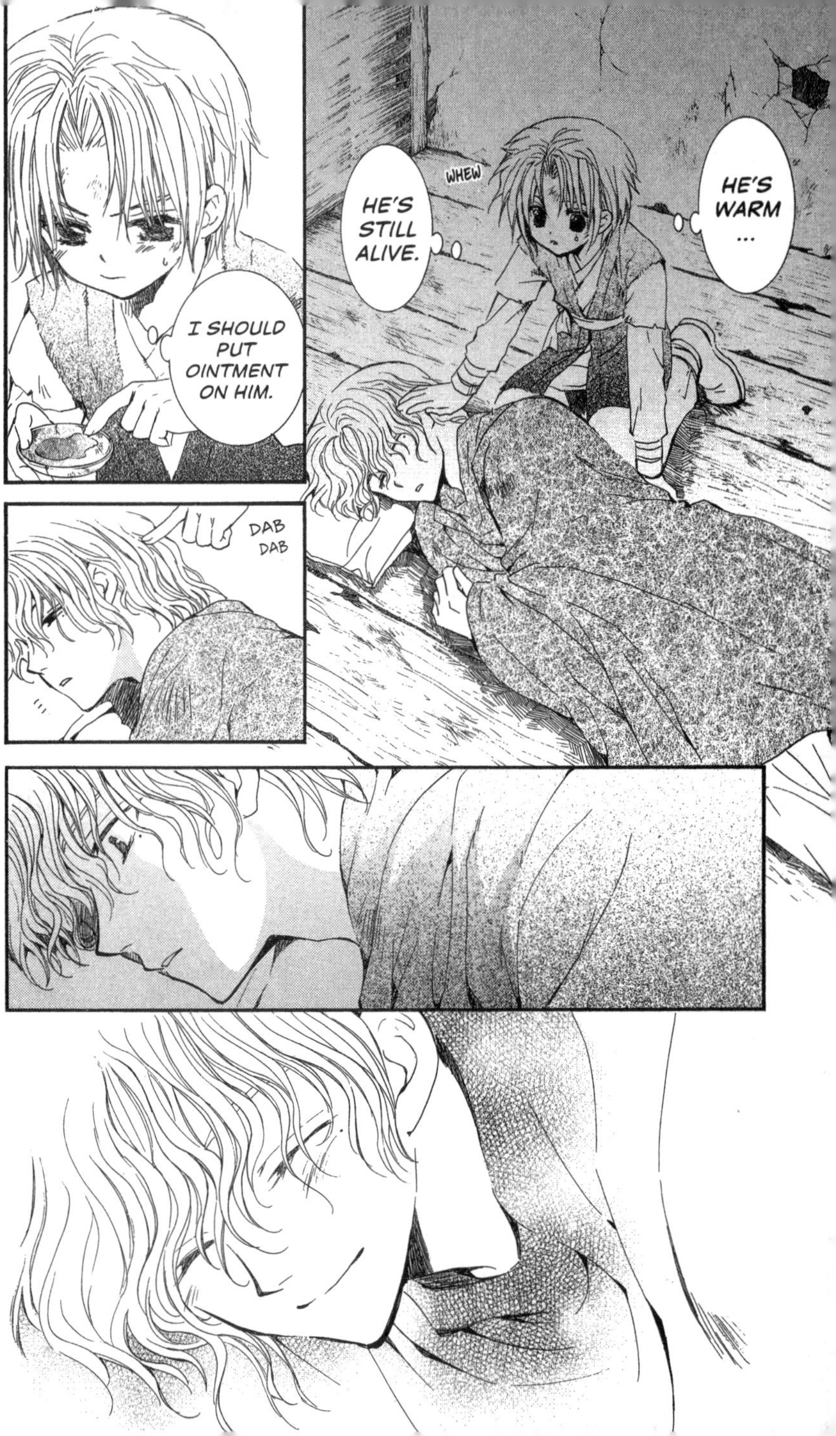
HE'S WARM ...
WHEW
HE'S STILL ALIVE.
I SHOULD PUT OINTMENT ON HIM.
DAB DAB

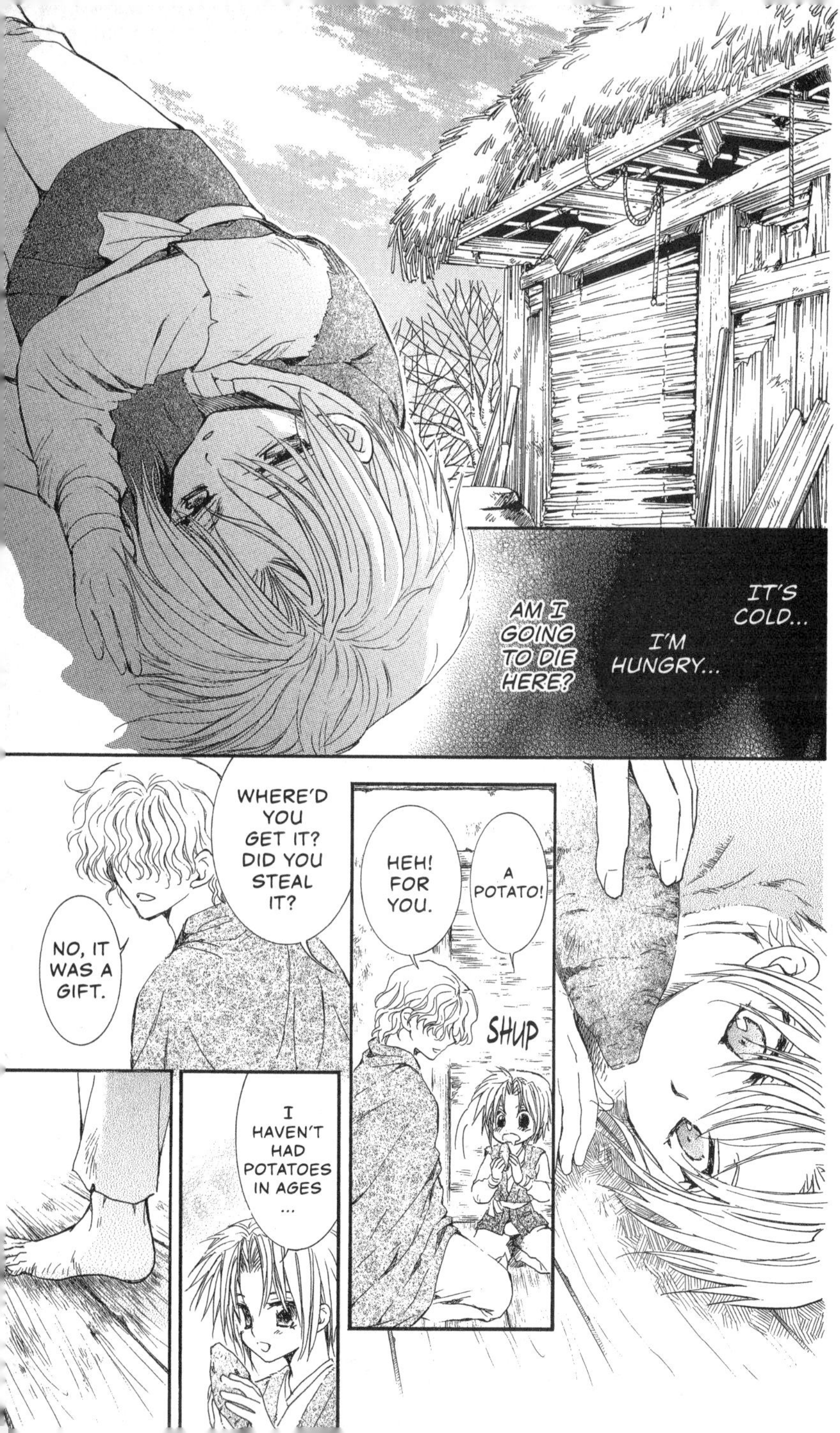
IT'S COLD...
I'M HUNGRY...
AM I GOING TO DIE HERE?
A POTATO!
HEH! FOR YOU.
SHUP
WHERE'D YOU GET IT? DID YOU STEAL IT?
NO, IT WAS A GIFT.
I HAVEN'T HAD POTATOES IN AGES ...

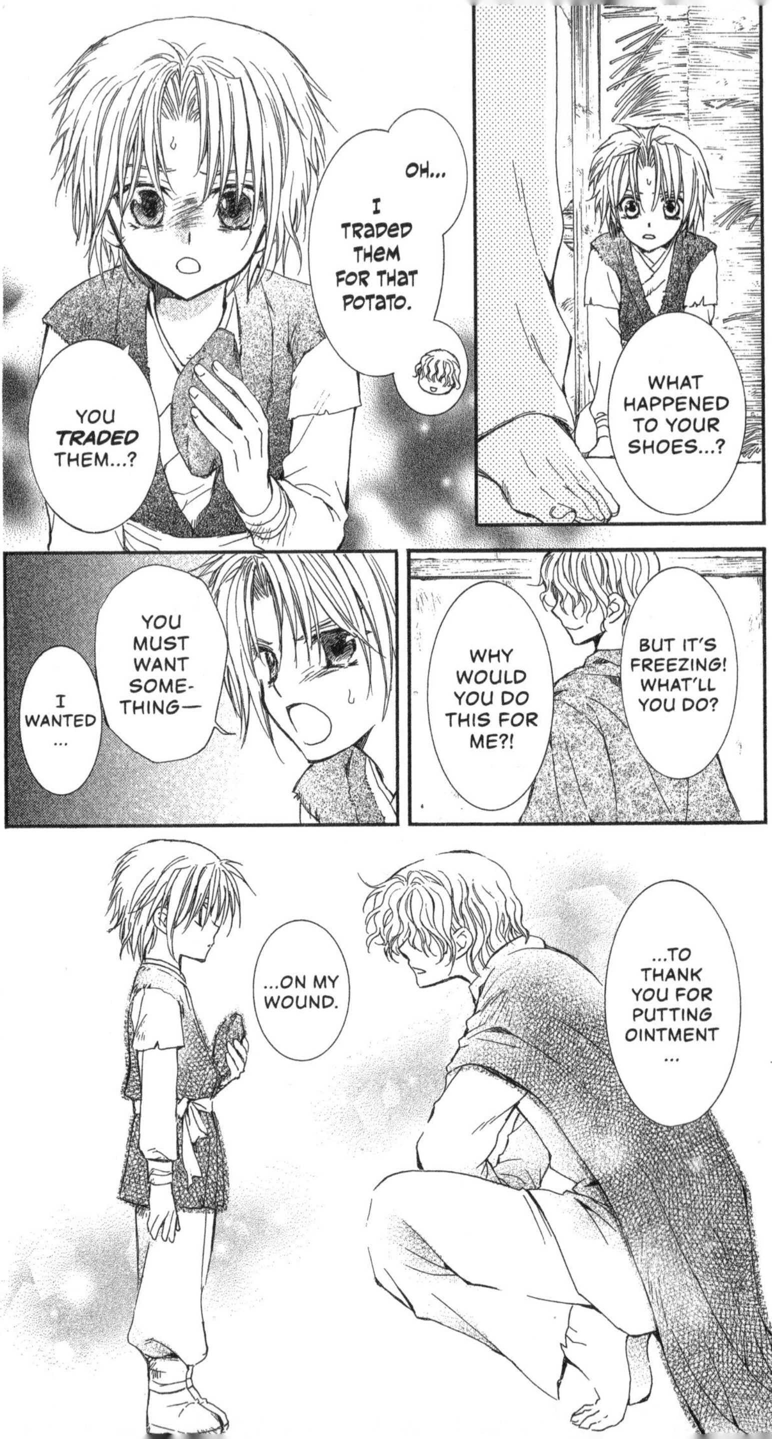
WHAT HAPPENED TO YOUR SHOES...?
OH... I TRADED THEM FOR THAT POTATO.
YOU *TRADED* THEM...?
BUT IT'S FREEZING! WHAT'LL YOU DO?
WHY WOULD YOU DO THIS FOR ME?!
YOU MUST WANT SOME-THING—
I WANTED ...
...TO THANK YOU FOR PUTTING OINTMENT ...
...ON MY WOUND.

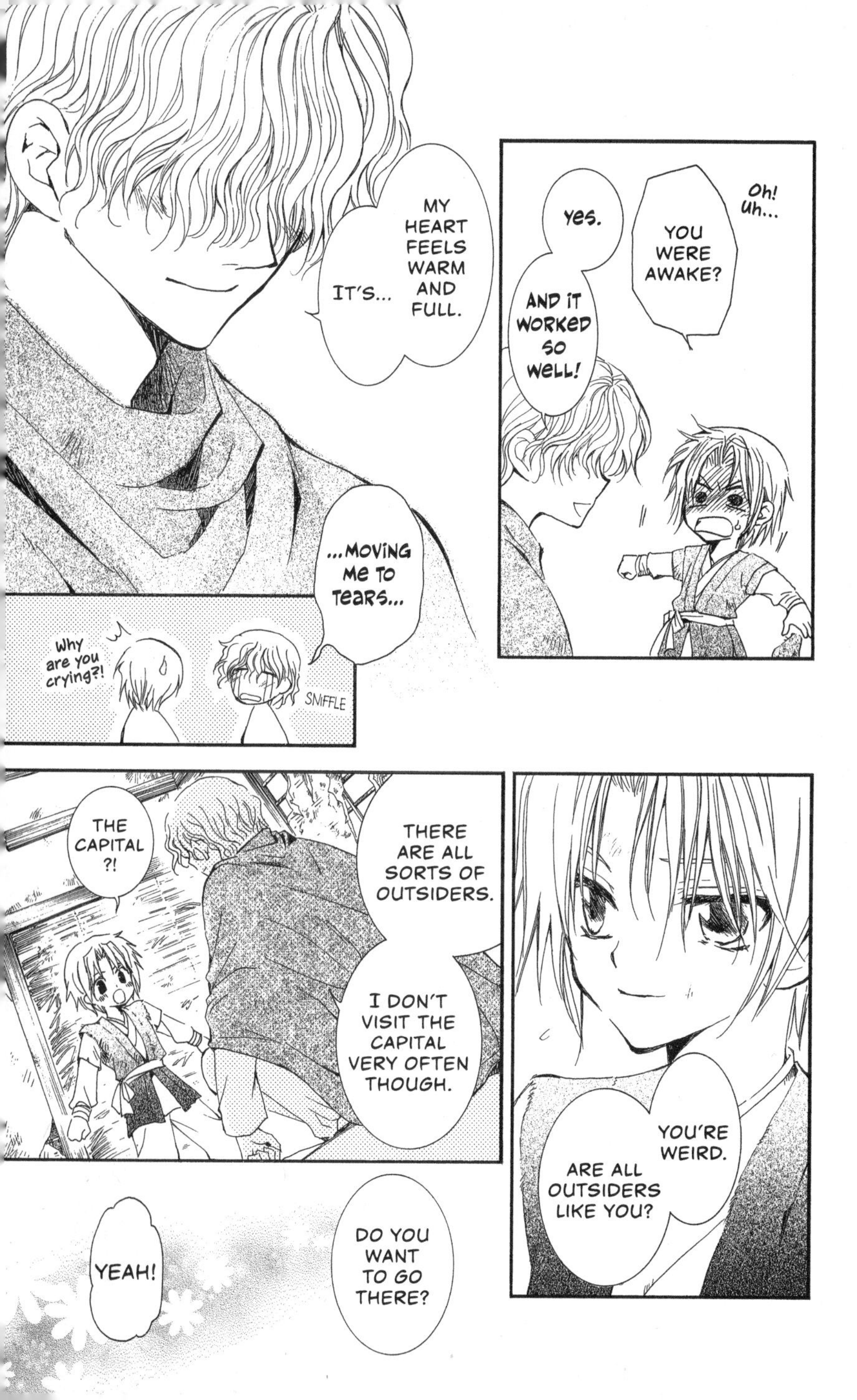
Oh! Uh...
YOU WERE AWAKE?
Yes.
AND IT WORKED SO WELL!
MY HEART FEELS WARM AND FULL.
IT'S...
...MOVING ME TO TEARS...
Why are you crying?!
SNIFFLE
YOU'RE WEIRD.
ARE ALL OUTSIDERS LIKE YOU?
THERE ARE ALL SORTS OF OUTSIDERS.
I DON'T VISIT THE CAPITAL VERY OFTEN THOUGH.
THE CAPITAL?!
DO YOU WANT TO GO THERE?
YEAH!

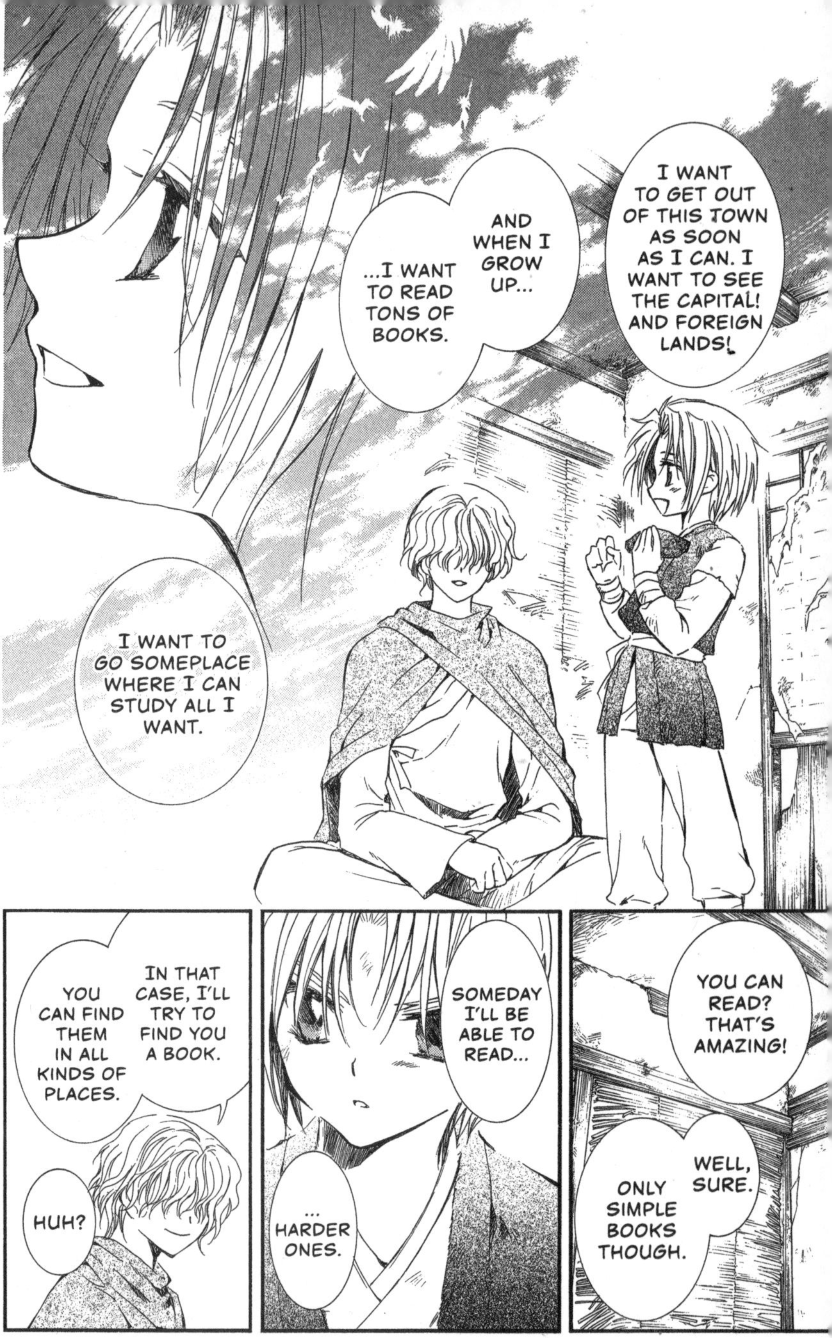
I WANT TO GET OUT OF THIS TOWN AS SOON AS I CAN. I WANT TO SEE THE CAPITAL! AND FOREIGN LANDS!
AND WHEN I GROW UP...
...I WANT TO READ TONS OF BOOKS.
I WANT TO GO SOMEPLACE WHERE I CAN STUDY ALL I WANT.
YOU CAN READ? THAT'S AMAZING!
WELL, SURE.
ONLY SIMPLE BOOKS THOUGH.
SOMEDAY I'LL BE ABLE TO READ...
... HARDER ONES.
IN THAT CASE, I'LL TRY TO FIND YOU A BOOK.
YOU CAN FIND THEM IN ALL KINDS OF PLACES.
HUH?

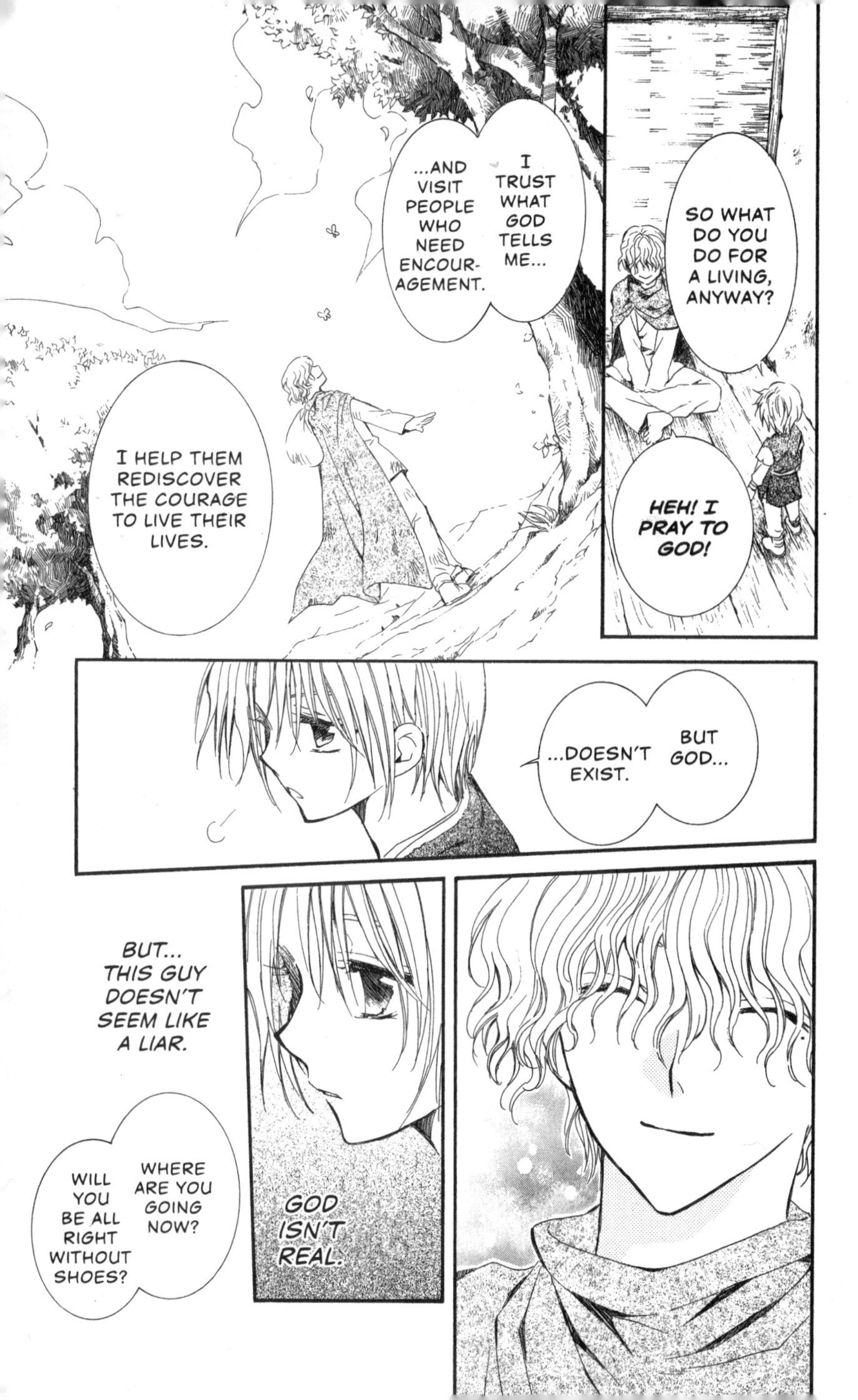
SO WHAT DO YOU DO FOR A LIVING, ANYWAY?
HEH! I PRAY TO GOD!
I TRUST WHAT GOD TELLS ME...
...AND VISIT PEOPLE WHO NEED ENCOURAGEMENT.
I HELP THEM REDISCOVER THE COURAGE TO LIVE THEIR LIVES.
BUT GOD...
...DOESN'T EXIST.
BUT... THIS GUY DOESN'T SEEM LIKE A LIAR.
GOD ISN'T REAL.
WHERE ARE YOU GOING NOW?
WILL YOU BE ALL RIGHT WITHOUT SHOES?

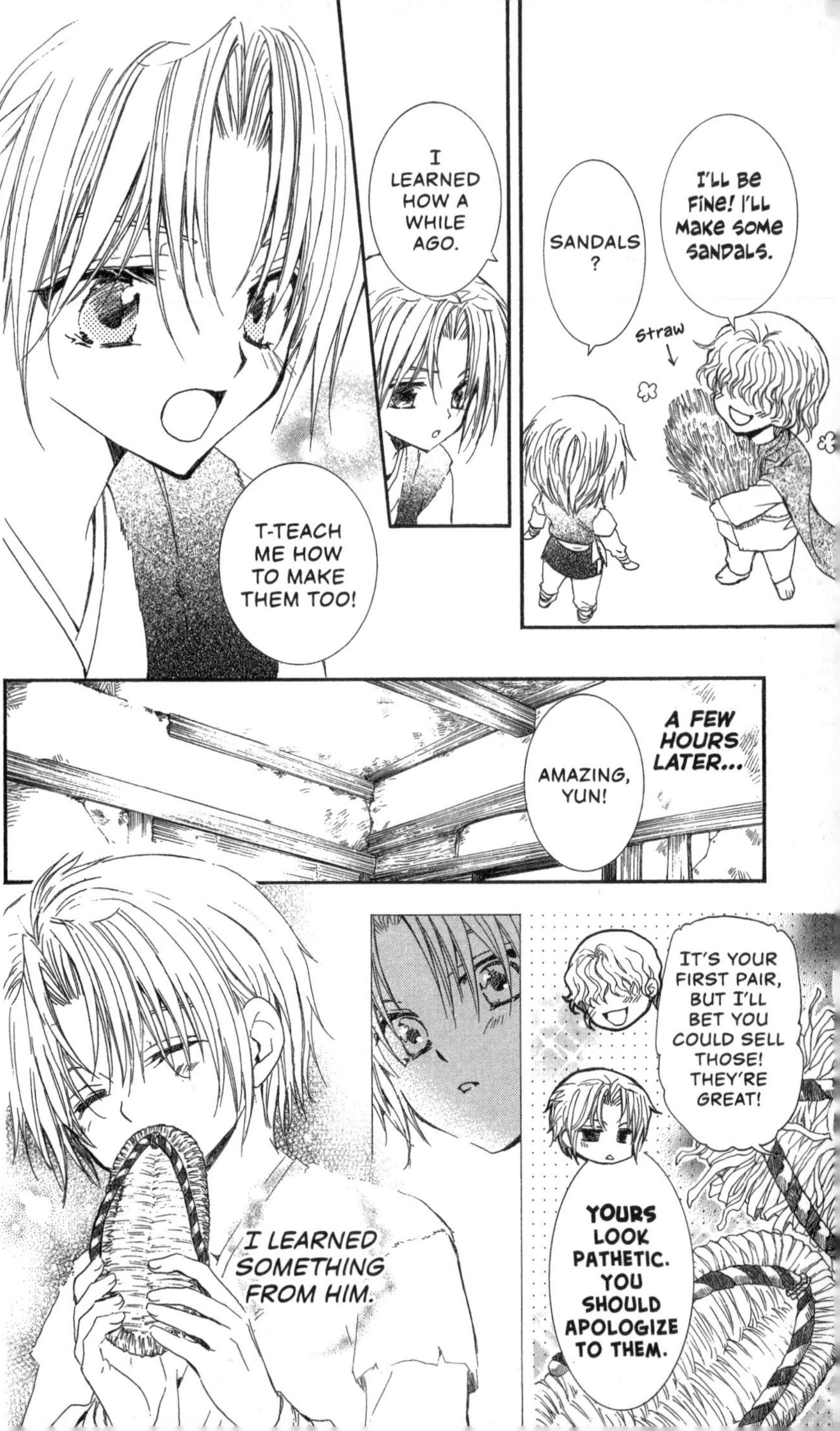
I'LL BE FINE! I'LL MAKE SOME SANDALS.
SANDALS?
STRAW
I LEARNED HOW A WHILE AGO.
T-TEACH ME HOW TO MAKE THEM TOO!
A FEW HOURS LATER...
AMAZING, YUN!
IT'S YOUR FIRST PAIR, BUT I'LL BET YOU COULD SELL THOSE! THEY'RE GREAT!
YOURS LOOK PATHETIC. YOU SHOULD APOLOGIZE TO THEM.
I LEARNED SOMETHING FROM HIM.

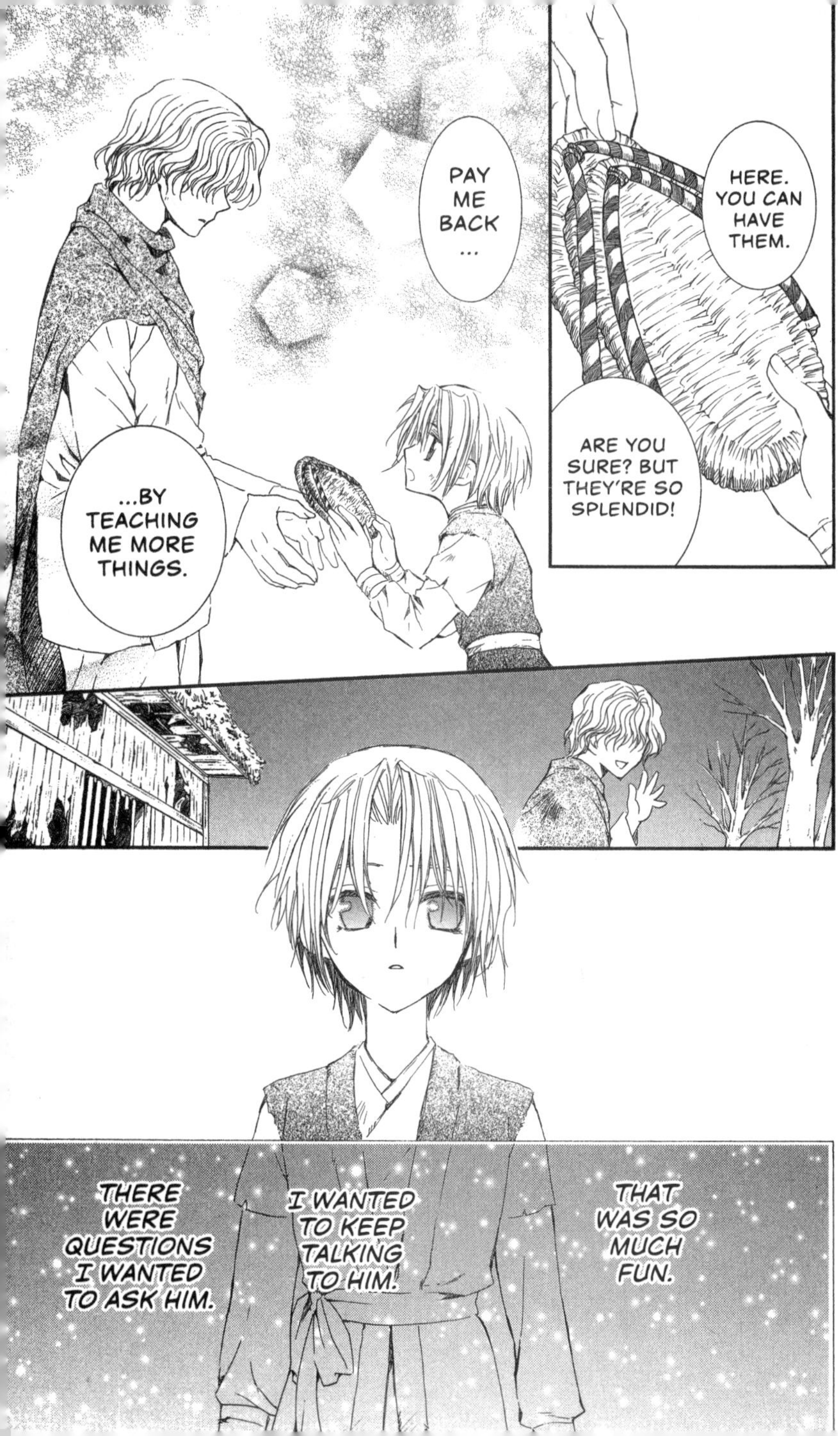
HERE. YOU CAN HAVE THEM.
ARE YOU SURE? BUT THEY'RE SO SPLENDID!
PAY ME BACK ...
...BY TEACHING ME MORE THINGS.
THAT WAS SO MUCH FUN.
I WANTED TO KEEP TALKING TO HIM.
THERE WERE QUESTIONS I WANTED TO ASK HIM.

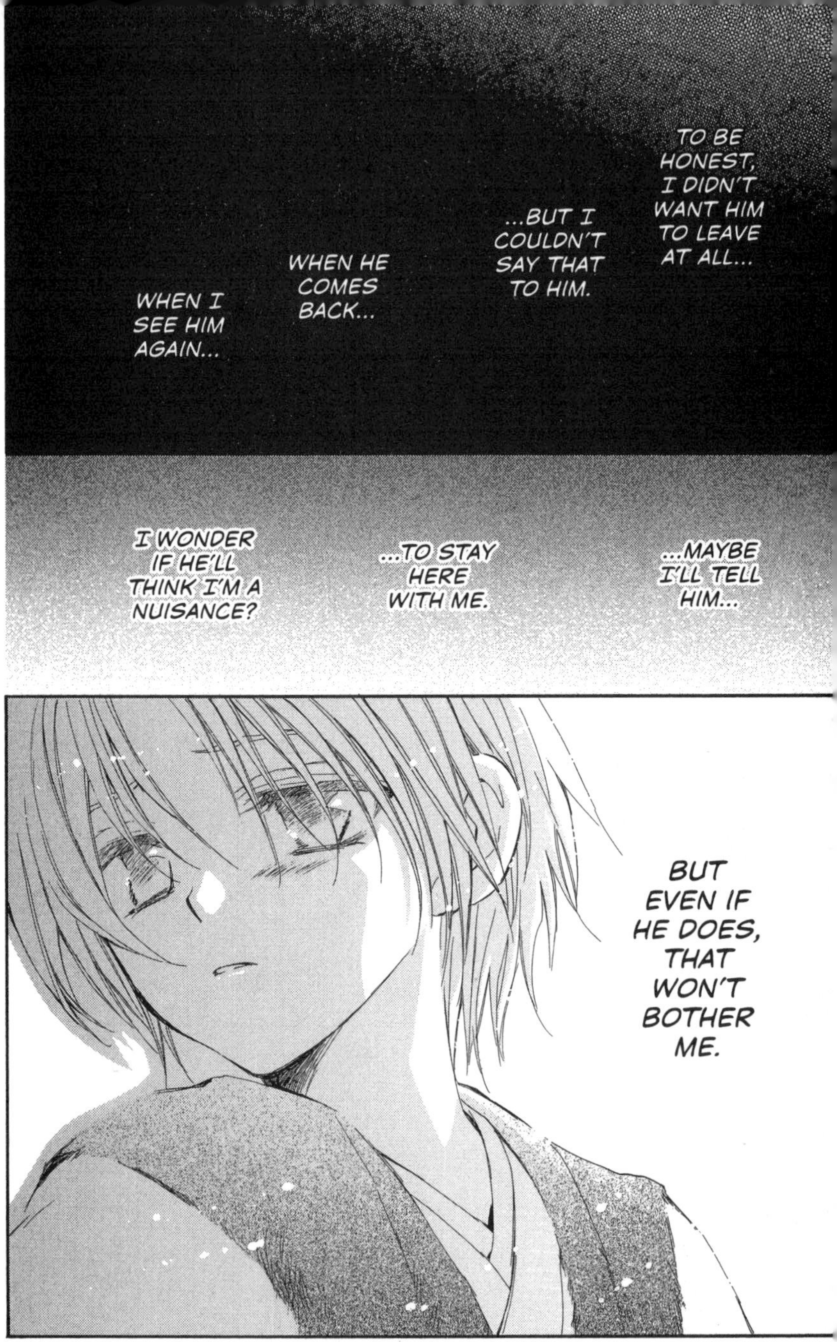
TO BE HONEST, I DIDN'T WANT HIM TO LEAVE AT ALL...
...BUT I COULDN'T SAY THAT TO HIM.
WHEN HE COMES BACK...
WHEN I SEE HIM AGAIN...
...MAYBE I'LL TELL HIM...
...TO STAY HERE WITH ME.
I WONDER IF HE'LL THINK I'M A NUISANCE?
BUT EVEN IF HE DOES, THAT WON'T BOTHER ME.

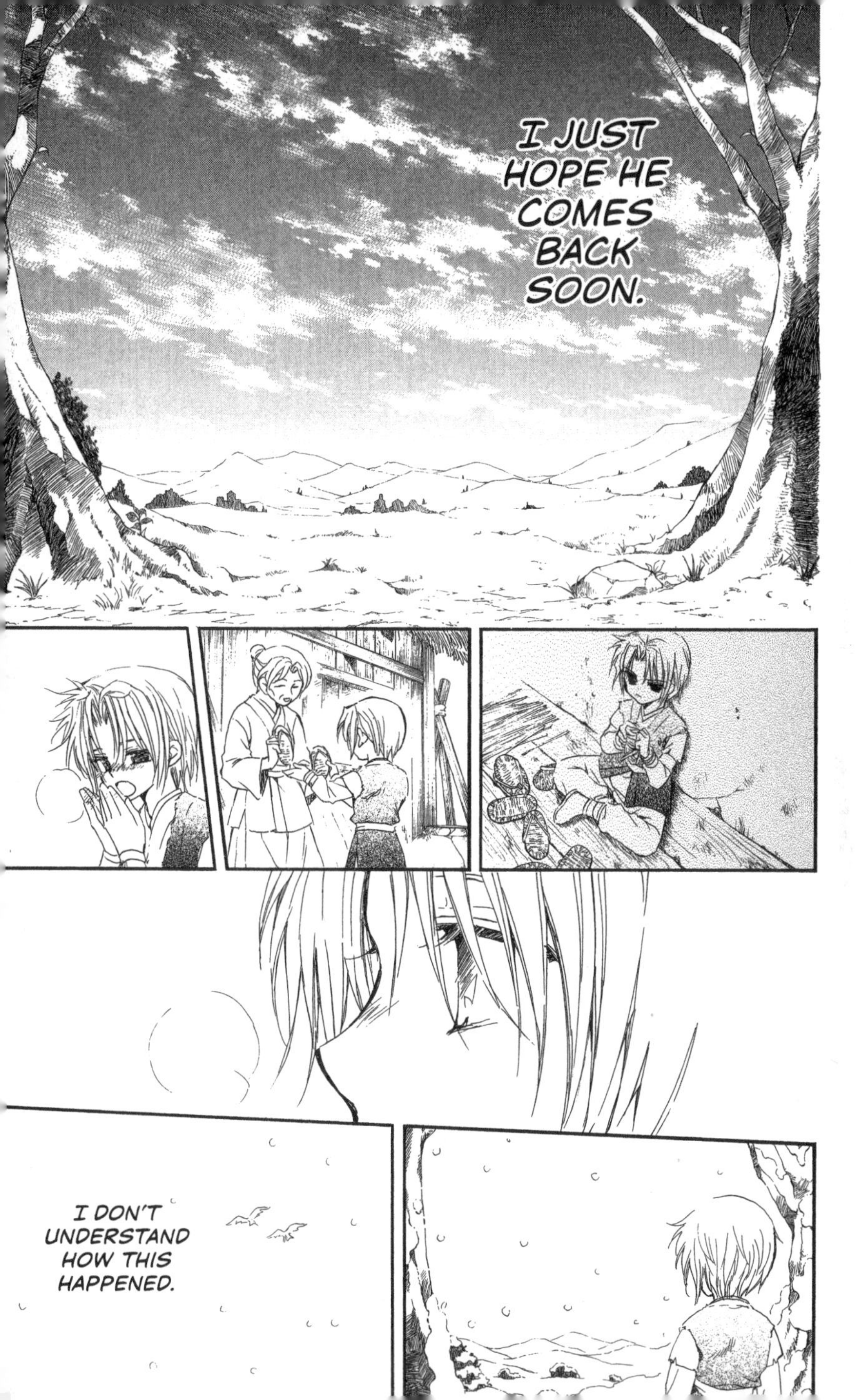
I JUST HOPE HE COMES BACK SOON.
I DON'T UNDERSTAND HOW THIS HAPPENED.

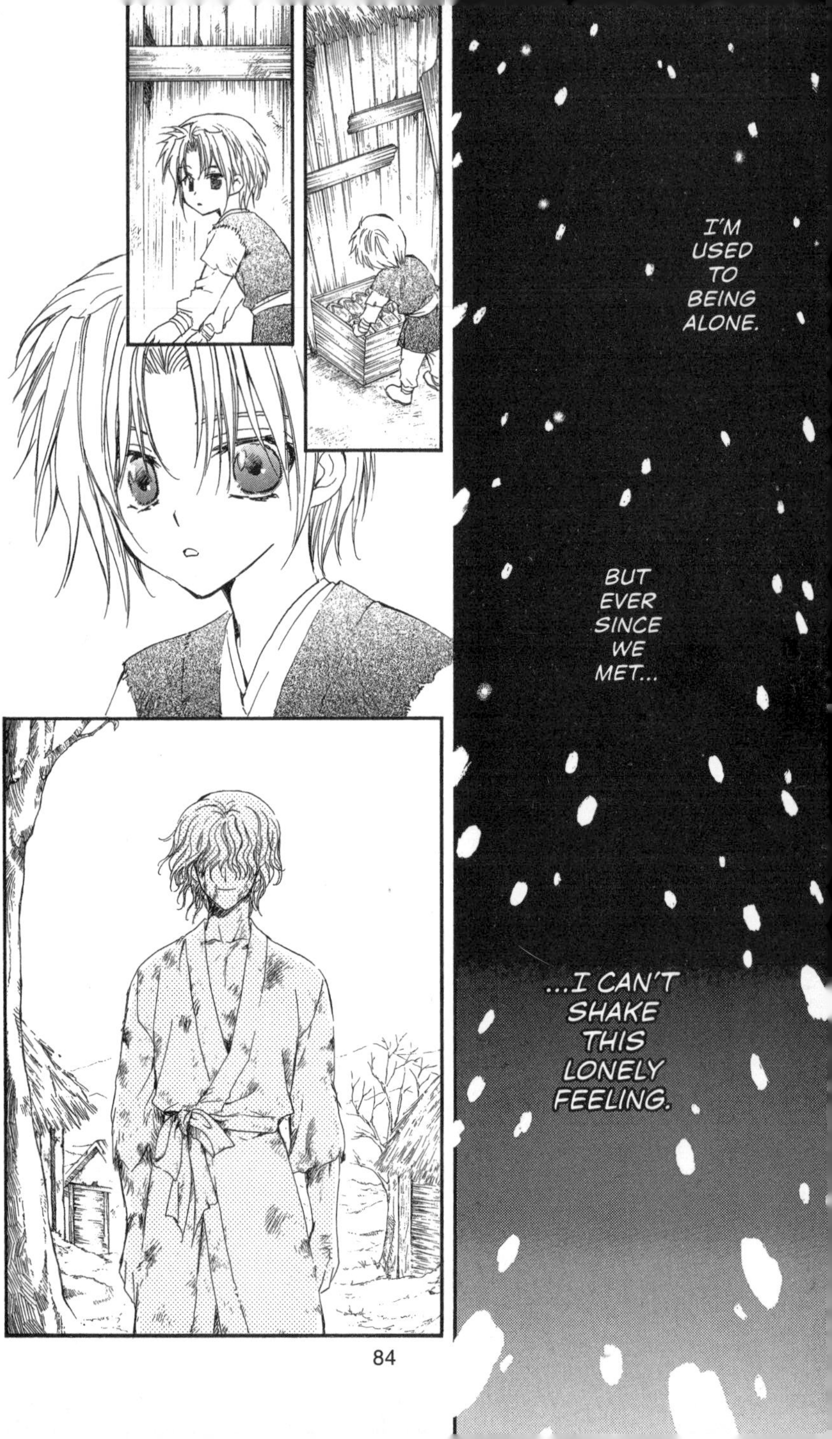
I'M USED TO BEING ALONE.
BUT EVER SINCE WE MET...
...I CAN'T SHAKE THIS LONELY FEELING.

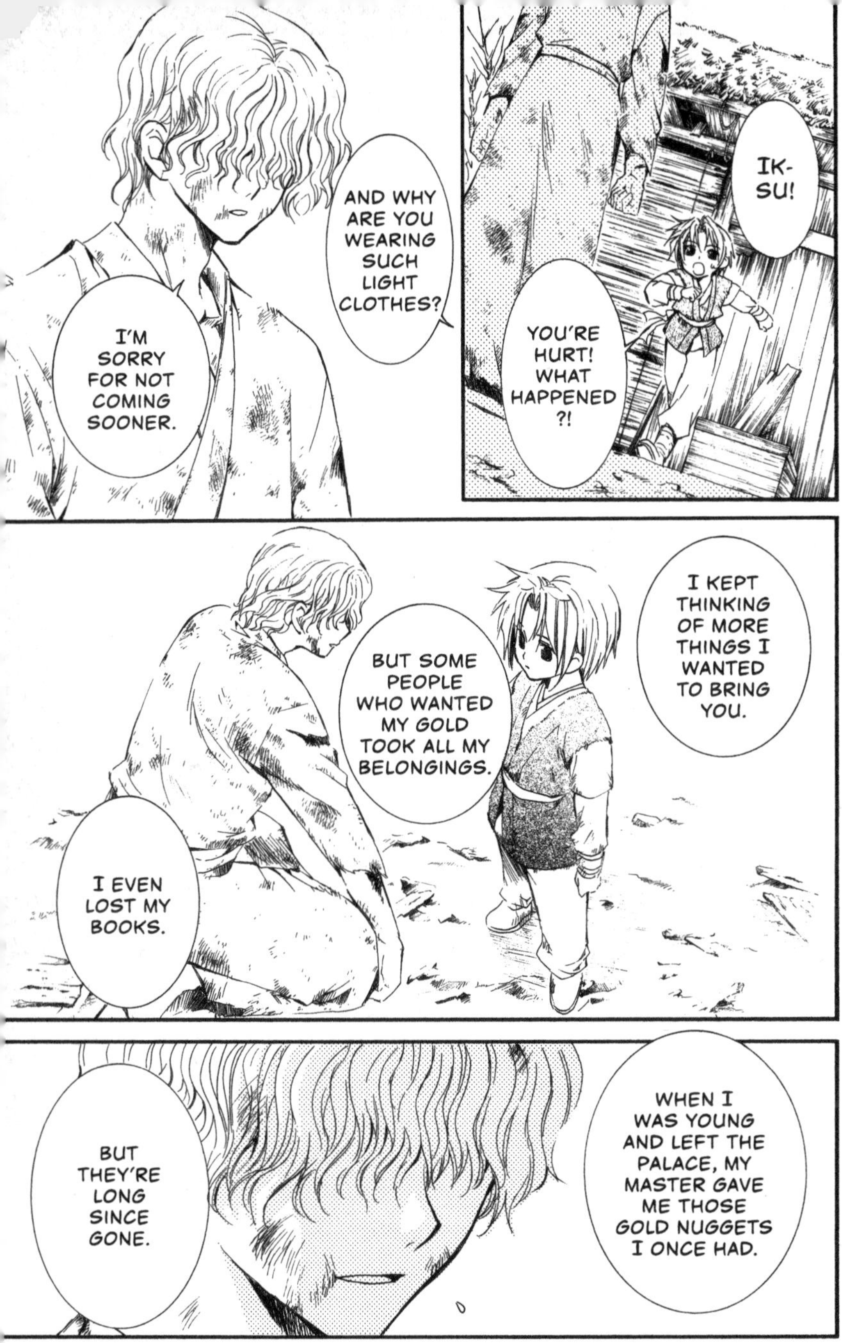
IK-SU!
YOU'RE HURT! WHAT HAPPENED?!
AND WHY ARE YOU WEARING SUCH LIGHT CLOTHES?
I'M SORRY FOR NOT COMING SOONER.
I KEPT THINKING OF MORE THINGS I WANTED TO BRING YOU.
BUT SOME PEOPLE WHO WANTED MY GOLD TOOK ALL MY BELONGINGS.
I EVEN LOST MY BOOKS.
WHEN I WAS YOUNG AND LEFT THE PALACE, MY MASTER GAVE ME THOSE GOLD NUGGETS I ONCE HAD.
BUT THEY'RE LONG SINCE GONE.

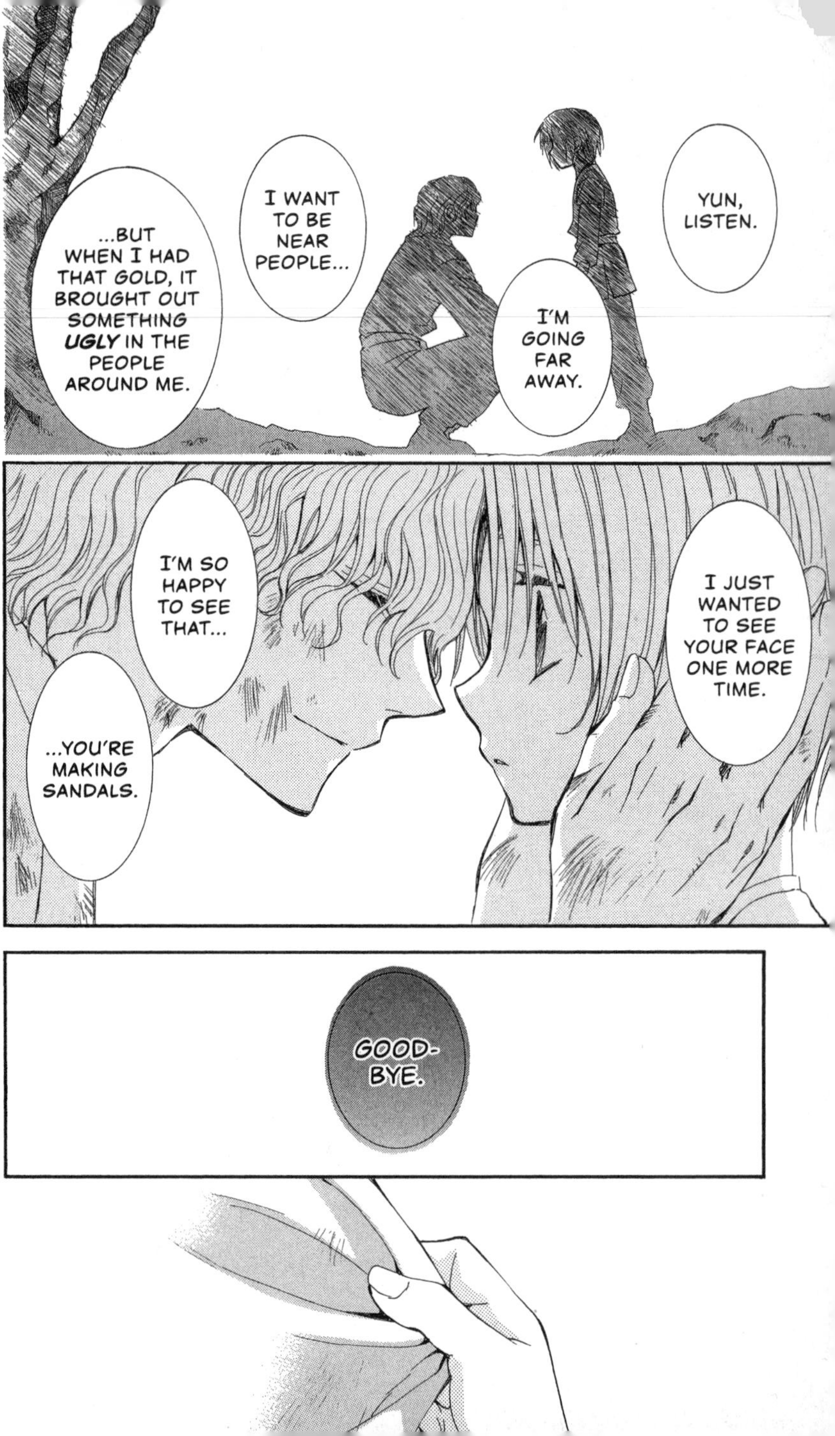
YUN, LISTEN.
I'M GOING FAR AWAY.
I WANT TO BE NEAR PEOPLE...
...BUT WHEN I HAD THAT GOLD, IT BROUGHT OUT SOMETHING UGLY IN THE PEOPLE AROUND ME.
I JUST WANTED TO SEE YOUR FACE ONE MORE TIME.
I'M SO HAPPY TO SEE THAT...
...YOU'RE MAKING SANDALS.
GOOD-BYE.

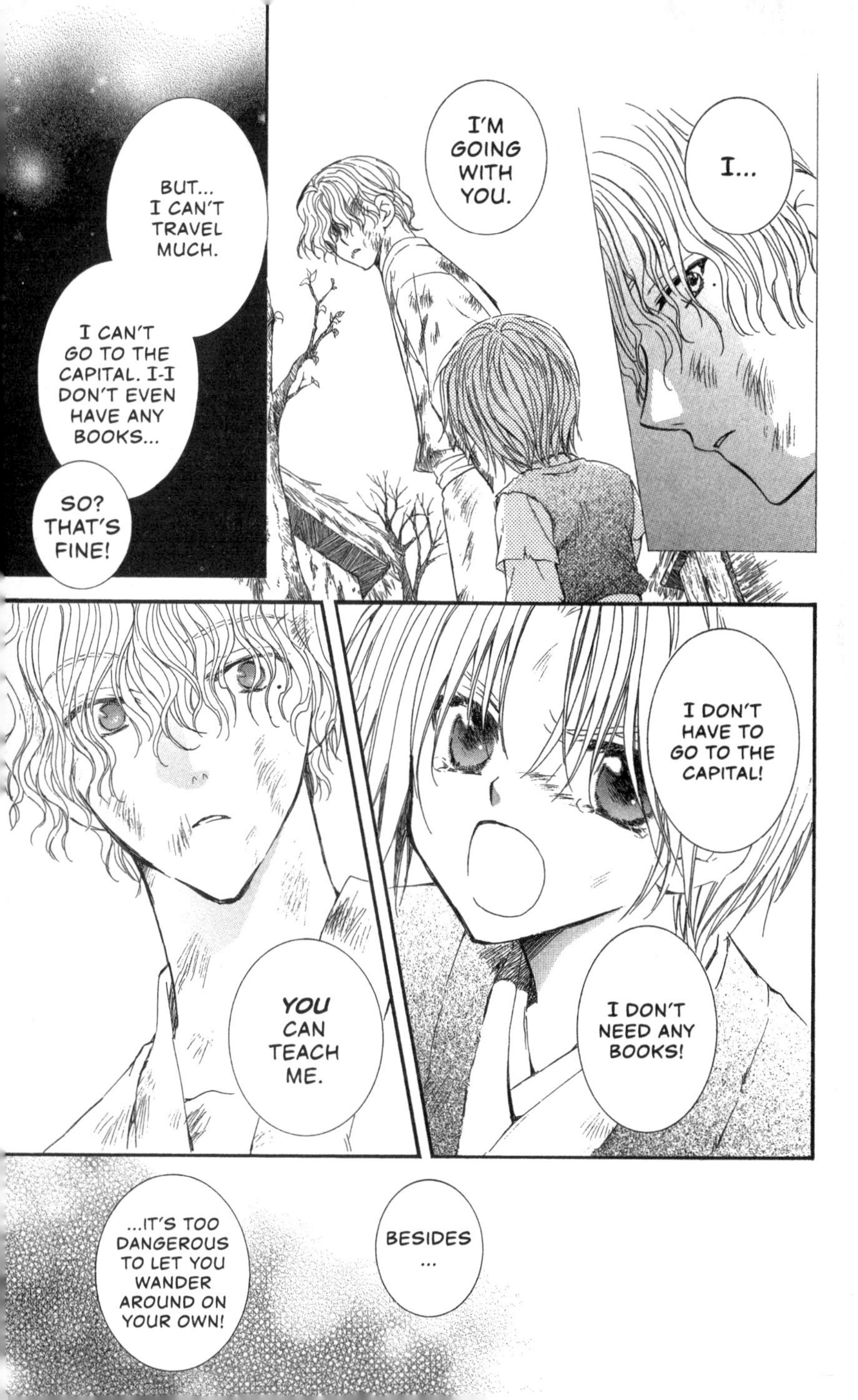
I...
I'M GOING WITH YOU.
BUT... I CAN'T TRAVEL MUCH.
I CAN'T GO TO THE CAPITAL. I-I DON'T EVEN HAVE ANY BOOKS...
SO? THAT'S FINE!
I DON'T HAVE TO GO TO THE CAPITAL!
I DON'T NEED ANY BOOKS!
YOU CAN TEACH ME.
BESIDES...
...IT'S TOO DANGEROUS TO LET YOU WANDER AROUND ON YOUR OWN!

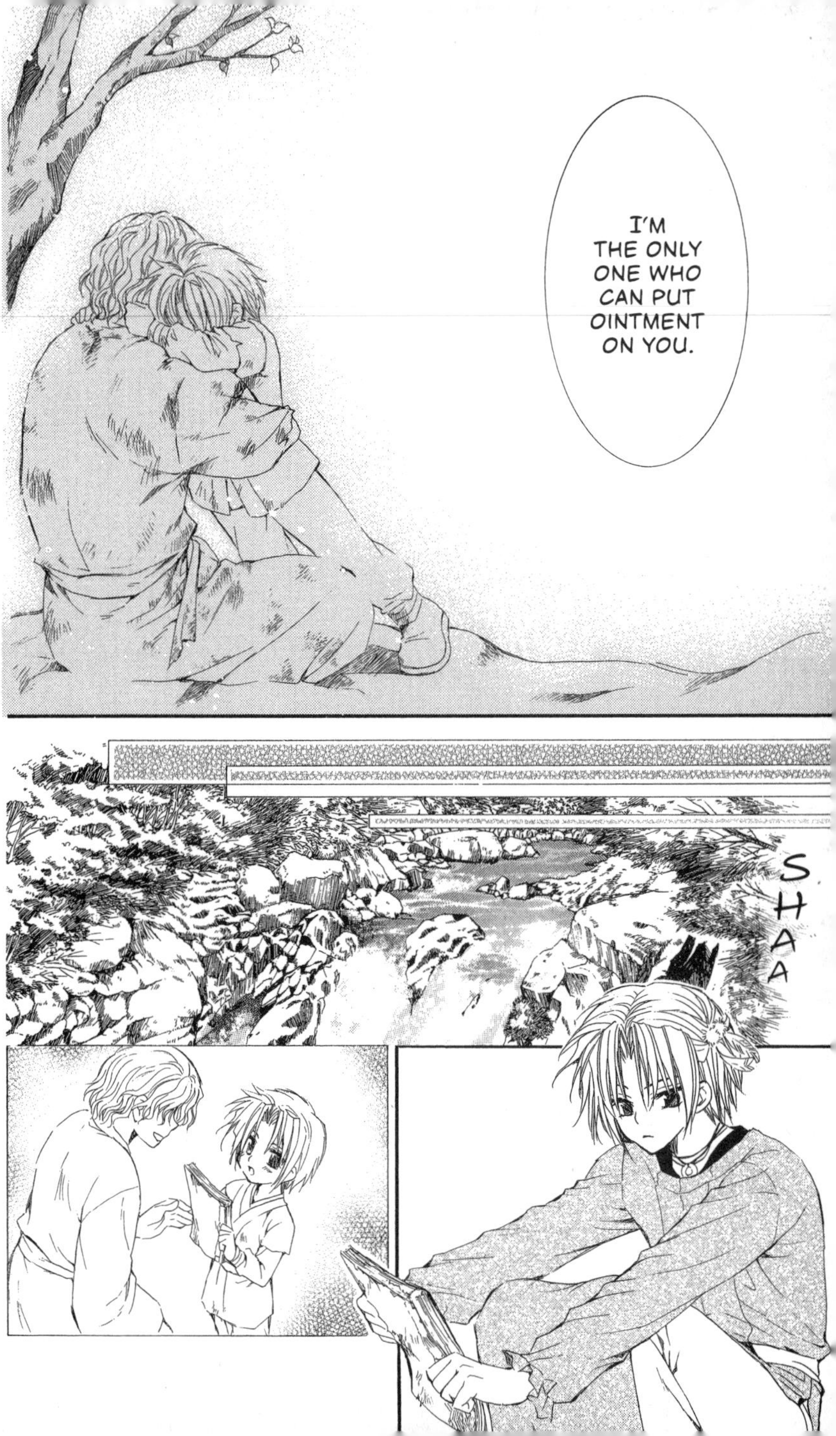
I'M THE ONLY ONE WHO CAN PUT OINTMENT ON YOU.
SHAA

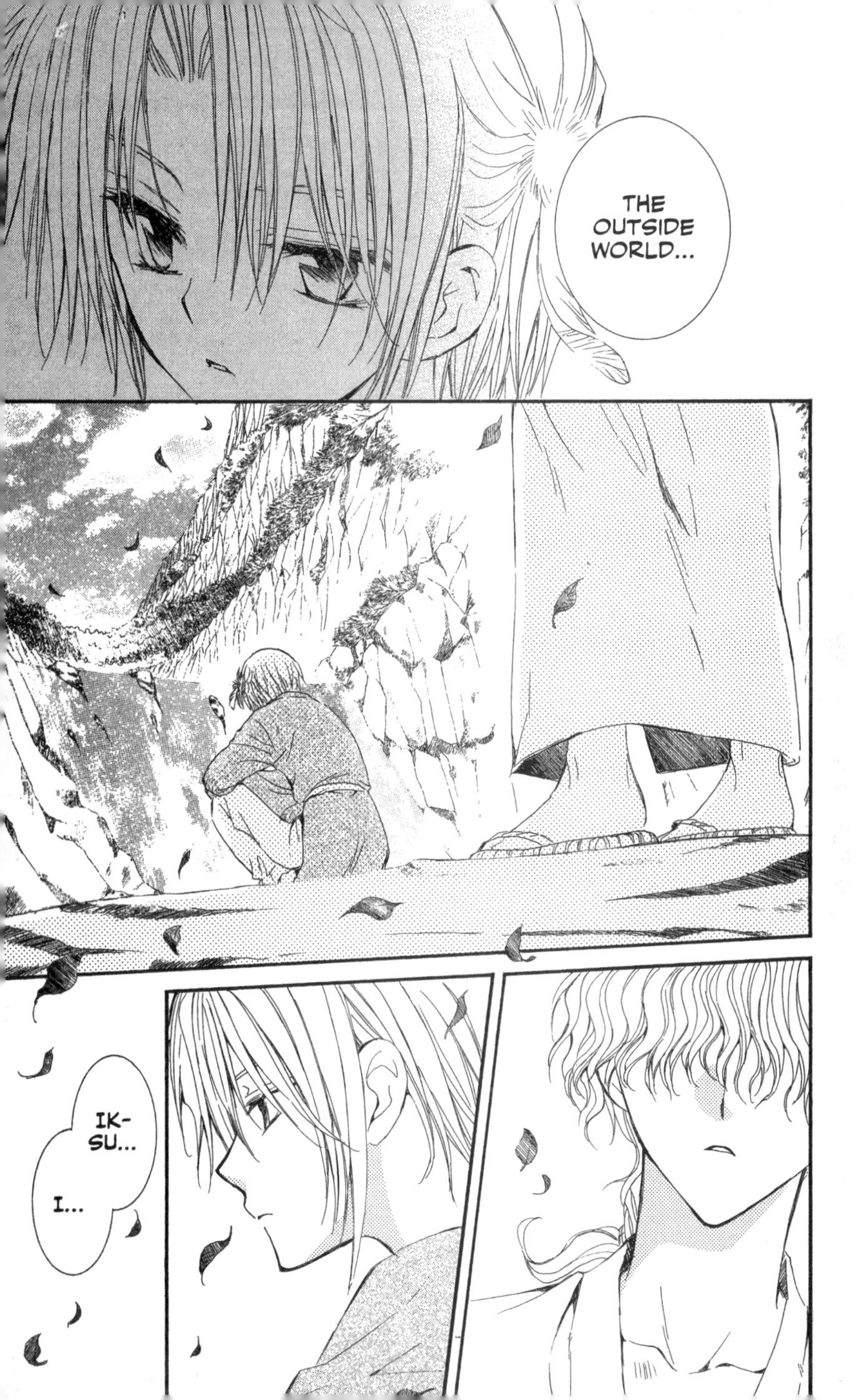
THE OUTSIDE WORLD...
IK-SU...
I...

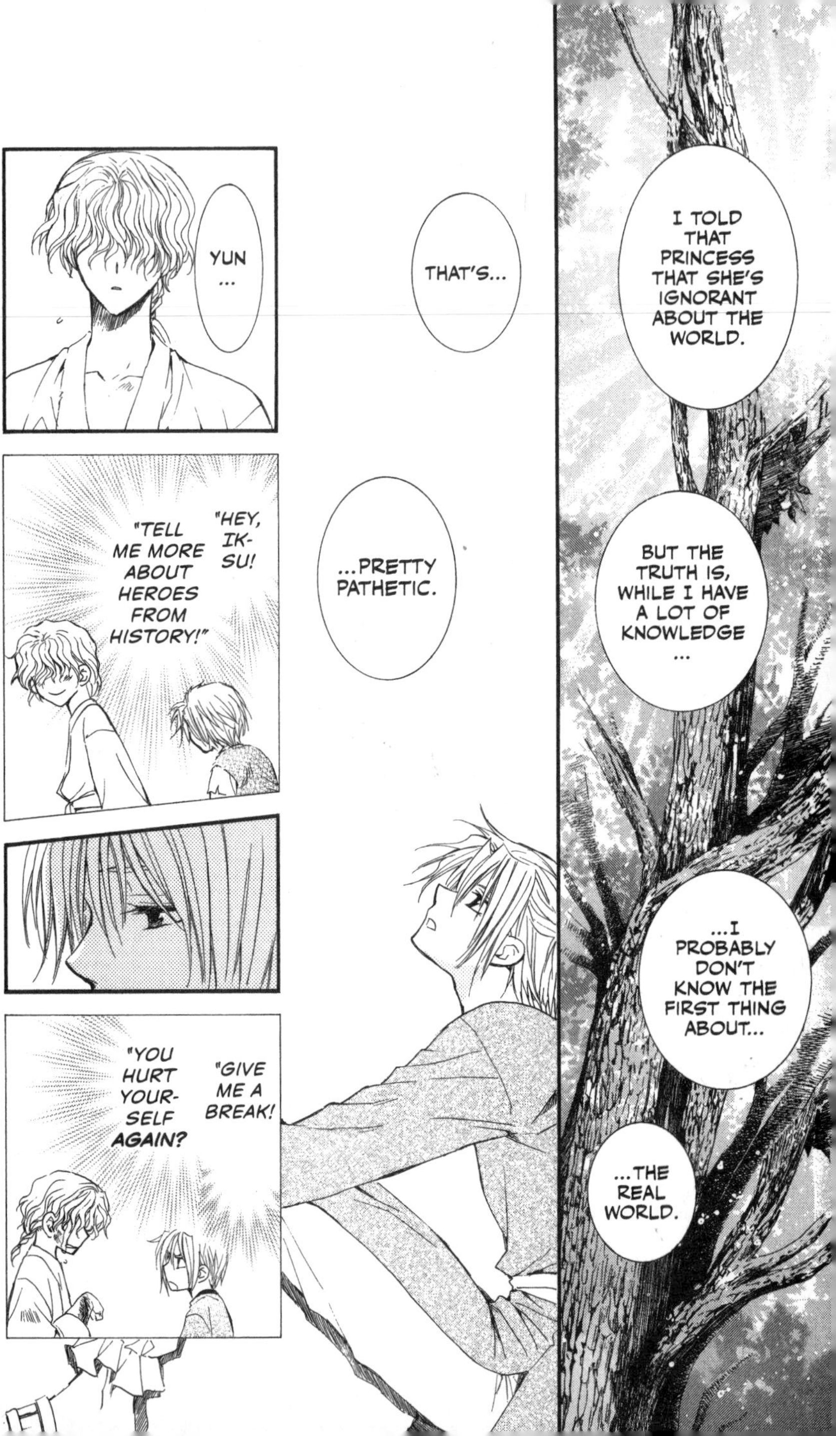

I TOLD THAT PRINCESS THAT SHE'S IGNORANT ABOUT THE WORLD.
BUT THE TRUTH IS, WHILE I HAVE A LOT OF KNOWLEDGE...
...I PROBABLY DON'T KNOW THE FIRST THING ABOUT...
...THE REAL WORLD.
THAT'S...
...PRETTY PATHETIC.
YUN...
"HEY, IK-SU!
"TELL ME MORE ABOUT HEROES FROM HISTORY!"
"GIVE ME A BREAK!
"YOU HURT YOUR-SELF **AGAIN**?

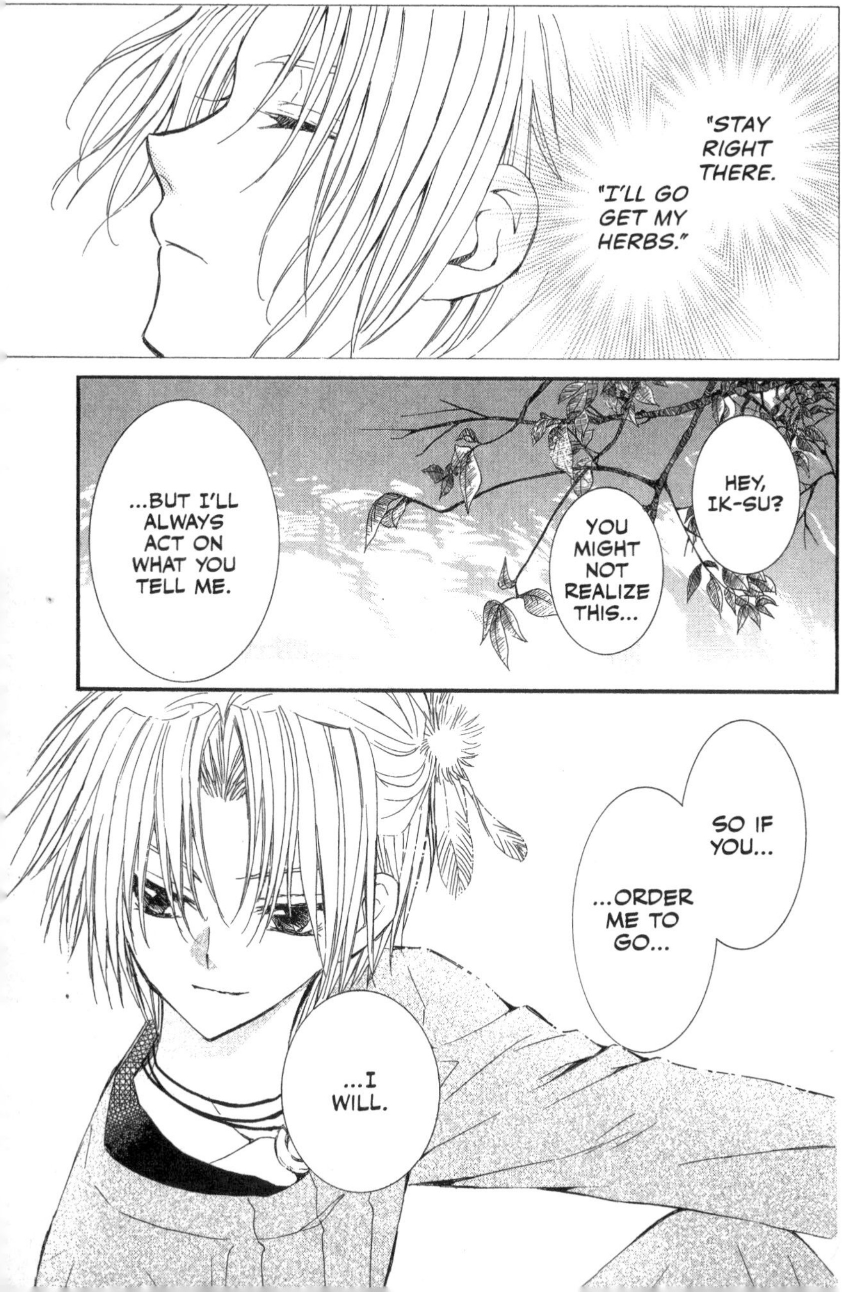
"STAY RIGHT THERE.
"I'LL GO GET MY HERBS."
HEY, IK-SU?
YOU MIGHT NOT REALIZE THIS...
...BUT I'LL ALWAYS ACT ON WHAT YOU TELL ME.
SO IF YOU...
...ORDER ME TO GO...
...I WILL.

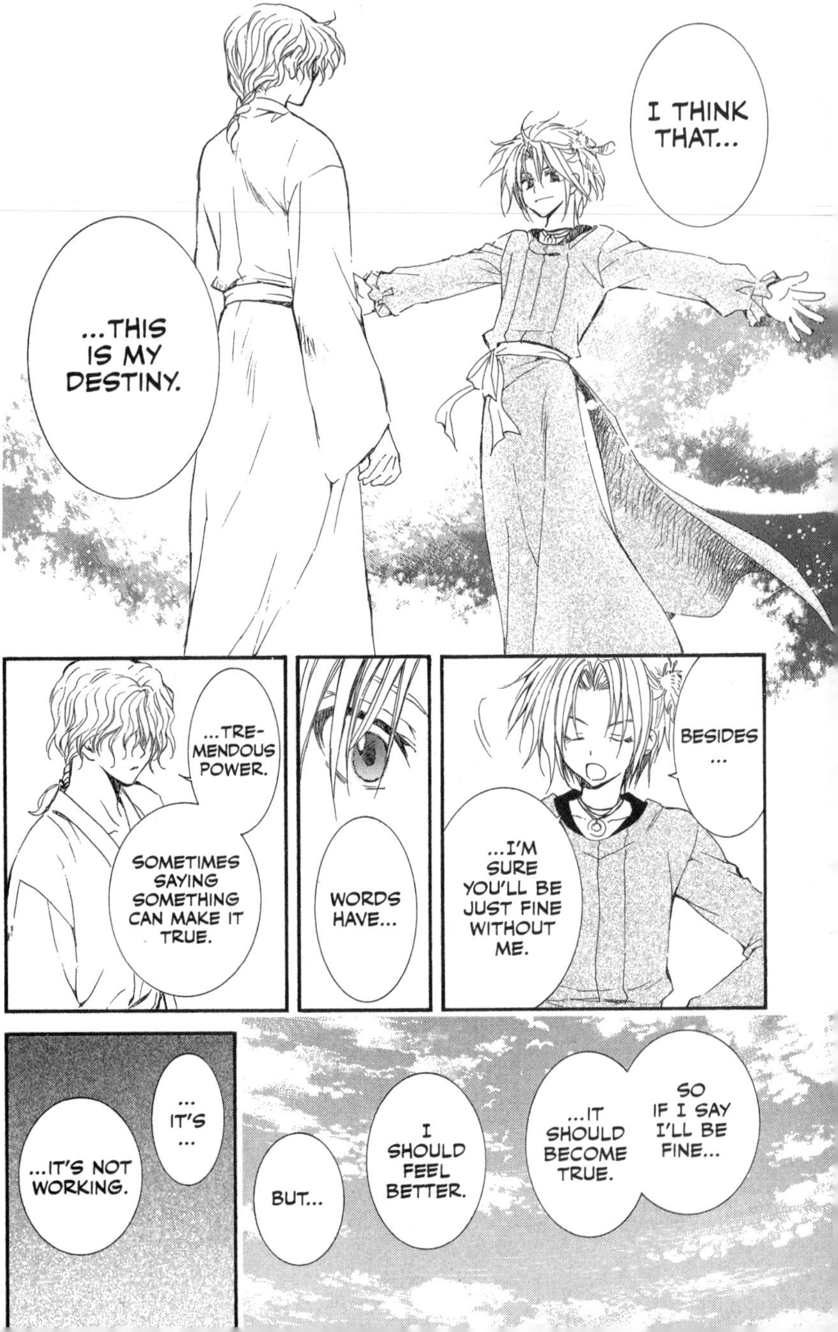
I THINK THAT...
...THIS IS MY DESTINY.
BESIDES...
...I'M SURE YOU'LL BE JUST FINE WITHOUT ME.
WORDS HAVE...
...TREMENDOUS POWER.
SOMETIMES SAYING SOMETHING CAN MAKE IT TRUE.
SO IF I SAY I'LL BE FINE...
...IT SHOULD BECOME TRUE.
I SHOULD FEEL BETTER.
BUT...
...IT'S...
...IT'S NOT WORKING.

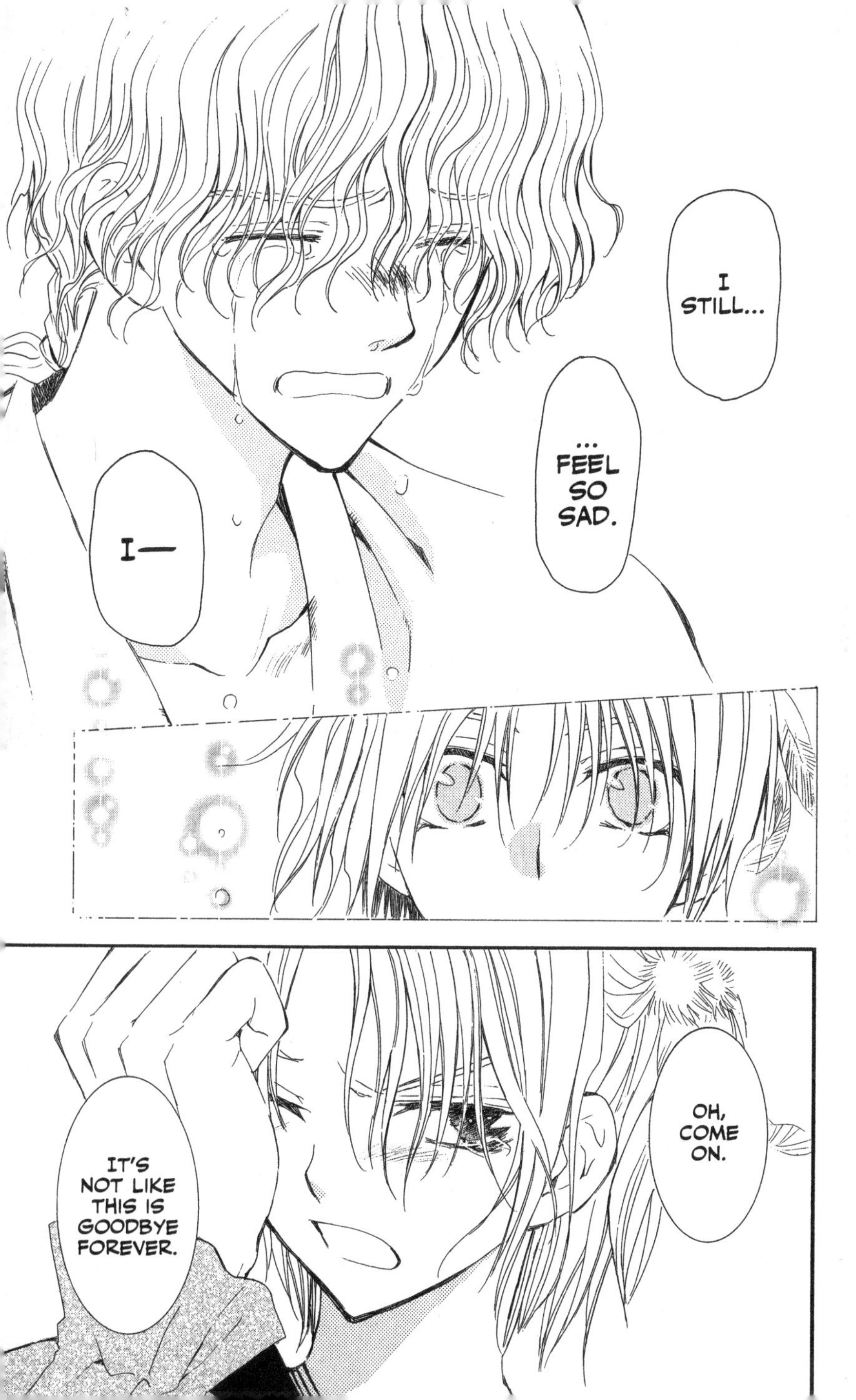
I STILL...
...FEEL SO SAD.
I—
OH, COME ON.
IT'S NOT LIKE THIS IS GOODBYE FOREVER.

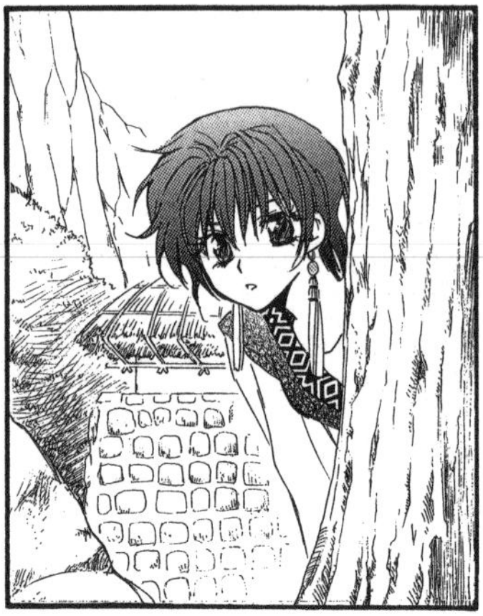
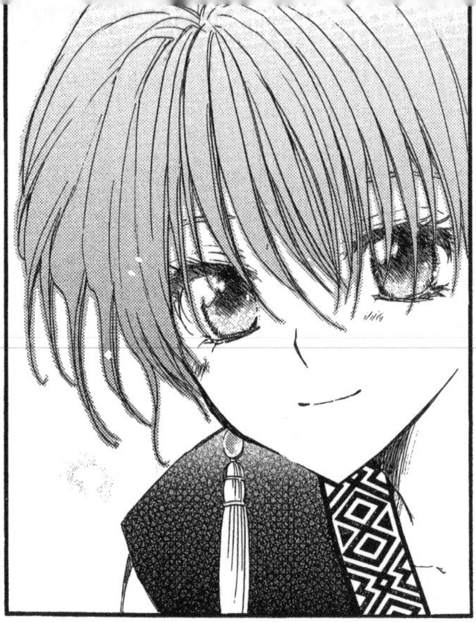
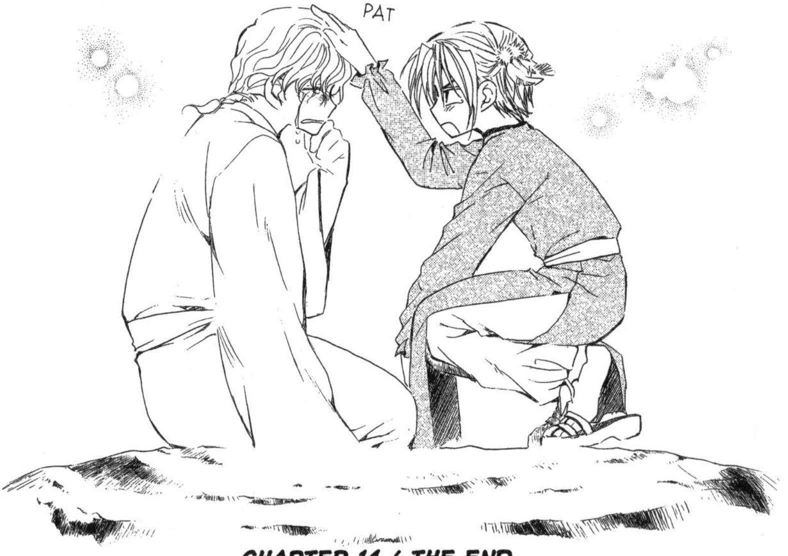
PAT

CHAPTER 14 / THE END

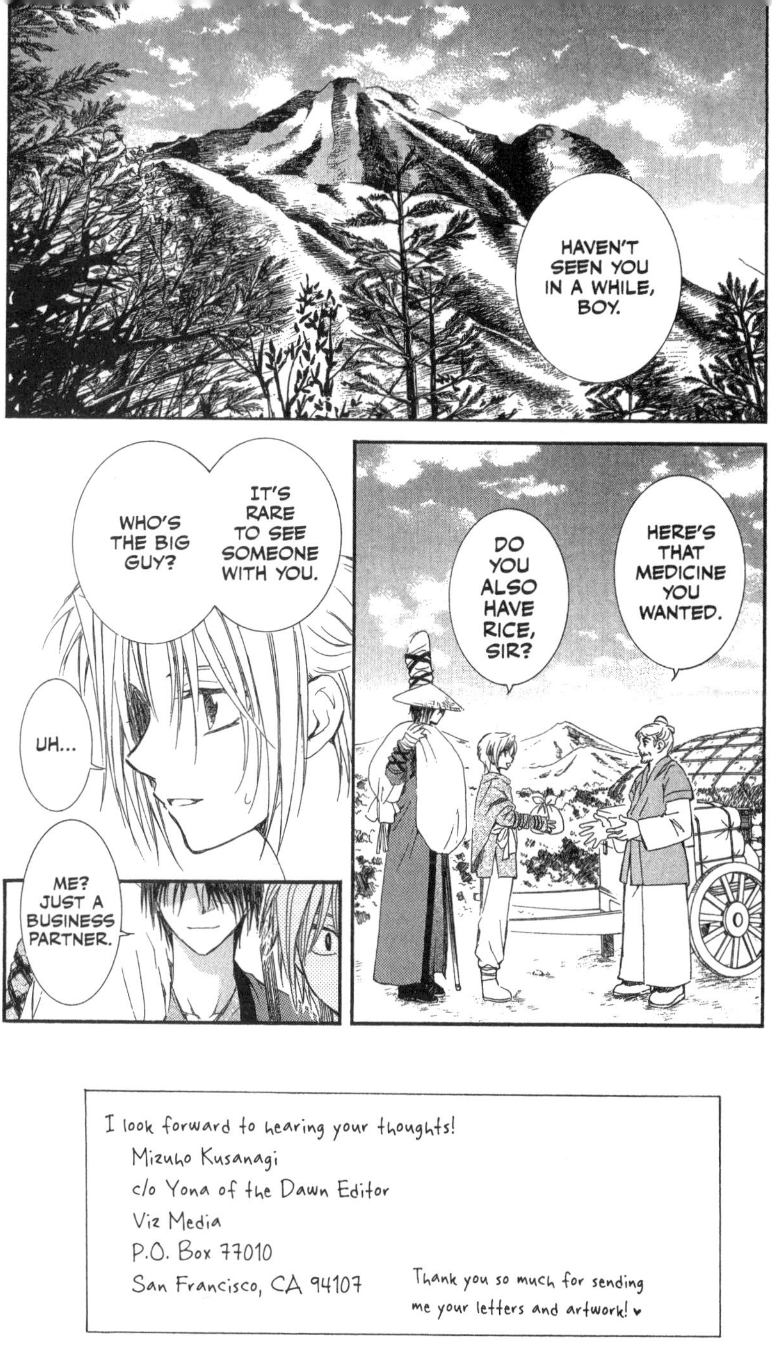
HAVEN'T SEEN YOU IN A WHILE, BOY.
HERE'S THAT MEDICINE YOU WANTED.
DO YOU ALSO HAVE RICE, SIR?
IT'S RARE TO SEE SOMEONE WITH YOU.
WHO'S THE BIG GUY?
UH...
ME? JUST A BUSINESS PARTNER.

I look forward to hearing your thoughts!

Mizuho Kusanagi
c/o Yona of the Dawn Editor
Viz Media
P.O. Box 77010
San Francisco, CA 94107

Thank you so much for sending me your letters and artwork! ♥

CHAPTER 15: WAVERING DETERMINATION

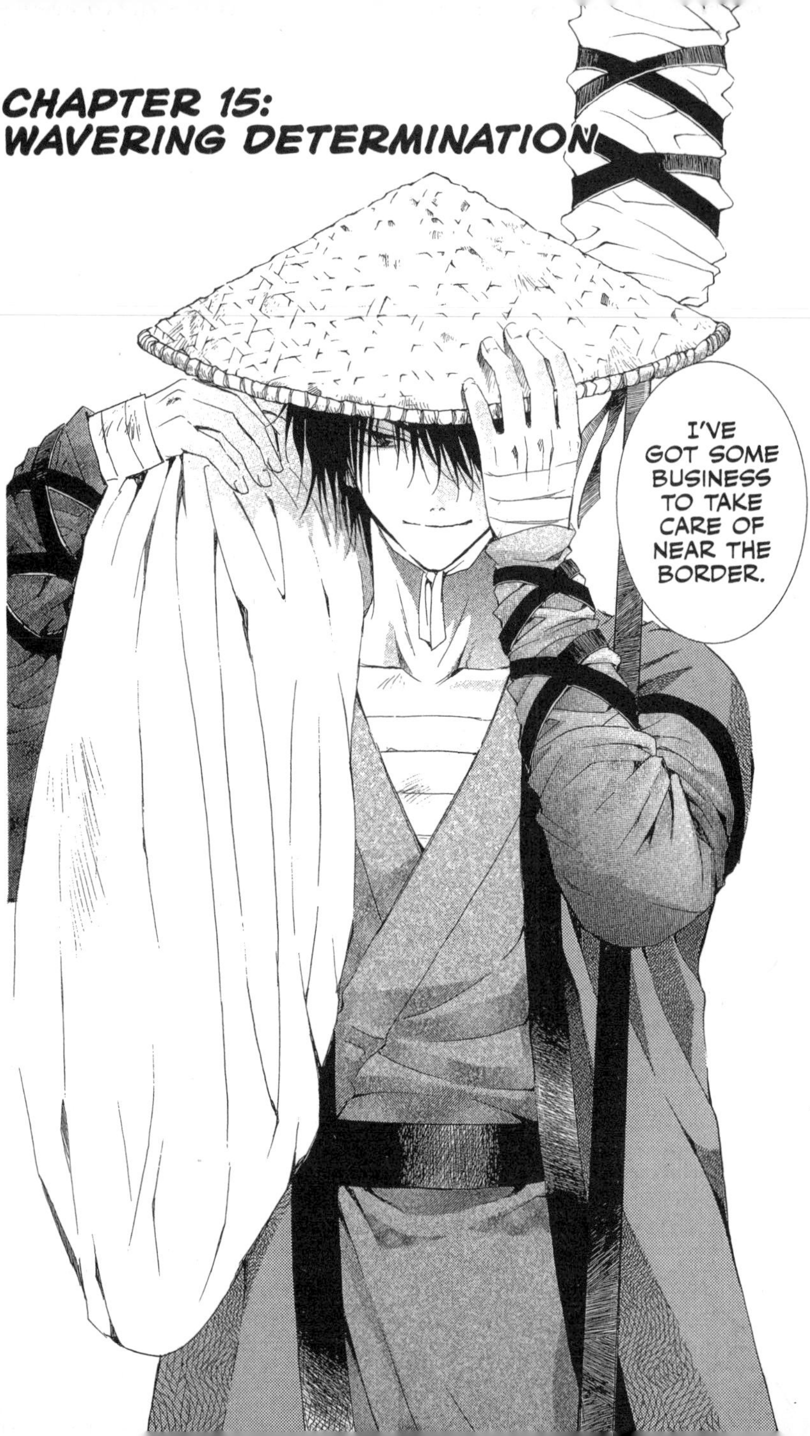
I'VE GOT SOME BUSINESS TO TAKE CARE OF NEAR THE BORDER.

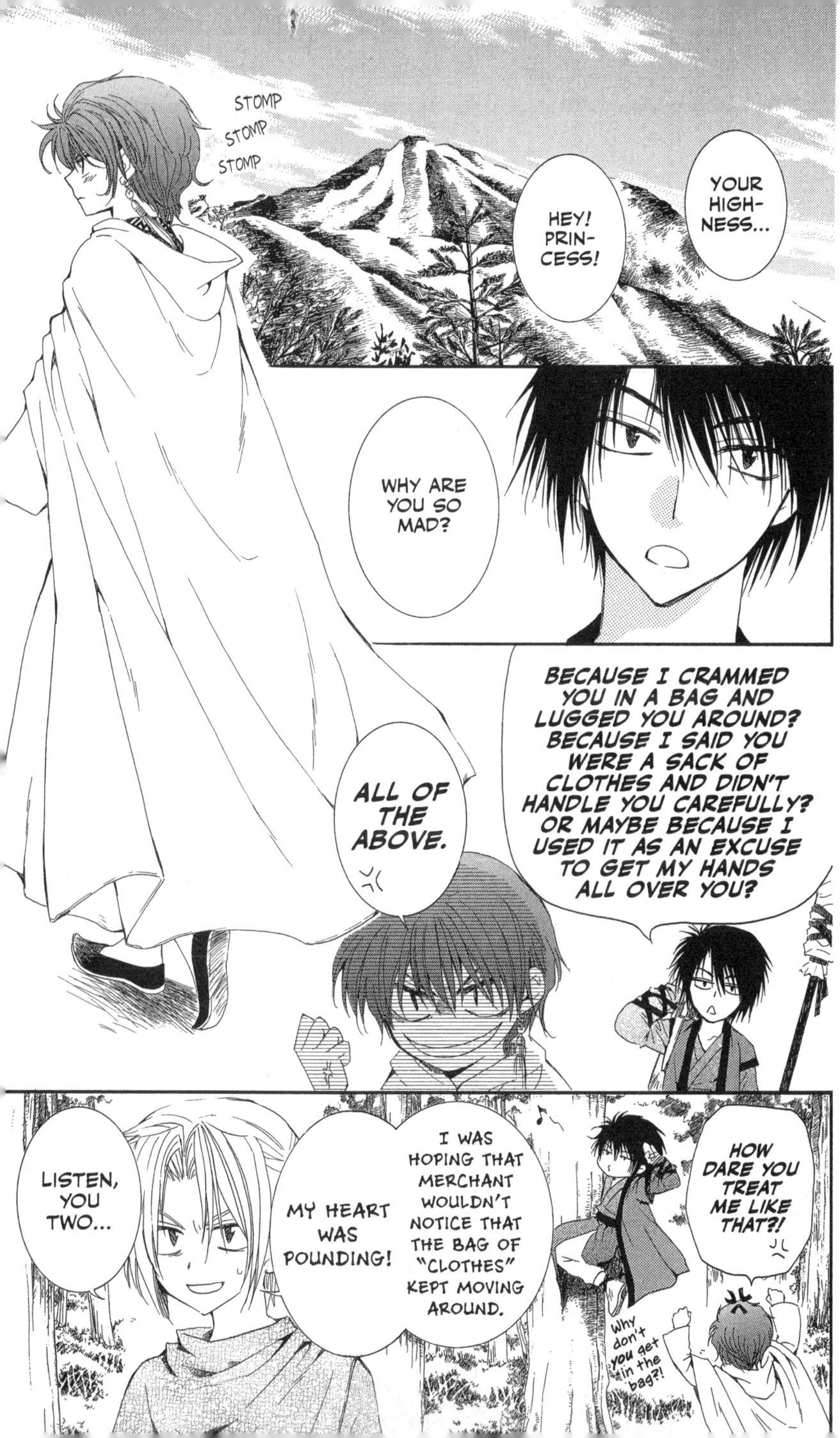
YOUR HIGHNESS...
HEY! PRINCESS!
STOMP STOMP STOMP
WHY ARE YOU SO MAD?
BECAUSE I CRAMMED YOU IN A BAG AND LUGGED YOU AROUND? BECAUSE I SAID YOU WERE A SACK OF CLOTHES AND DIDN'T HANDLE YOU CAREFULLY? OR MAYBE BECAUSE I USED IT AS AN EXCUSE TO GET MY HANDS ALL OVER YOU?
ALL OF THE ABOVE.
HOW DARE YOU TREAT ME LIKE THAT?!
Why don't you get in the bag?!
I WAS HOPING THAT MERCHANT WOULDN'T NOTICE THAT THE BAG OF "CLOTHES" KEPT MOVING AROUND.
MY HEART WAS POUNDING!
LISTEN, YOU TWO...

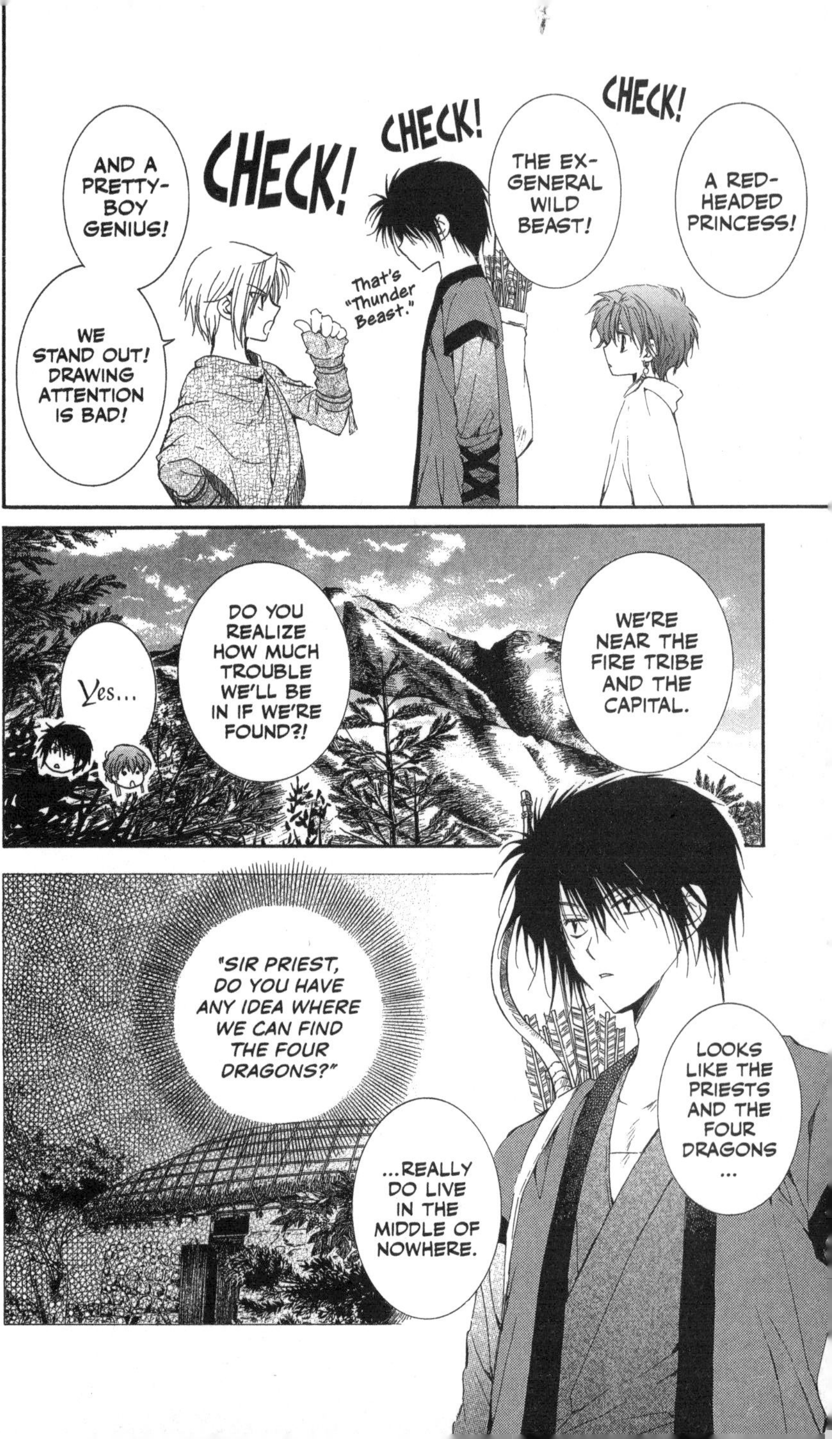
A RED-HEADED PRINCESS!
CHECK!
THE EX-GENERAL WILD BEAST!
CHECK!
That's "Thunder Beast."
CHECK!
AND A PRETTY-BOY GENIUS!
WE STAND OUT! DRAWING ATTENTION IS BAD!
WE'RE NEAR THE FIRE TRIBE AND THE CAPITAL.
DO YOU REALIZE HOW MUCH TROUBLE WE'LL BE IN IF WE'RE FOUND?!
Yes...
"SIR PRIEST, DO YOU HAVE ANY IDEA WHERE WE CAN FIND THE FOUR DRAGONS?"
LOOKS LIKE THE PRIESTS AND THE FOUR DRAGONS...
...REALLY DO LIVE IN THE MIDDLE OF NOWHERE.

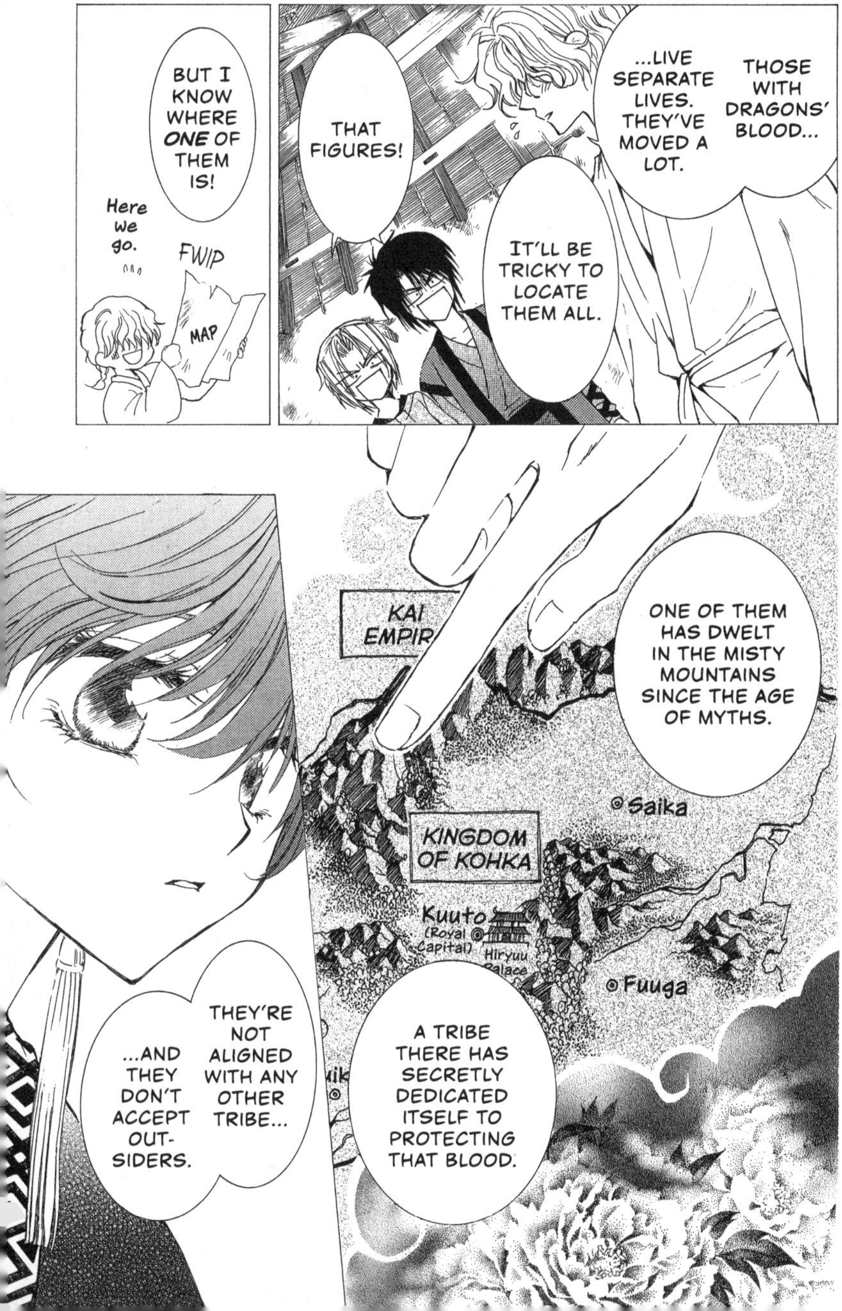
THOSE WITH DRAGONS' BLOOD...
...LIVE SEPARATE LIVES. THEY'VE MOVED A LOT.
IT'LL BE TRICKY TO LOCATE THEM ALL.
THAT FIGURES!
BUT I KNOW WHERE *ONE* OF THEM IS!
Here we go.
FWIP
MAP
ONE OF THEM HAS DWELT IN THE MISTY MOUNTAINS SINCE THE AGE OF MYTHS.
KAI EMPIR
KINGDOM OF KOHKA
Saika
Kuuto (Royal Capital)
Hiryuu Palace
Fuuga
A TRIBE THERE HAS SECRETLY DEDICATED ITSELF TO PROTECTING THAT BLOOD.
THEY'RE NOT ALIGNED WITH ANY OTHER TRIBE...
...AND THEY DON'T ACCEPT OUT-SIDERS.

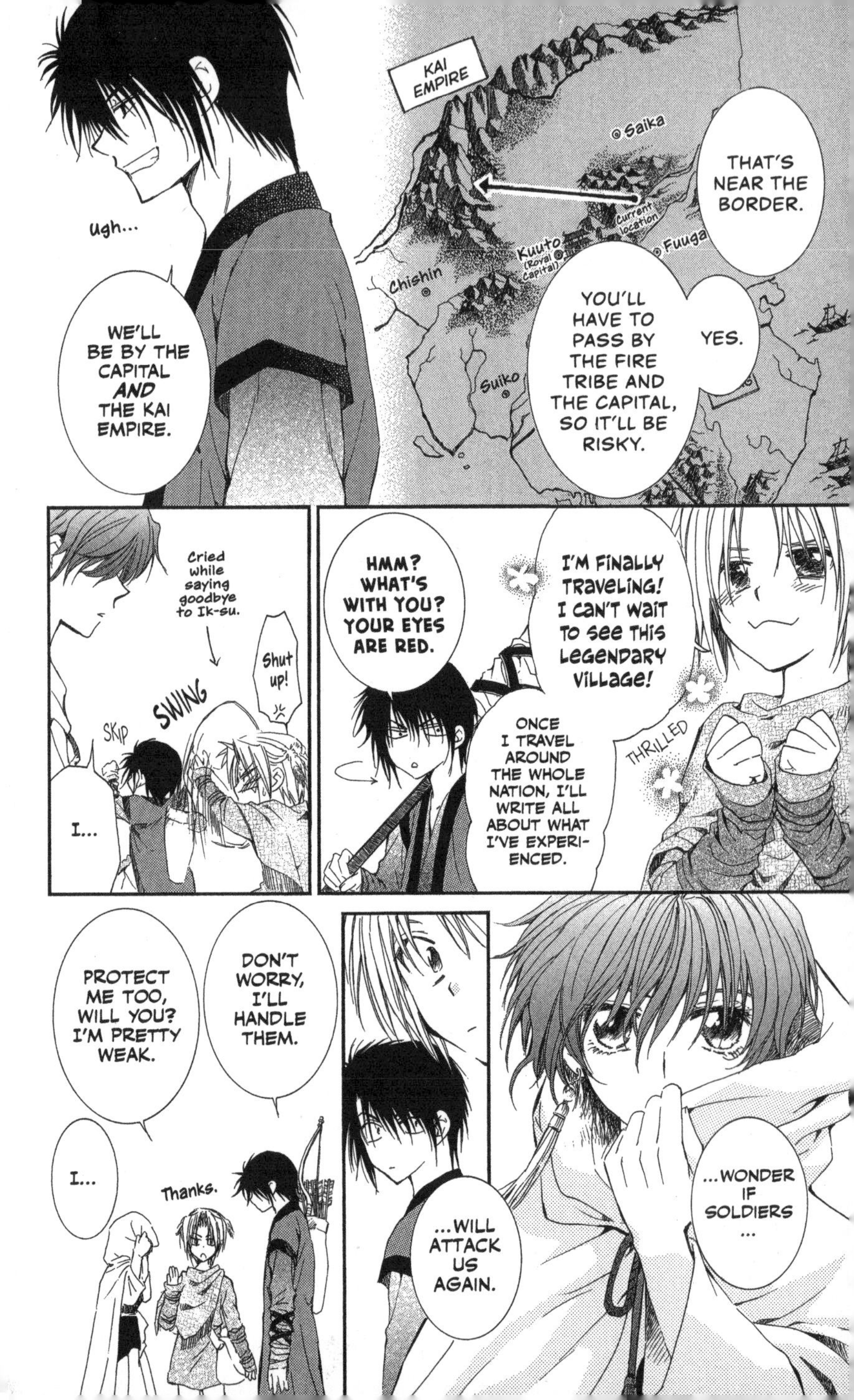
KAI EMPIRE
Saika
Current location
Kuuto (Royal Capital)
Fuuga
Chishin
Suiko
THAT'S NEAR THE BORDER.
YES.
YOU'LL HAVE TO PASS BY THE FIRE TRIBE AND THE CAPITAL, SO IT'LL BE RISKY.
Ugh...
WE'LL BE BY THE CAPITAL *AND* THE KAI EMPIRE.
I'M FINALLY TRAVELING! I CAN'T WAIT TO SEE THIS LEGENDARY VILLAGE!
THRILLED
ONCE I TRAVEL AROUND THE WHOLE NATION, I'LL WRITE ALL ABOUT WHAT I'VE EXPERIENCED.
HMM? WHAT'S WITH YOU? YOUR EYES ARE RED.
Cried while saying goodbye to Ik-su.
Shut up!
SWING
SKIP
I...
...WONDER IF SOLDIERS...
...WILL ATTACK US AGAIN.
DON'T WORRY, I'LL HANDLE THEM.
PROTECT ME TOO, WILL YOU? I'M PRETTY WEAK.
Thanks.
I...

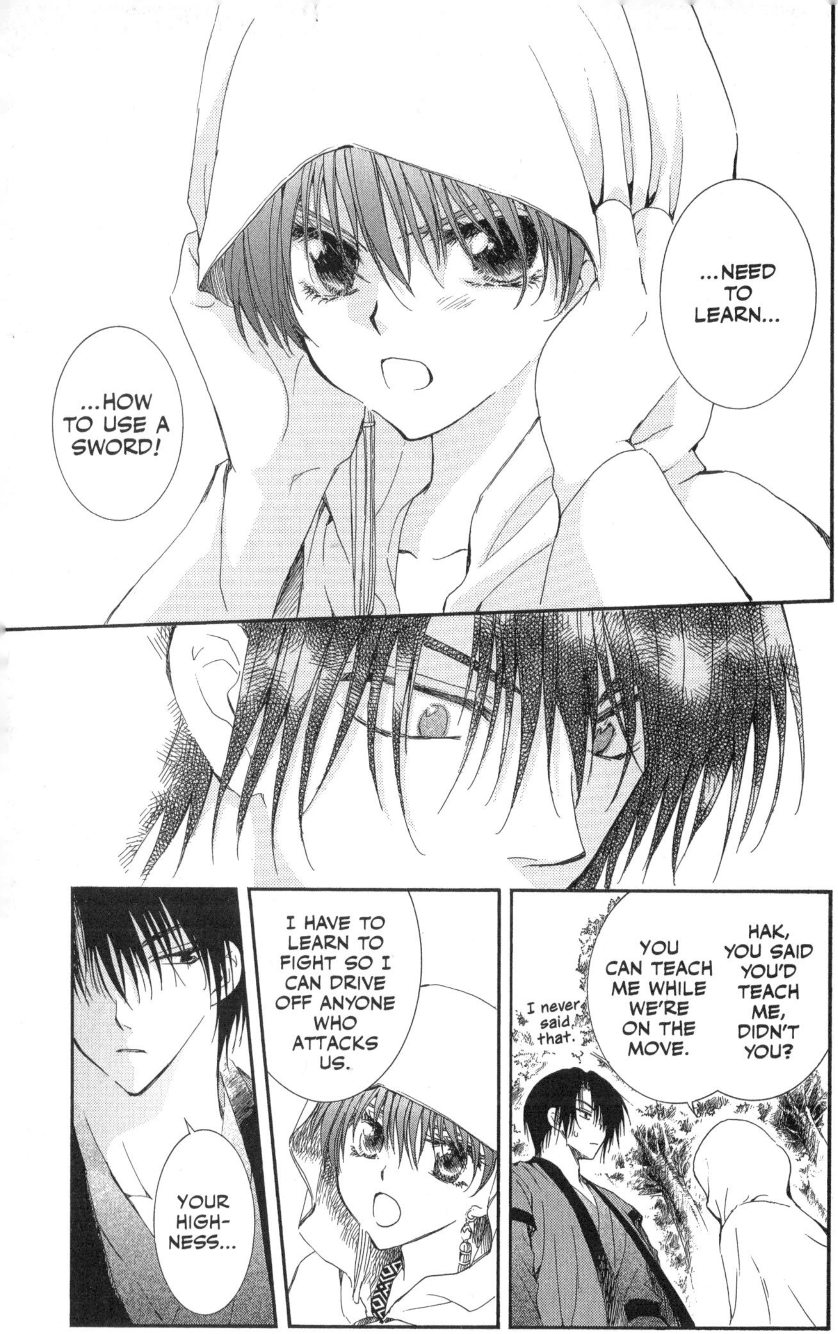
...NEED TO LEARN...
...HOW TO USE A SWORD!
HAK, YOU SAID YOU'D TEACH ME, DIDN'T YOU?
YOU CAN TEACH ME WHILE WE'RE ON THE MOVE.
I never said that.
I HAVE TO LEARN TO FIGHT SO I CAN DRIVE OFF ANYONE WHO ATTACKS US.
YOUR HIGHNESS...

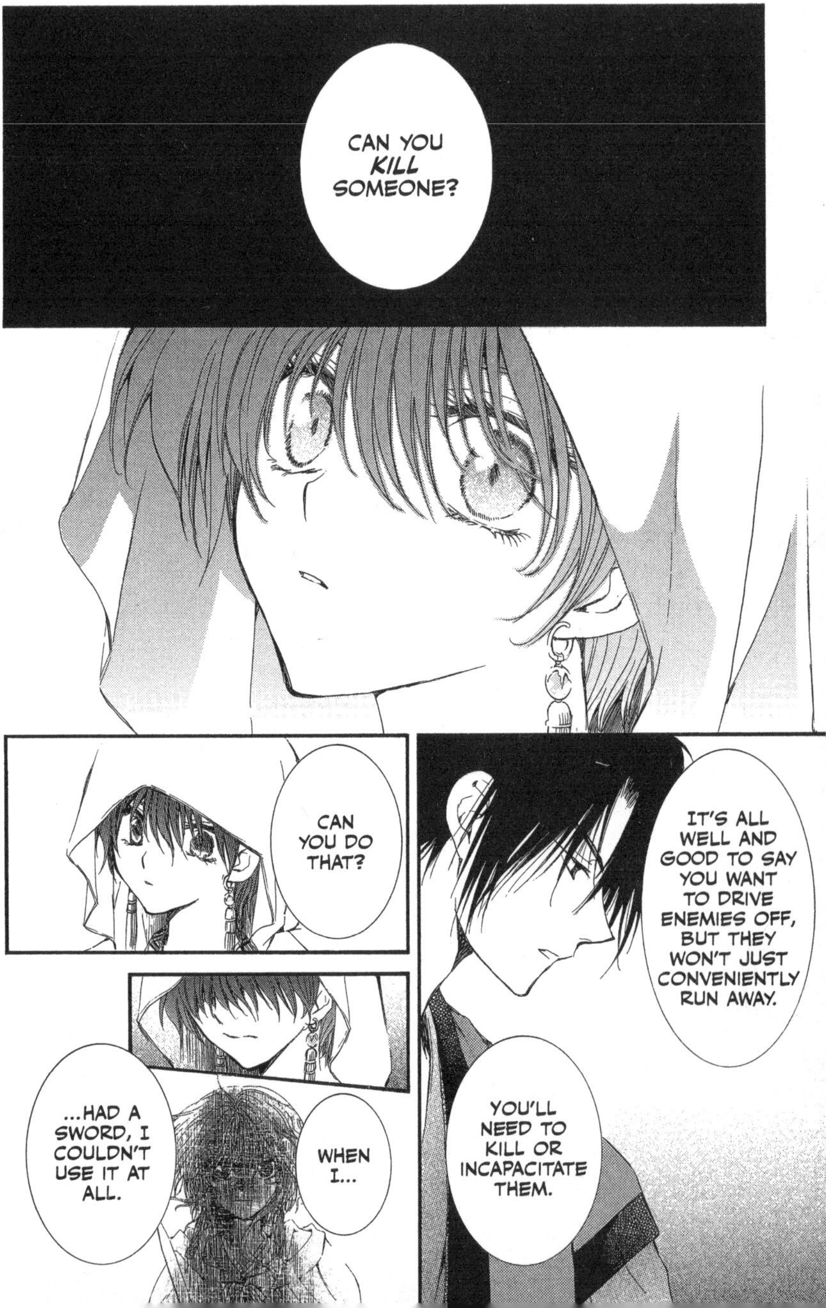
CAN YOU KILL SOMEONE?
IT'S ALL WELL AND GOOD TO SAY YOU WANT TO DRIVE ENEMIES OFF, BUT THEY WON'T JUST CONVENIENTLY RUN AWAY.
YOU'LL NEED TO KILL OR INCAPACITATE THEM.
CAN YOU DO THAT?
WHEN I...
...HAD A SWORD, I COULDN'T USE IT AT ALL.

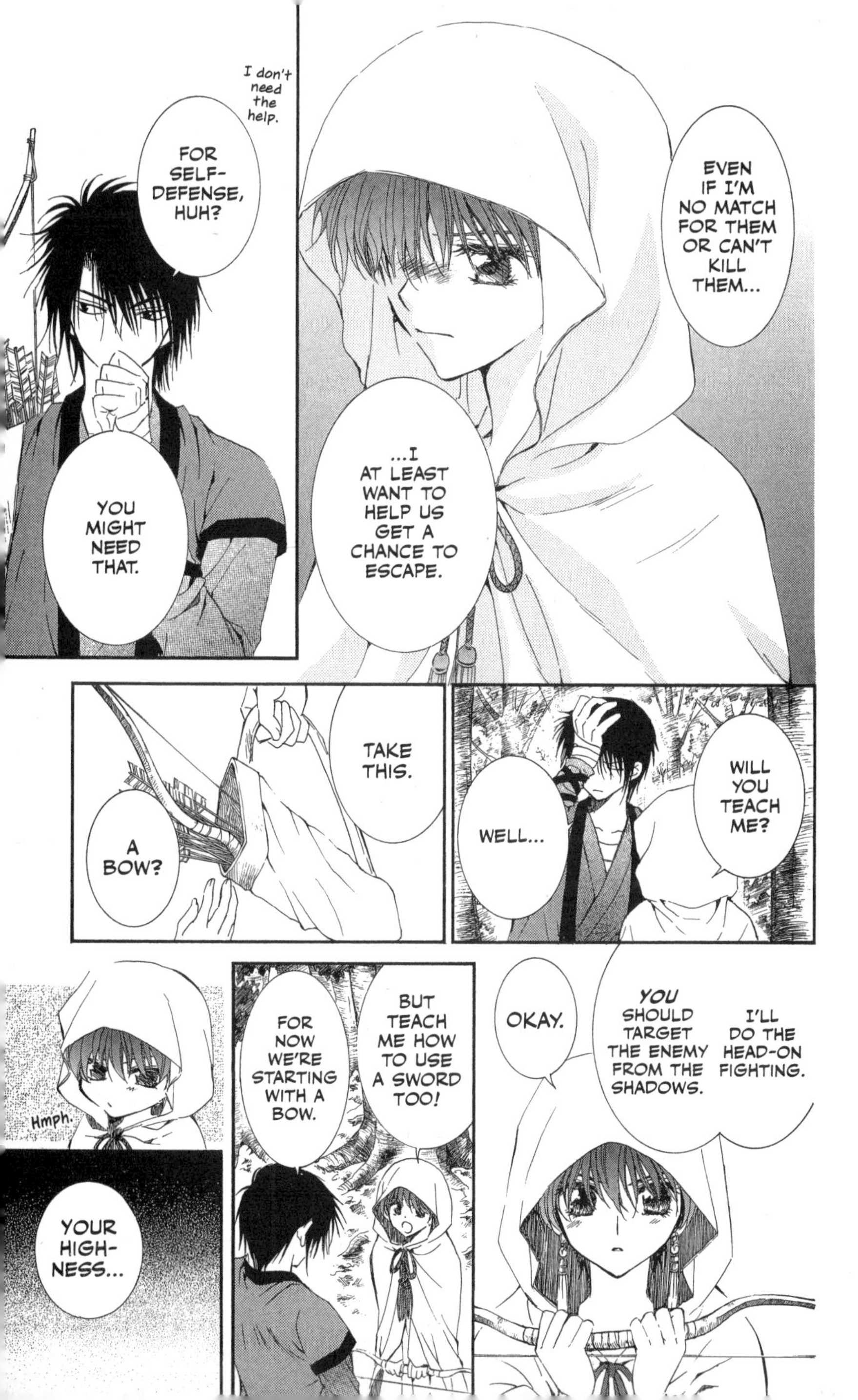
EVEN IF I'M NO MATCH FOR THEM OR CAN'T KILL THEM...
...I AT LEAST WANT TO HELP US GET A CHANCE TO ESCAPE.
I don't need the help.
FOR SELF-DEFENSE, HUH?
YOU MIGHT NEED THAT.
WILL YOU TEACH ME?
WELL...
TAKE THIS.
A BOW?
I'LL DO THE HEAD-ON FIGHTING.
YOU SHOULD TARGET THE ENEMY FROM THE SHADOWS.
OKAY.
BUT TEACH ME HOW TO USE A SWORD TOO!
FOR NOW WE'RE STARTING WITH A BOW.
Hmph.
YOUR HIGHNESS...

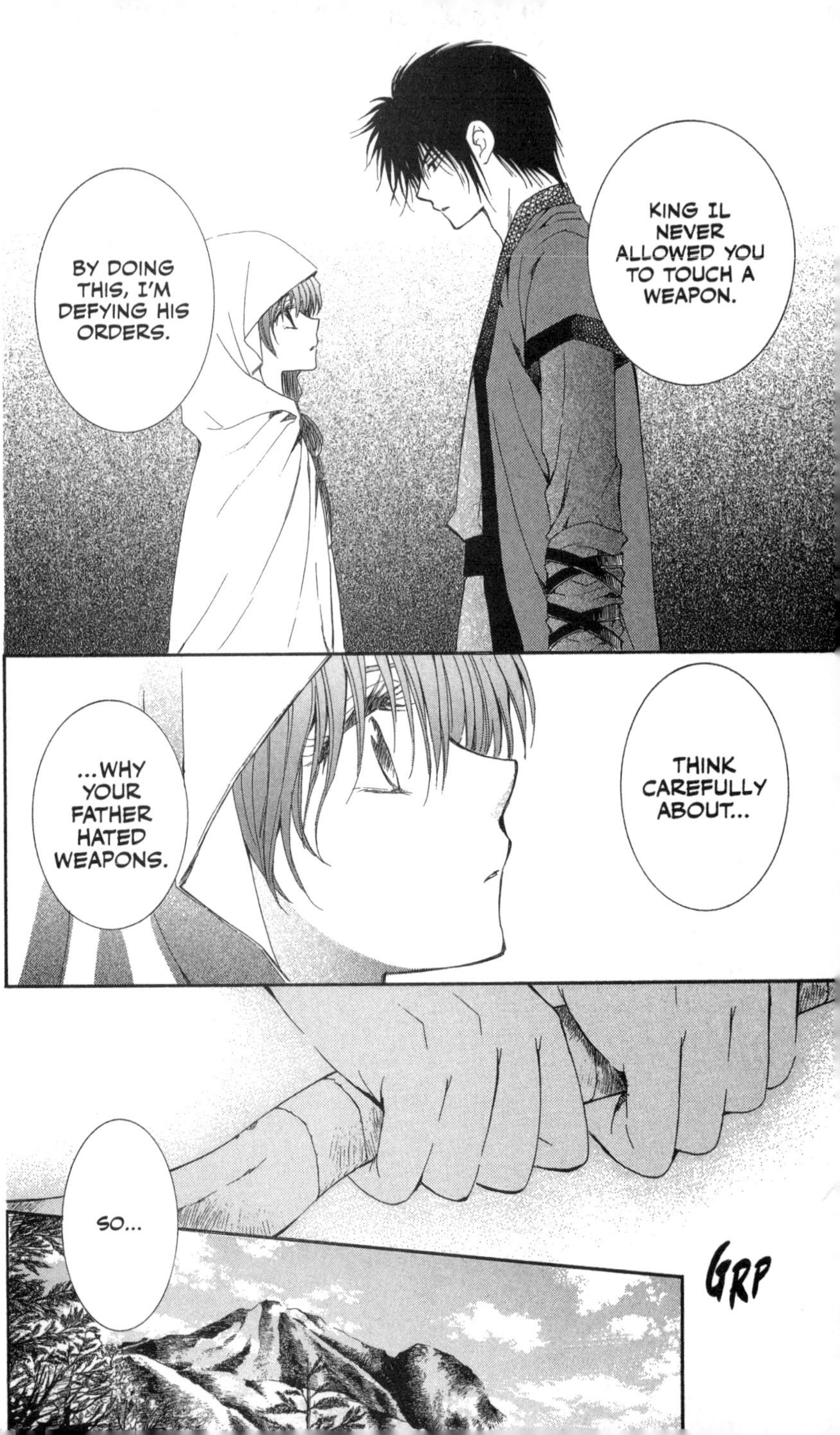
KING IL NEVER ALLOWED YOU TO TOUCH A WEAPON.
BY DOING THIS, I'M DEFYING HIS ORDERS.
THINK CAREFULLY ABOUT...
...WHY YOUR FATHER HATED WEAPONS.
GRP
SO...

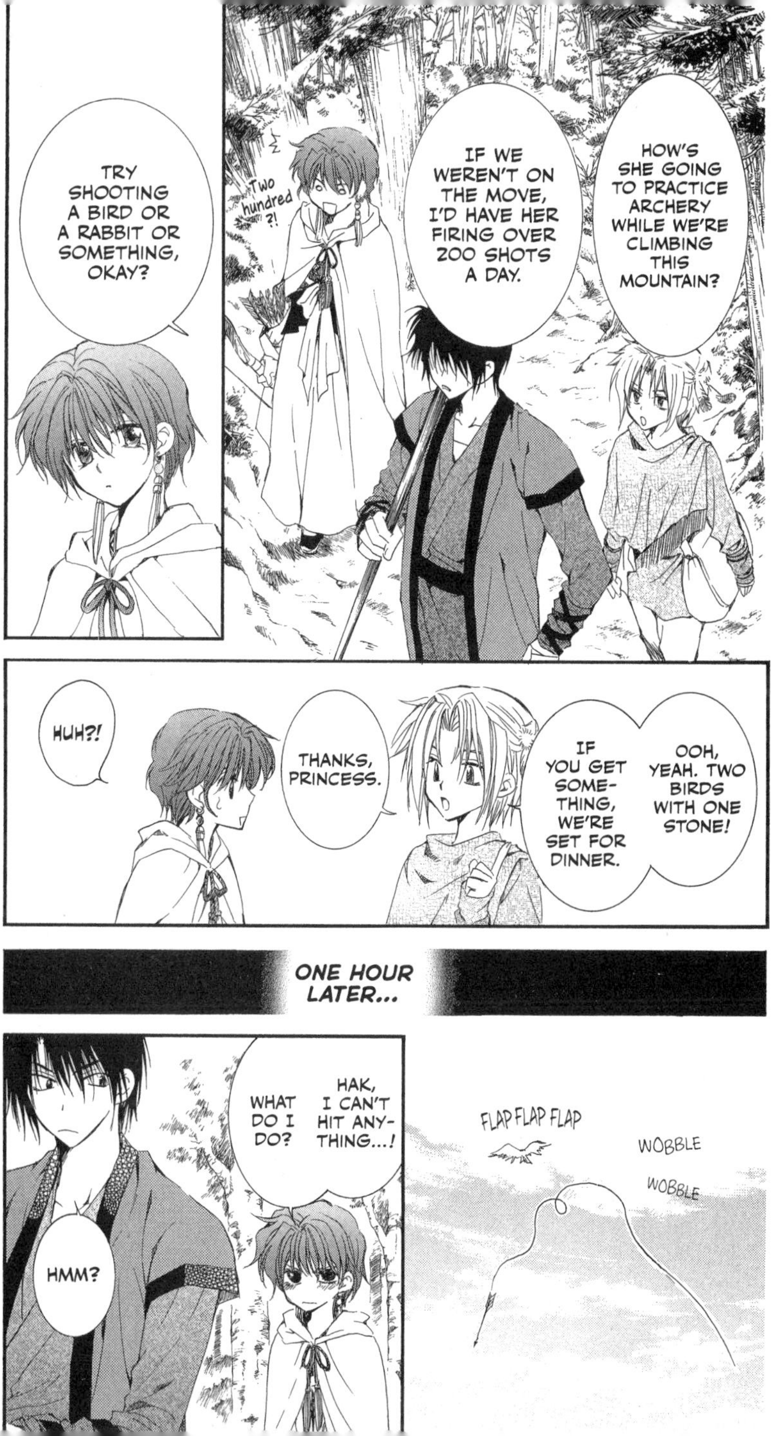
HOW'S SHE GOING TO PRACTICE ARCHERY WHILE WE'RE CLIMBING THIS MOUNTAIN?
IF WE WEREN'T ON THE MOVE, I'D HAVE HER FIRING OVER 200 SHOTS A DAY.
Two hundred ?!
TRY SHOOTING A BIRD OR A RABBIT OR SOMETHING, OKAY?
OOH, YEAH. TWO BIRDS WITH ONE STONE!
IF YOU GET SOME-THING, WE'RE SET FOR DINNER.
THANKS, PRINCESS.
HUH?!
ONE HOUR LATER...
FLAP FLAP FLAP
WOBBLE
WOBBLE
HAK, I CAN'T HIT ANY-THING...!
WHAT DO I DO?
HMM?

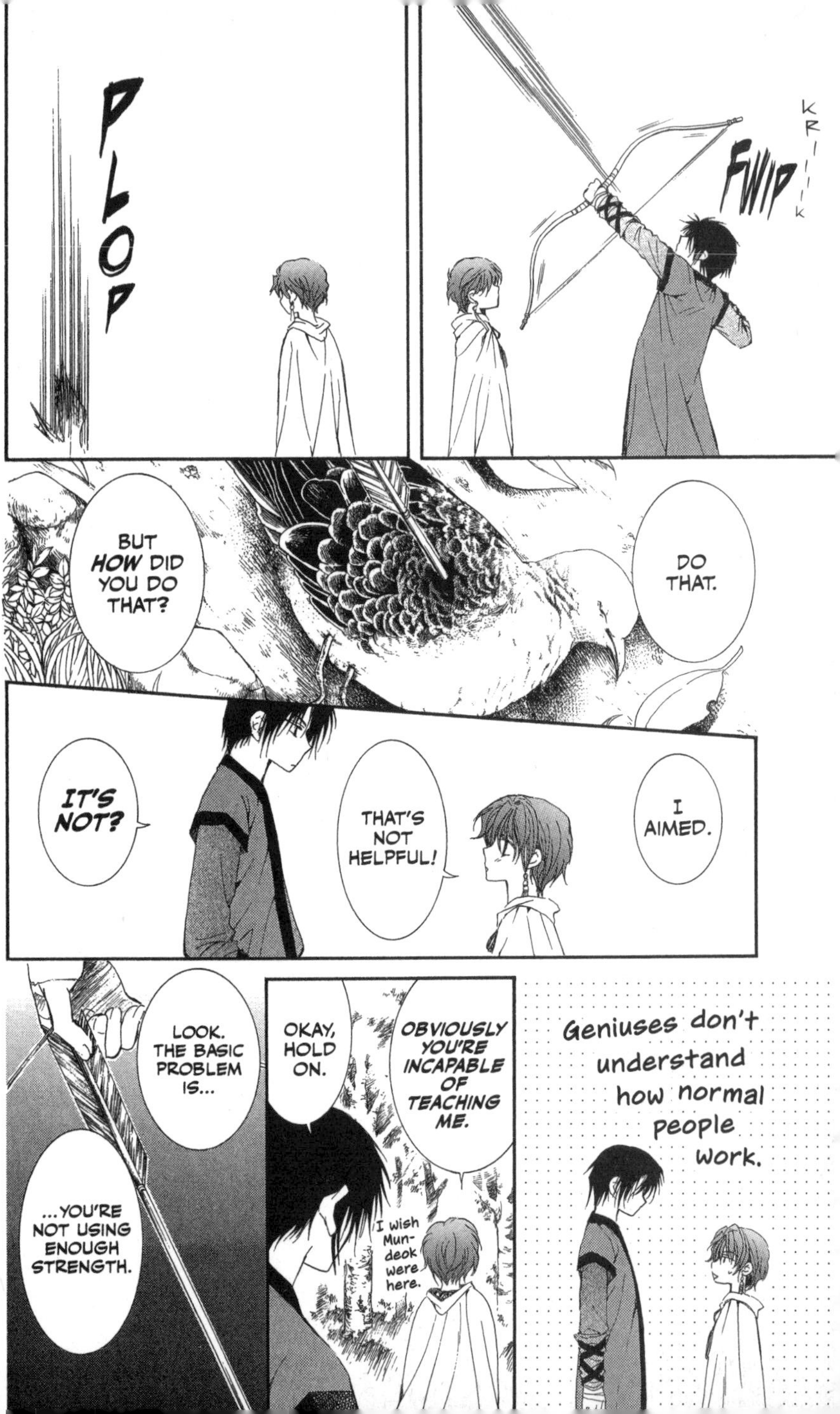
KRIIIK
FWIP
PLOP
DO THAT.
BUT HOW DID YOU DO THAT?
I AIMED.
THAT'S NOT HELPFUL!
IT'S NOT?
Geniuses don't understand how normal people work.
OBVIOUSLY YOU'RE INCAPABLE OF TEACHING ME.
OKAY, HOLD ON.
I wish Mun-deok were here.
LOOK. THE BASIC PROBLEM IS...
...YOU'RE NOT USING ENOUGH STRENGTH.

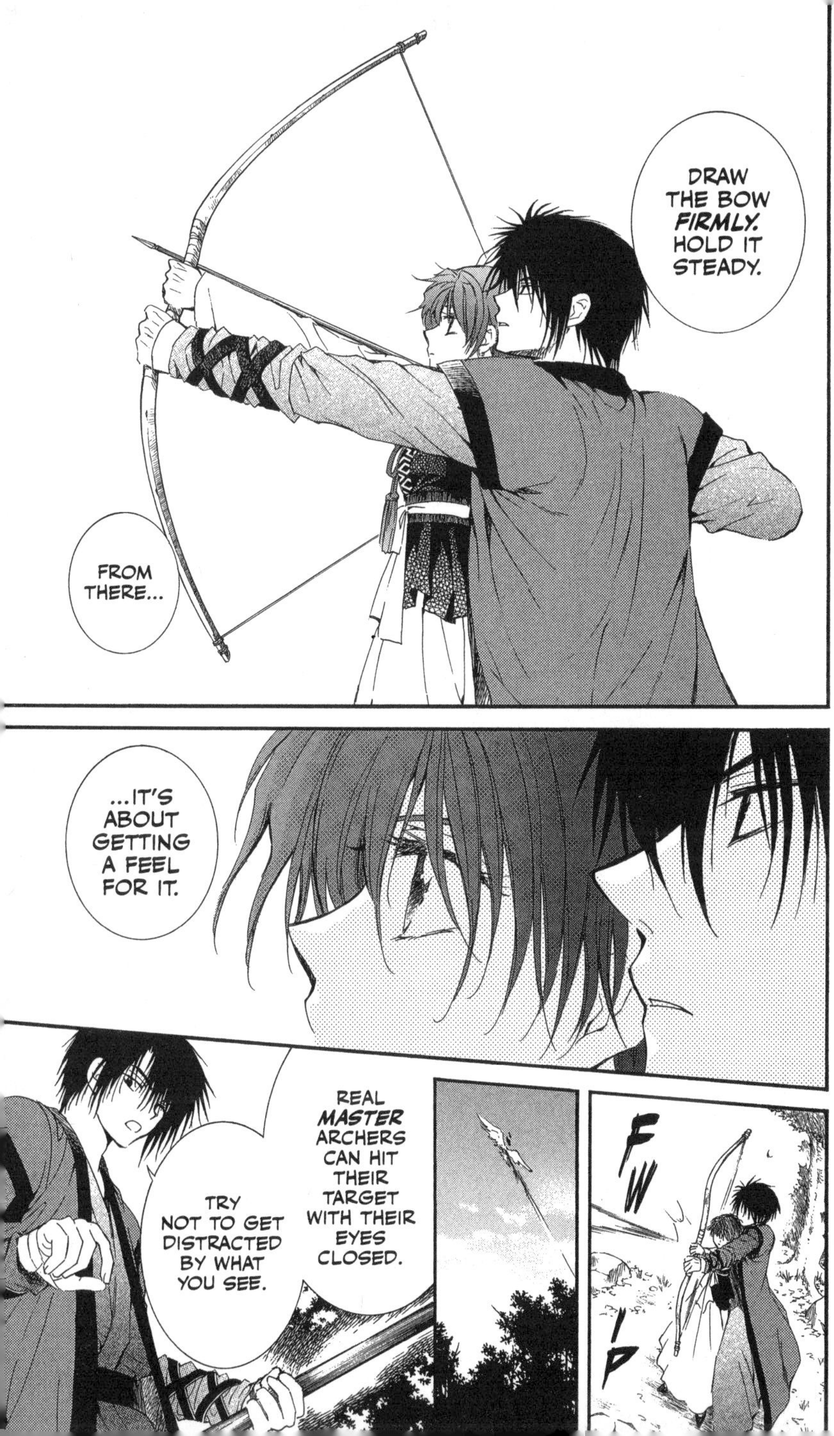
DRAW THE BOW *FIRMLY.* HOLD IT STEADY.
FROM THERE...
...IT'S ABOUT GETTING A FEEL FOR IT.
FWIP
REAL *MASTER* ARCHERS CAN HIT THEIR TARGET WITH THEIR EYES CLOSED.
TRY NOT TO GET DISTRACTED BY WHAT YOU SEE.

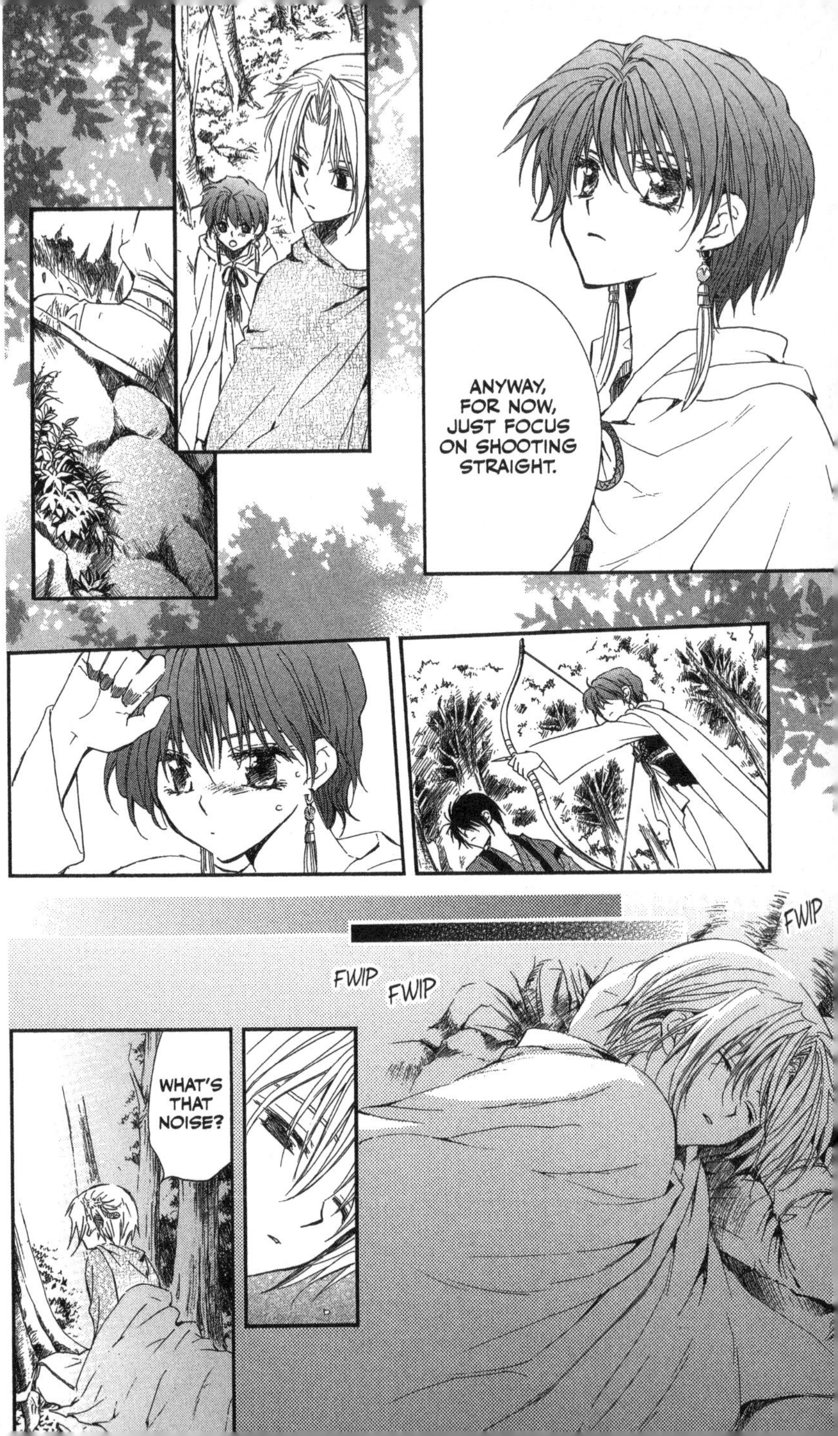
ANYWAY, FOR NOW, JUST FOCUS ON SHOOTING STRAIGHT.
FWIP
FWIP
FWIP
WHAT'S THAT NOISE?

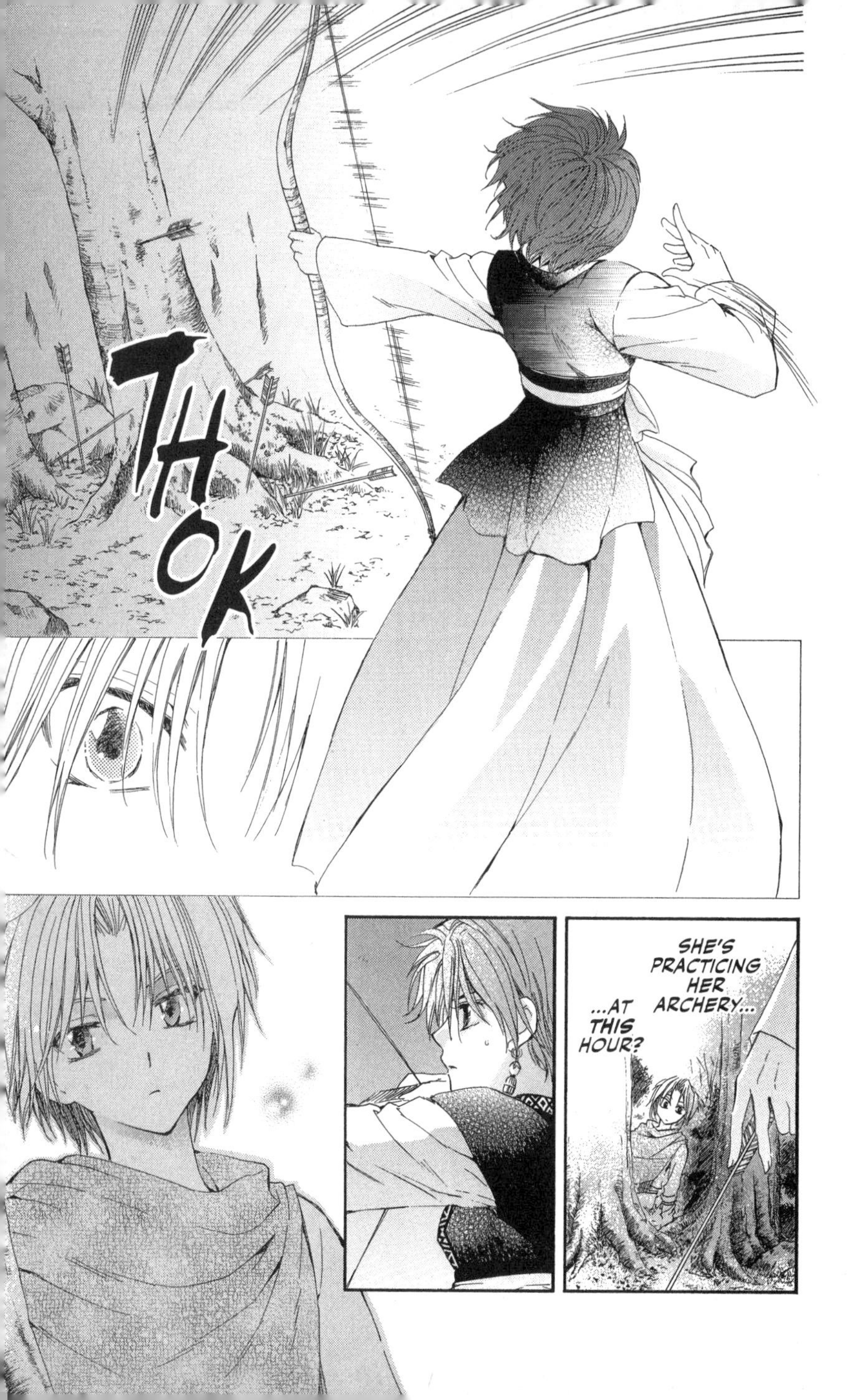

THOK
SHE'S PRACTICING HER ARCHERY...
...AT THIS HOUR?

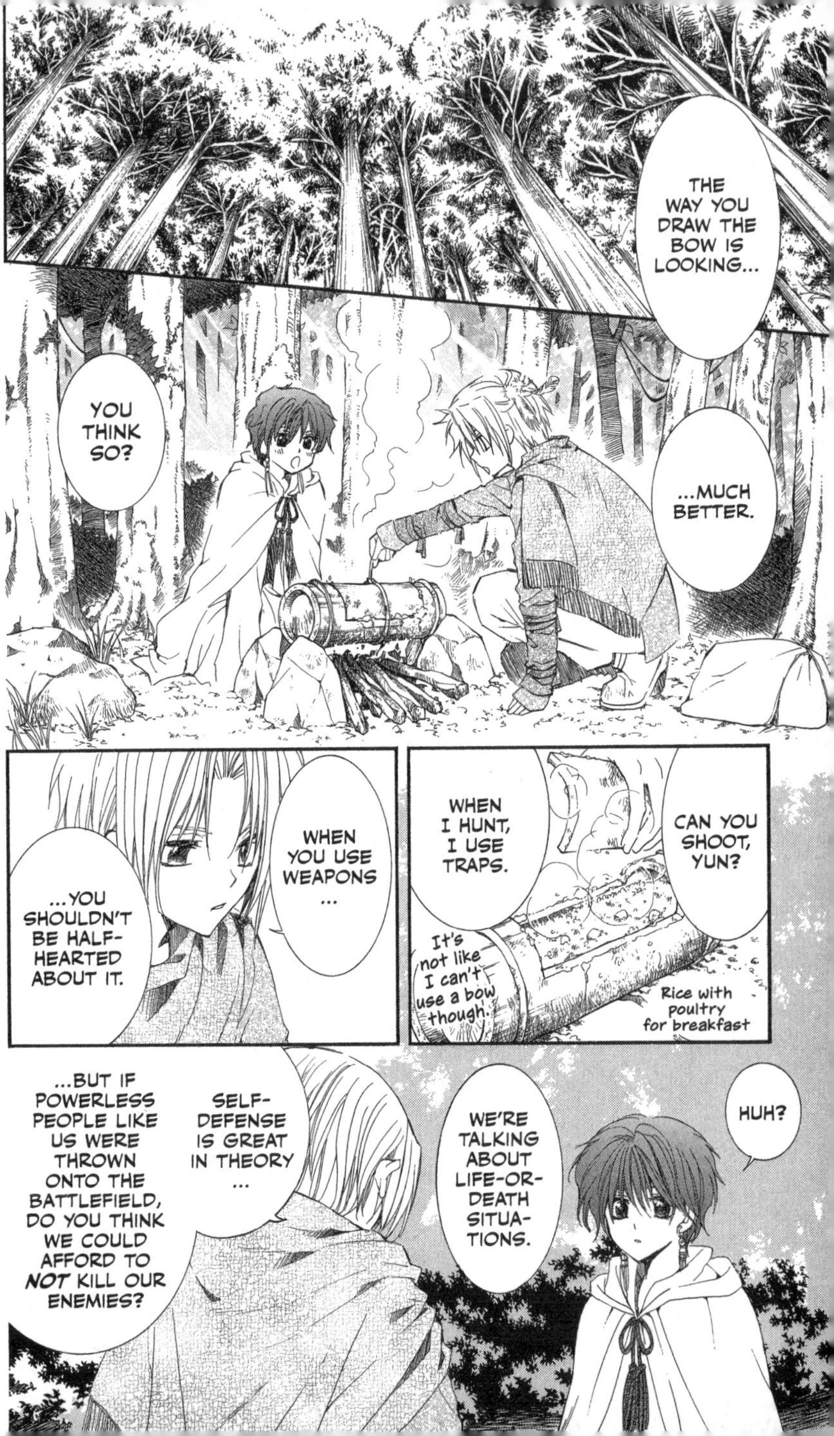
THE WAY YOU DRAW THE BOW IS LOOKING...
...MUCH BETTER.
YOU THINK SO?
CAN YOU SHOOT, YUN?
WHEN I HUNT, I USE TRAPS.
It's not like I can't use a bow though.
Rice with poultry for breakfast
WHEN YOU USE WEAPONS...
...YOU SHOULDN'T BE HALF-HEARTED ABOUT IT.
HUH?
WE'RE TALKING ABOUT LIFE-OR-DEATH SITUATIONS.
SELF-DEFENSE IS GREAT IN THEORY...
...BUT IF POWERLESS PEOPLE LIKE US WERE THROWN ONTO THE BATTLEFIELD, DO YOU THINK WE COULD AFFORD TO *NOT* KILL OUR ENEMIES?

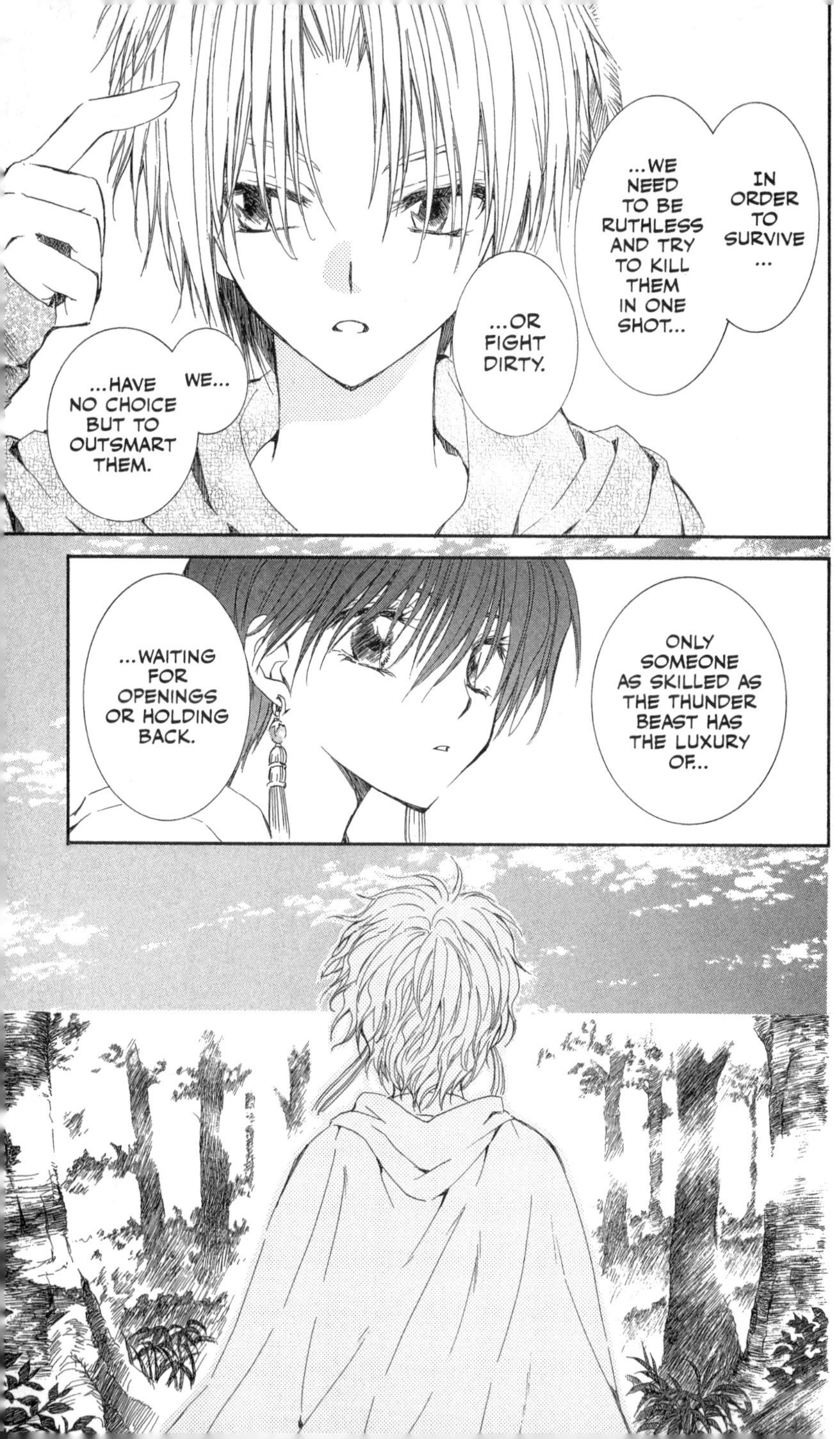
IN ORDER TO SURVIVE...
...WE NEED TO BE RUTHLESS AND TRY TO KILL THEM IN ONE SHOT...
...OR FIGHT DIRTY.
WE...
...HAVE NO CHOICE BUT TO OUTSMART THEM.
ONLY SOMEONE AS SKILLED AS THE THUNDER BEAST HAS THE LUXURY OF...
...WAITING FOR OPENINGS OR HOLDING BACK.

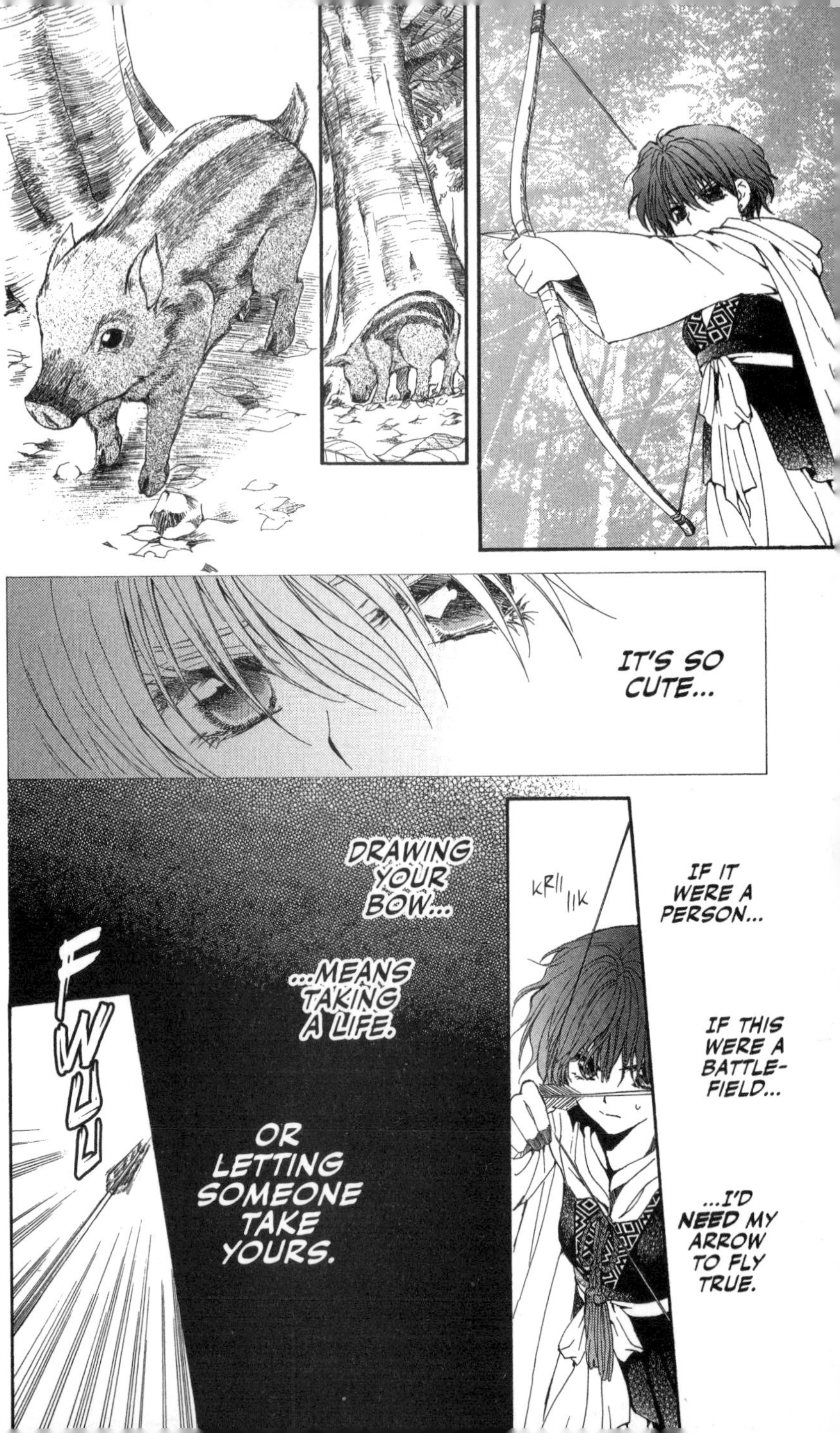
IT'S SO CUTE...
IF IT WERE A PERSON...
KRII IIK
IF THIS WERE A BATTLE-FIELD...
...I'D NEED MY ARROW TO FLY TRUE.
DRAWING YOUR BOW...
...MEANS TAKING A LIFE.
OR LETTING SOMEONE TAKE YOURS.
FWUU

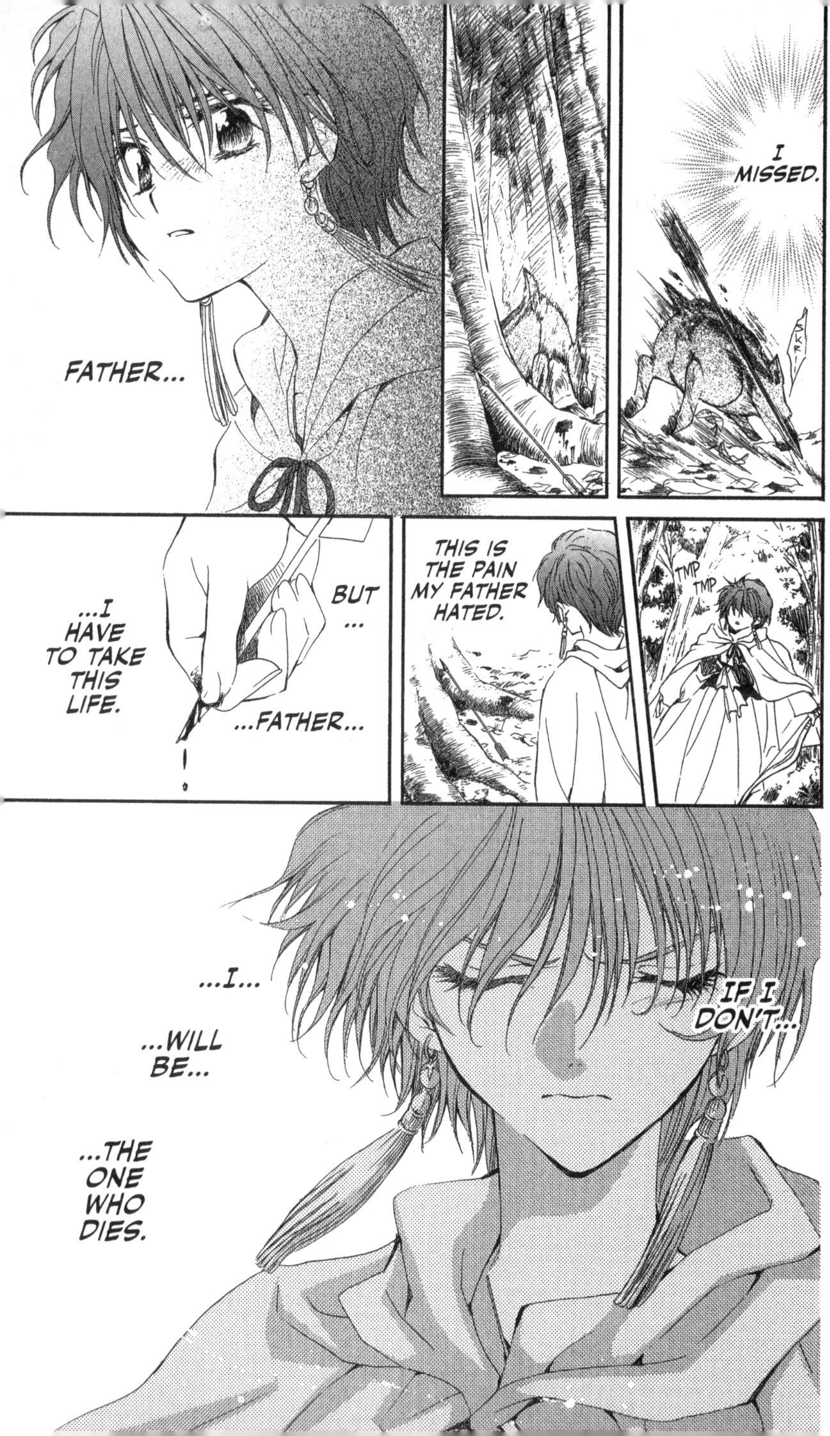
I MISSED.
FATHER...
TMP TMP
THIS IS THE PAIN MY FATHER HATED.
BUT...
...FATHER...
...I HAVE TO TAKE THIS LIFE.
IF I DON'T...
...I...
...WILL BE...
...THE ONE WHO DIES.

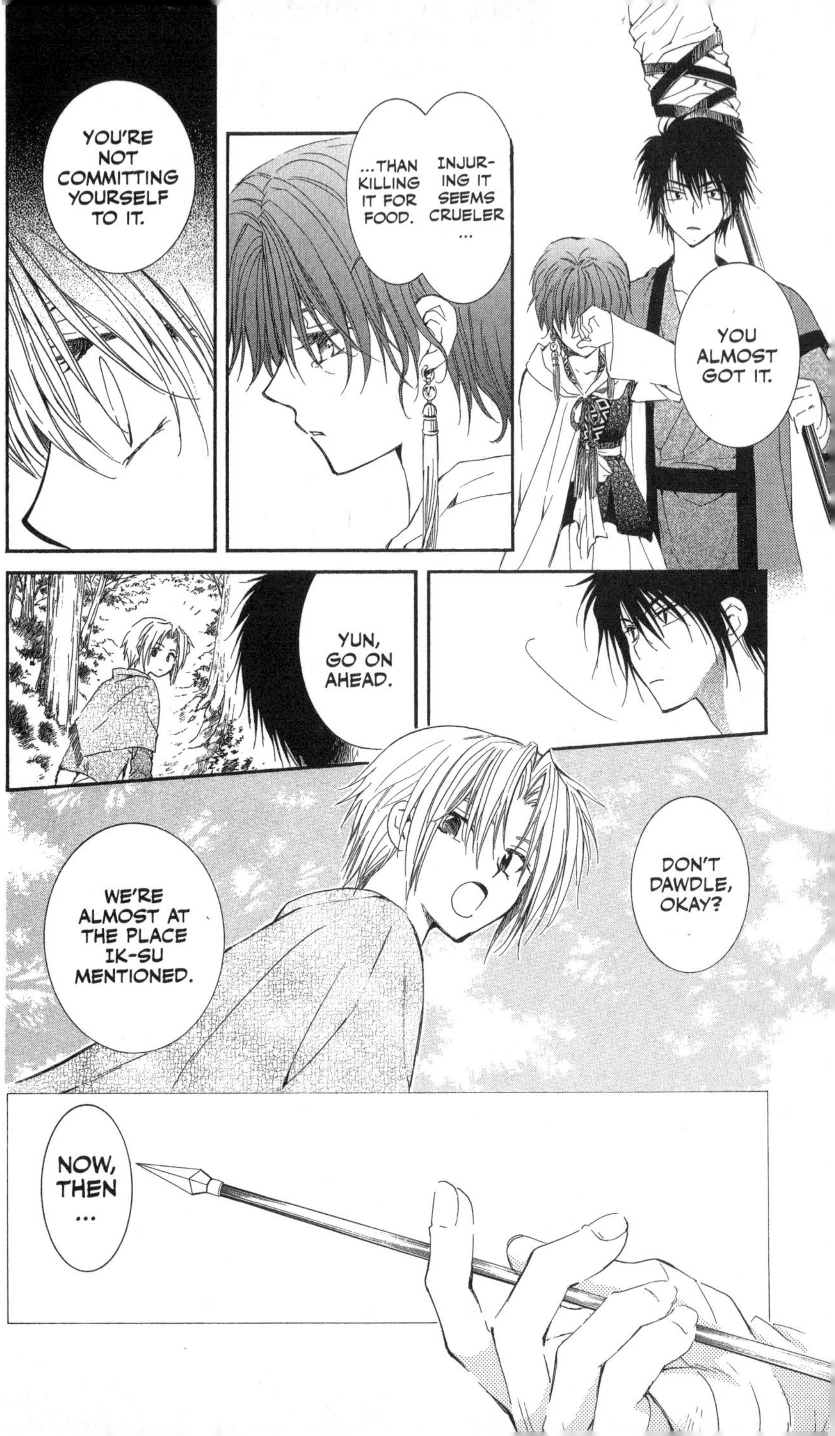
YOU ALMOST GOT IT.
INJURING IT SEEMS CRUELER...
...THAN KILLING IT FOR FOOD.
YOU'RE NOT COMMITTING YOURSELF TO IT.
YUN, GO ON AHEAD.
DON'T DAWDLE, OKAY?
WE'RE ALMOST AT THE PLACE IK-SU MENTIONED.
NOW, THEN...

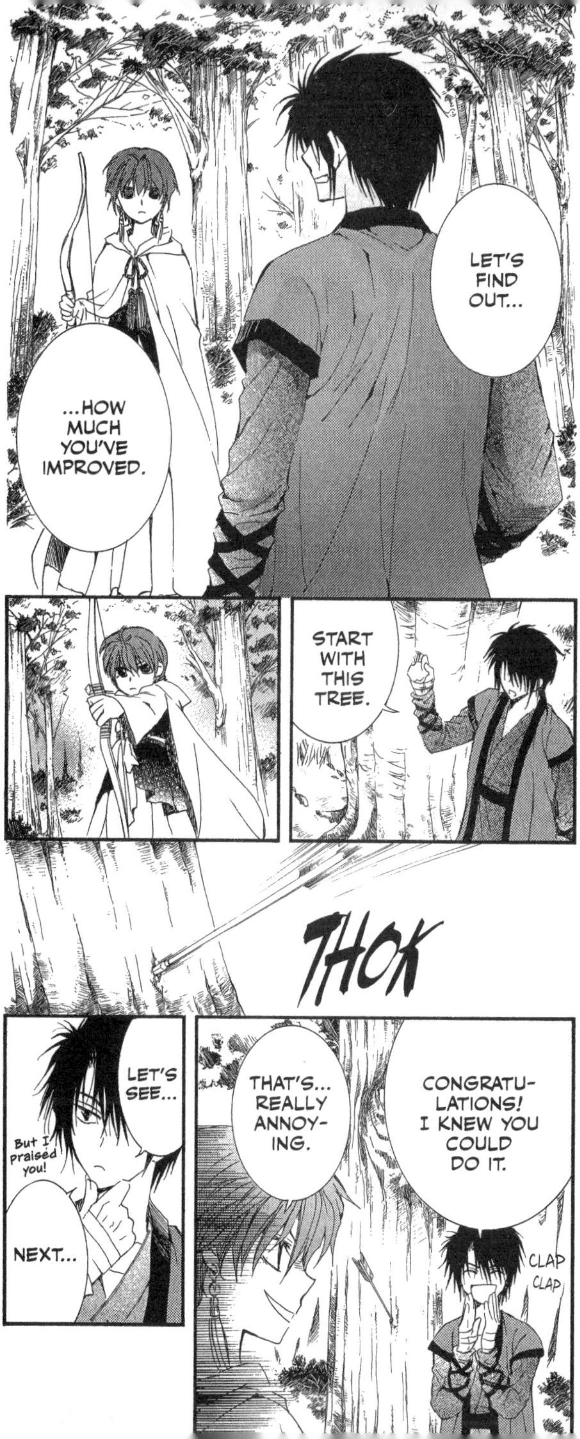
LET'S FIND OUT...
...HOW MUCH YOU'VE IMPROVED.
START WITH THIS TREE.
THOK
CONGRATU-LATIONS! I KNEW YOU COULD DO IT.
CLAP CLAP
THAT'S... REALLY ANNOY-ING.
LET'S SEE...
But I praised you!
NEXT...

Talking to My Editor

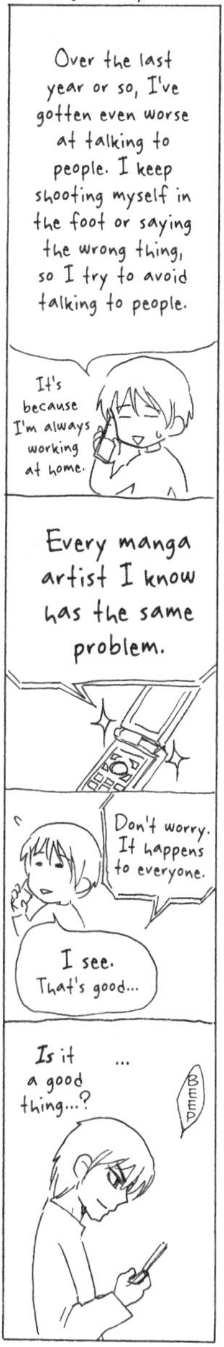
Over the last year or so, I've gotten even worse at talking to people. I keep shooting myself in the foot or saying the wrong thing, so I try to avoid talking to people.
It's because I'm always working at home.
Every manga artist I know has the same problem.
Don't worry. It happens to everyone.
I see. That's good...
Is it a good thing...?
...
BEEP

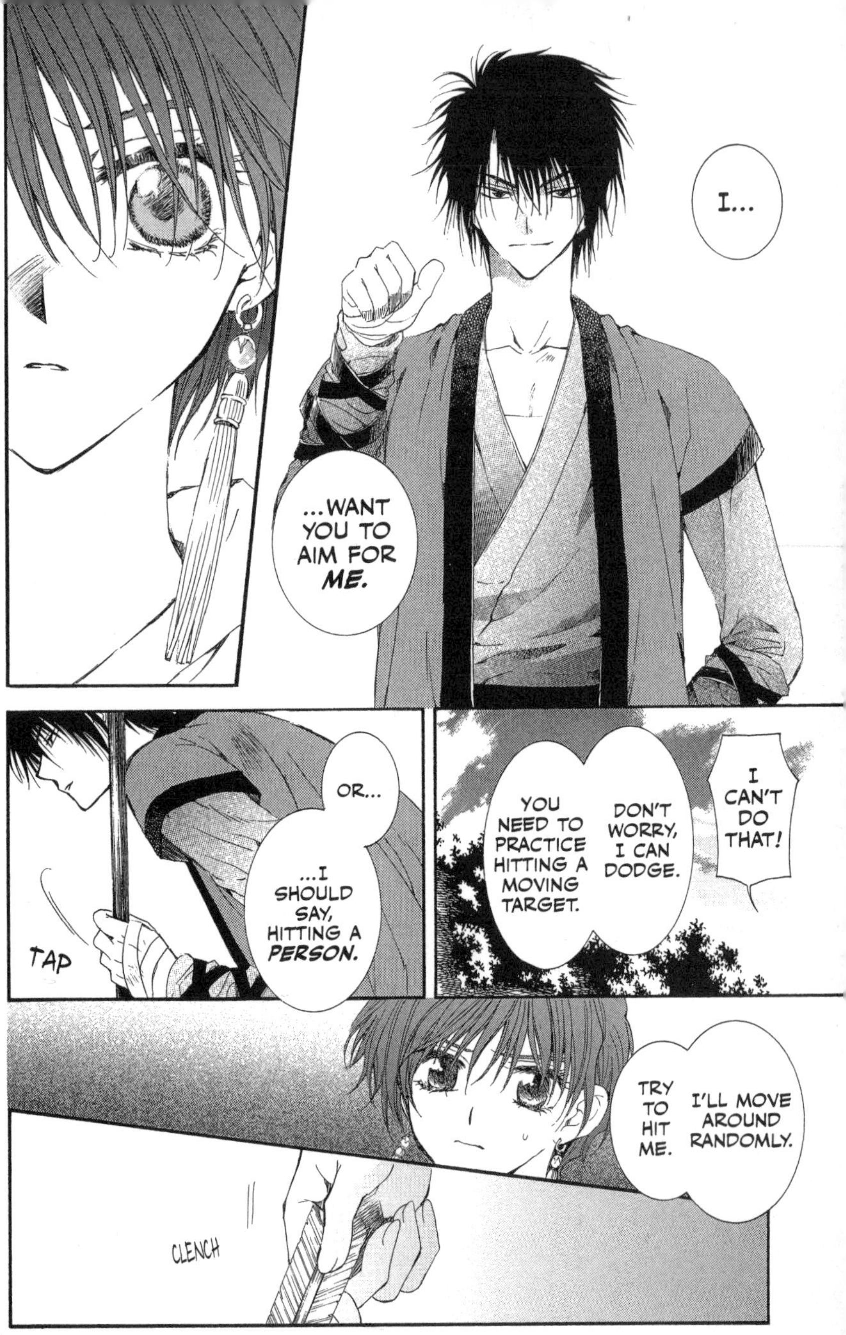
I...
...WANT YOU TO AIM FOR *ME.*
I CAN'T DO THAT!
DON'T WORRY, I CAN DODGE.
YOU NEED TO PRACTICE HITTING A MOVING TARGET.
OR...
...I SHOULD SAY, HITTING A *PERSON.*
TAP
I'LL MOVE AROUND RANDOMLY.
TRY TO HIT ME.
CLENCH

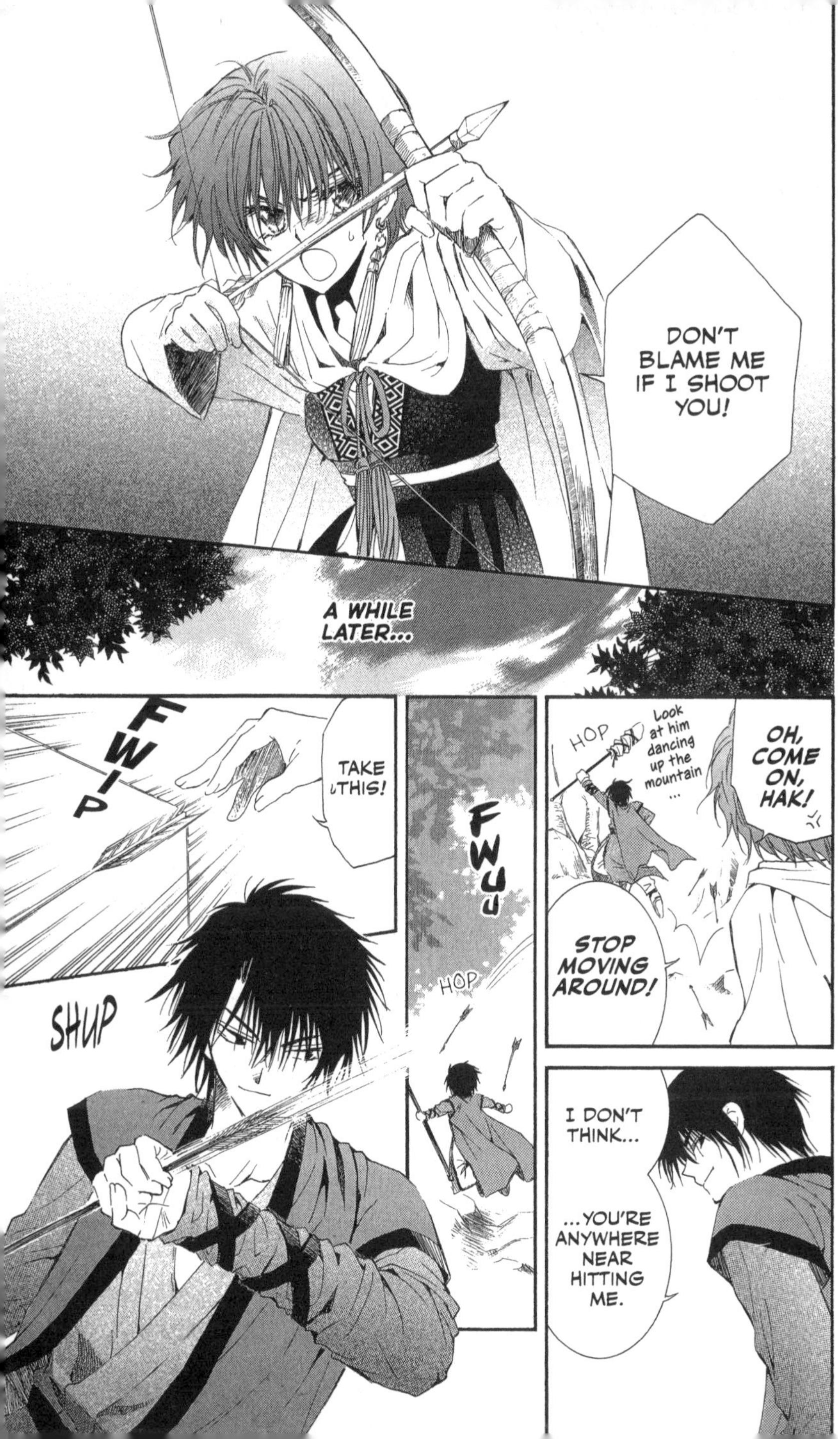
DON'T BLAME ME IF I SHOOT YOU!
A WHILE LATER...
OH, COME ON, HAK!
Look at him dancing up the mountain...
HOP
STOP MOVING AROUND!
I DON'T THINK...
...YOU'RE ANYWHERE NEAR HITTING ME.
FWUU
HOP
TAKE THIS!
FWIP
SHUP

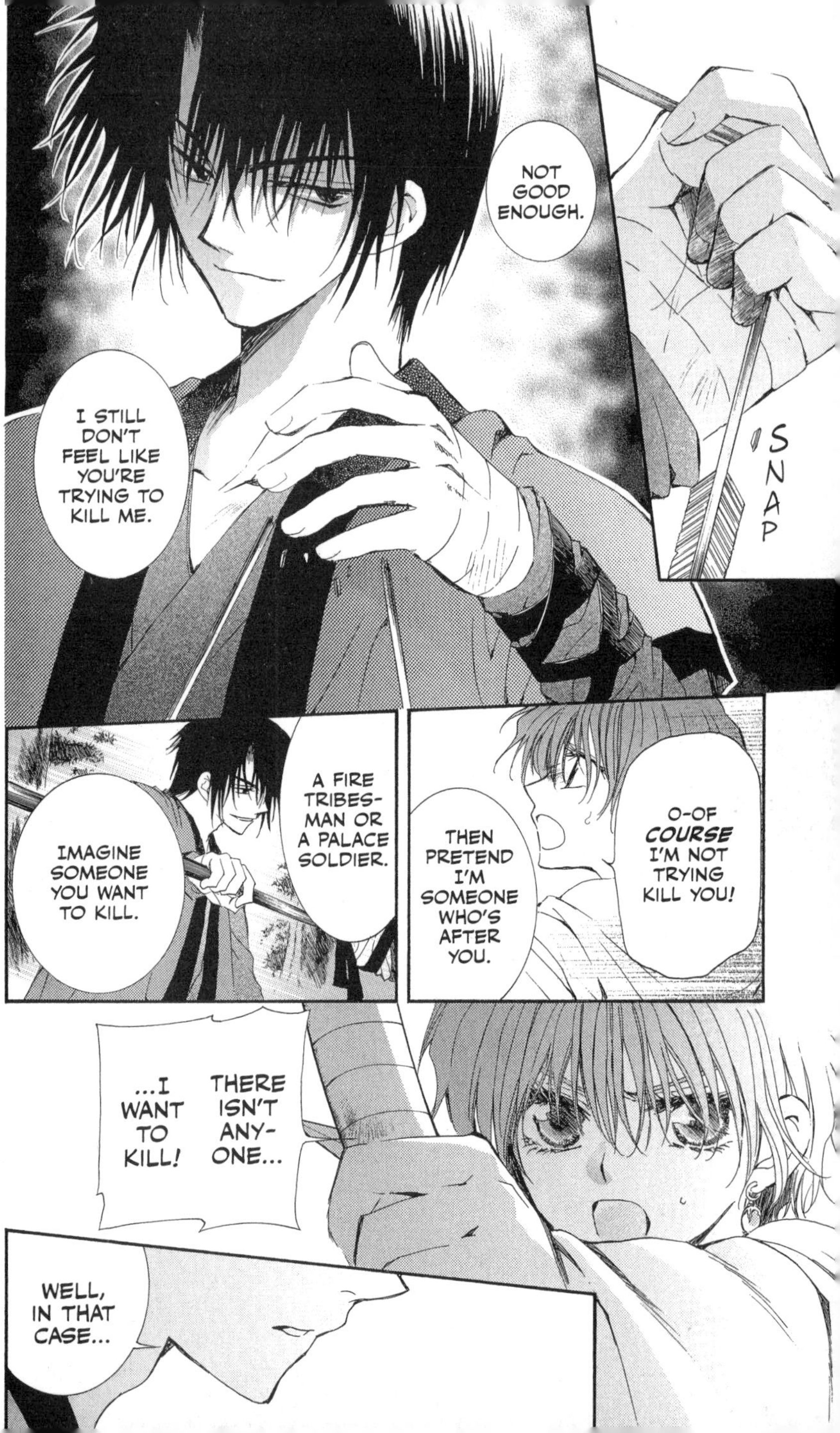
SNAP
NOT GOOD ENOUGH.
I STILL DON'T FEEL LIKE YOU'RE TRYING TO KILL ME.
O-OF *COURSE* I'M NOT TRYING KILL YOU!
THEN PRETEND I'M SOMEONE WHO'S AFTER YOU.
A FIRE TRIBESMAN OR A PALACE SOLDIER.
IMAGINE SOMEONE YOU WANT TO KILL.
THERE ISN'T ANYONE... ...I WANT TO KILL!
WELL, IN THAT CASE...

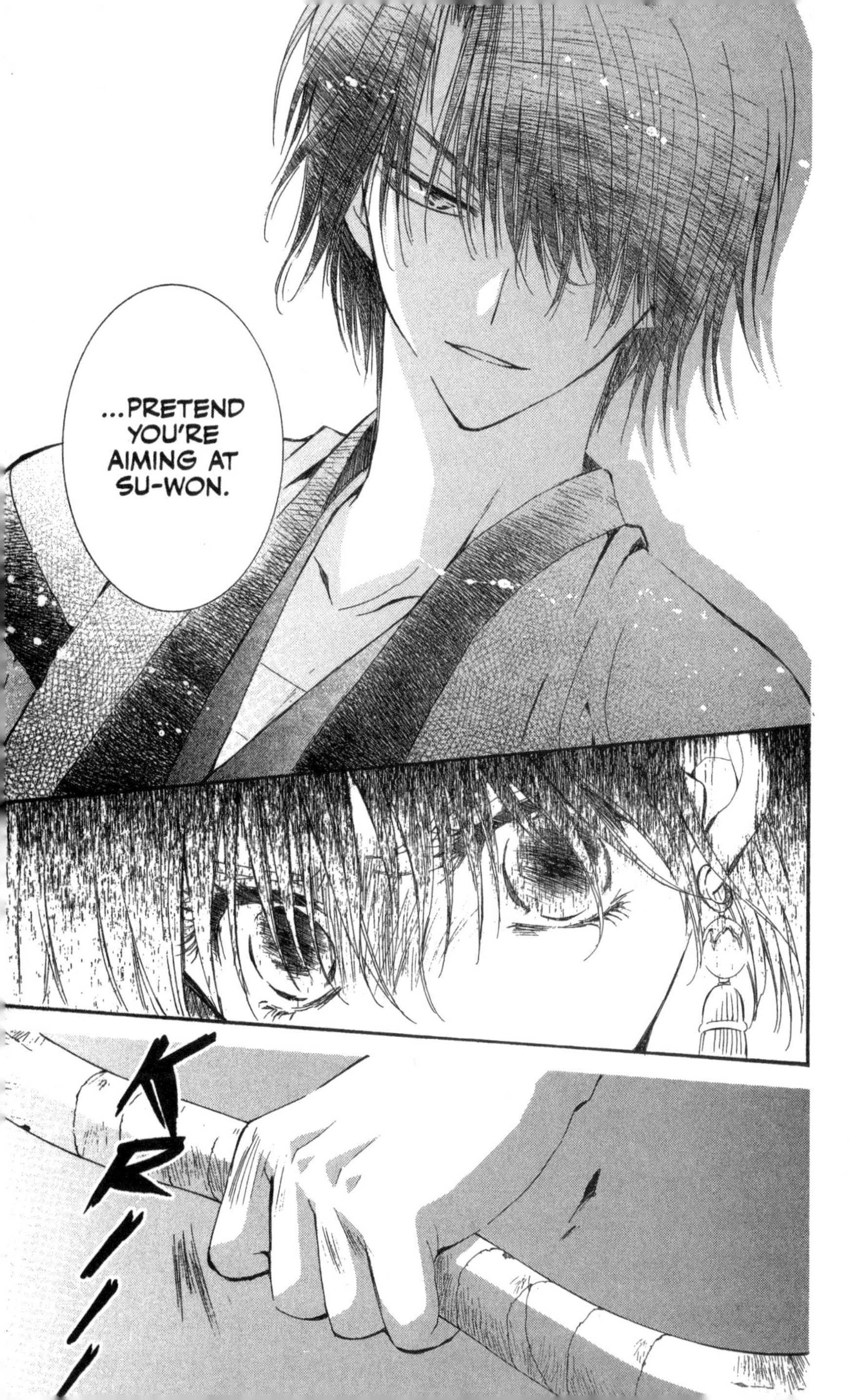
...PRETEND YOU'RE AIMING AT SU-WON.
KRR--

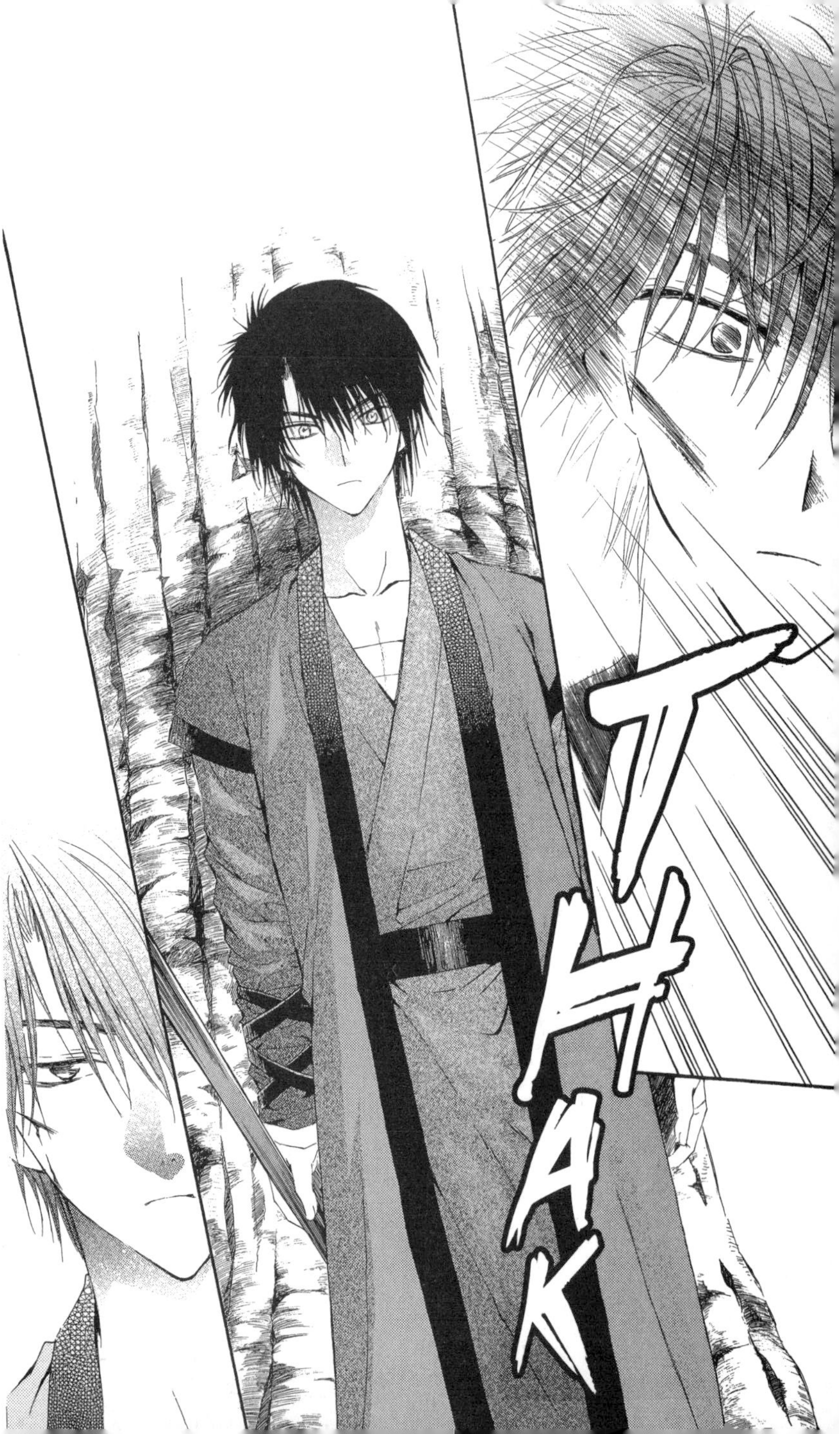
THAK

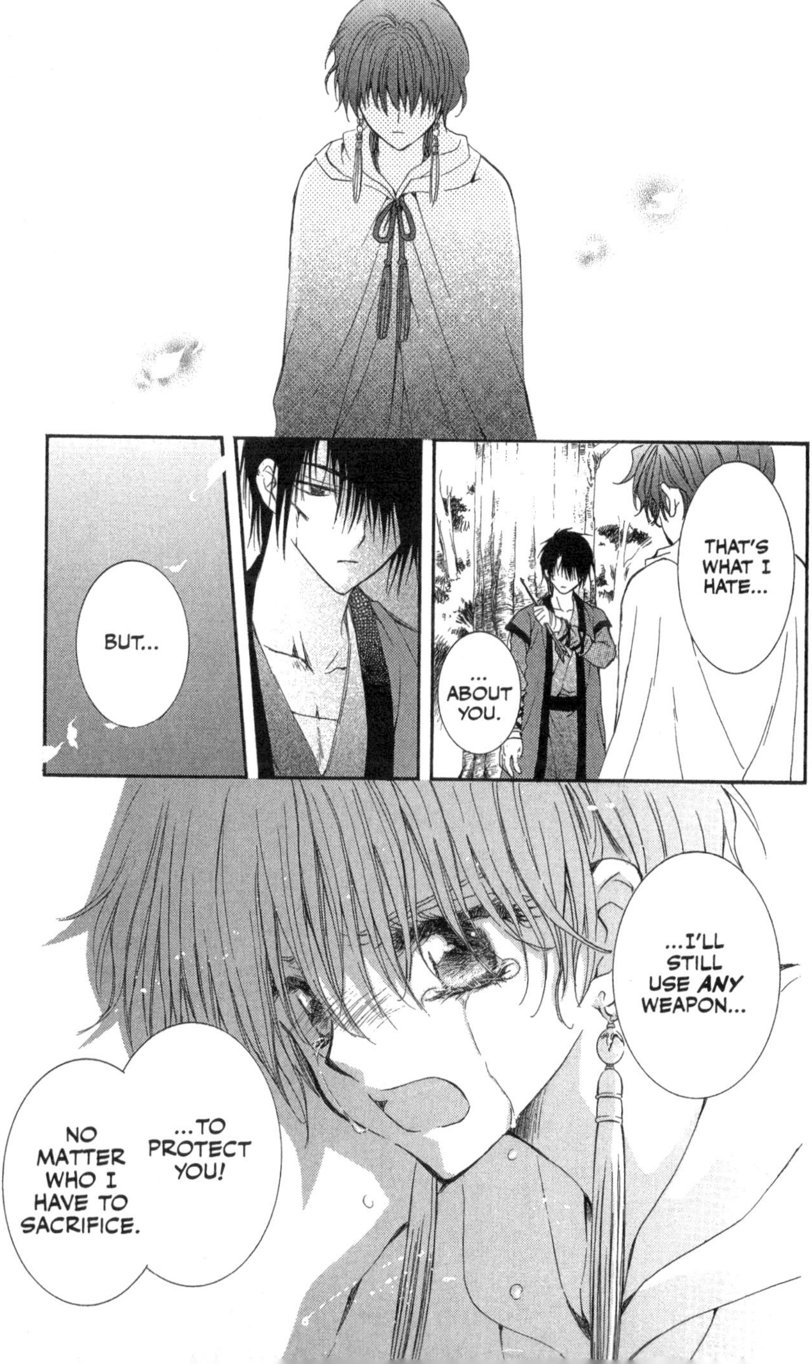
THAT'S WHAT I HATE...
...ABOUT YOU.
BUT...
...I'LL STILL USE ANY WEAPON...
NO MATTER WHO I HAVE TO SACRIFICE.
...TO PROTECT YOU!

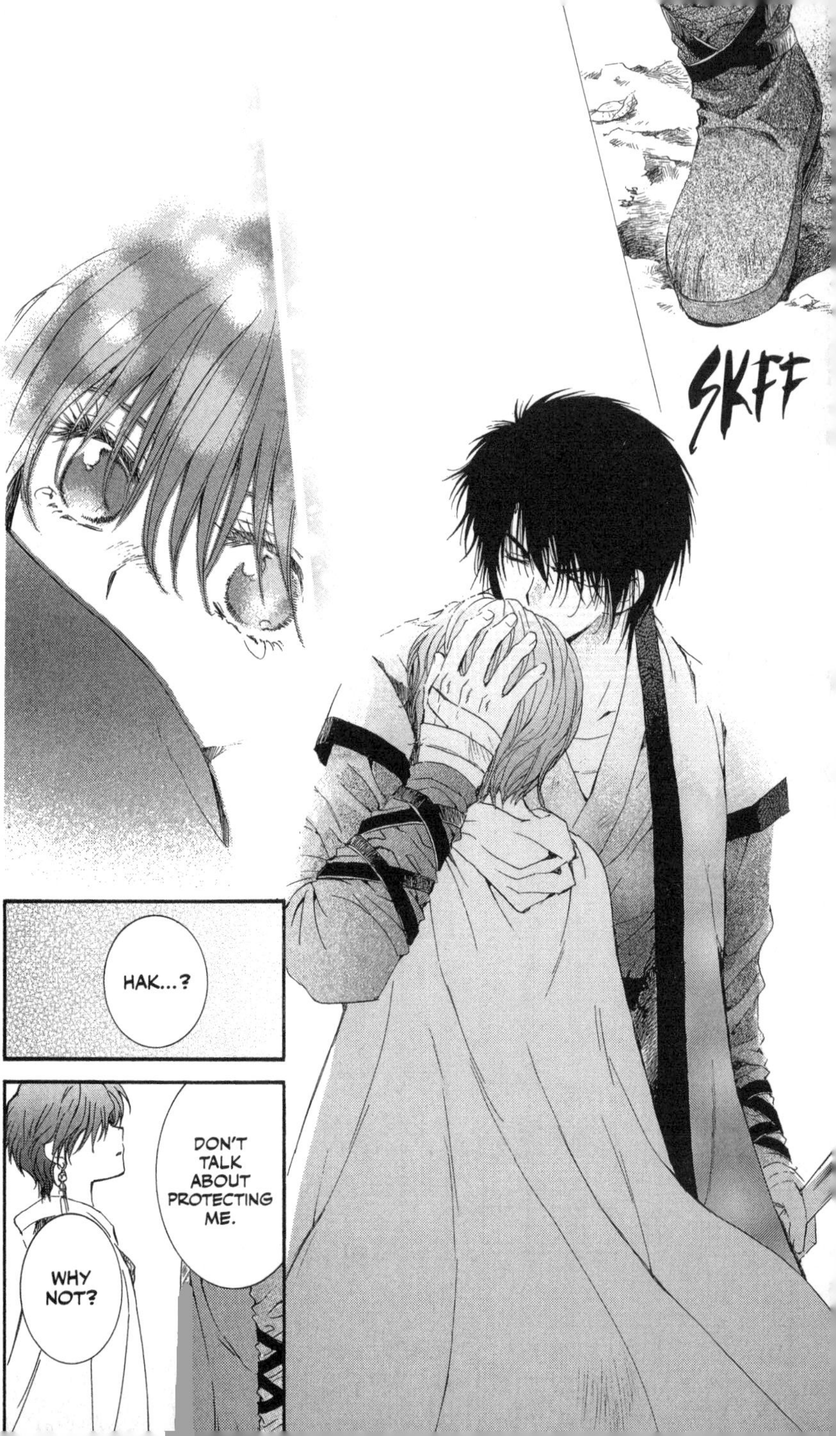
SKFF
HAK...?
DON'T TALK ABOUT PROTECTING ME.
WHY NOT?

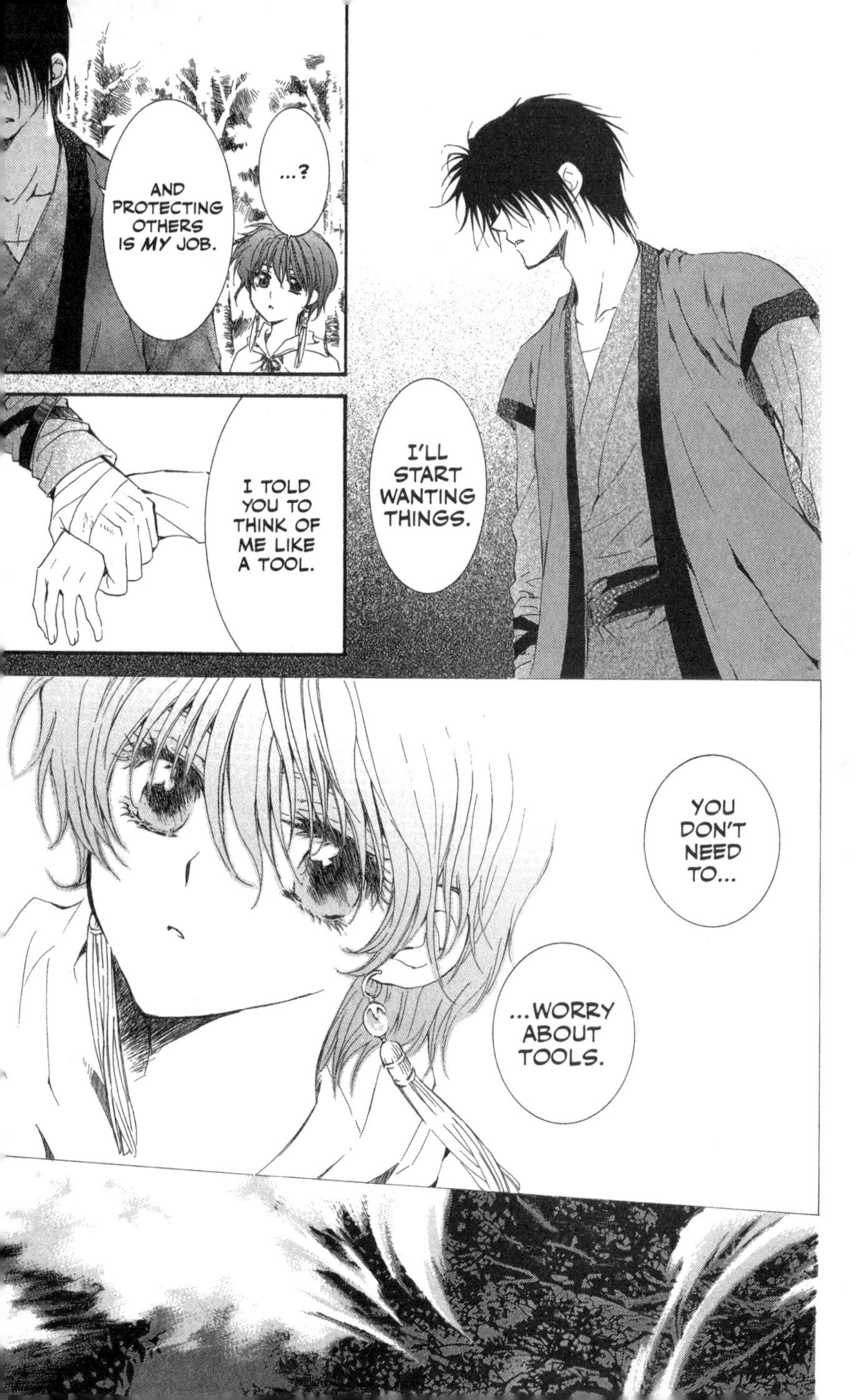
I'LL START WANTING THINGS.
...?
AND PROTECTING OTHERS IS *MY* JOB.
I TOLD YOU TO THINK OF ME LIKE A TOOL.
YOU DON'T NEED TO...
...WORRY ABOUT TOOLS.

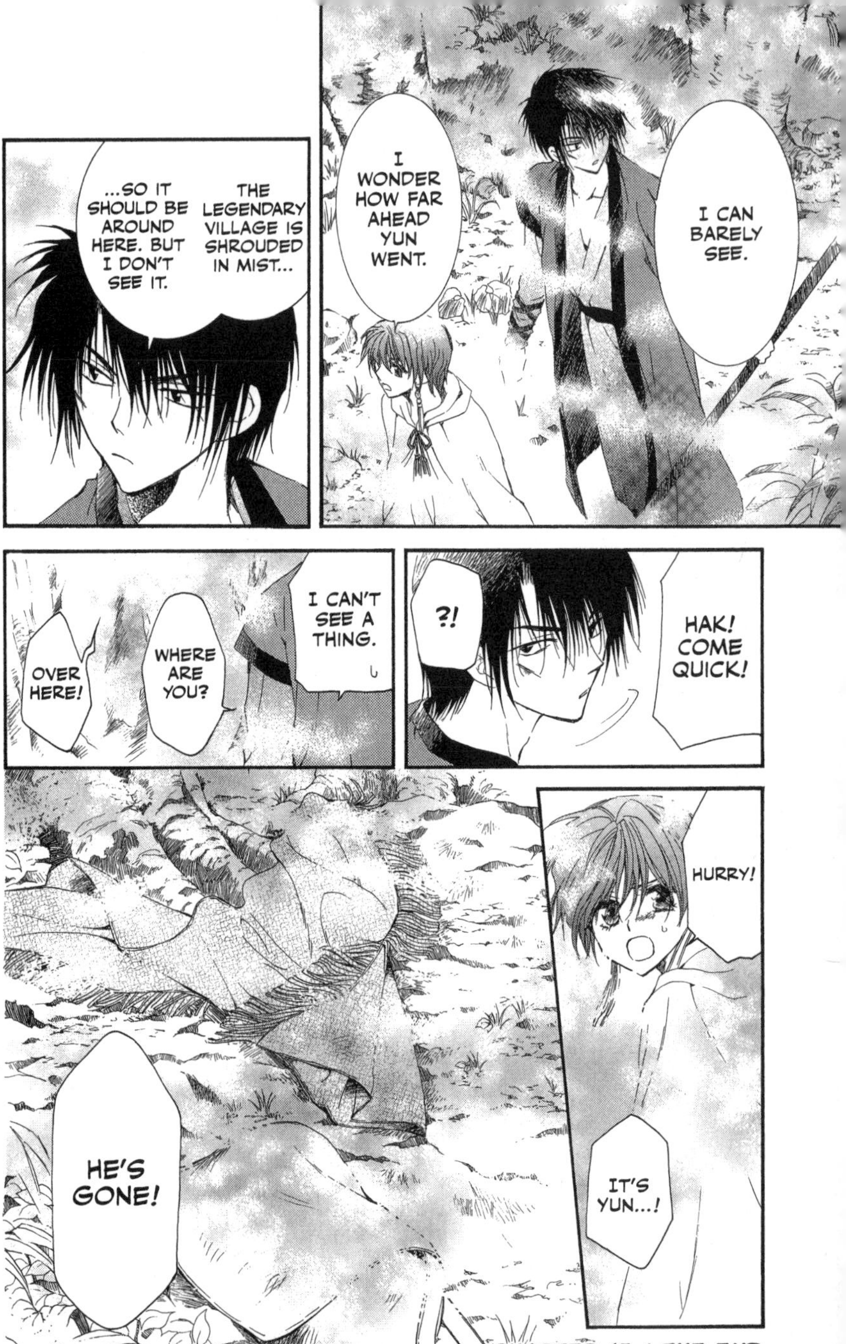
I CAN BARELY SEE.
I WONDER HOW FAR AHEAD YUN WENT.
THE LEGENDARY VILLAGE IS SHROUDED IN MIST...
...SO IT SHOULD BE AROUND HERE. BUT I DON'T SEE IT.
HAK! COME QUICK!
?!
I CAN'T SEE A THING.
WHERE ARE YOU?
OVER HERE!
HURRY!
IT'S YUN...!
HE'S GONE!

CHAPTER 15 / THE END

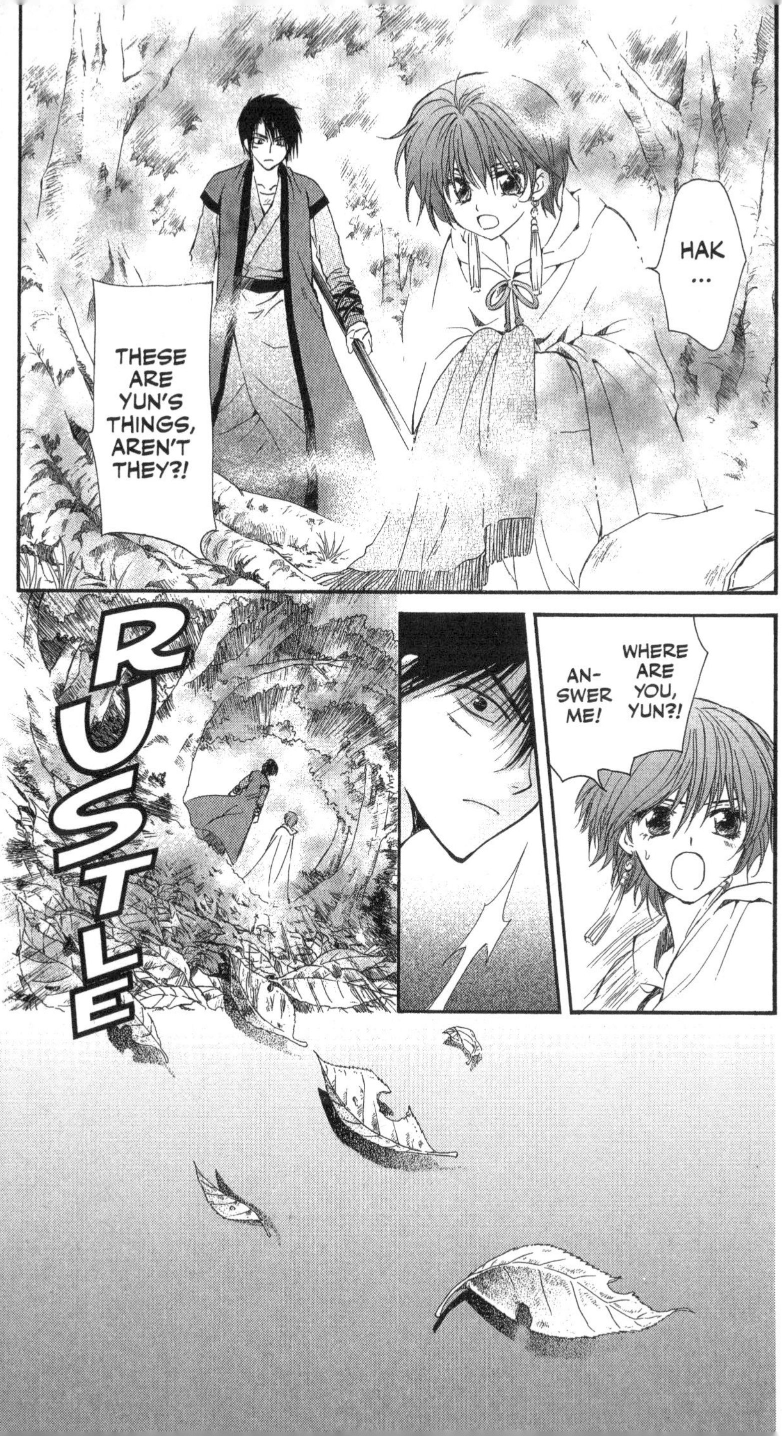
HAK ...
THESE ARE YUN'S THINGS, AREN'T THEY?!
WHERE ARE YOU, YUN?!
AN-SWER ME!
RUSTLE

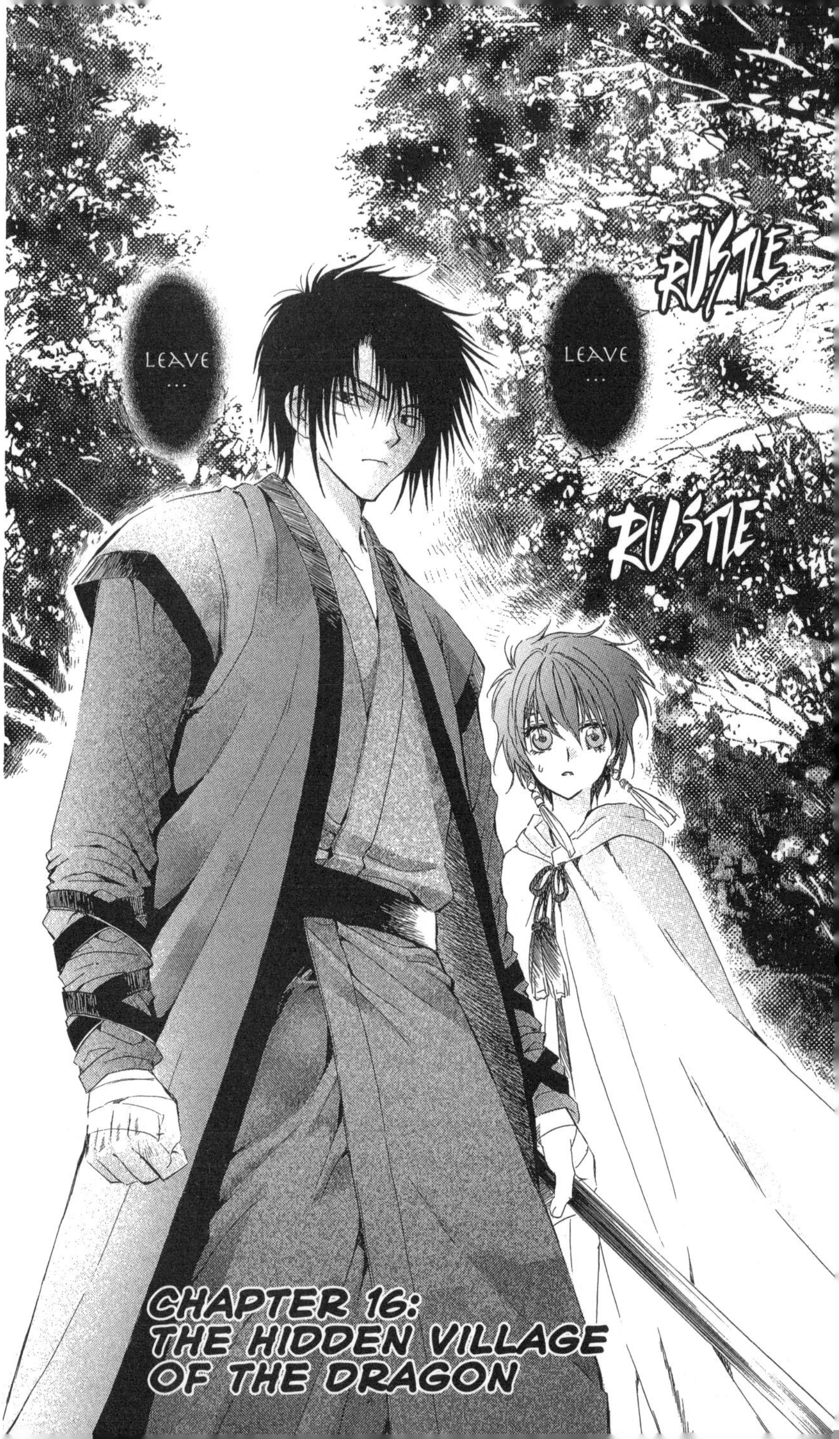
RUSTLE
LEAVE...
LEAVE...
RUSTLE

CHAPTER 16: THE HIDDEN VILLAGE OF THE DRAGON

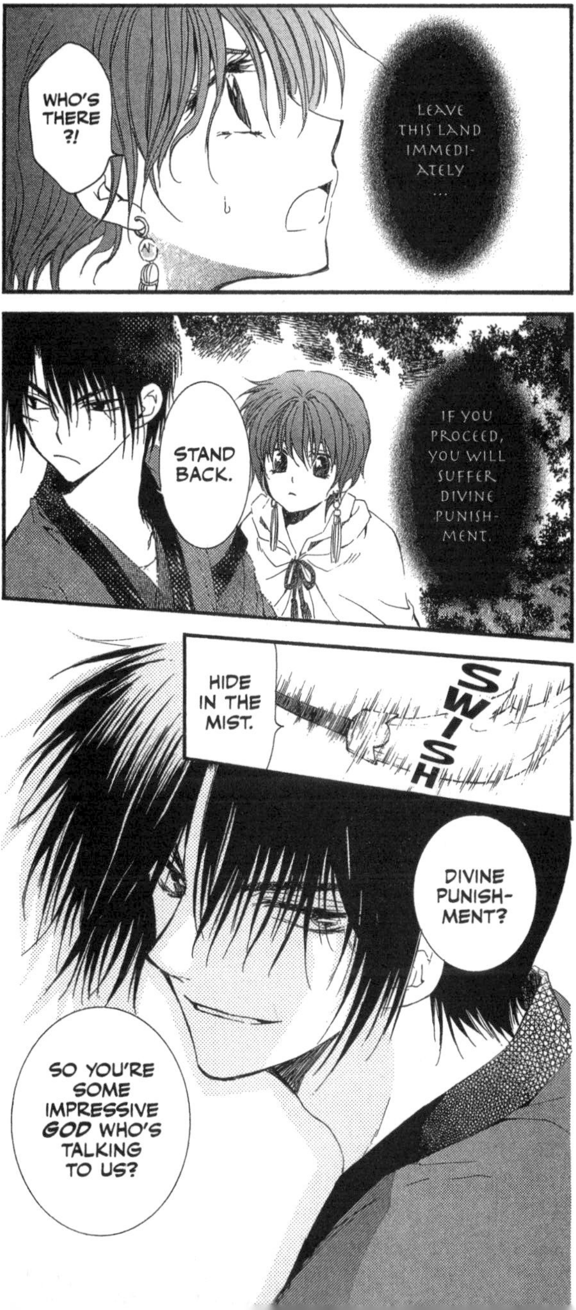
LEAVE THIS LAND IMMEDIATELY ...
WHO'S THERE ?!
IF YOU PROCEED, YOU WILL SUFFER DIVINE PUNISHMENT.
STAND BACK.
SWISH
HIDE IN THE MIST.
DIVINE PUNISHMENT?
SO YOU'RE SOME IMPRESSIVE GOD WHO'S TALKING TO US?

What is a Thunder Beast?

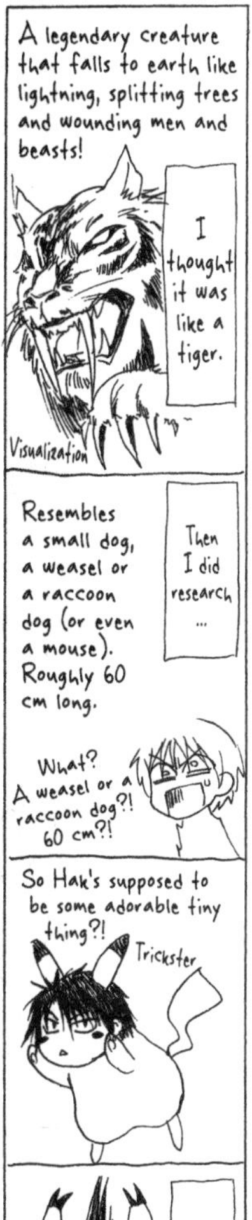
A legendary creature that falls to earth like lightning, splitting trees and wounding men and beasts!
I thought it was like a tiger.
Visualization
Resembles a small dog, a weasel or a raccoon dog (or even a mouse). Roughly 60 cm long.
Then I did research ...
What? A weasel or a raccoon dog?! 60 cm?!
So Hak's supposed to be some adorable tiny thing?!
Trickster
After searching online...
Thunder Beast Illustration
A weasel?
??
...

So in the world of Yona of the Dawn, just pretend a Thunder Beast looks like a tiger.

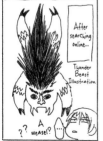

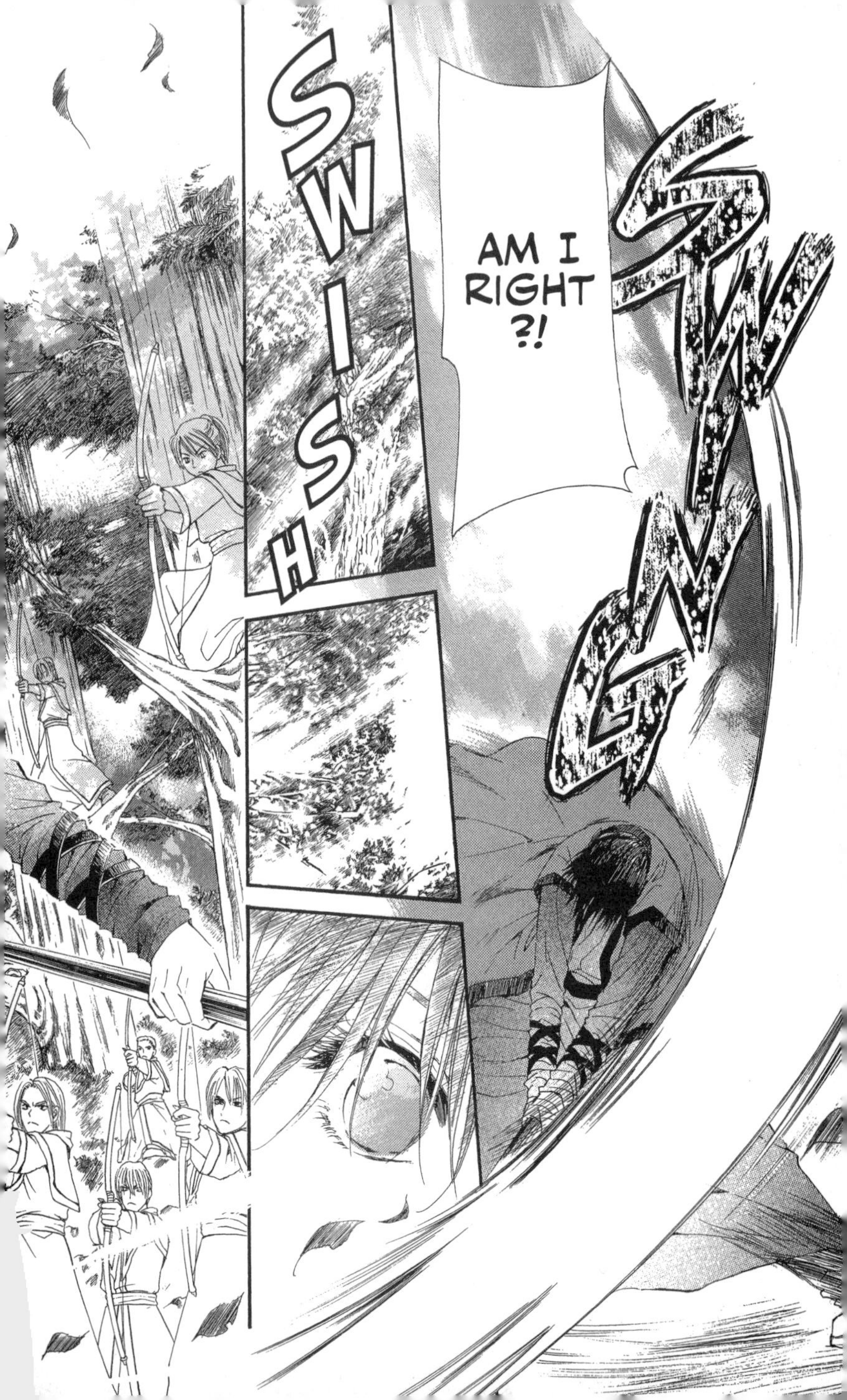

SWING
AM I RIGHT ?!
SWISH

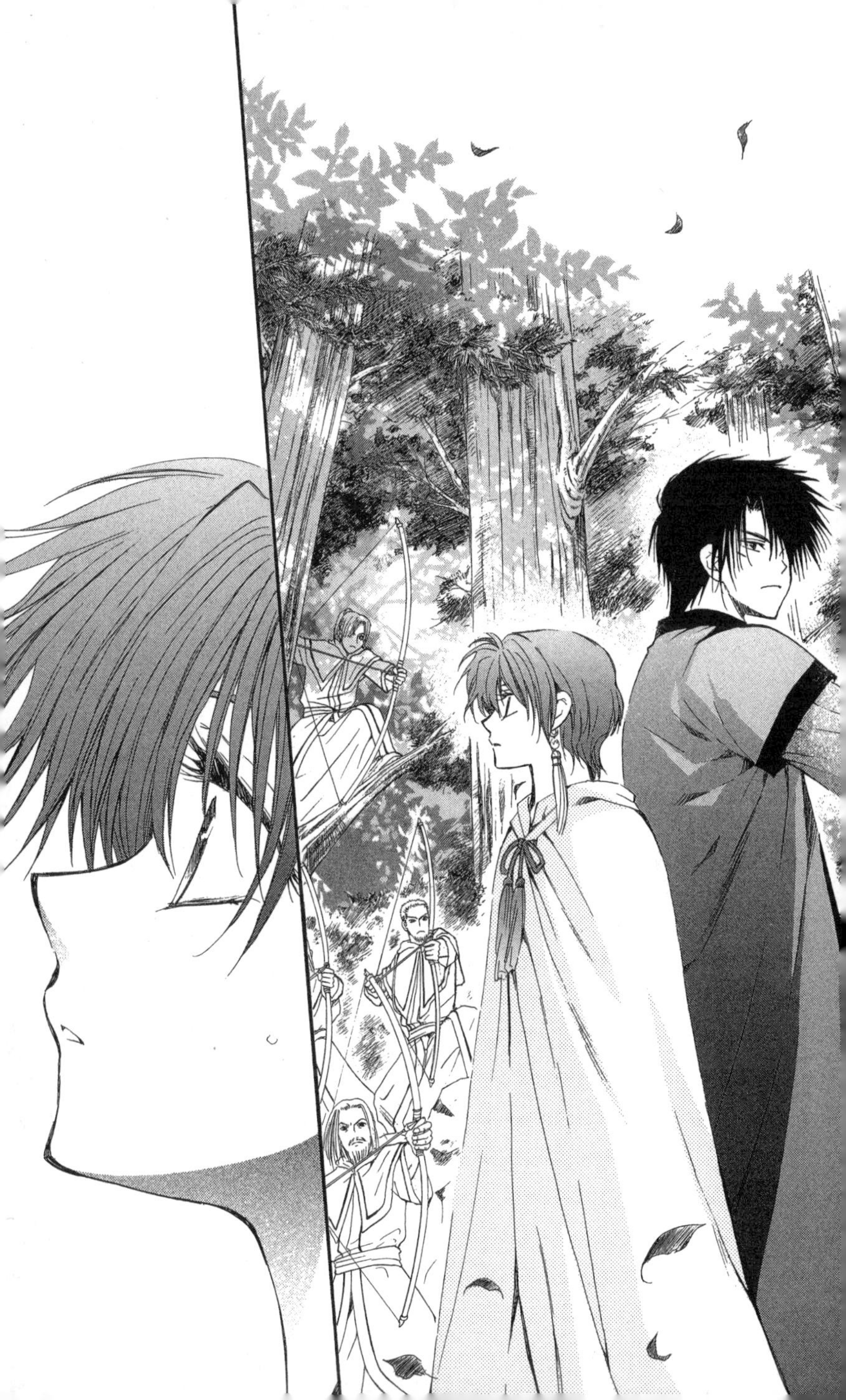

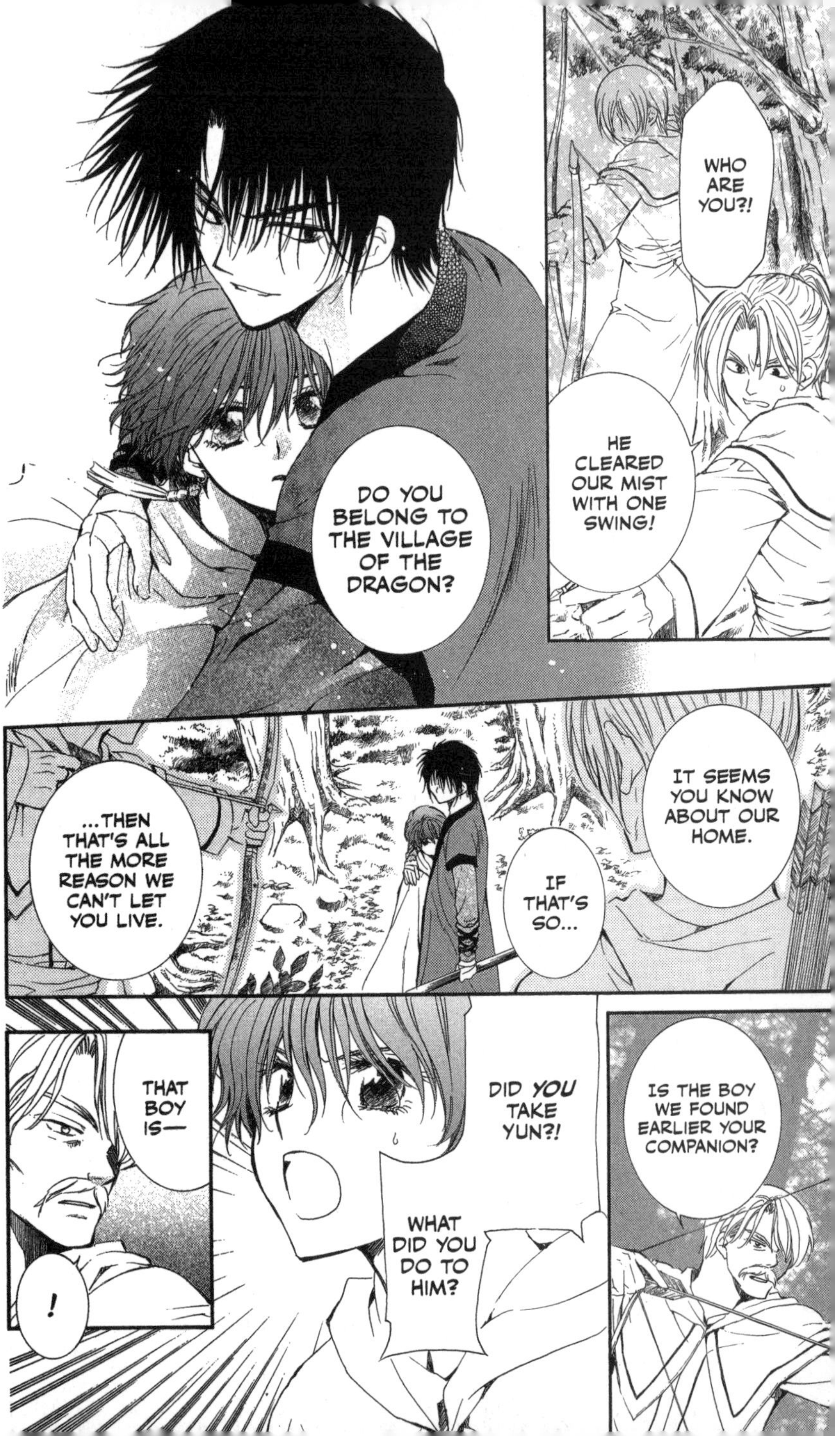
WHO ARE YOU?!
HE CLEARED OUR MIST WITH ONE SWING!
DO YOU BELONG TO THE VILLAGE OF THE DRAGON?
IT SEEMS YOU KNOW ABOUT OUR HOME.
IF THAT'S SO...
...THEN THAT'S ALL THE MORE REASON WE CAN'T LET YOU LIVE.
IS THE BOY WE FOUND EARLIER YOUR COMPANION?
DID *YOU* TAKE YUN?!
WHAT DID YOU DO TO HIM?
THAT BOY IS—
!

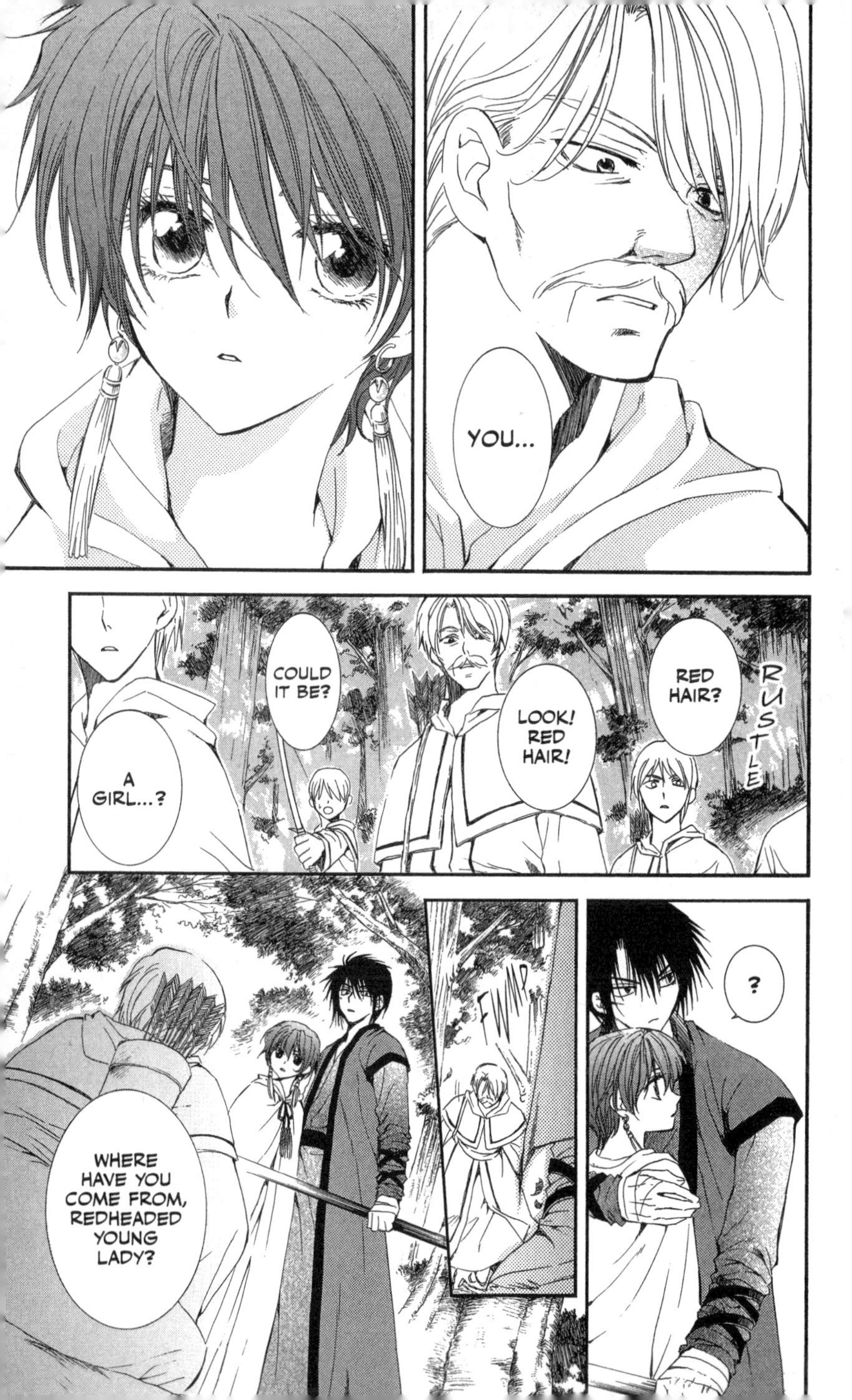
YOU...
RED HAIR?
RUSTLE
LOOK! RED HAIR!
COULD IT BE?
A GIRL...?
?
FWMP
WHERE HAVE YOU COME FROM, REDHEADED YOUNG LADY?

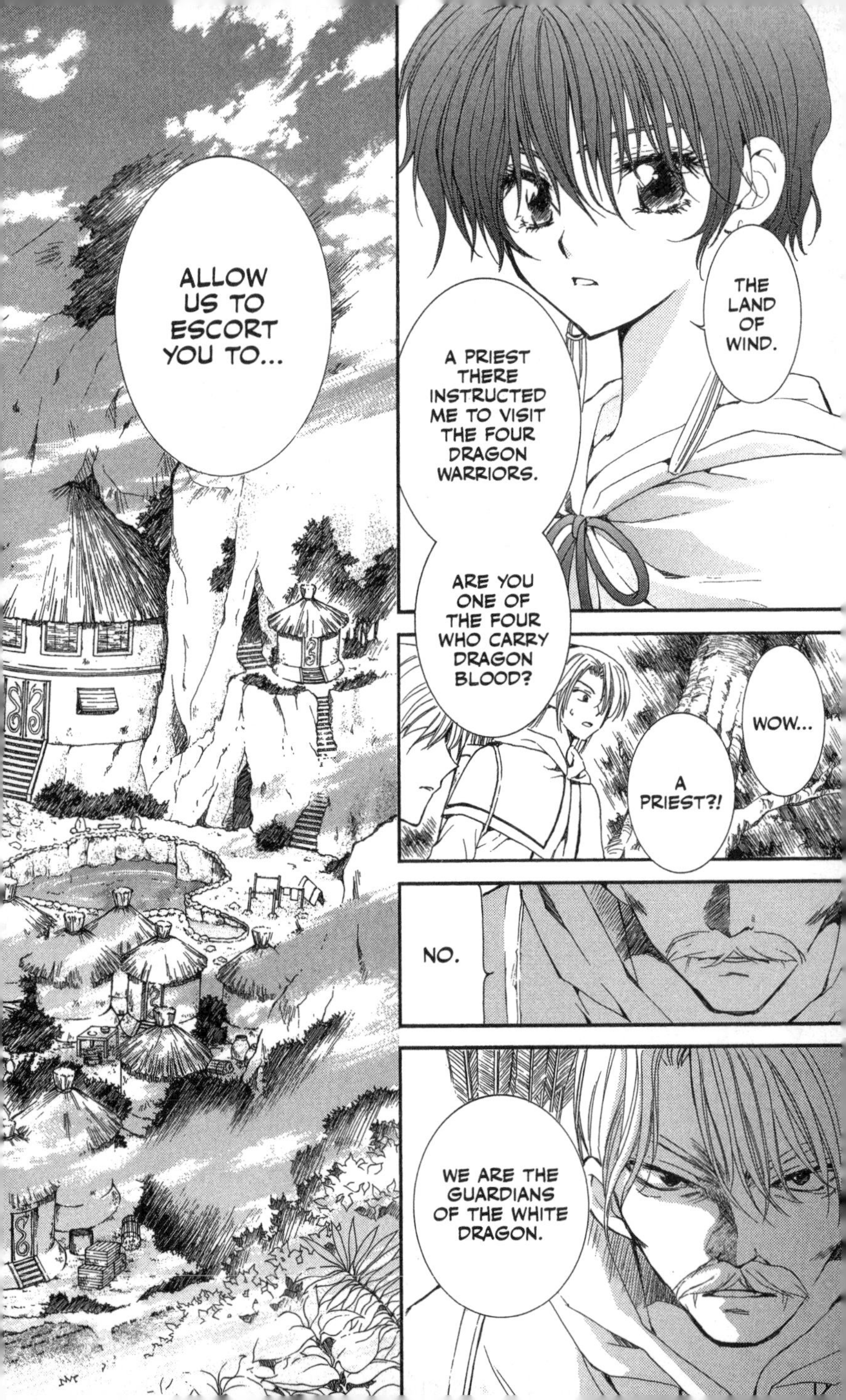
THE LAND OF WIND.
A PRIEST THERE INSTRUCTED ME TO VISIT THE FOUR DRAGON WARRIORS.
ARE YOU ONE OF THE FOUR WHO CARRY DRAGON BLOOD?
WOW...
A PRIEST?!
NO.
WE ARE THE GUARDIANS OF THE WHITE DRAGON.
ALLOW US TO ESCORT YOU TO...

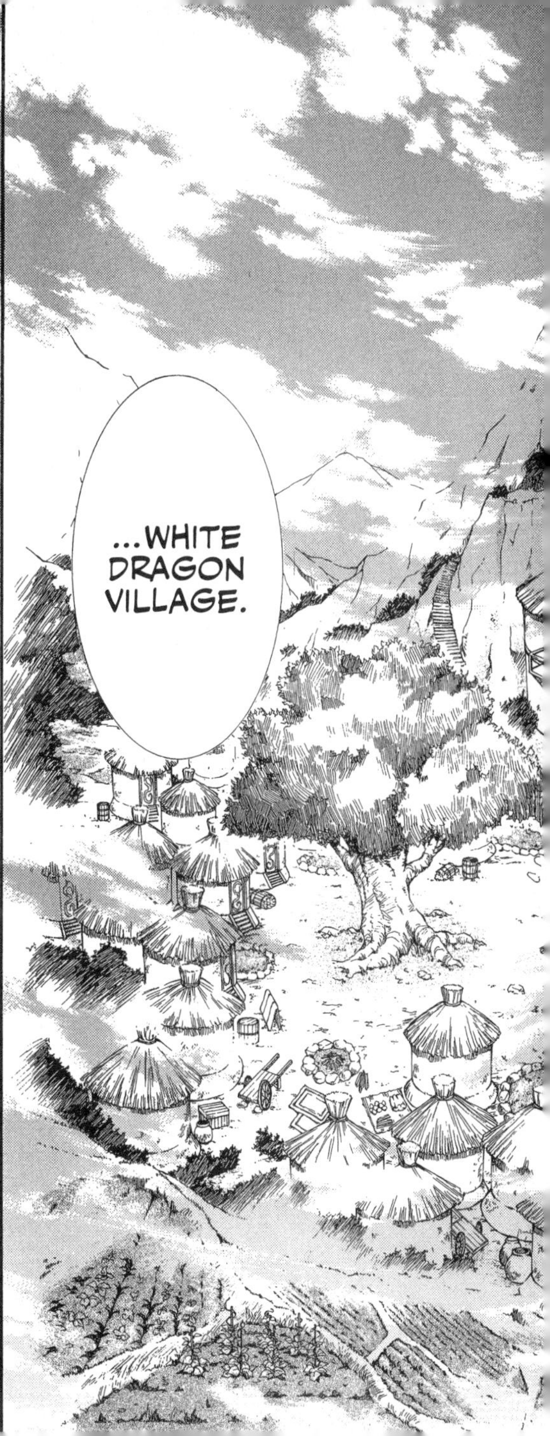
...WHITE DRAGON VILLAGE.
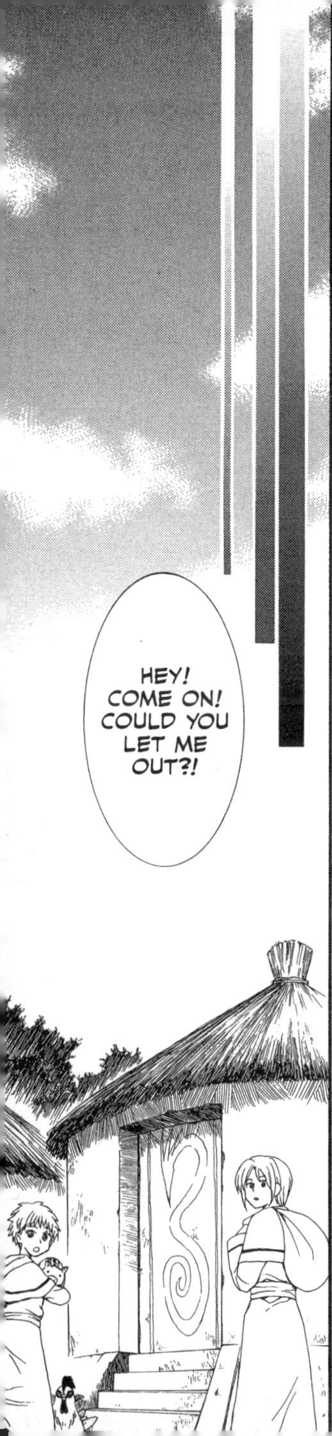
HEY! COME ON! COULD YOU LET ME OUT?!

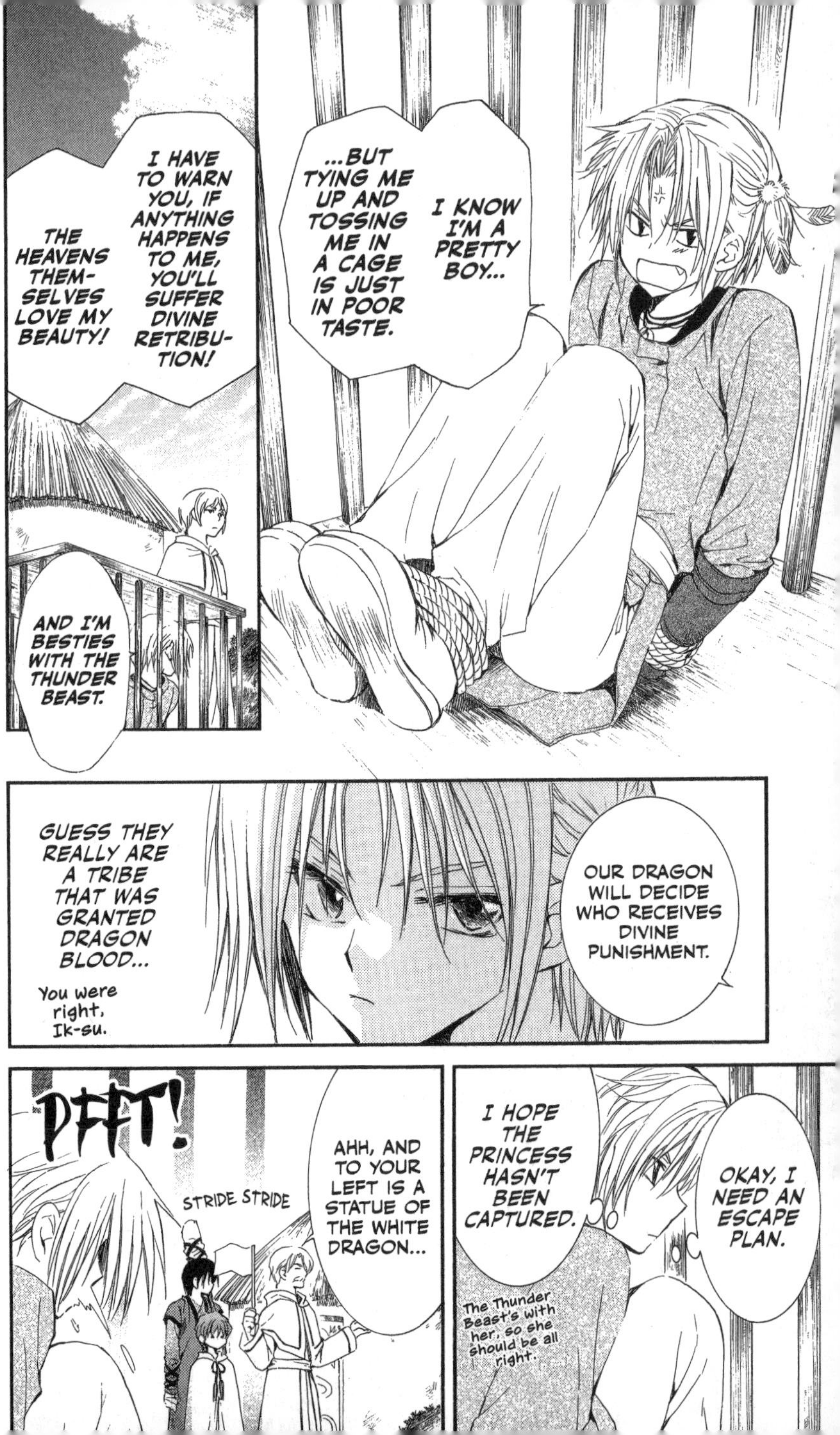
I KNOW I'M A PRETTY BOY...
...BUT TYING ME UP AND TOSSING ME IN A CAGE IS JUST IN POOR TASTE.
I HAVE TO WARN YOU, IF ANYTHING HAPPENS TO ME, YOU'LL SUFFER DIVINE RETRIBUTION!
THE HEAVENS THEMSELVES LOVE MY BEAUTY!
AND I'M BESTIES WITH THE THUNDER BEAST.
OUR DRAGON WILL DECIDE WHO RECEIVES DIVINE PUNISHMENT.
GUESS THEY REALLY ARE A TRIBE THAT WAS GRANTED DRAGON BLOOD...
You were right, Ik-su.
OKAY, I NEED AN ESCAPE PLAN.
I HOPE THE PRINCESS HASN'T BEEN CAPTURED.
The Thunder Beast's with her, so she should be all right.
AHH, AND TO YOUR LEFT IS A STATUE OF THE WHITE DRAGON...
STRIDE STRIDE
PFFT!

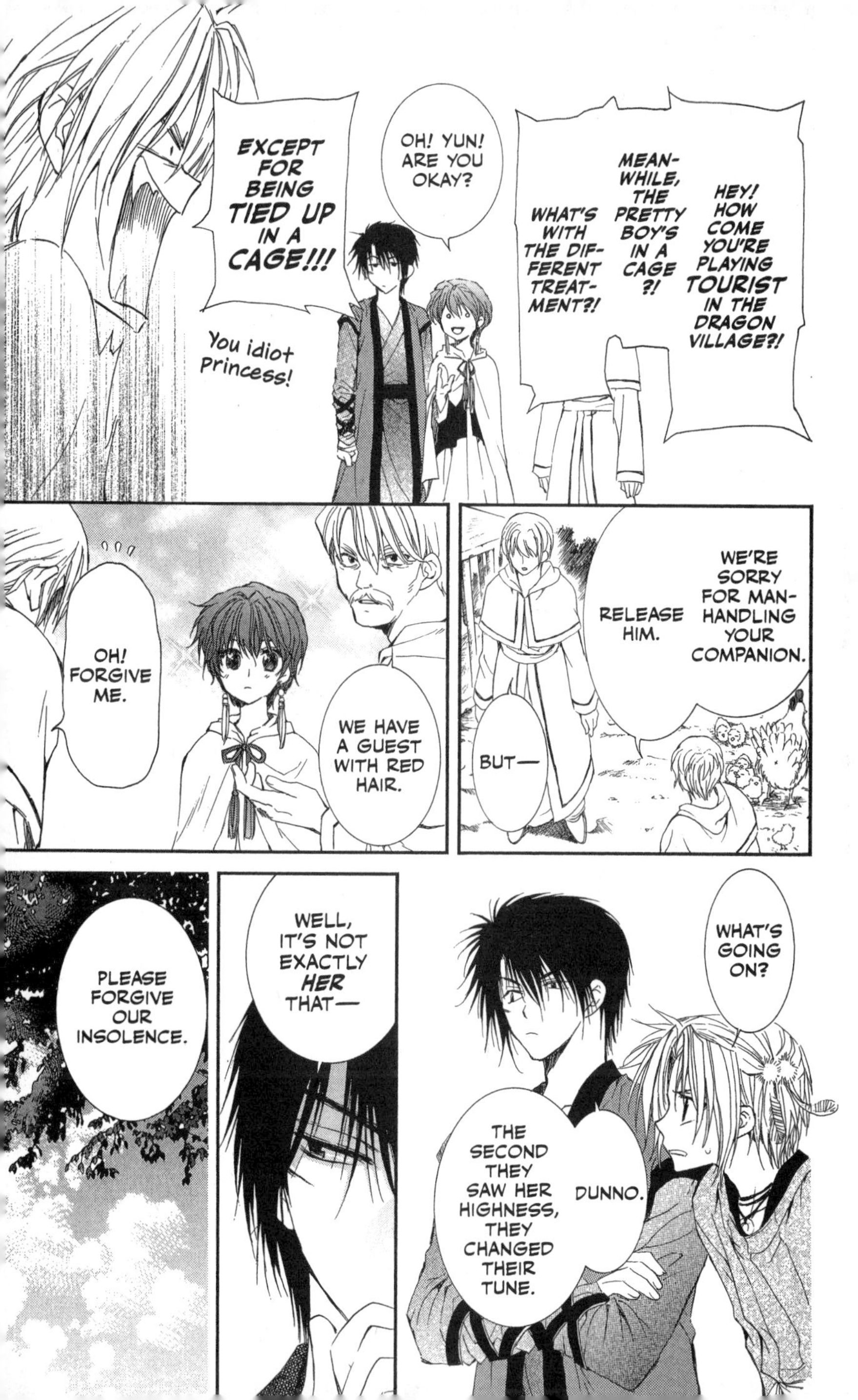
HEY! HOW COME YOU'RE PLAYING TOURIST IN THE DRAGON VILLAGE?!
MEANWHILE, THE PRETTY BOY'S IN A CAGE?!
WHAT'S WITH THE DIFFERENT TREATMENT?!
OH! YUN! ARE YOU OKAY?
EXCEPT FOR BEING TIED UP IN A CAGE!!!
You idiot Princess!
WE'RE SORRY FOR MANHANDLING YOUR COMPANION.
RELEASE HIM.
BUT—
WE HAVE A GUEST WITH RED HAIR.
OH! FORGIVE ME.
WHAT'S GOING ON?
DUNNO.
THE SECOND THEY SAW HER HIGHNESS, THEY CHANGED THEIR TUNE.
WELL, IT'S NOT EXACTLY HER THAT—
PLEASE FORGIVE OUR INSOLENCE.

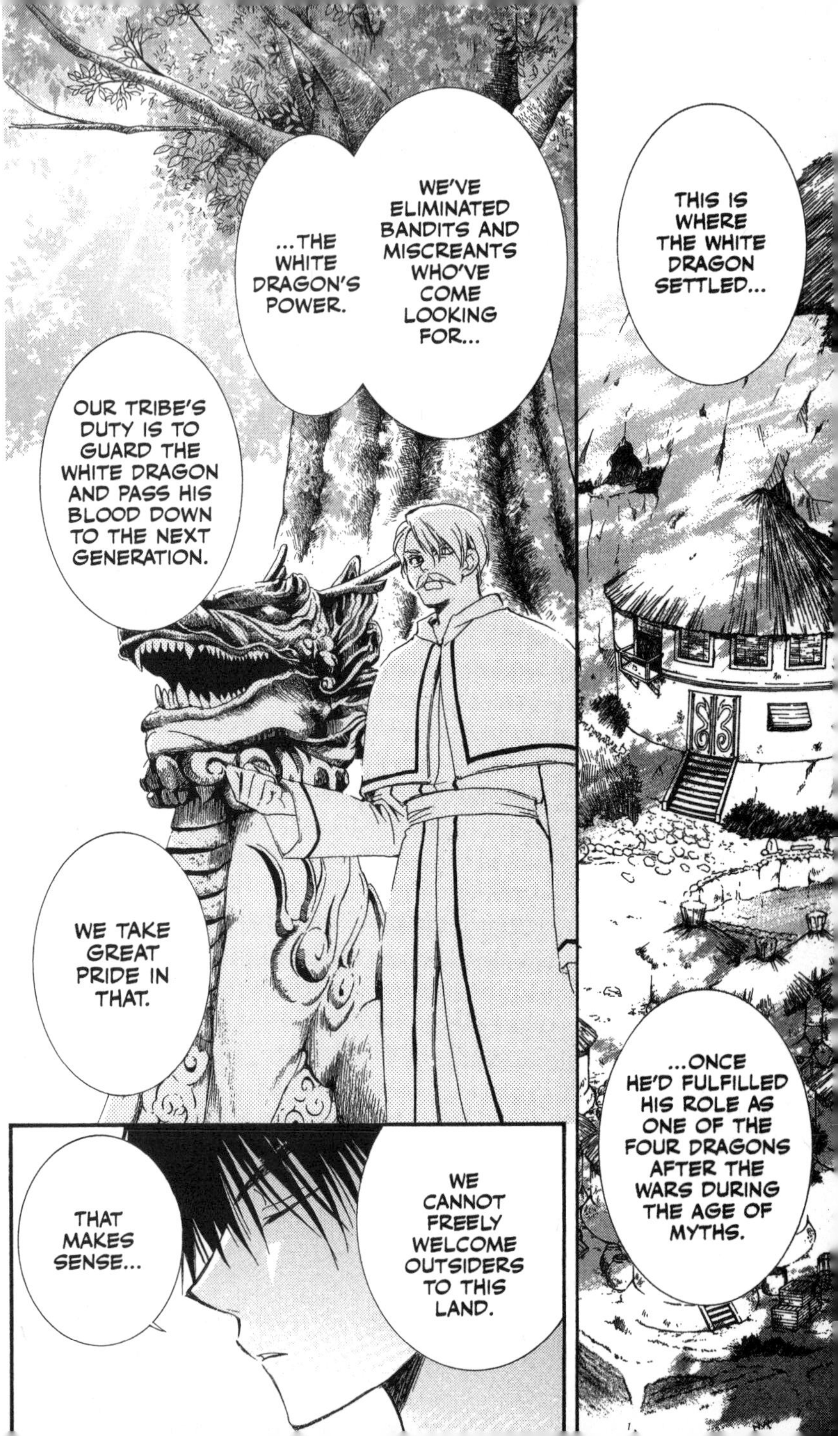
THIS IS WHERE THE WHITE DRAGON SETTLED...
...ONCE HE'D FULFILLED HIS ROLE AS ONE OF THE FOUR DRAGONS AFTER THE WARS DURING THE AGE OF MYTHS.
WE'VE ELIMINATED BANDITS AND MISCREANTS WHO'VE COME LOOKING FOR...
...THE WHITE DRAGON'S POWER.
OUR TRIBE'S DUTY IS TO GUARD THE WHITE DRAGON AND PASS HIS BLOOD DOWN TO THE NEXT GENERATION.
WE TAKE GREAT PRIDE IN THAT.
WE CANNOT FREELY WELCOME OUTSIDERS TO THIS LAND.
THAT MAKES SENSE...

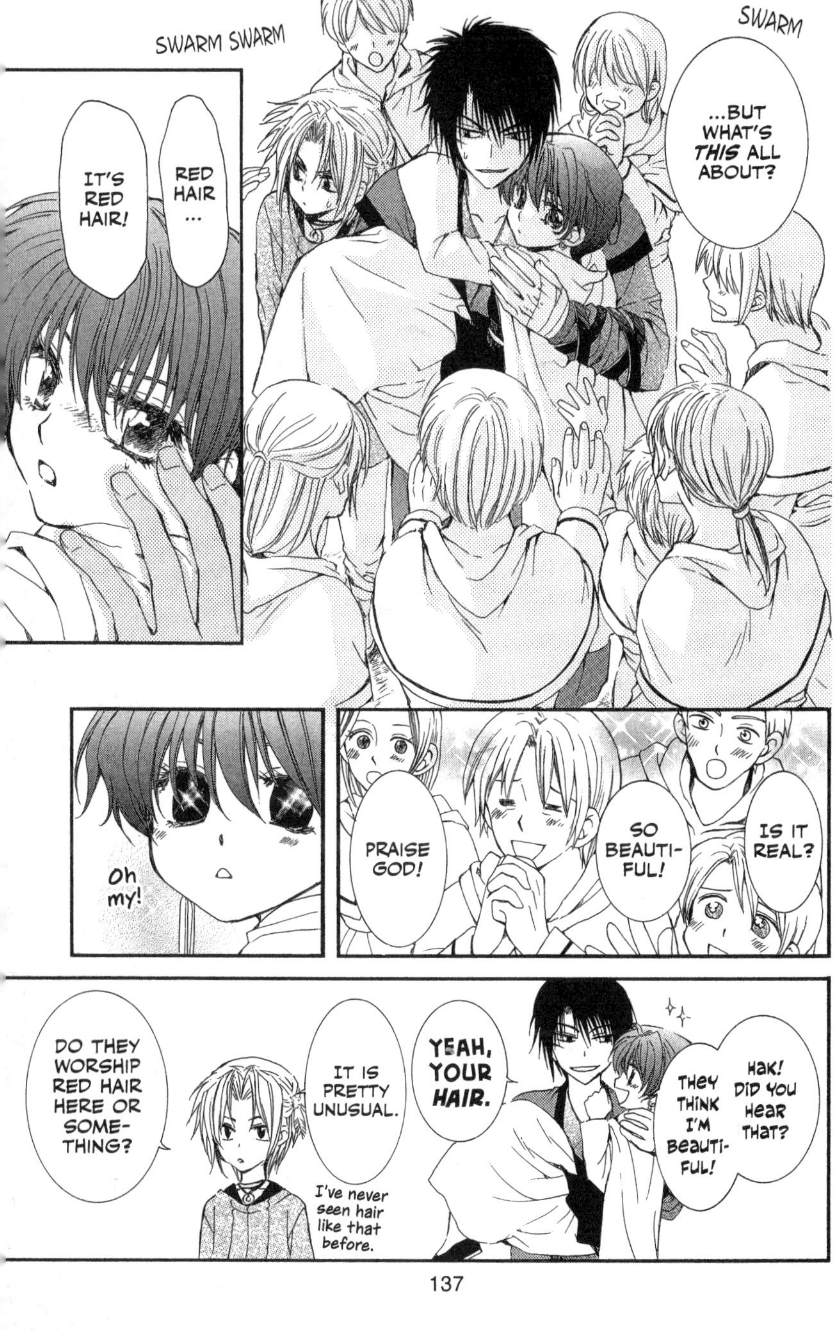
SWARM
SWARM SWARM
...BUT WHAT'S THIS ALL ABOUT?
RED HAIR...
IT'S RED HAIR!
IS IT REAL?
SO BEAUTIFUL!
PRAISE GOD!
Oh my!
Hak! Did you hear that?
They think I'm beautiful!
YEAH, YOUR HAIR.
IT IS PRETTY UNUSUAL.
I've never seen hair like that before.
DO THEY WORSHIP RED HAIR HERE OR SOMETHING?

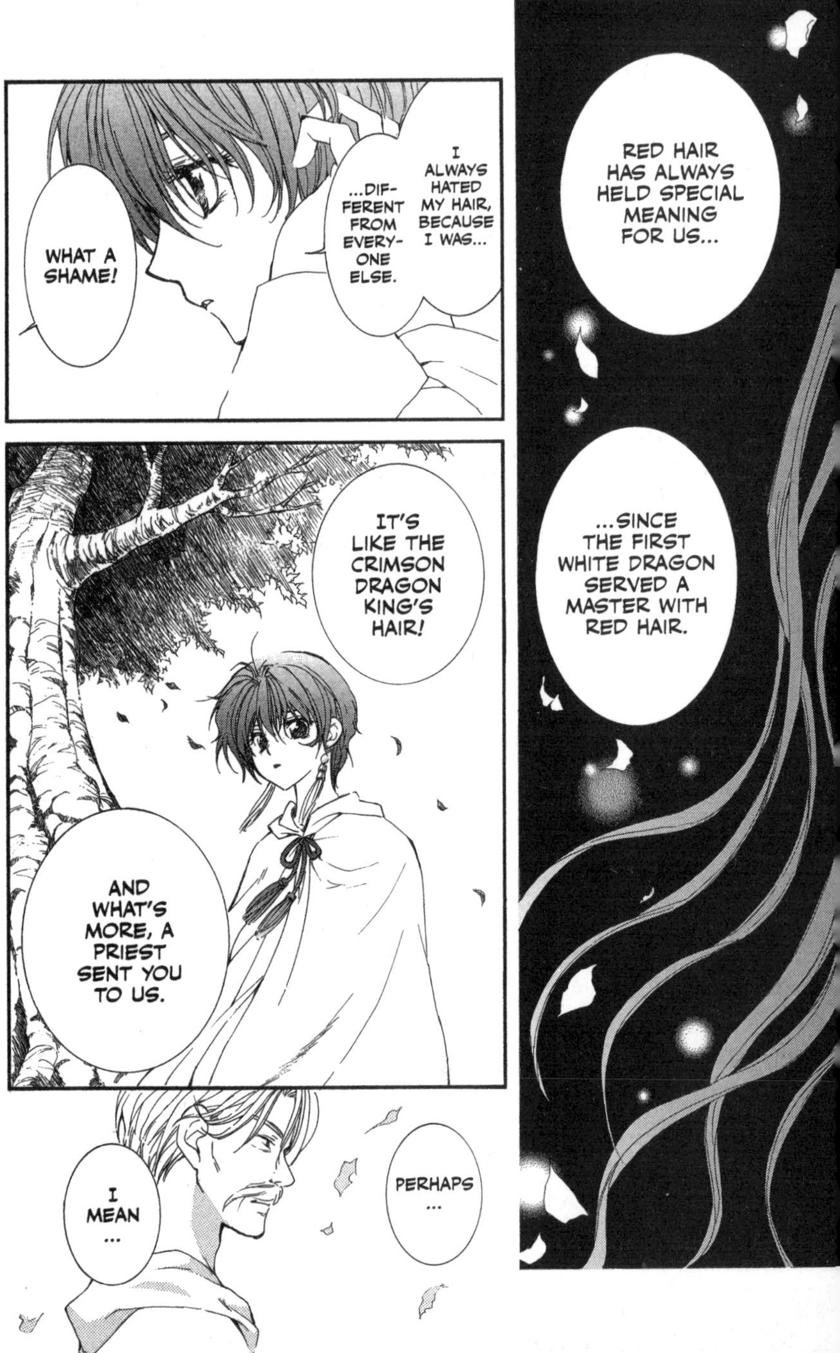
RED HAIR HAS ALWAYS HELD SPECIAL MEANING FOR US...
...SINCE THE FIRST WHITE DRAGON SERVED A MASTER WITH RED HAIR.
I ALWAYS HATED MY HAIR, BECAUSE I WAS...
...DIF-FERENT FROM EVERY-ONE ELSE.
WHAT A SHAME!
IT'S LIKE THE CRIMSON DRAGON KING'S HAIR!
AND WHAT'S MORE, A PRIEST SENT YOU TO US.
PERHAPS...
I MEAN...

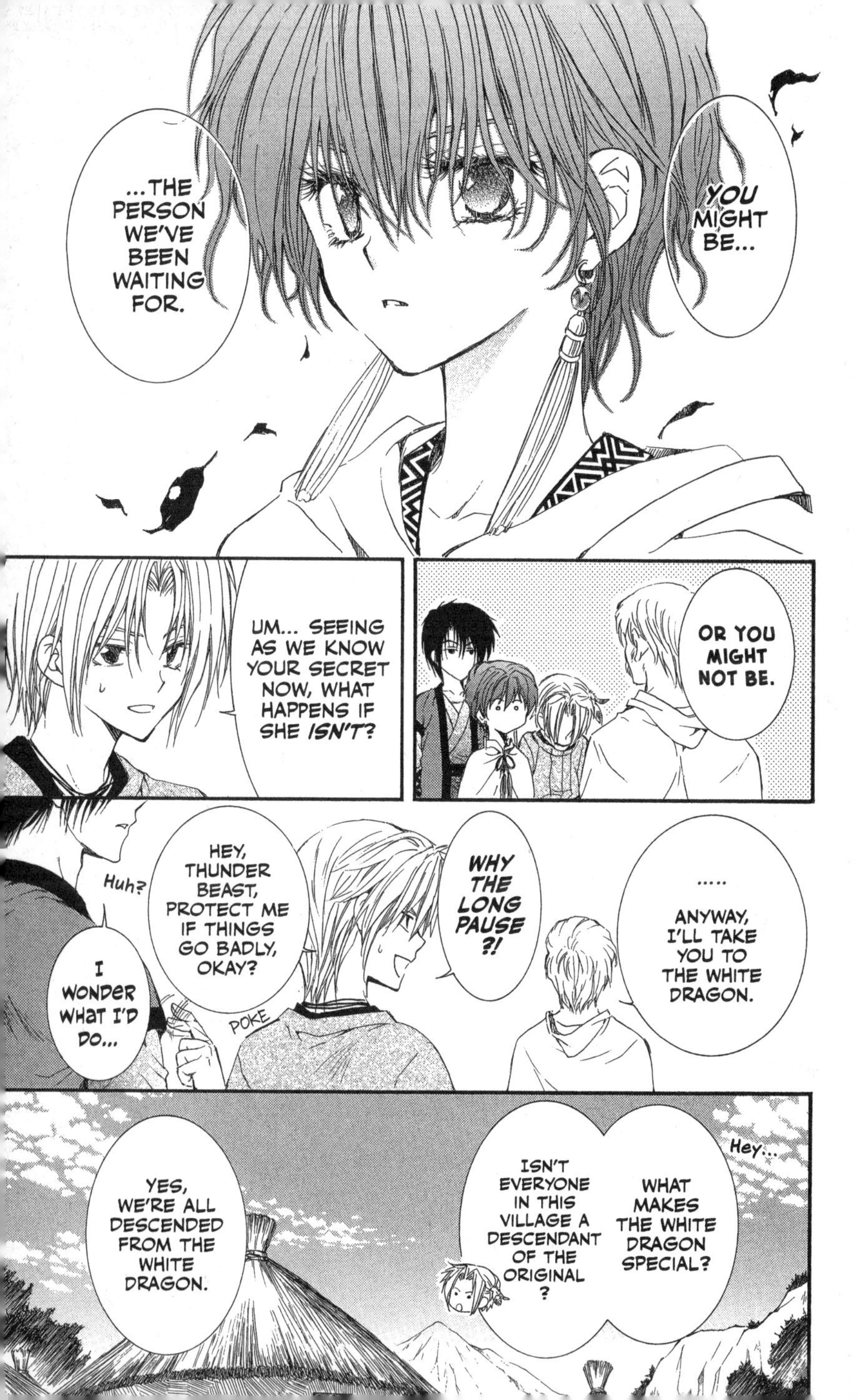
YOU MIGHT BE...
...THE PERSON WE'VE BEEN WAITING FOR.
OR YOU MIGHT NOT BE.
UM... SEEING AS WE KNOW YOUR SECRET NOW, WHAT HAPPENS IF SHE ISN'T?
.....
ANYWAY, I'LL TAKE YOU TO THE WHITE DRAGON.
WHY THE LONG PAUSE?!
HEY, THUNDER BEAST, PROTECT ME IF THINGS GO BADLY, OKAY?
POKE
Huh?
I WONDER WHAT I'D DO...
Hey...
WHAT MAKES THE WHITE DRAGON SPECIAL?
ISN'T EVERYONE IN THIS VILLAGE A DESCENDANT OF THE ORIGINAL?
YES, WE'RE ALL DESCENDED FROM THE WHITE DRAGON.

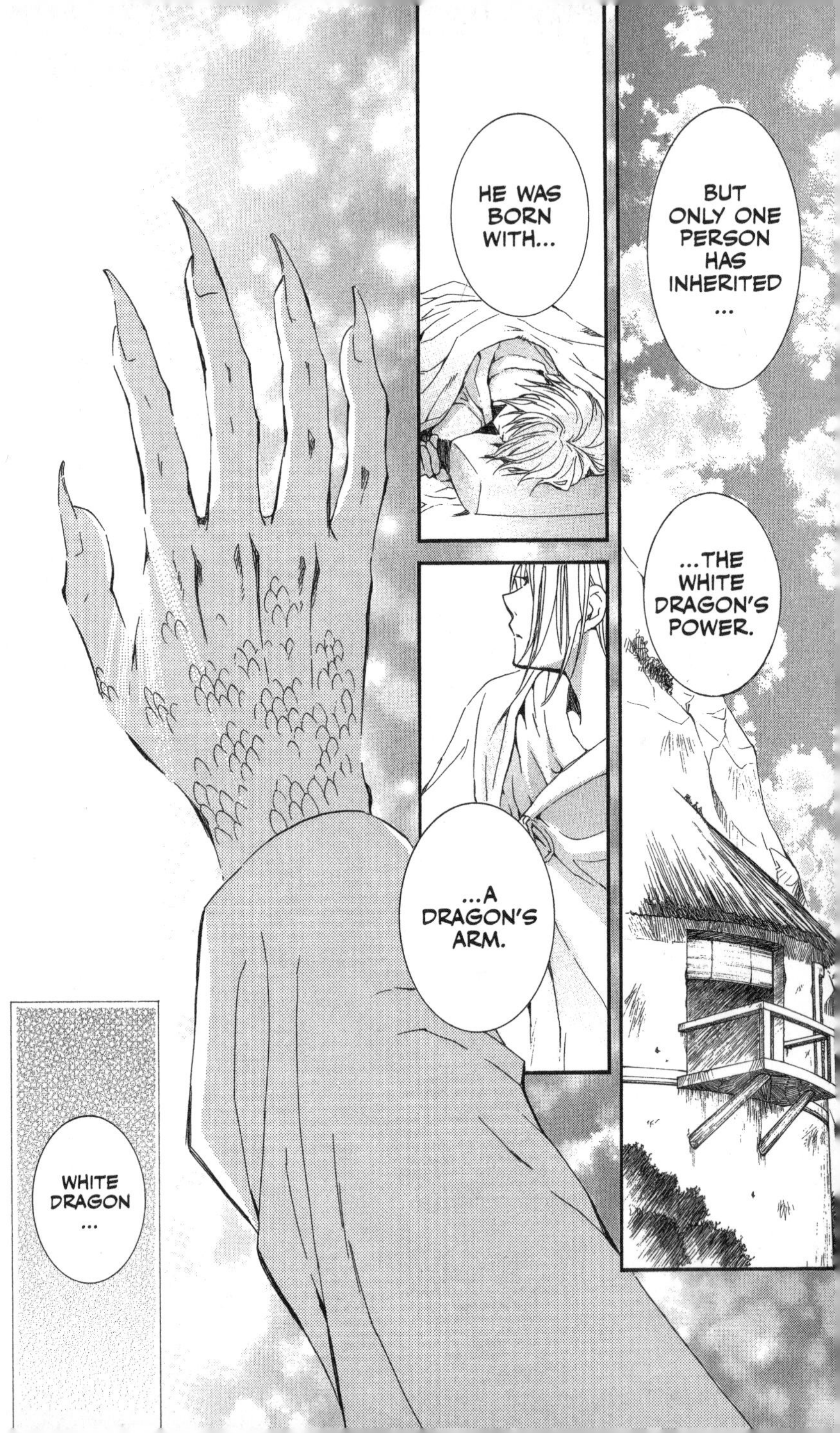
BUT ONLY ONE PERSON HAS INHERITED ...
...THE WHITE DRAGON'S POWER.
HE WAS BORN WITH...
...A DRAGON'S ARM.
WHITE DRAGON ...

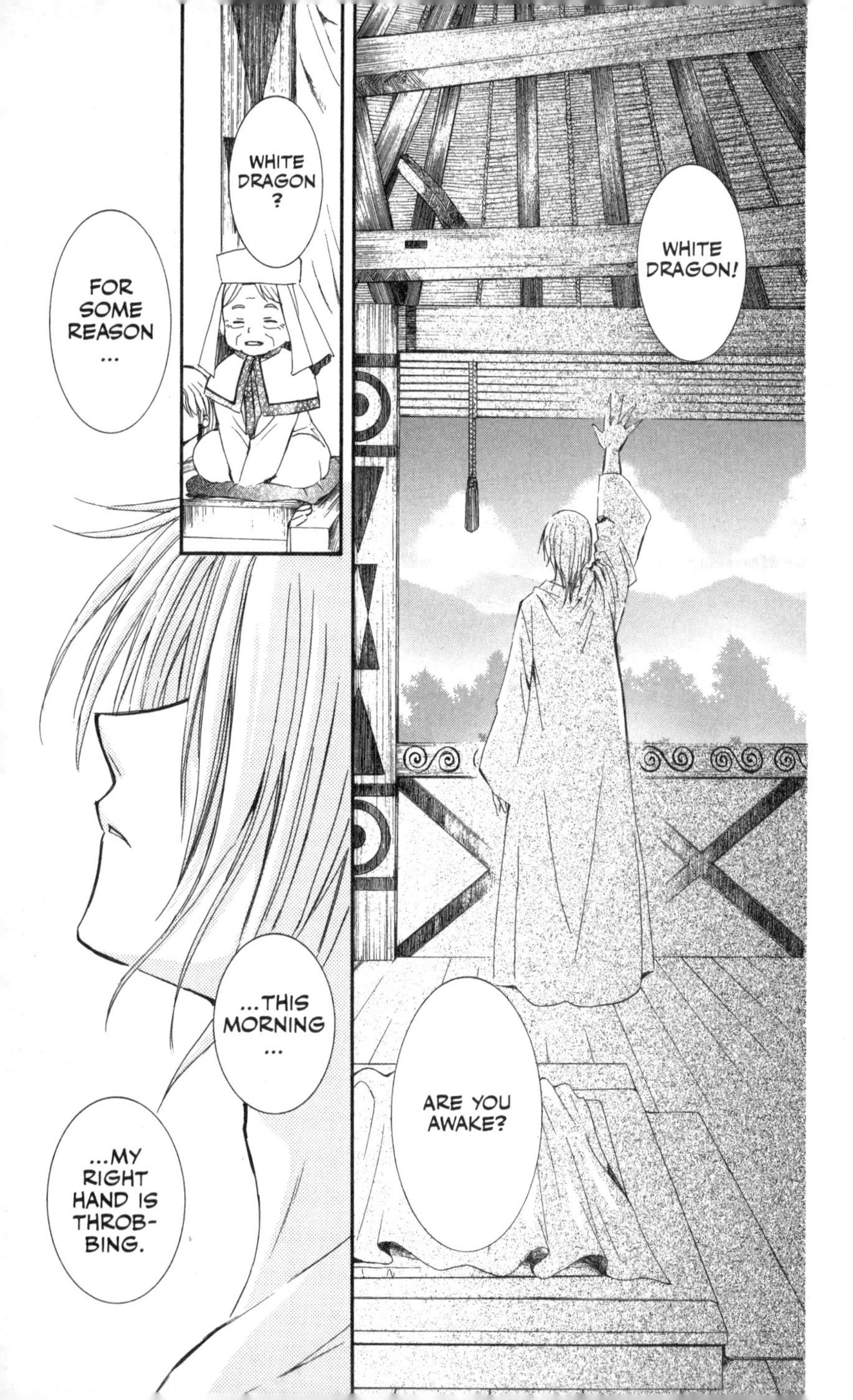
WHITE DRAGON!
ARE YOU AWAKE?
WHITE DRAGON?
FOR SOME REASON...
...THIS MORNING...
...MY RIGHT HAND IS THROBBING.

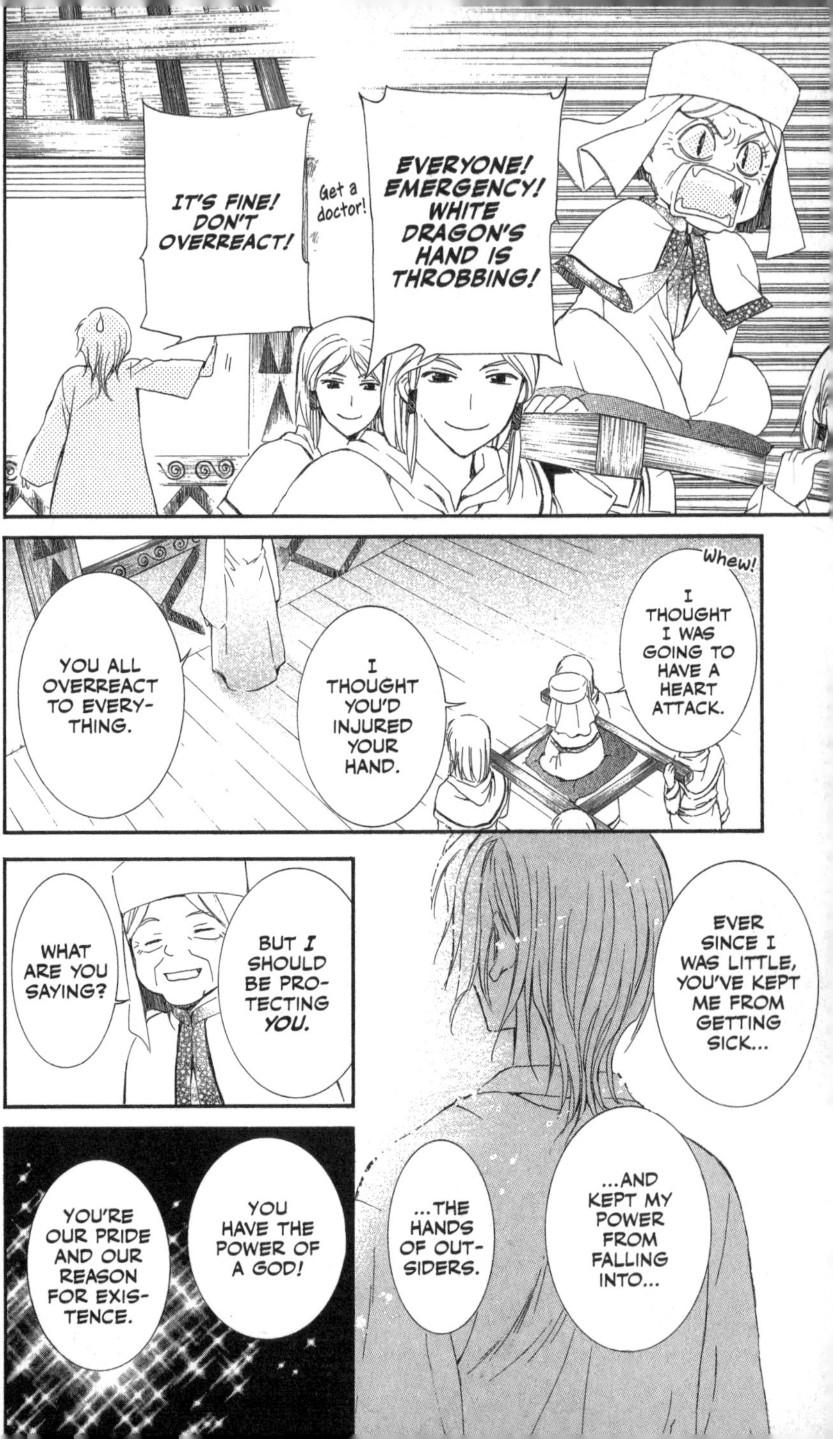
EVERYONE! EMERGENCY! WHITE DRAGON'S HAND IS THROBBING!
Get a doctor!
IT'S FINE! DON'T OVERREACT!
Whew!
I THOUGHT I WAS GOING TO HAVE A HEART ATTACK.
I THOUGHT YOU'D INJURED YOUR HAND.
YOU ALL OVERREACT TO EVERYTHING.
EVER SINCE I WAS LITTLE, YOU'VE KEPT ME FROM GETTING SICK...
...AND KEPT MY POWER FROM FALLING INTO...
...THE HANDS OF OUTSIDERS.
BUT *I* SHOULD BE PROTECTING *YOU*.
WHAT ARE YOU SAYING?
YOU HAVE THE POWER OF A GOD!
YOU'RE OUR PRIDE AND OUR REASON FOR EXISTENCE.

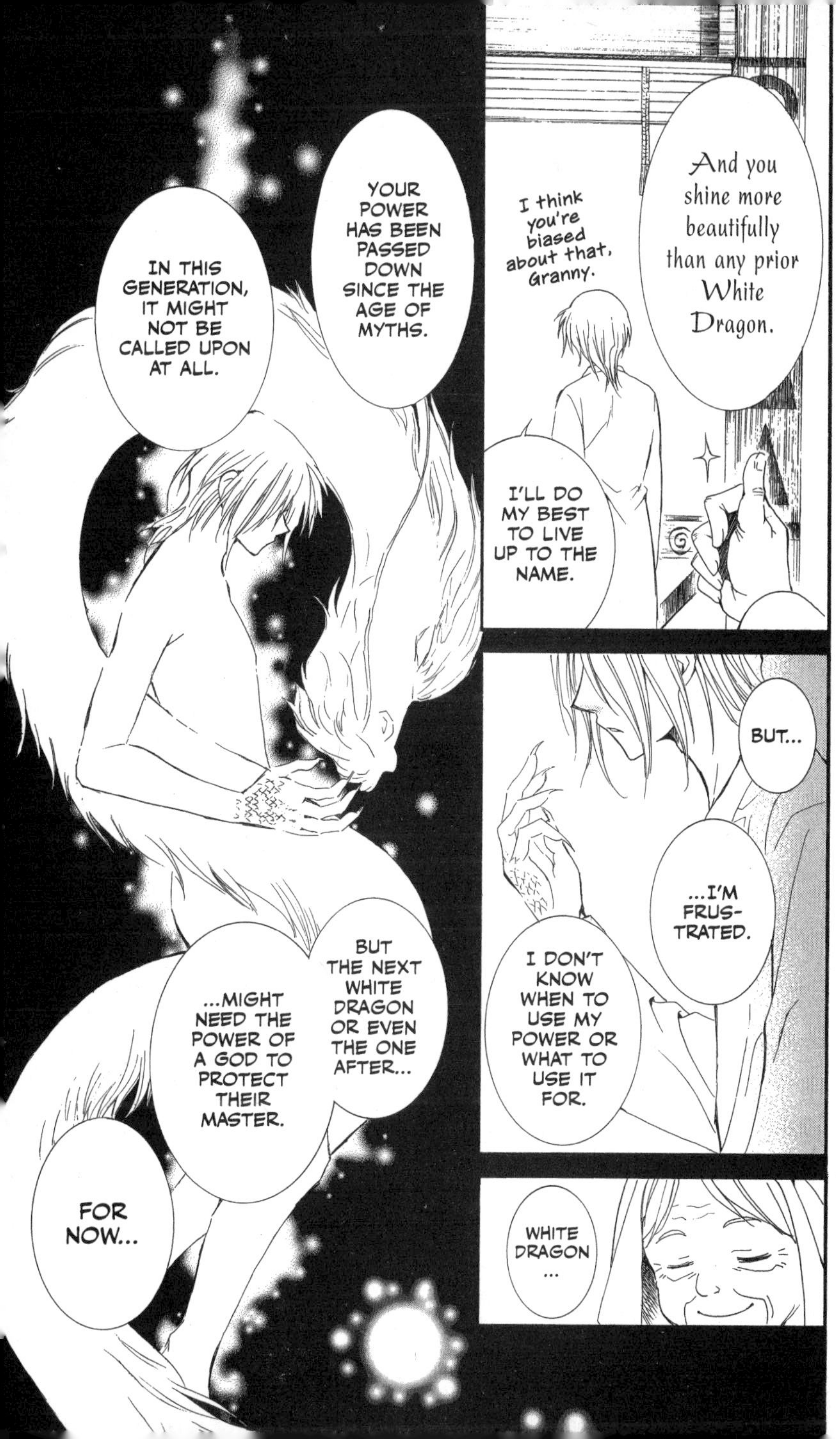
And you shine more beautifully than any prior White Dragon.
I think you're biased about that, Granny.
I'LL DO MY BEST TO LIVE UP TO THE NAME.
BUT...
...I'M FRUS-TRATED.
I DON'T KNOW WHEN TO USE MY POWER OR WHAT TO USE IT FOR.
WHITE DRAGON...
YOUR POWER HAS BEEN PASSED DOWN SINCE THE AGE OF MYTHS.
IN THIS GENERATION, IT MIGHT NOT BE CALLED UPON AT ALL.
BUT THE NEXT WHITE DRAGON OR EVEN THE ONE AFTER...
...MIGHT NEED THE POWER OF A GOD TO PROTECT THEIR MASTER.
FOR NOW...

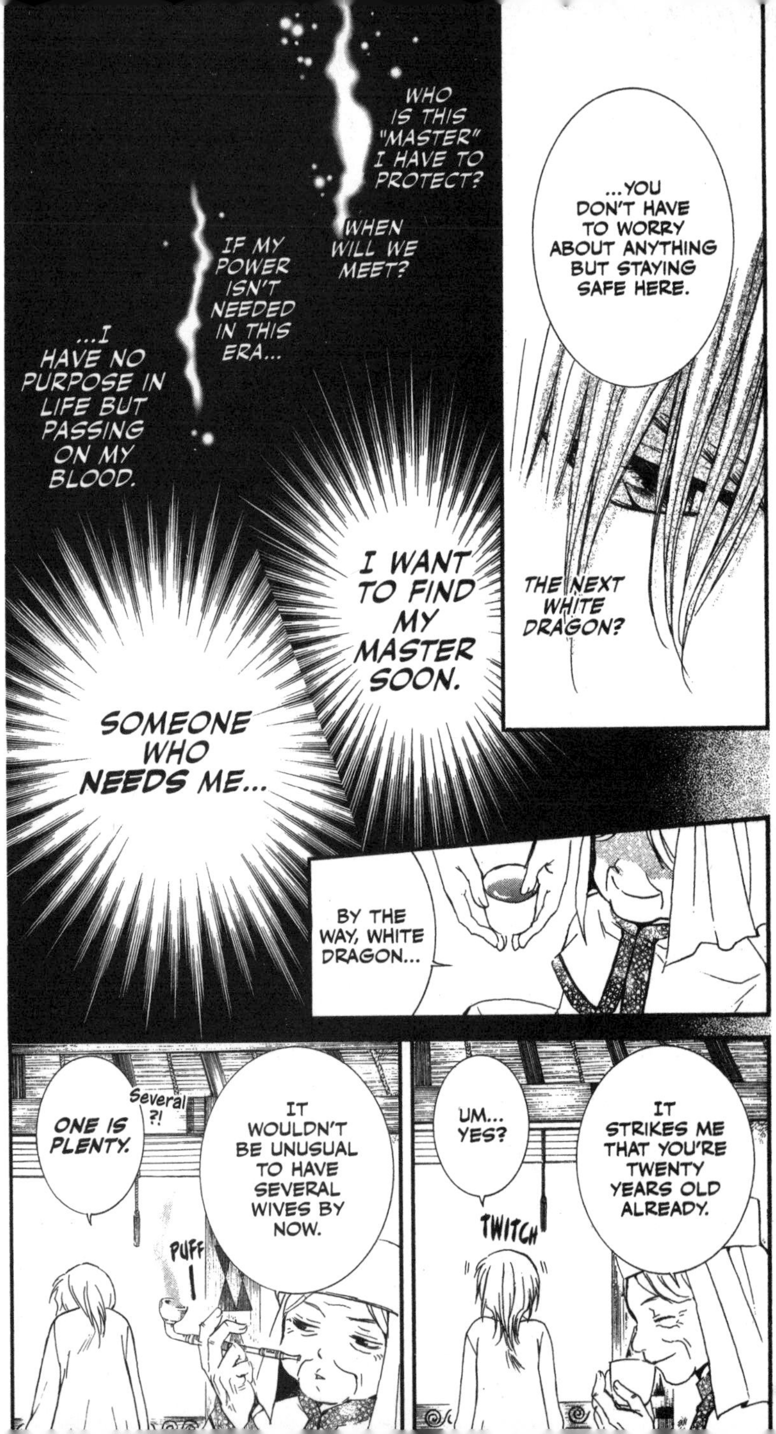
...YOU DON'T HAVE TO WORRY ABOUT ANYTHING BUT STAYING SAFE HERE.
THE NEXT WHITE DRAGON?
WHO IS THIS "MASTER" I HAVE TO PROTECT?
WHEN WILL WE MEET?
IF MY POWER ISN'T NEEDED IN THIS ERA...
...I HAVE NO PURPOSE IN LIFE BUT PASSING ON MY BLOOD.
I WANT TO FIND MY MASTER SOON.
SOMEONE WHO NEEDS ME...
BY THE WAY, WHITE DRAGON...
IT STRIKES ME THAT YOU'RE TWENTY YEARS OLD ALREADY.
UM... YES?
TWITCH
IT WOULDN'T BE UNUSUAL TO HAVE SEVERAL WIVES BY NOW.
PUFF
Several ?!
ONE IS PLENTY.

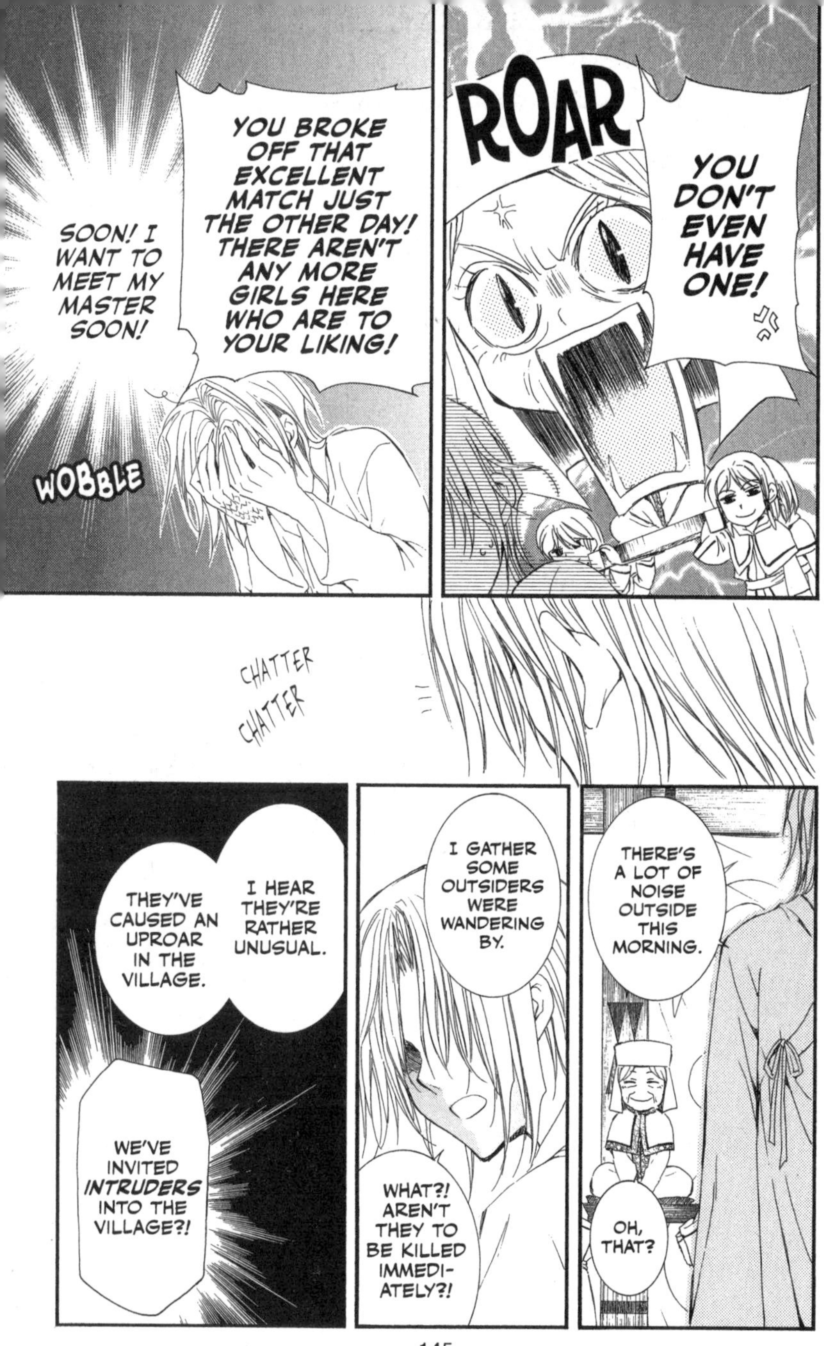
ROAR
YOU DON'T EVEN HAVE ONE!
YOU BROKE OFF THAT EXCELLENT MATCH JUST THE OTHER DAY! THERE AREN'T ANY MORE GIRLS HERE WHO ARE TO YOUR LIKING!
SOON! I WANT TO MEET MY MASTER SOON!
WOBBLE
CHATTER
CHATTER
THERE'S A LOT OF NOISE OUTSIDE THIS MORNING.
OH, THAT?
I GATHER SOME OUTSIDERS WERE WANDERING BY.
WHAT?! AREN'T THEY TO BE KILLED IMMEDI-ATELY?!
I HEAR THEY'RE RATHER UNUSUAL.
THEY'VE CAUSED AN UPROAR IN THE VILLAGE.
WE'VE INVITED *INTRUDERS* INTO THE VILLAGE?!

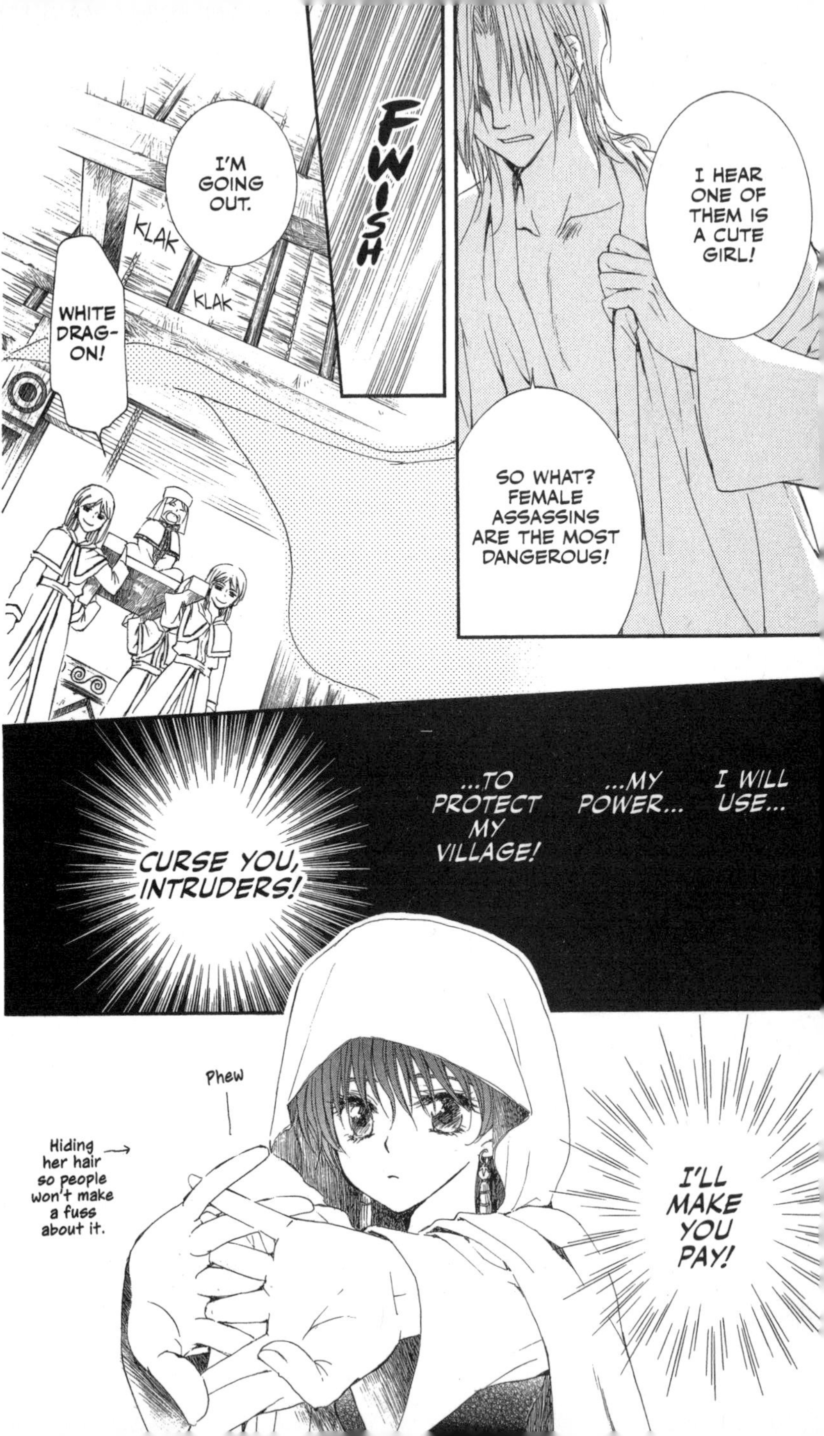
I HEAR ONE OF THEM IS A CUTE GIRL!
SO WHAT? FEMALE ASSASSINS ARE THE MOST DANGEROUS!
FWISH
I'M GOING OUT.
KLAK
KLAK
WHITE DRAG-ON!
I WILL USE...
...MY POWER...
...TO PROTECT MY VILLAGE!
CURSE YOU, INTRUDERS!
I'LL MAKE YOU PAY!
Phew
Hiding her hair so people won't make a fuss about it.

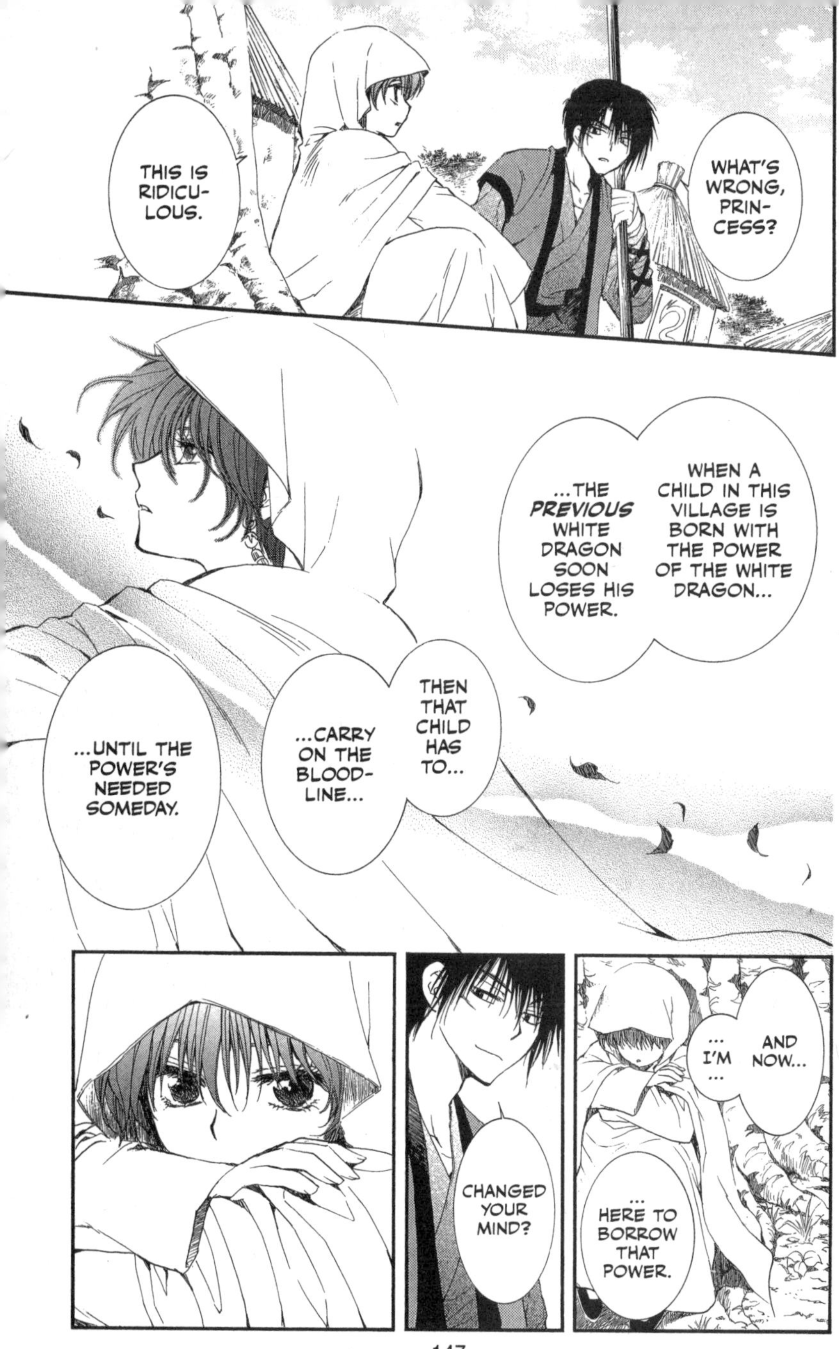
WHAT'S WRONG, PRIN-CESS?
THIS IS RIDICU-LOUS.
WHEN A CHILD IN THIS VILLAGE IS BORN WITH THE POWER OF THE WHITE DRAGON...
...THE *PREVIOUS* WHITE DRAGON SOON LOSES HIS POWER.
THEN THAT CHILD HAS TO...
...CARRY ON THE BLOOD-LINE...
...UNTIL THE POWER'S NEEDED SOMEDAY.
AND NOW...
... I'M ...
... HERE TO BORROW THAT POWER.
CHANGED YOUR MIND?

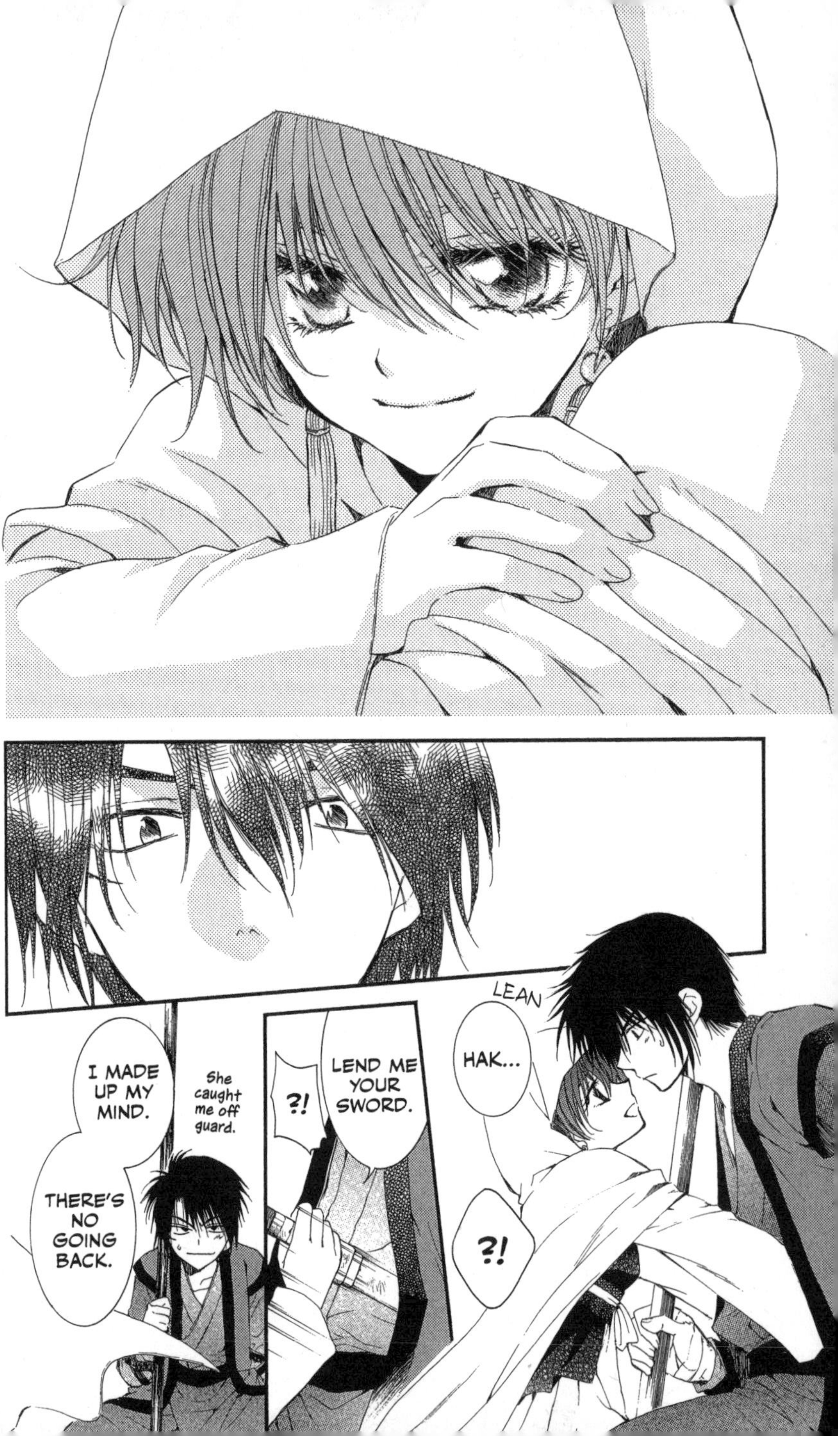
LEAN
HAK...
?!
LEND ME YOUR SWORD.
?!
She caught me off guard.
I MADE UP MY MIND.
THERE'S NO GOING BACK.

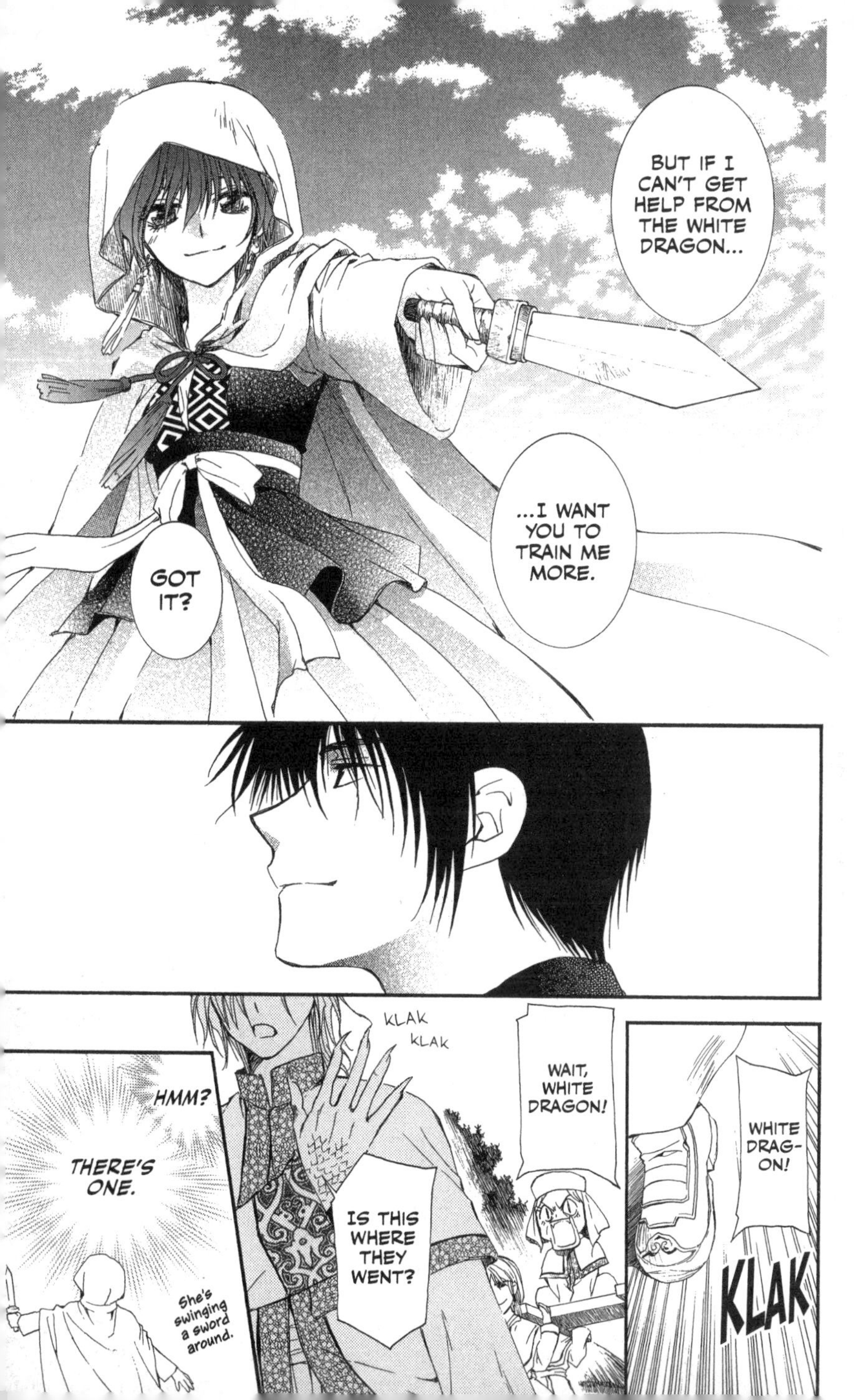
BUT IF I CAN'T GET HELP FROM THE WHITE DRAGON...
...I WANT YOU TO TRAIN ME MORE.
GOT IT?
WHITE DRAG-ON!
KLAK
WAIT, WHITE DRAGON!
KLAK KLAK
IS THIS WHERE THEY WENT?
HMM?
THERE'S ONE.
She's swinging a sword around.

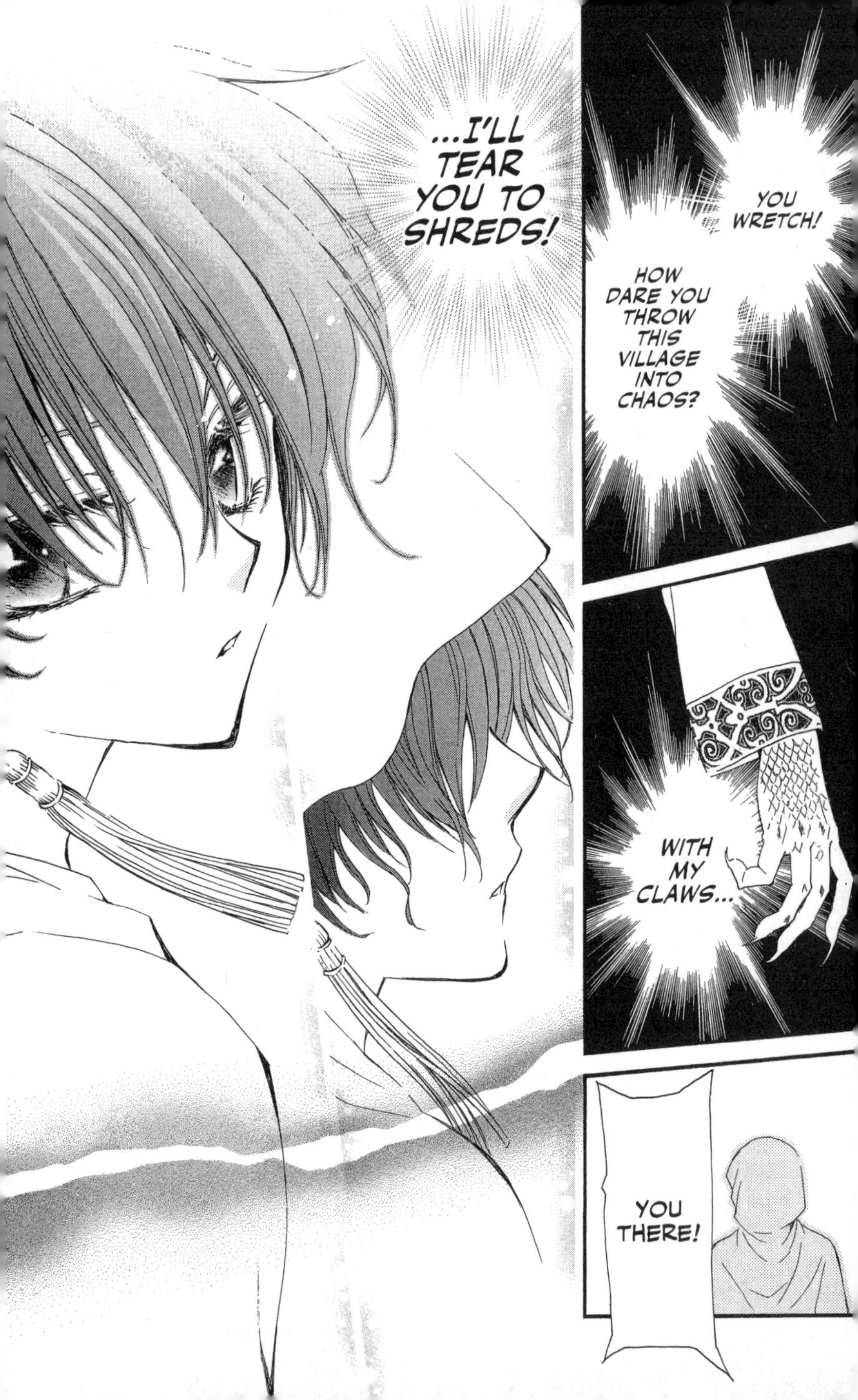
YOU WRETCH!
HOW DARE YOU THROW THIS VILLAGE INTO CHAOS?
WITH MY CLAWS...
YOU THERE!
...I'LL TEAR YOU TO SHREDS!

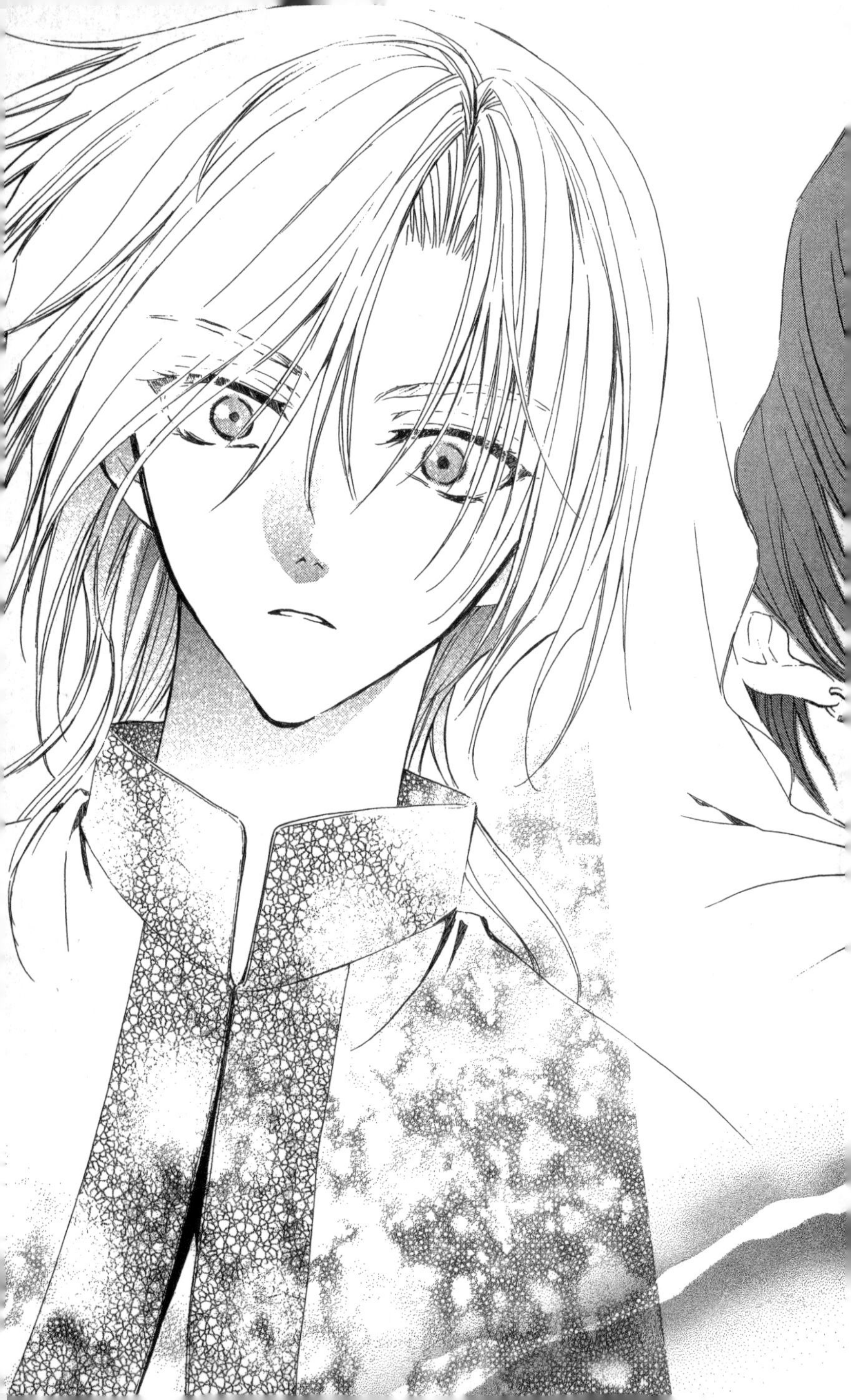

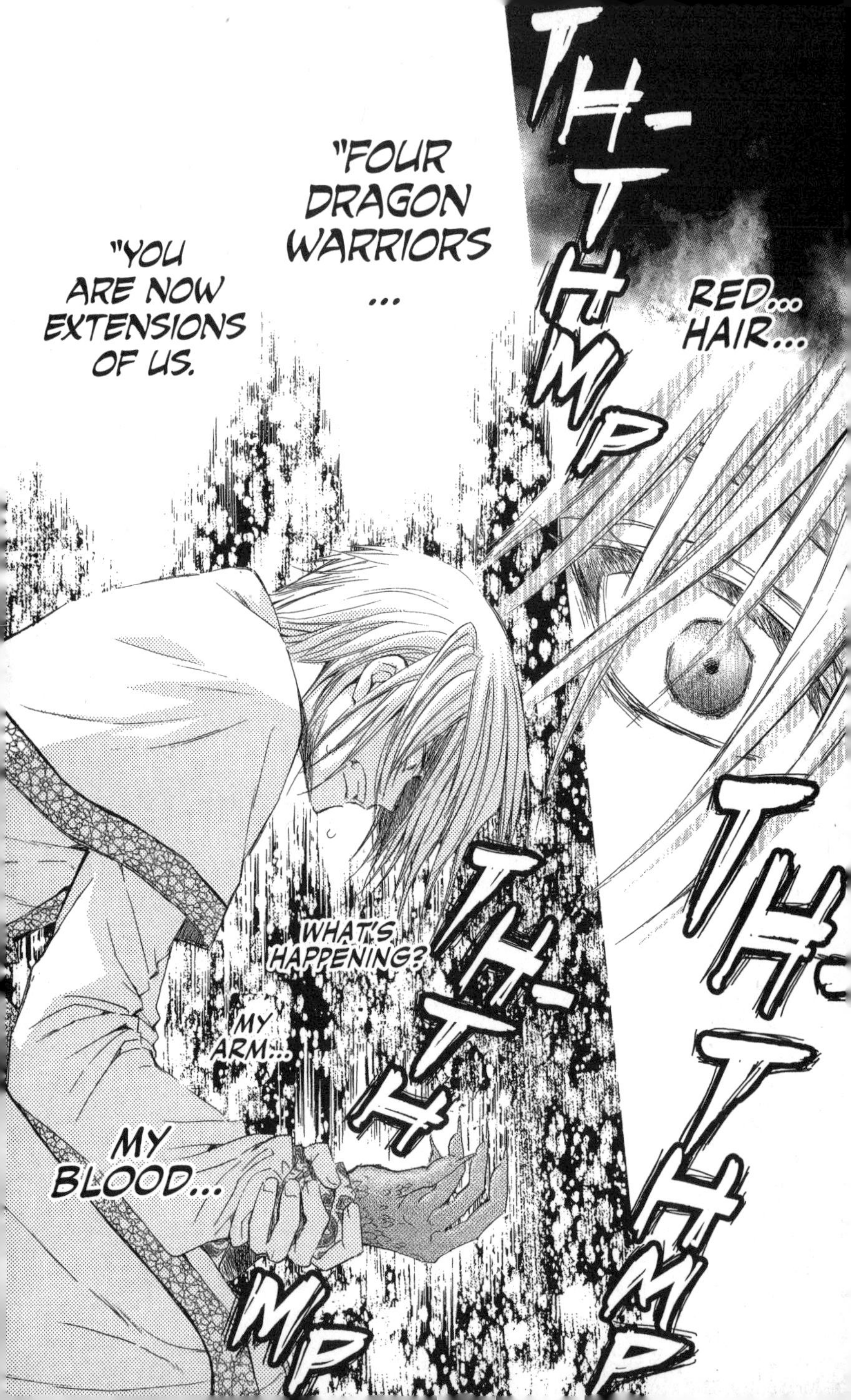
TH-THUMP
RED... HAIR...
"FOUR DRAGON WARRIORS ...
"YOU ARE NOW EXTENSIONS OF US.
TH-THUMP
TH-THUMP
WHAT'S HAPPENING?
MY ARM...
MY BLOOD...

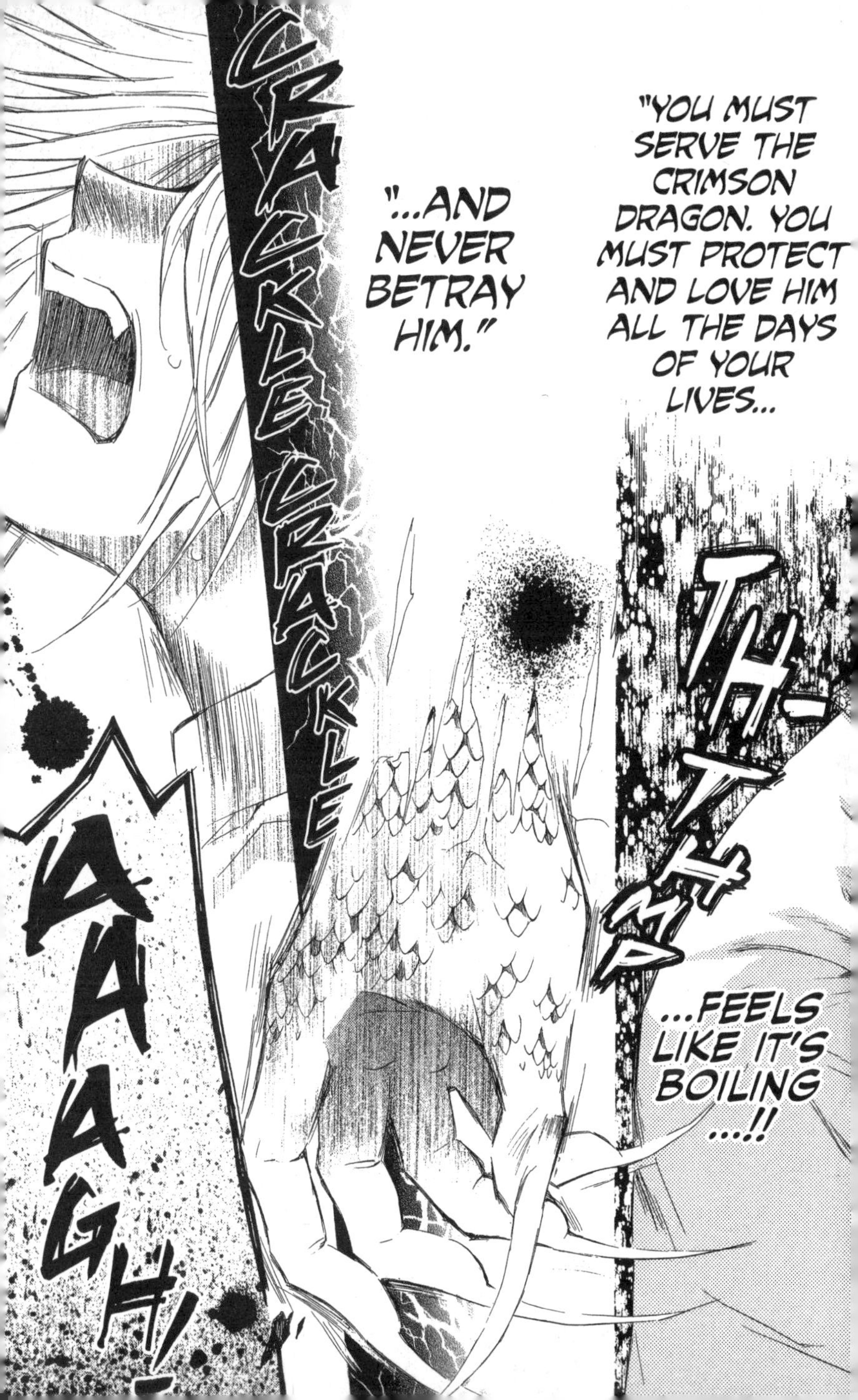
"YOU MUST SERVE THE CRIMSON DRAGON. YOU MUST PROTECT AND LOVE HIM ALL THE DAYS OF YOUR LIVES...
"...AND NEVER BETRAY HIM."
CRACKLE CRACKLE
TH-THMP
...FEELS LIKE IT'S BOILING ...!!
AAAGH!

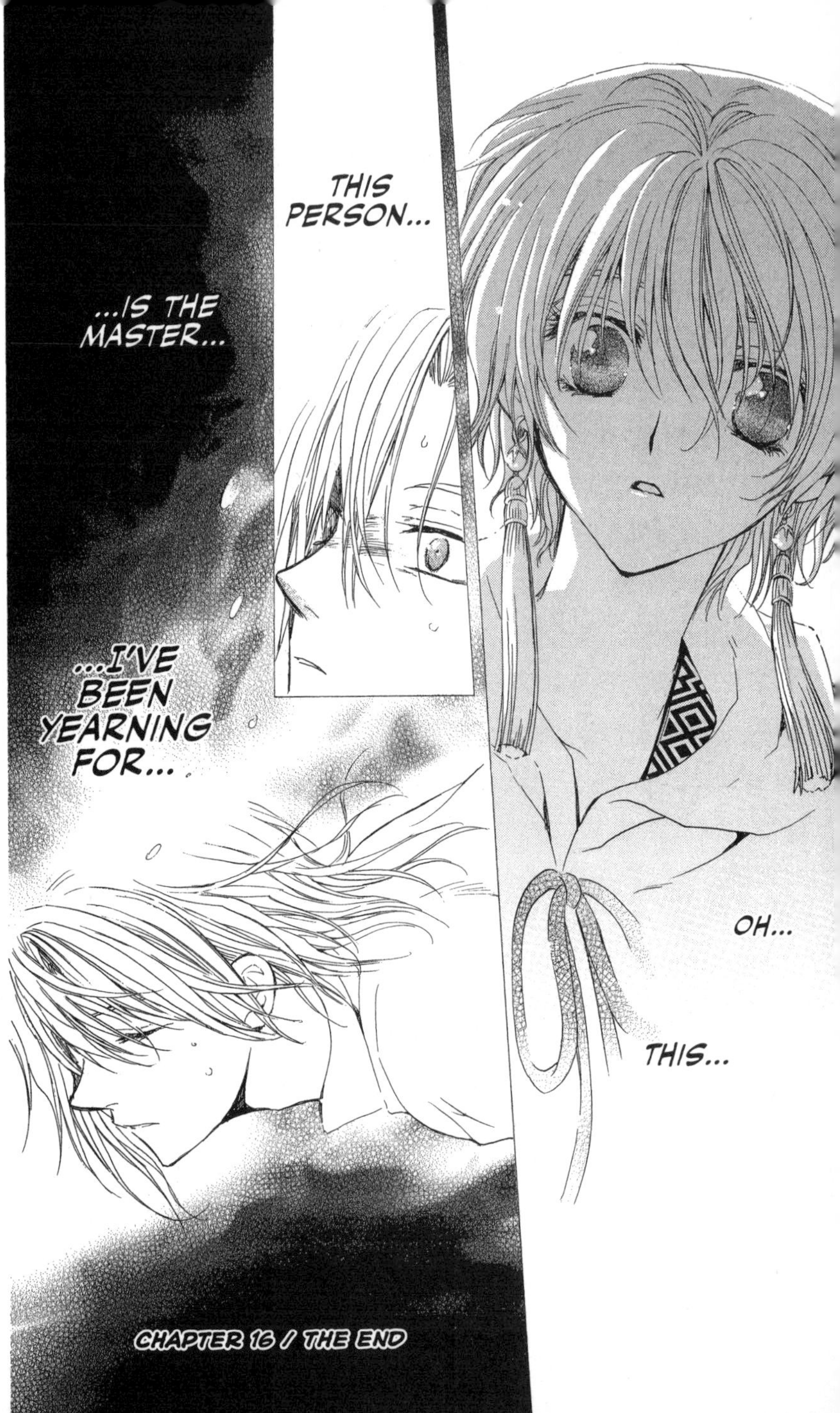
OH...
THIS...
THIS PERSON...
...IS THE MASTER...
...I'VE BEEN YEARNING FOR...
CHAPTER 16 / THE END

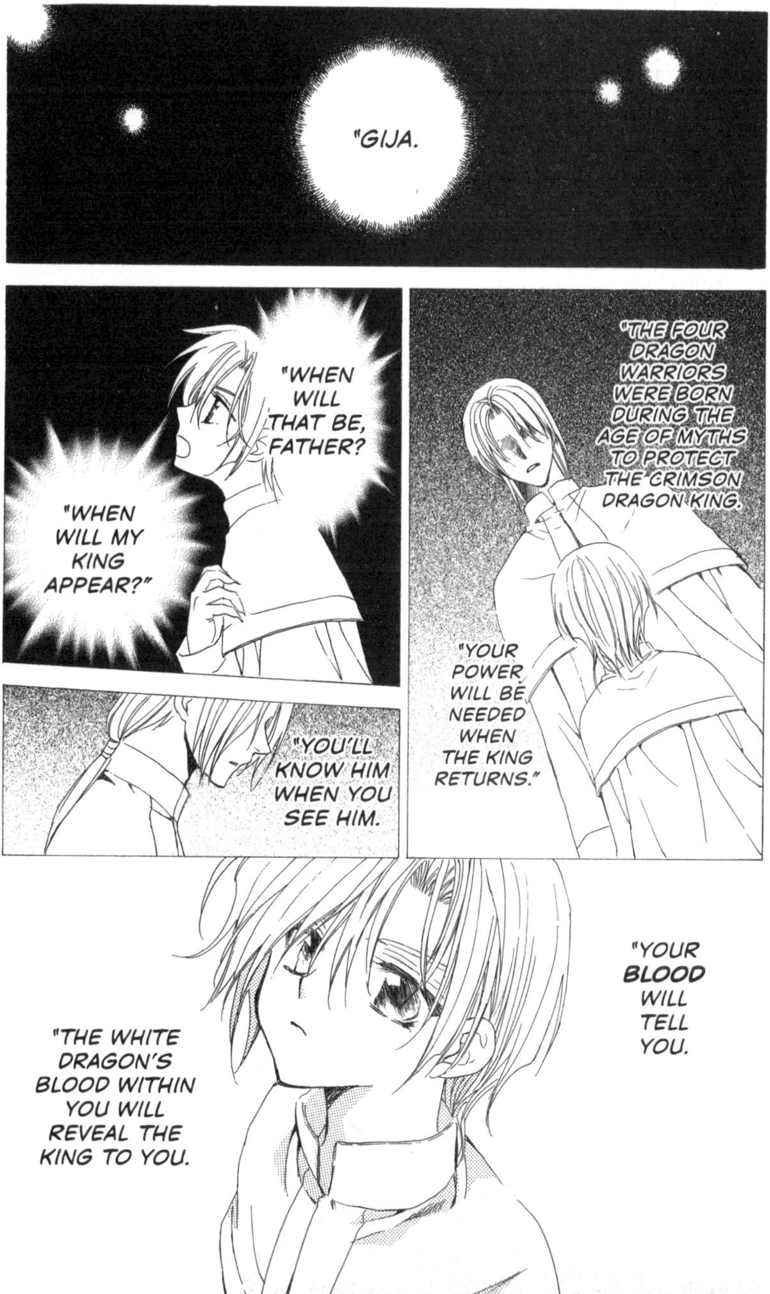
"GIJA.
"THE FOUR DRAGON WARRIORS WERE BORN DURING THE AGE OF MYTHS TO PROTECT THE CRIMSON DRAGON KING.
"YOUR POWER WILL BE NEEDED WHEN THE KING RETURNS."
"WHEN WILL THAT BE, FATHER?
"WHEN WILL MY KING APPEAR?"
"YOU'LL KNOW HIM WHEN YOU SEE HIM.
"YOUR **BLOOD** WILL TELL YOU.
"THE WHITE DRAGON'S BLOOD WITHIN YOU WILL REVEAL THE KING TO YOU.

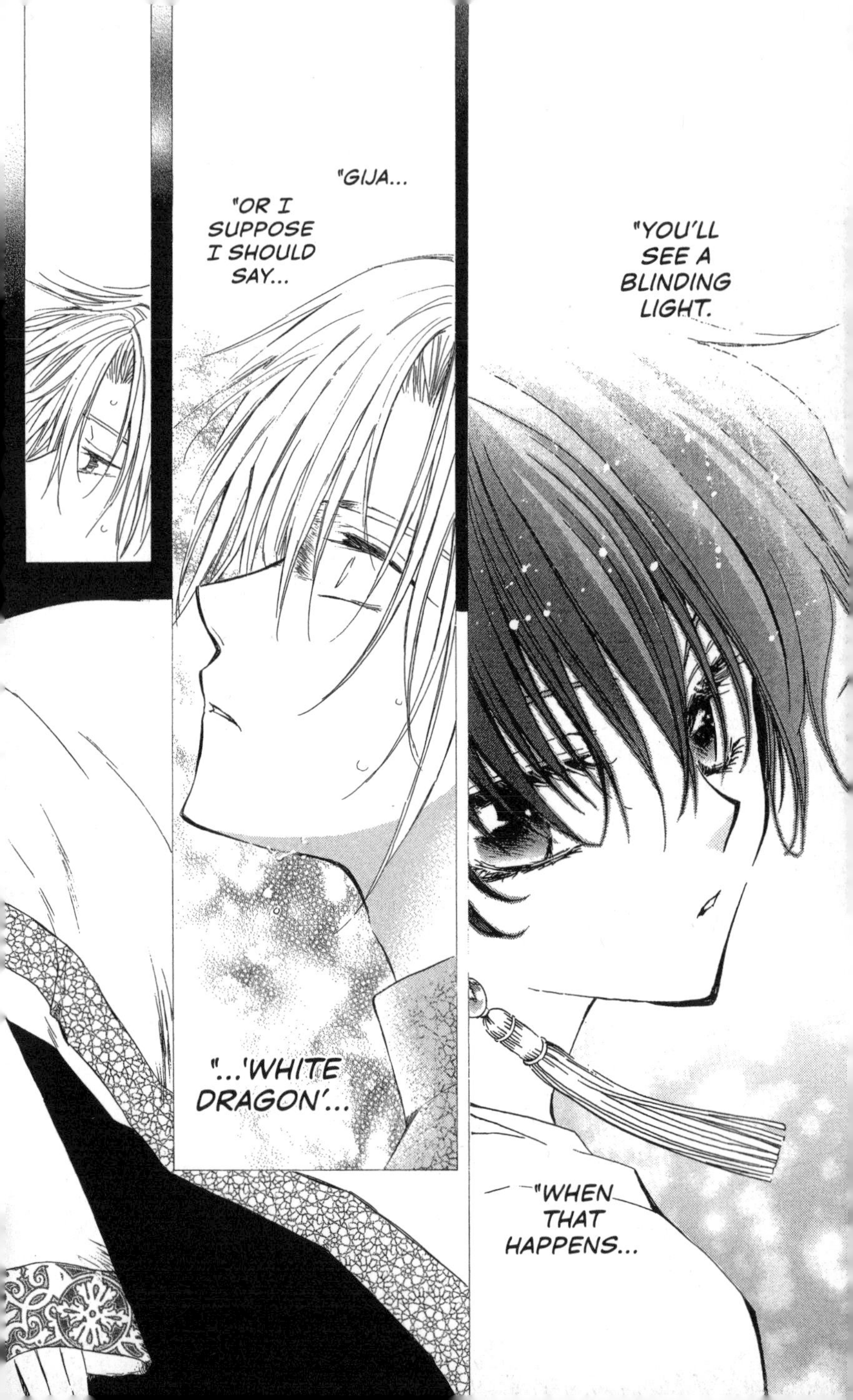
"YOU'LL SEE A BLINDING LIGHT.
"WHEN THAT HAPPENS...
"GIJA...
"OR I SUPPOSE I SHOULD SAY...
"...'WHITE DRAGON'...

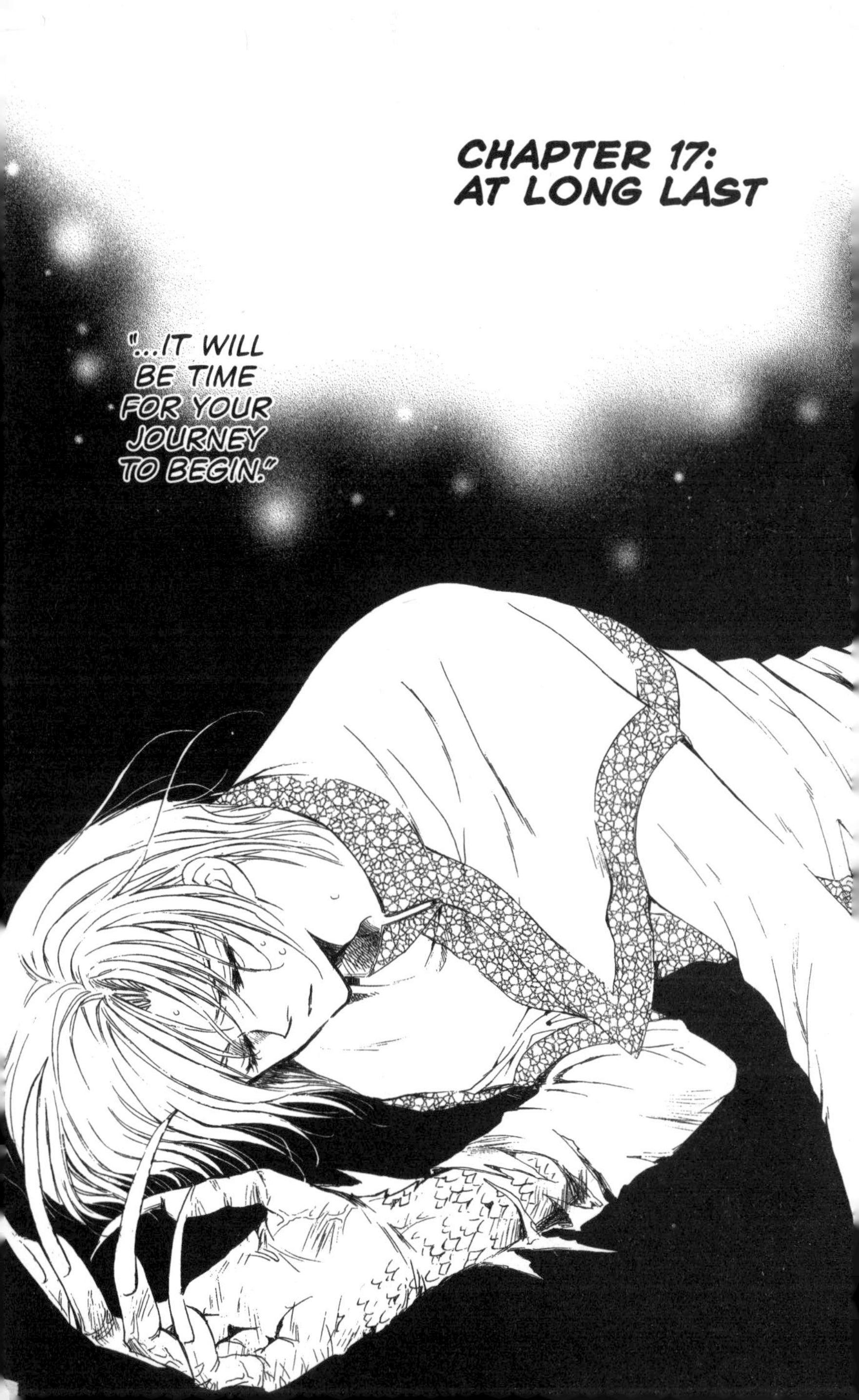
CHAPTER 17:
AT LONG LAST
"...IT WILL BE TIME FOR YOUR JOURNEY TO BEGIN."

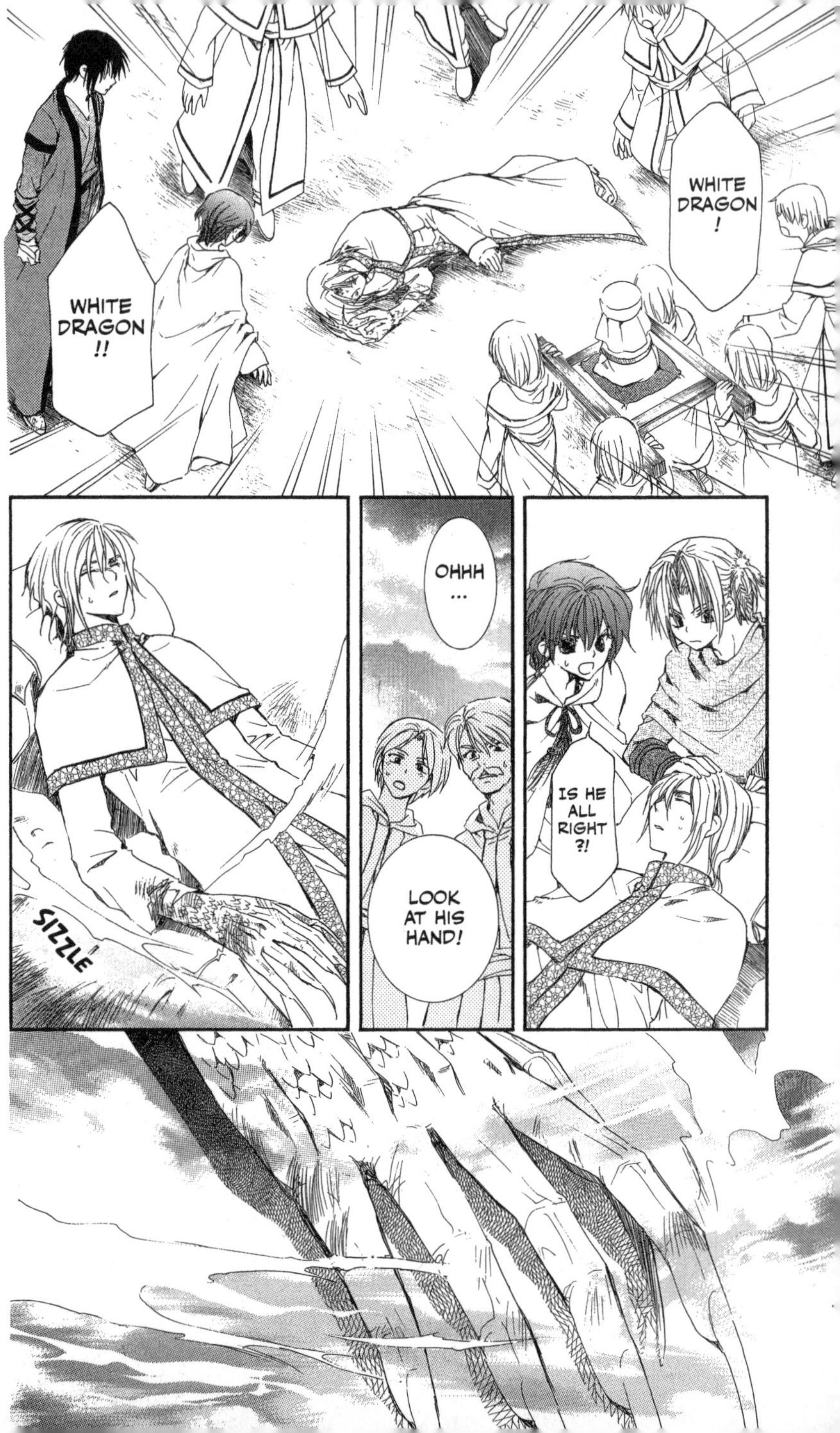
WHITE DRAGON !
WHITE DRAGON !!
IS HE ALL RIGHT ?!
OHHH ...
LOOK AT HIS HAND!
SIZZLE

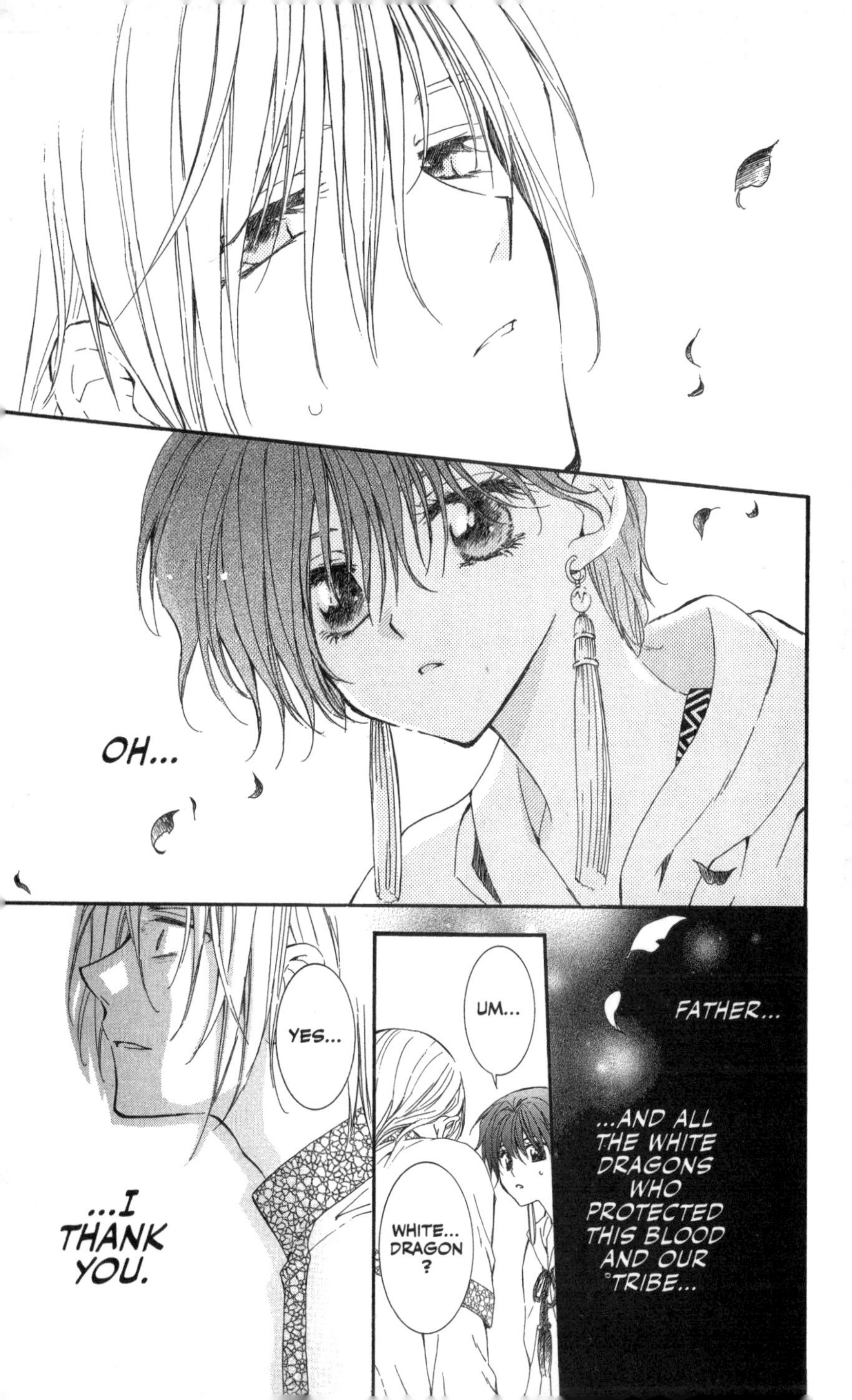
OH...
FATHER...
...AND ALL THE WHITE DRAGONS WHO PROTECTED THIS BLOOD AND OUR TRIBE...
UM...
WHITE... DRAGON?
YES...
...I THANK YOU.

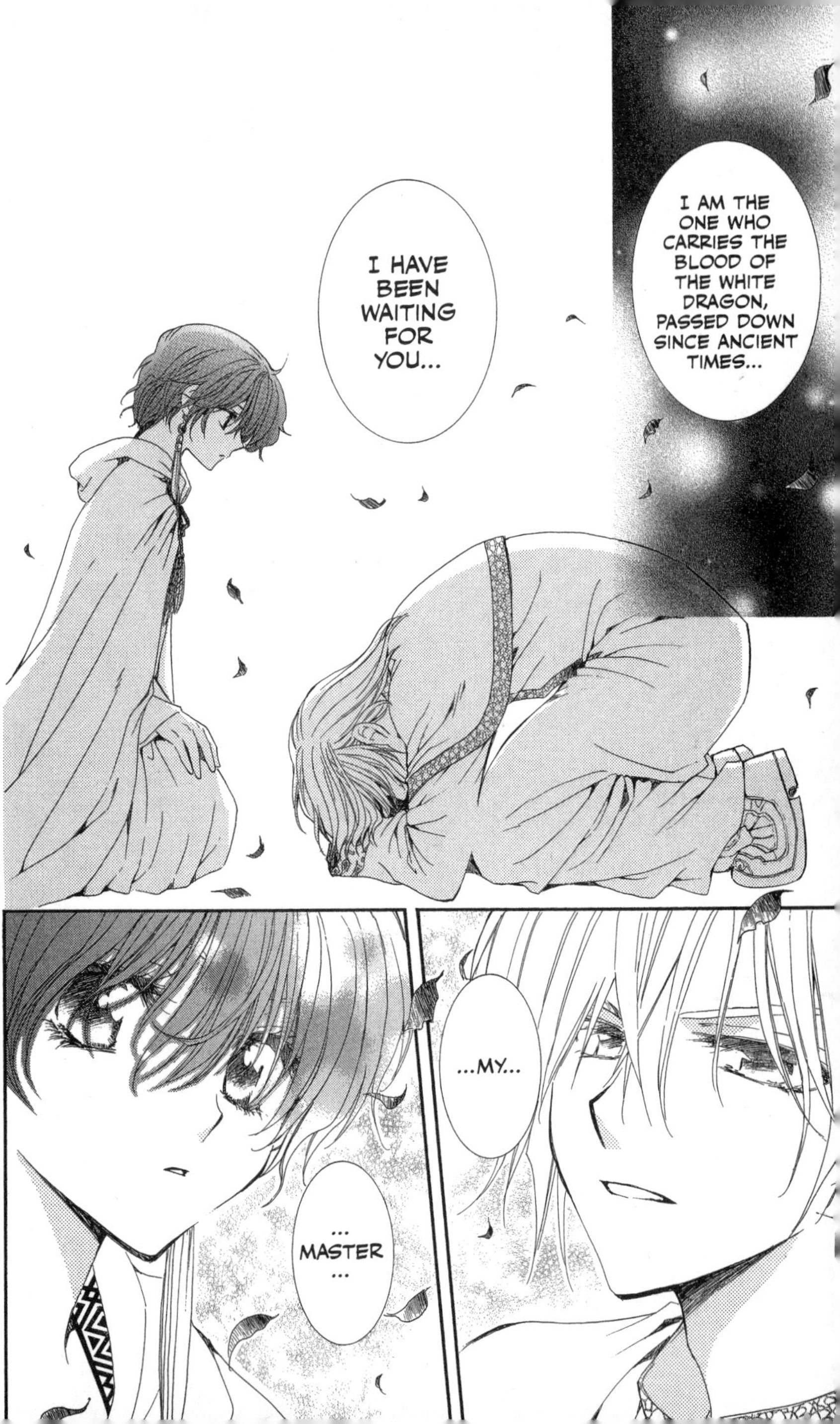
I AM THE ONE WHO CARRIES THE BLOOD OF THE WHITE DRAGON, PASSED DOWN SINCE ANCIENT TIMES...
I HAVE BEEN WAITING FOR YOU...
...MY...
...MASTER...

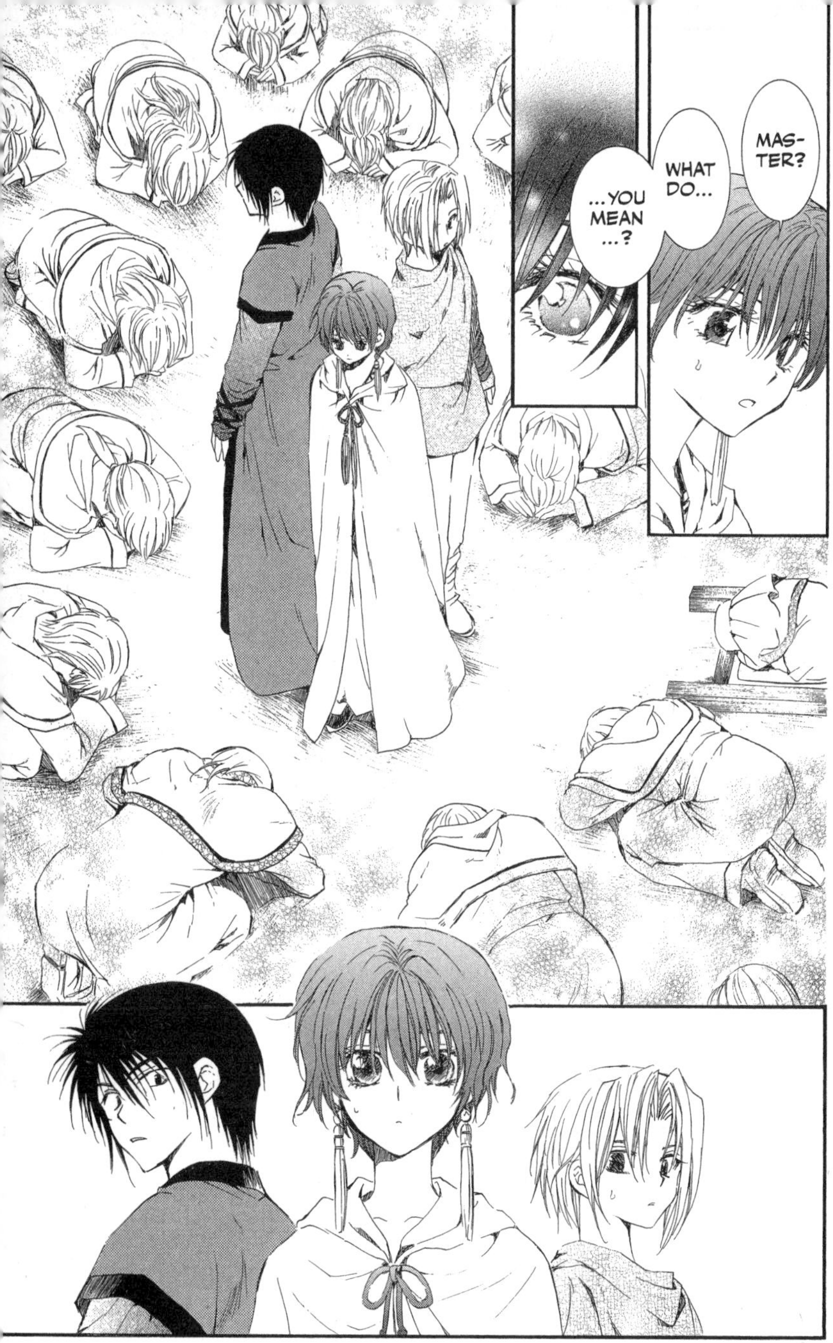
MAS-TER?
WHAT DO...
...YOU MEAN ...?

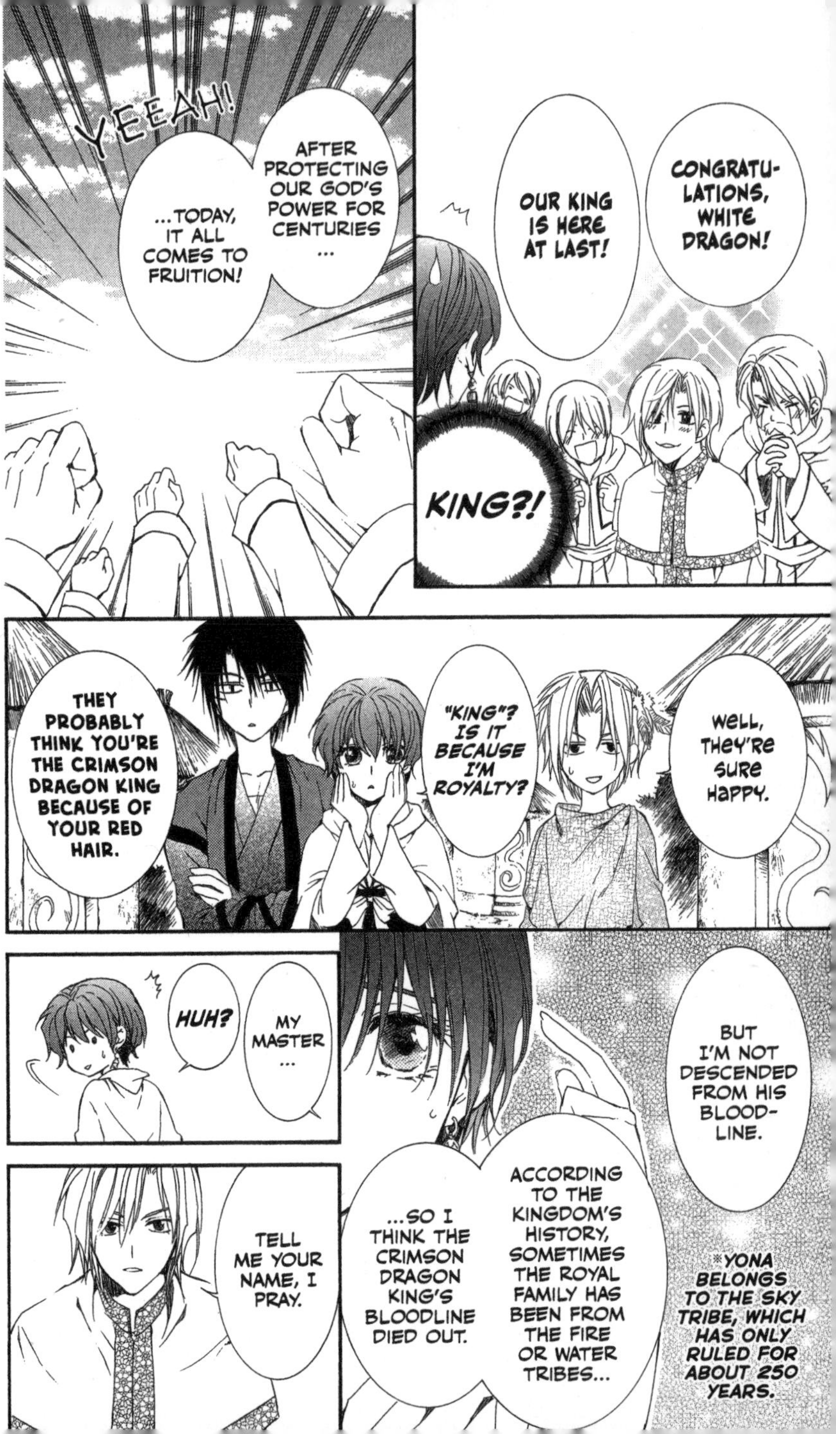
CONGRATU-LATIONS, WHITE DRAGON!
OUR KING IS HERE AT LAST!
KING?!
AFTER PROTECTING OUR GOD'S POWER FOR CENTURIES ...
...TODAY, IT ALL COMES TO FRUITION!
YEEAH!
WELL, THEY'RE SURE HAPPY.
"KING"? IS IT BECAUSE I'M ROYALTY?
THEY PROBABLY THINK YOU'RE THE CRIMSON DRAGON KING BECAUSE OF YOUR RED HAIR.
BUT I'M NOT DESCENDED FROM HIS BLOOD-LINE.
ACCORDING TO THE KINGDOM'S HISTORY, SOMETIMES THE ROYAL FAMILY HAS BEEN FROM THE FIRE OR WATER TRIBES...
...SO I THINK THE CRIMSON DRAGON KING'S BLOODLINE DIED OUT.
※YONA BELONGS TO THE SKY TRIBE, WHICH HAS ONLY RULED FOR ABOUT 250 YEARS.
MY MASTER ...
HUH?
TELL ME YOUR NAME, I PRAY.

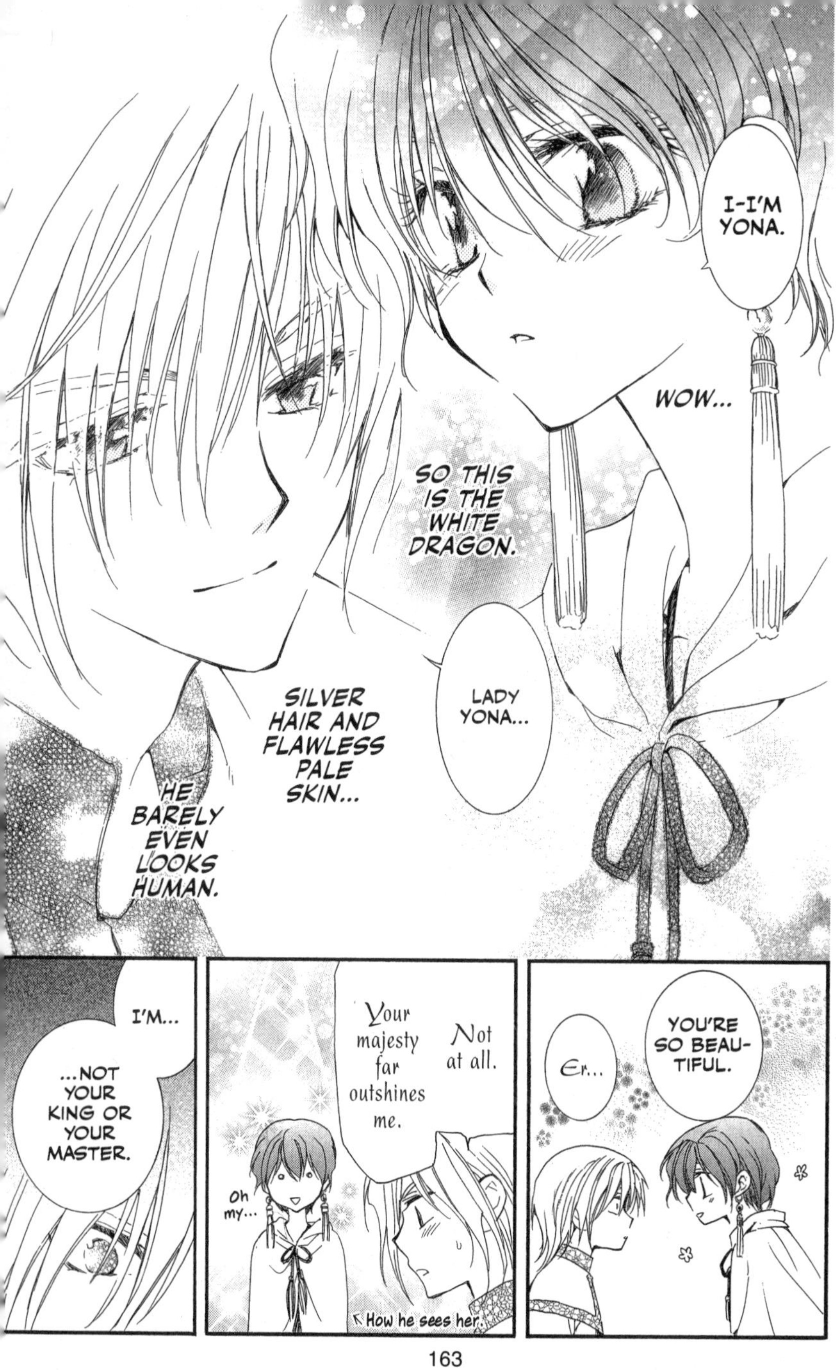
I-I'M YONA.
WOW...
SO THIS IS THE WHITE DRAGON.
LADY YONA...
SILVER HAIR AND FLAWLESS PALE SKIN...
HE BARELY EVEN LOOKS HUMAN.
YOU'RE SO BEAU-TIFUL.
Er...
Not at all.
Your majesty far outshines me.
Oh my...
How he sees her.
I'M...
...NOT YOUR KING OR YOUR MASTER.

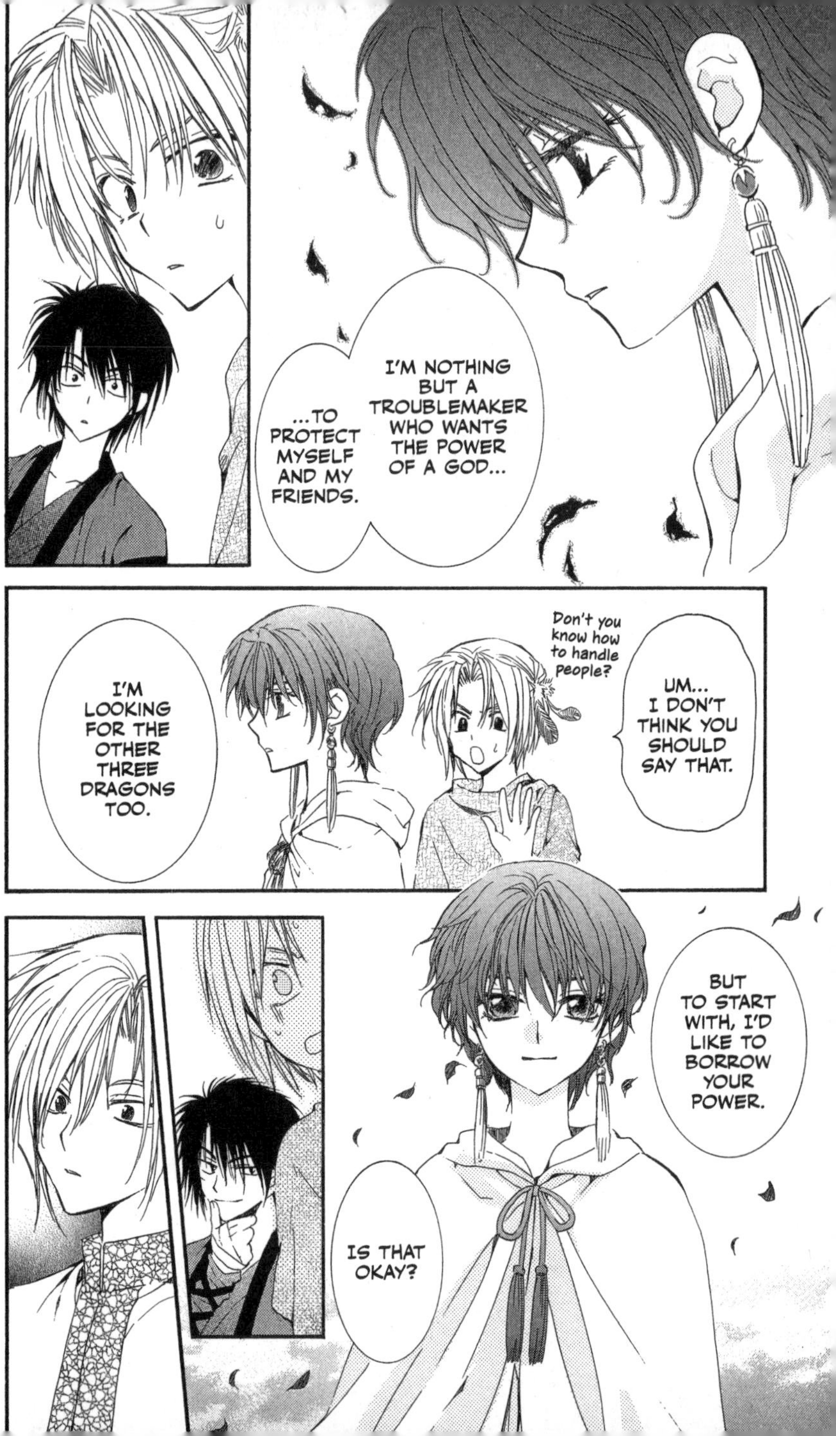
I'M NOTHING BUT A TROUBLEMAKER WHO WANTS THE POWER OF A GOD...
...TO PROTECT MYSELF AND MY FRIENDS.
UM... I DON'T THINK YOU SHOULD SAY THAT.
Don't you know how to handle people?
I'M LOOKING FOR THE OTHER THREE DRAGONS TOO.
BUT TO START WITH, I'D LIKE TO BORROW YOUR POWER.
IS THAT OKAY?

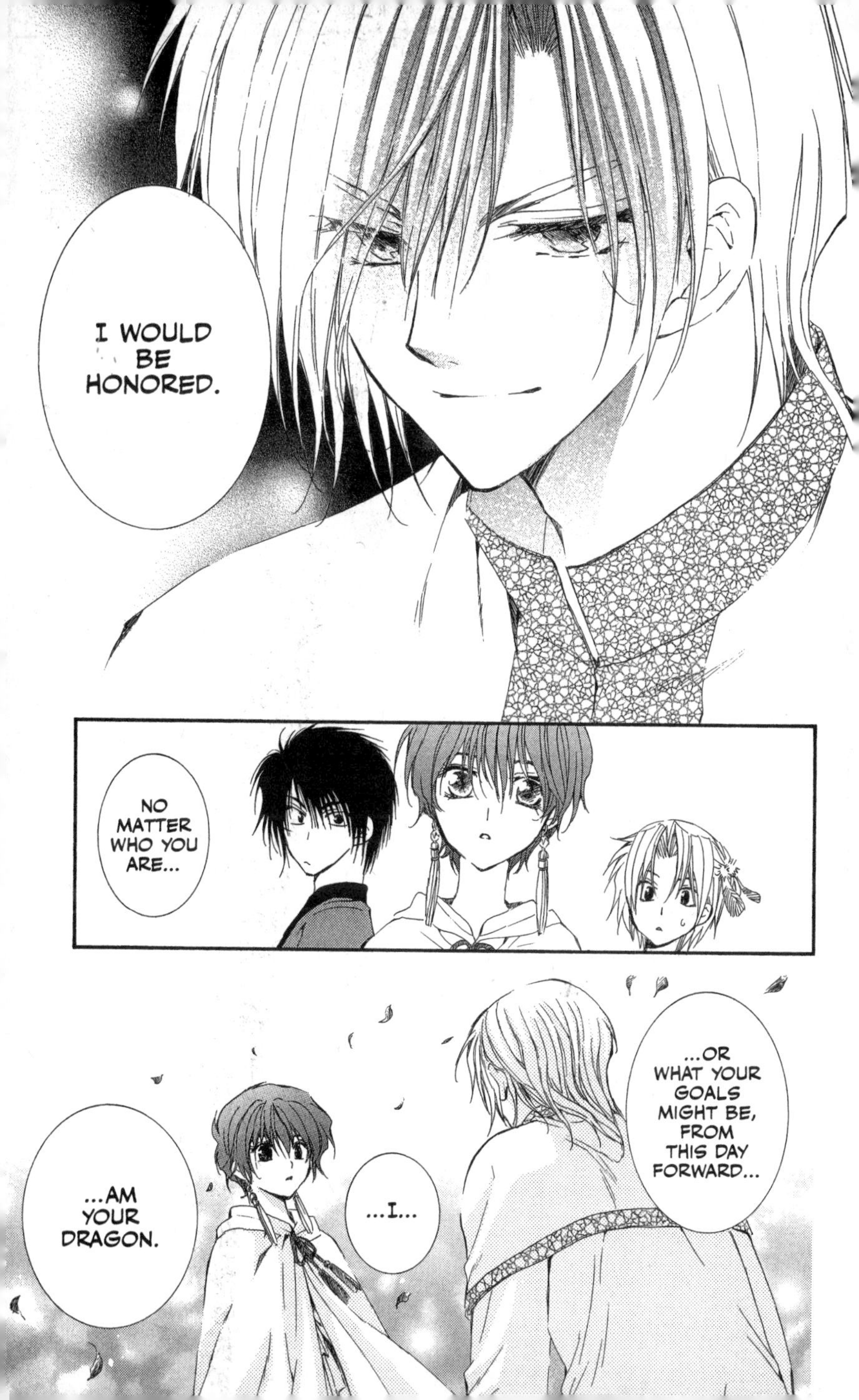
I WOULD BE HONORED.
NO MATTER WHO YOU ARE...
...OR WHAT YOUR GOALS MIGHT BE, FROM THIS DAY FORWARD...
...I...
...AM YOUR DRAGON.

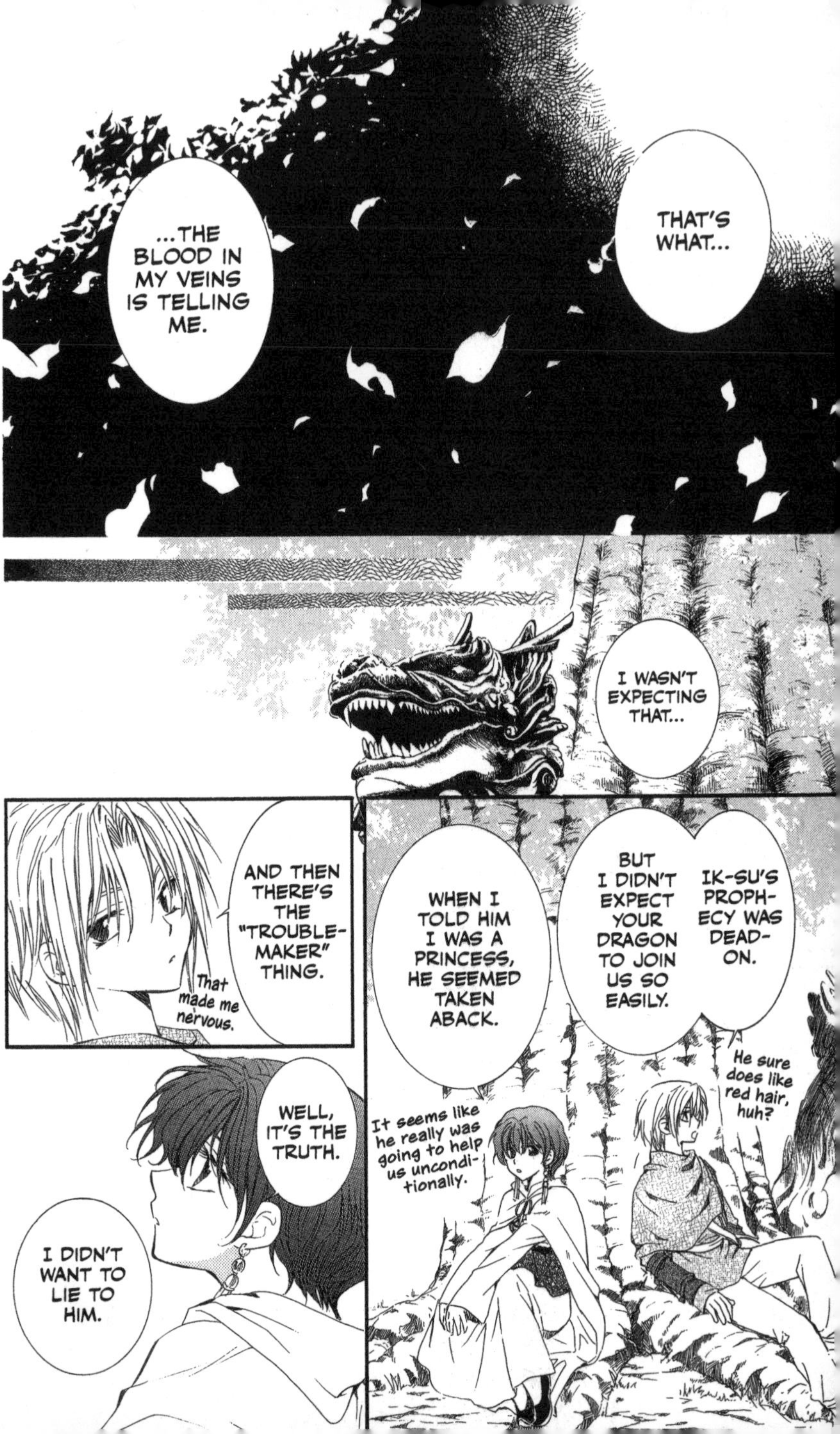
THAT'S WHAT...
...THE BLOOD IN MY VEINS IS TELLING ME.
I WASN'T EXPECTING THAT...
IK-SU'S PROPHECY WAS DEAD-ON.
BUT I DIDN'T EXPECT YOUR DRAGON TO JOIN US SO EASILY.
WHEN I TOLD HIM I WAS A PRINCESS, HE SEEMED TAKEN ABACK.
He sure does like red hair, huh?
It seems like he really was going to help us unconditionally.
AND THEN THERE'S THE "TROUBLEMAKER" THING.
That made me nervous.
WELL, IT'S THE TRUTH.
I DIDN'T WANT TO LIE TO HIM.

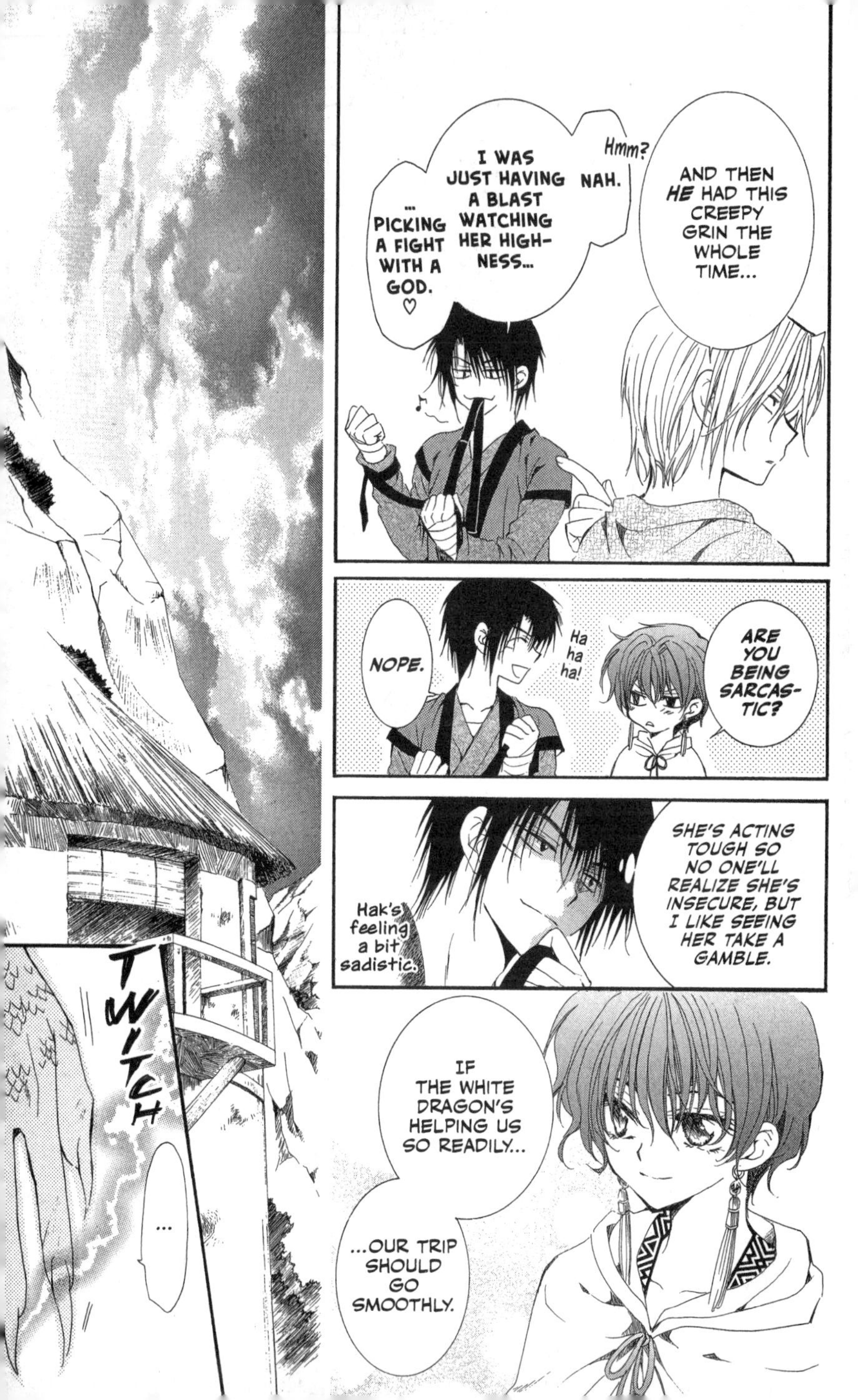
AND THEN HE HAD THIS CREEPY GRIN THE WHOLE TIME...
Hmm?
NAH.
I WAS JUST HAVING A BLAST WATCHING HER HIGHNESS...
...PICKING A FIGHT WITH A GOD. ♡
ARE YOU BEING SARCASTIC?
Ha ha ha!
NOPE.
SHE'S ACTING TOUGH SO NO ONE'LL REALIZE SHE'S INSECURE, BUT I LIKE SEEING HER TAKE A GAMBLE.
Hak's feeling a bit sadistic.
IF THE WHITE DRAGON'S HELPING US SO READILY...
...OUR TRIP SHOULD GO SMOOTHLY.
TWITCH
...

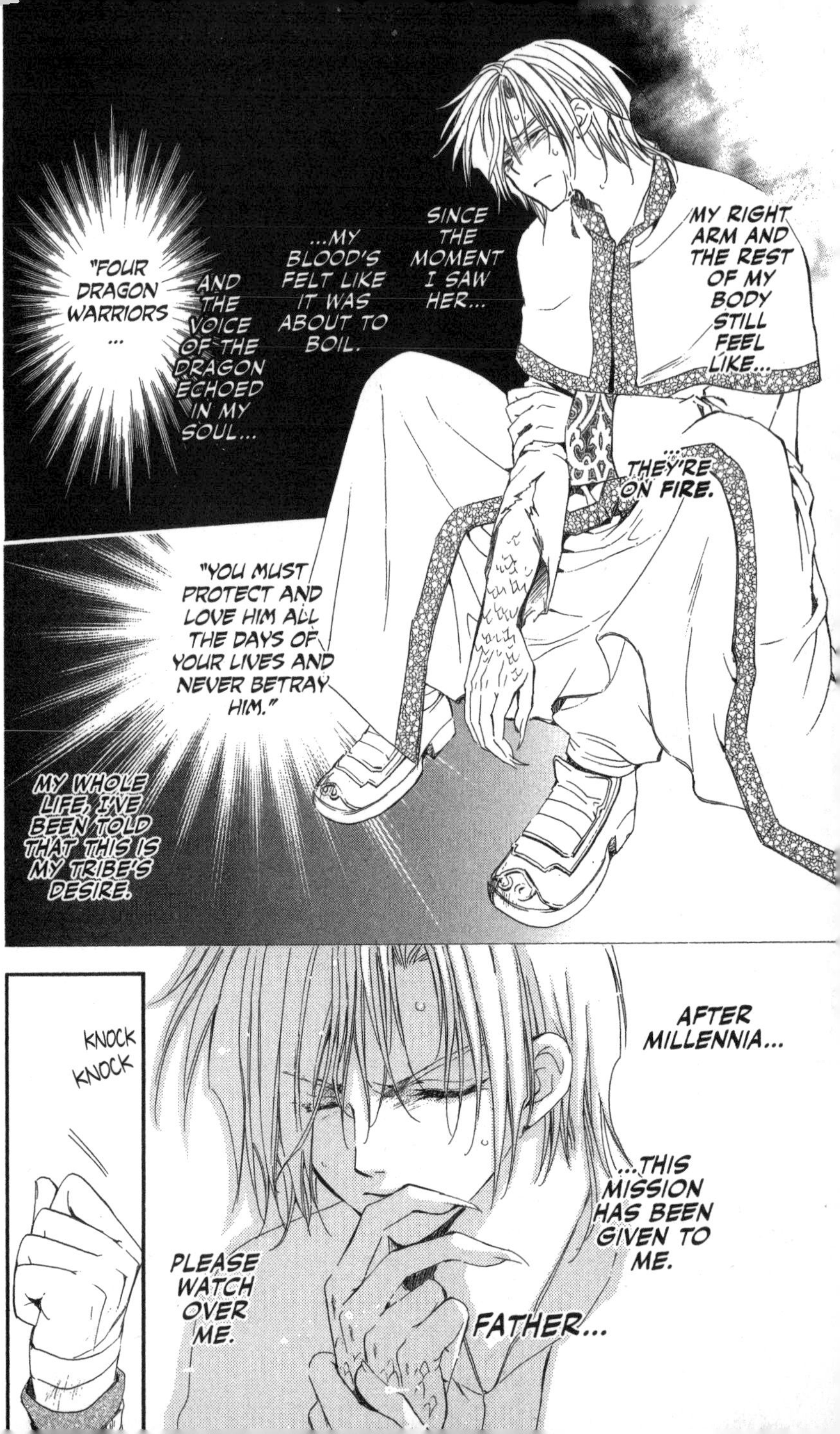
MY RIGHT ARM AND THE REST OF MY BODY STILL FEEL LIKE...
...THEY'RE ON FIRE.
SINCE THE MOMENT I SAW HER...
...MY BLOOD'S FELT LIKE IT WAS ABOUT TO BOIL.
AND THE VOICE OF THE DRAGON ECHOED IN MY SOUL...
"FOUR DRAGON WARRIORS...
"YOU MUST PROTECT AND LOVE HIM ALL THE DAYS OF YOUR LIVES AND NEVER BETRAY HIM."
MY WHOLE LIFE, I'VE BEEN TOLD THAT THIS IS MY TRIBE'S DESIRE.
AFTER MILLENNIA...
...THIS MISSION HAS BEEN GIVEN TO ME.
FATHER...
PLEASE WATCH OVER ME.
KNOCK KNOCK

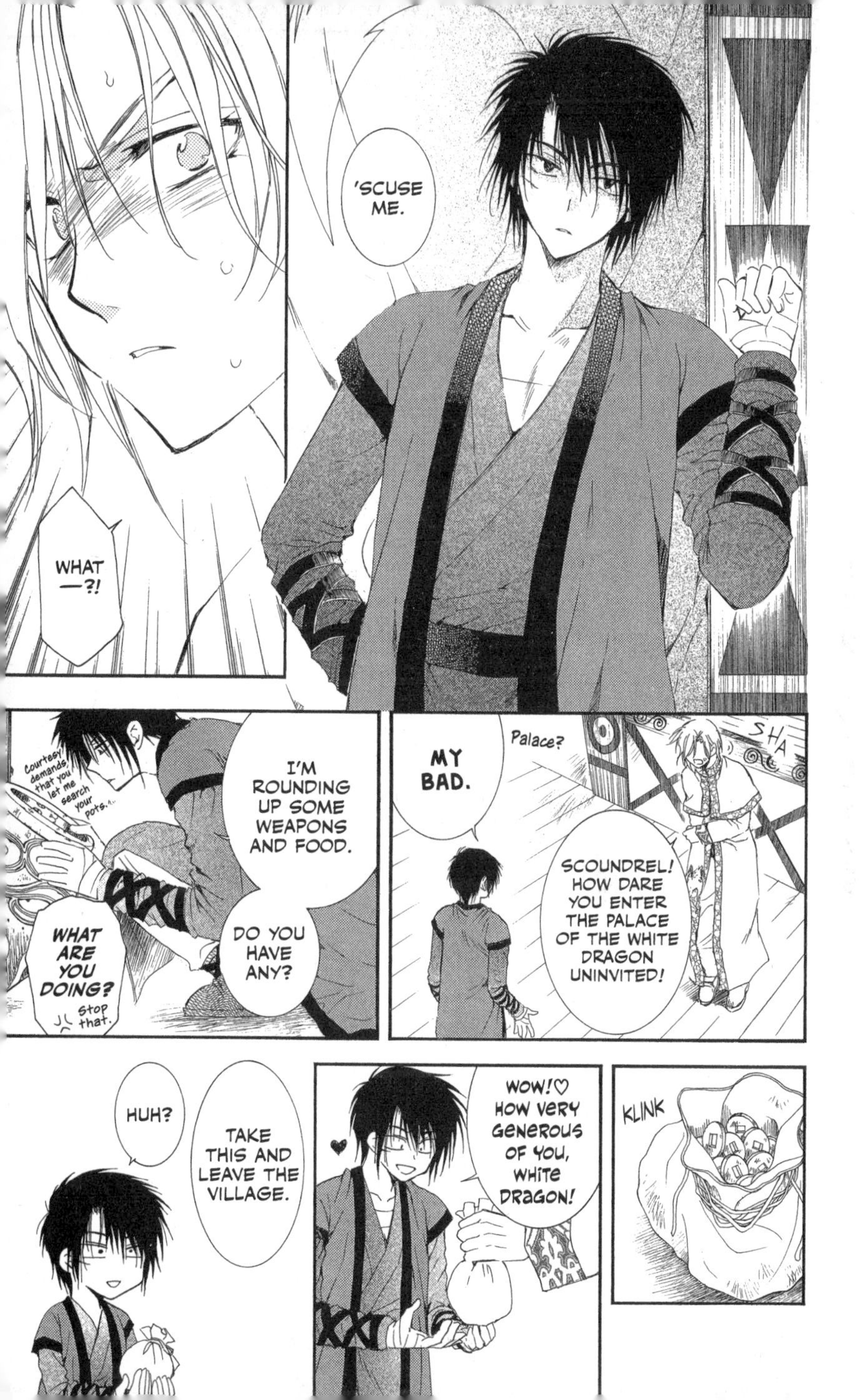
'SCUSE ME.
WHAT—?!
SHA
SCOUNDREL! HOW DARE YOU ENTER THE PALACE OF THE WHITE DRAGON UNINVITED!
Palace?
MY BAD.
I'M ROUNDING UP SOME WEAPONS AND FOOD.
DO YOU HAVE ANY?
Courtesy demands that you let me search your pots...
WHAT ARE YOU DOING?
Stop that.
KLINK
WOW!♡ HOW VERY GENEROUS OF YOU, WHITE DRAGON!
TAKE THIS AND LEAVE THE VILLAGE.
HUH?

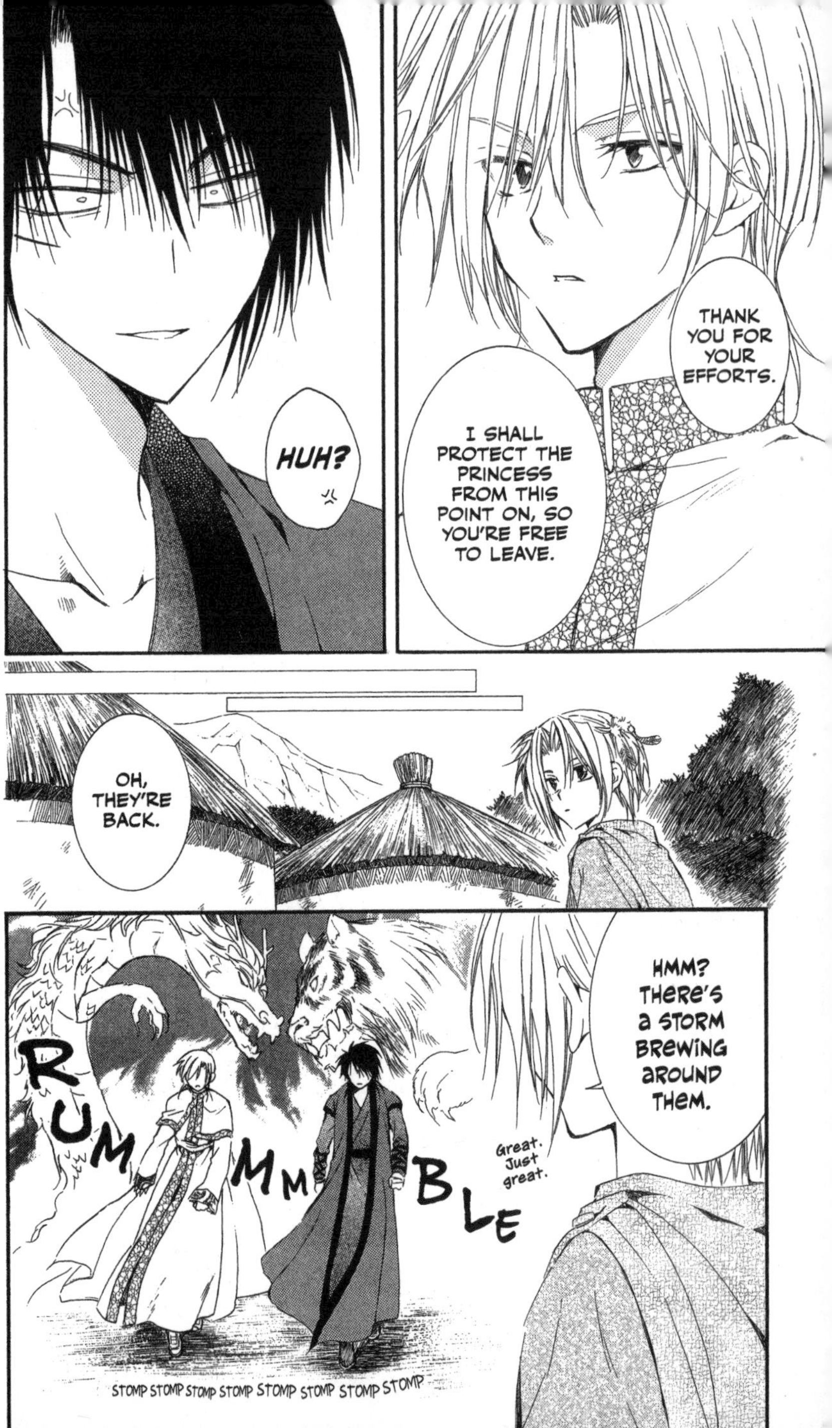
THANK YOU FOR YOUR EFFORTS.
I SHALL PROTECT THE PRINCESS FROM THIS POINT ON, SO YOU'RE FREE TO LEAVE.
HUH?
OH, THEY'RE BACK.
HMM? THERE'S A STORM BREWING AROUND THEM.
Great. Just great.
RUMMMBLE
STOMP STOMP STOMP STOMP STOMP STOMP STOMP STOMP

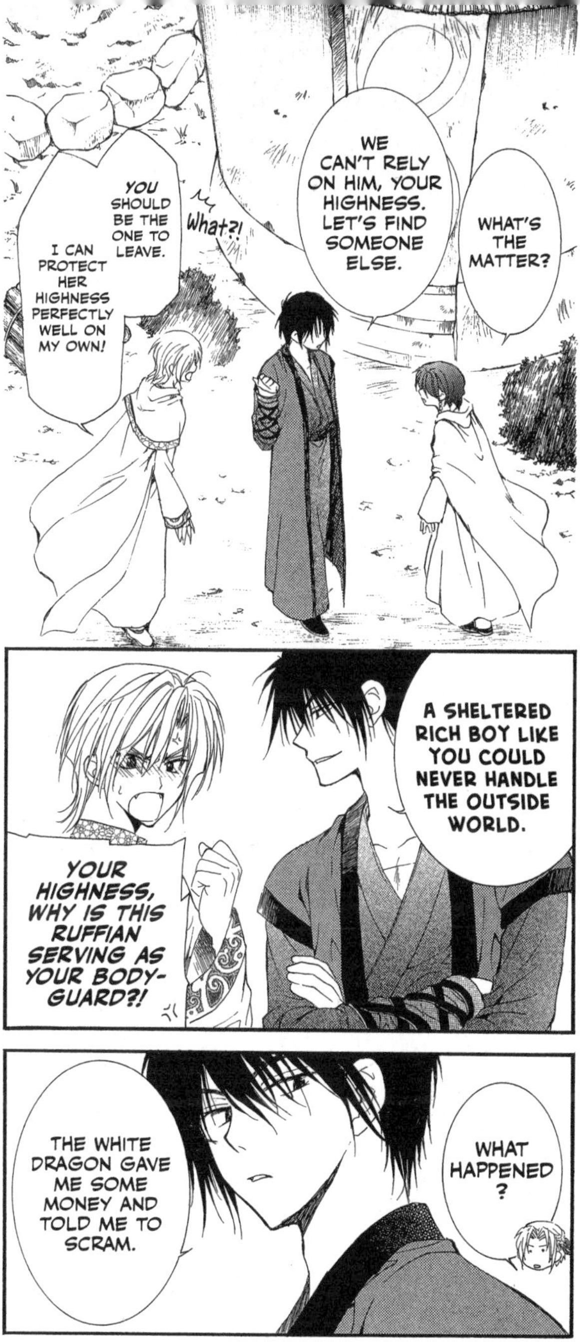
WHAT'S THE MATTER?
WE CAN'T RELY ON HIM, YOUR HIGHNESS. LET'S FIND SOMEONE ELSE.
What?!
YOU SHOULD BE THE ONE TO LEAVE.
I CAN PROTECT HER HIGHNESS PERFECTLY WELL ON MY OWN!
A SHELTERED RICH BOY LIKE YOU COULD NEVER HANDLE THE OUTSIDE WORLD.
YOUR HIGHNESS, WHY IS THIS RUFFIAN SERVING AS YOUR BODY-GUARD?!
WHAT HAPPENED?
THE WHITE DRAGON GAVE ME SOME MONEY AND TOLD ME TO SCRAM.

My assistants help me so much. Thank you for your incredible backgrounds and all the fun we have together. They're all wonderful people who ink very tidily and are excited about the world of Yona!

Special thanks to:
My assistants
- Mikorun
- Kyoko
- Rurunga
- Ryo Sakura
- My little sister

My Editor:
- Yamashita

The *Hana to Yume* editorial office
Naato
Everyone who helped me create and sell this manga.
The family and friends who've supported me.
And my readers!♥

Thank you for making me want to continue drawing this manga! I hope to see you in volume 4!

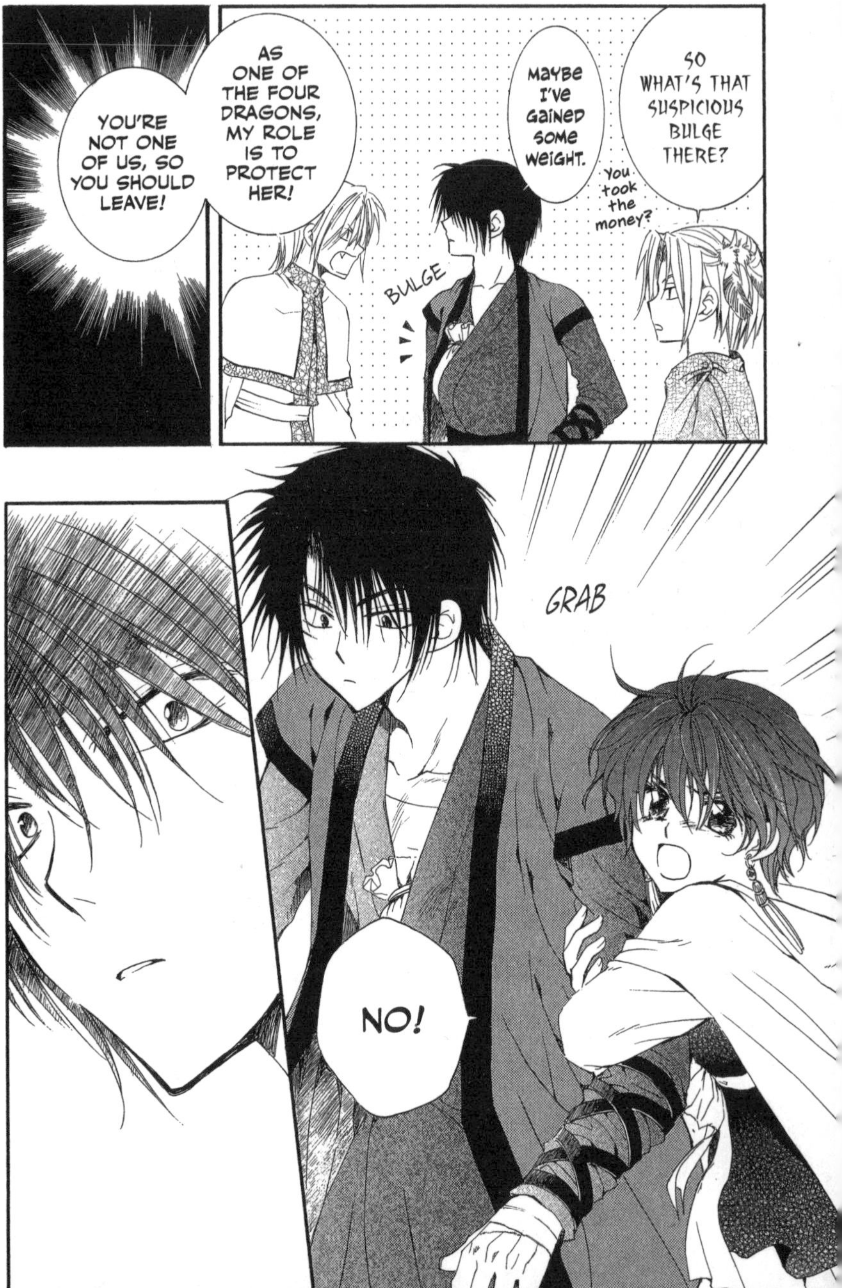
SO WHAT'S THAT SUSPICIOUS BULGE THERE?
You took the money?
Maybe I've gained some weight.
BULGE
AS ONE OF THE FOUR DRAGONS, MY ROLE IS TO PROTECT HER!
YOU'RE NOT ONE OF US, SO YOU SHOULD LEAVE!
GRAB
NO!

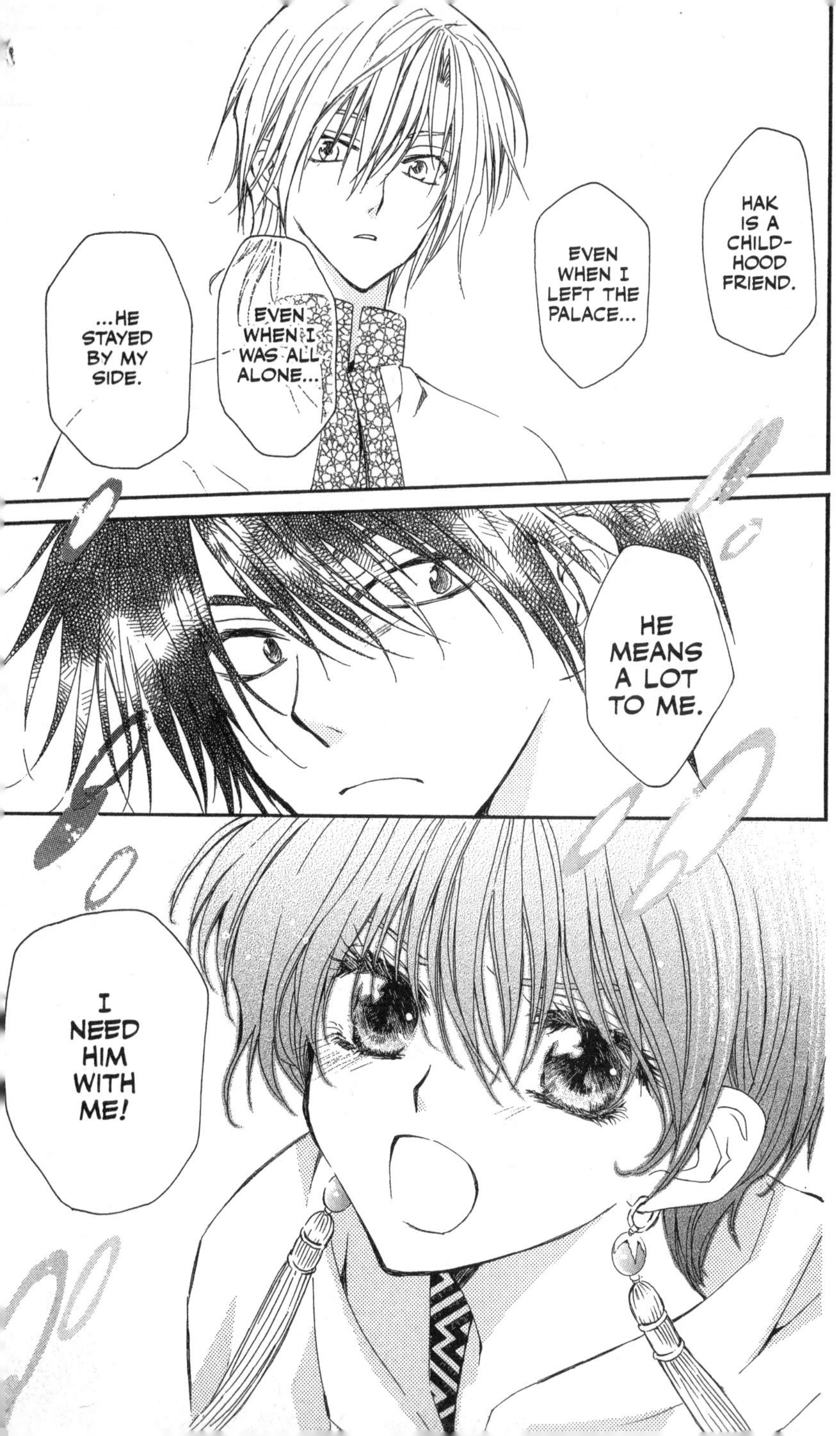
HAK IS A CHILD-HOOD FRIEND.
EVEN WHEN I LEFT THE PALACE...
EVEN WHEN I WAS ALL ALONE...
...HE STAYED BY MY SIDE.
HE MEANS A LOT TO ME.
I NEED HIM WITH ME!

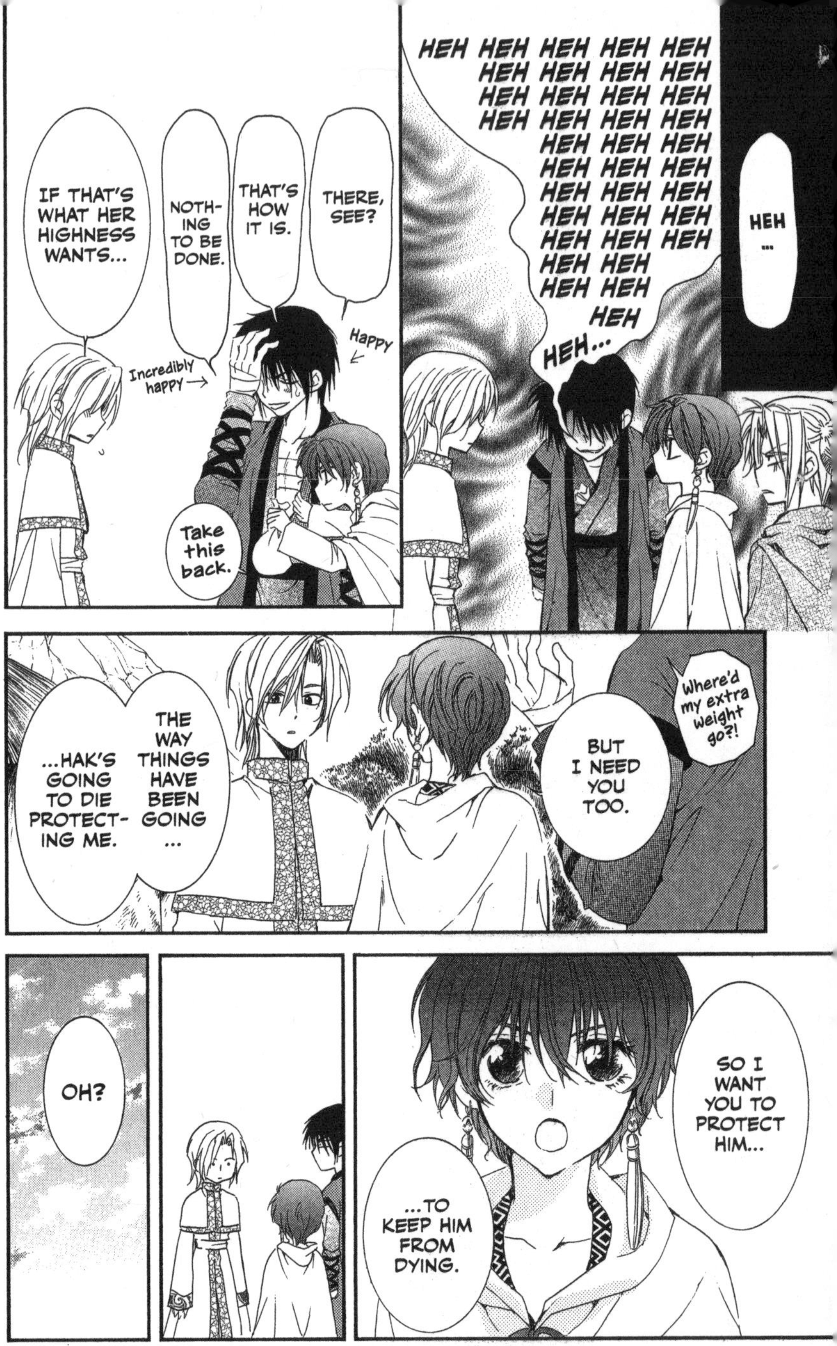
HEH ...
HEH HEH HEH HEH HEH
HEH HEH HEH HEH
HEH HEH HEH HEH
HEH HEH HEH HEH
HEH HEH HEH
HEH HEH HEH
HEH HEH HEH
HEH HEH HEH
HEH HEH HEH
HEH HEH
HEH HEH
HEH
HEH...
THERE, SEE?
Happy
THAT'S HOW IT IS.
NOTH-ING TO BE DONE.
Incredibly happy
IF THAT'S WHAT HER HIGHNESS WANTS...
Take this back.
Where'd my extra weight go?!
BUT I NEED YOU TOO.
THE WAY THINGS HAVE BEEN GOING...
...HAK'S GOING TO DIE PROTECT-ING ME.
SO I WANT YOU TO PROTECT HIM...
...TO KEEP HIM FROM DYING.
OH?

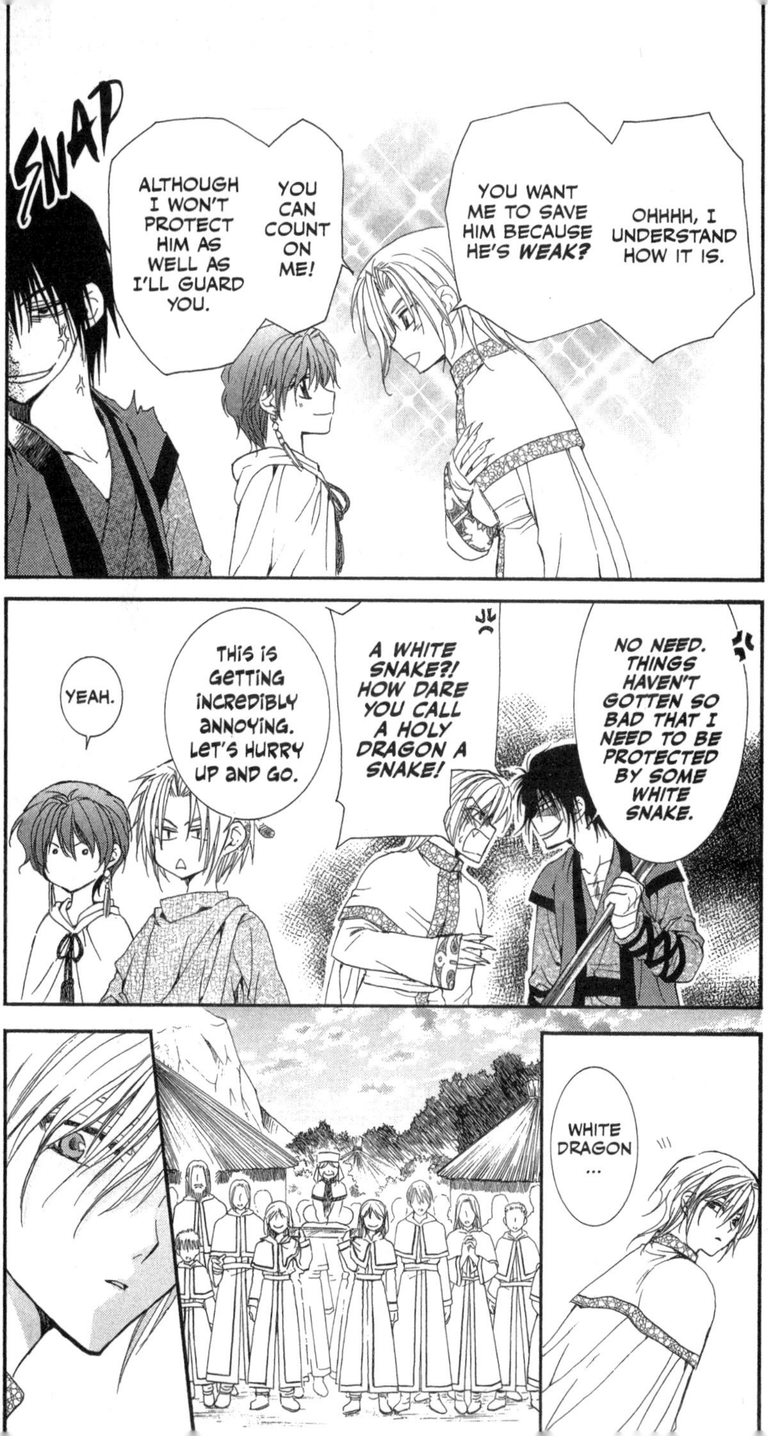
OHHHH, I UNDERSTAND HOW IT IS.
YOU WANT ME TO SAVE HIM BECAUSE HE'S *WEAK?*
YOU CAN COUNT ON ME!
ALTHOUGH I WON'T PROTECT HIM AS WELL AS I'LL GUARD YOU.
SNAP
NO NEED. THINGS HAVEN'T GOTTEN SO BAD THAT I NEED TO BE PROTECTED BY SOME WHITE SNAKE.
A WHITE SNAKE?! HOW DARE YOU CALL A HOLY DRAGON A SNAKE!
THIS IS GETTING INCREDIBLY ANNOYING. LET'S HURRY UP AND GO.
YEAH.
WHITE DRAGON...

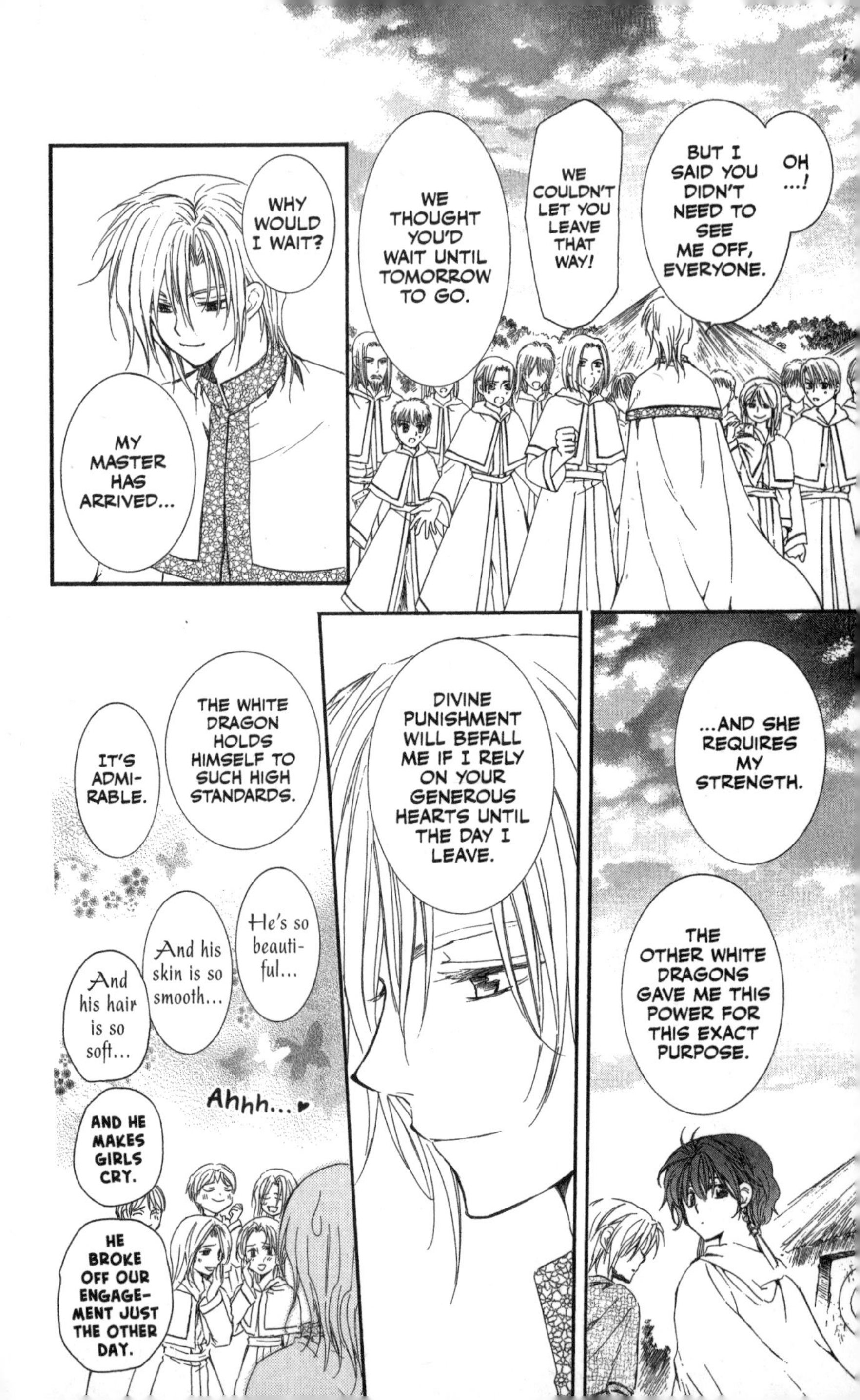
OH ...!
BUT I SAID YOU DIDN'T NEED TO SEE ME OFF, EVERYONE.
WE COULDN'T LET YOU LEAVE THAT WAY!
WE THOUGHT YOU'D WAIT UNTIL TOMORROW TO GO.
WHY WOULD I WAIT?
MY MASTER HAS ARRIVED...
...AND SHE REQUIRES MY STRENGTH.
THE OTHER WHITE DRAGONS GAVE ME THIS POWER FOR THIS EXACT PURPOSE.
DIVINE PUNISHMENT WILL BEFALL ME IF I RELY ON YOUR GENEROUS HEARTS UNTIL THE DAY I LEAVE.
THE WHITE DRAGON HOLDS HIMSELF TO SUCH HIGH STANDARDS.
IT'S ADMIRABLE.
He's so beautiful...
And his skin is so smooth...
And his hair is so soft...
Ahhh...
AND HE MAKES GIRLS CRY.
HE BROKE OFF OUR ENGAGEMENT JUST THE OTHER DAY.

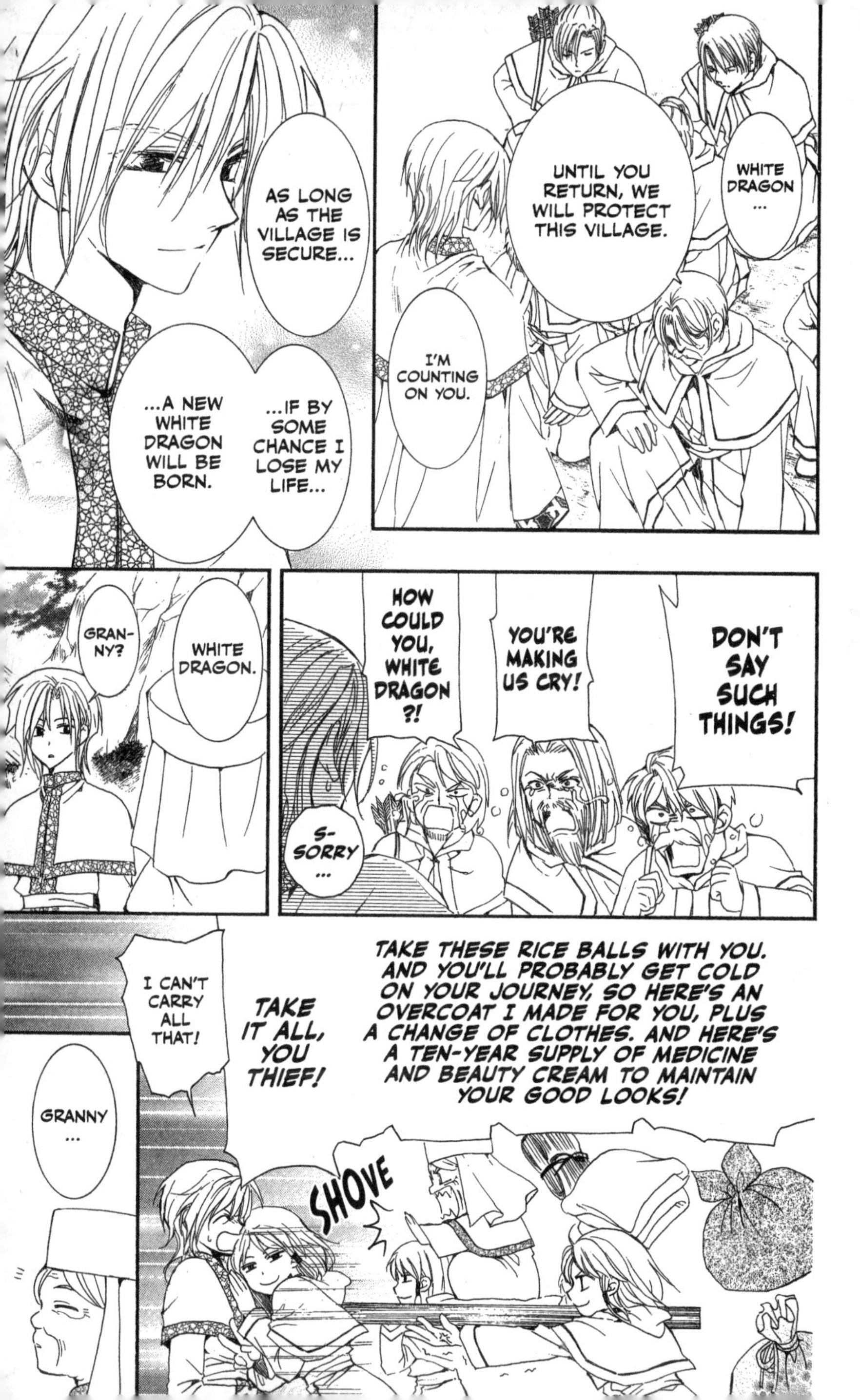
WHITE DRAGON...
UNTIL YOU RETURN, WE WILL PROTECT THIS VILLAGE.
I'M COUNTING ON YOU.
AS LONG AS THE VILLAGE IS SECURE...
...IF BY SOME CHANCE I LOSE MY LIFE...
...A NEW WHITE DRAGON WILL BE BORN.
DON'T SAY SUCH THINGS!
YOU'RE MAKING US CRY!
HOW COULD YOU, WHITE DRAGON?!
S-SORRY...
WHITE DRAGON.
GRAN-NY?
TAKE THESE RICE BALLS WITH YOU. AND YOU'LL PROBABLY GET COLD ON YOUR JOURNEY, SO HERE'S AN OVERCOAT I MADE FOR YOU, PLUS A CHANGE OF CLOTHES. AND HERE'S A TEN-YEAR SUPPLY OF MEDICINE AND BEAUTY CREAM TO MAINTAIN YOUR GOOD LOOKS!
TAKE IT ALL, YOU THIEF!
I CAN'T CARRY ALL THAT!
SHOVE
GRANNY...

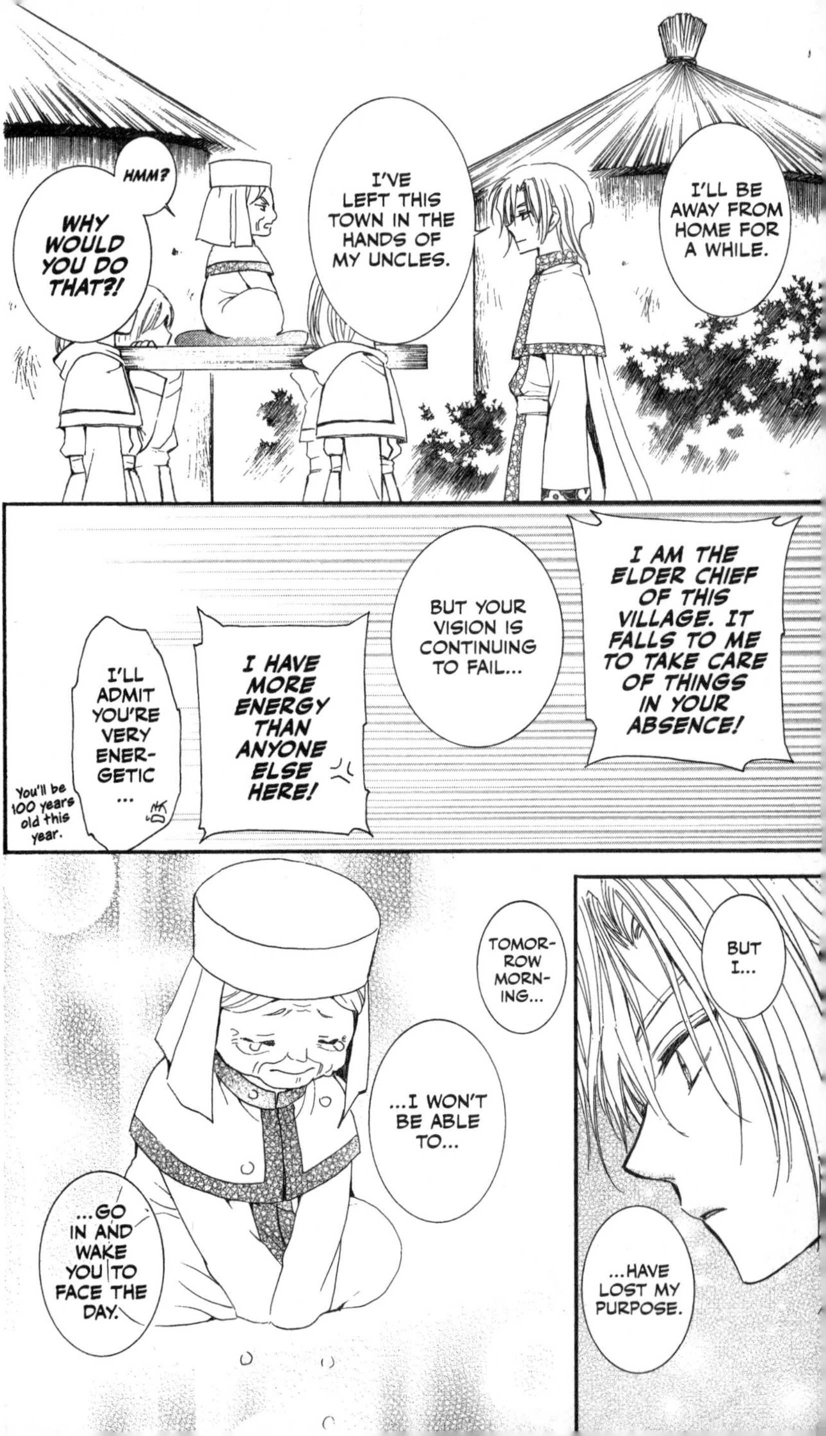
I'LL BE AWAY FROM HOME FOR A WHILE.
I'VE LEFT THIS TOWN IN THE HANDS OF MY UNCLES.
HMM?
WHY WOULD YOU DO THAT?!
I AM THE ELDER CHIEF OF THIS VILLAGE. IT FALLS TO ME TO TAKE CARE OF THINGS IN YOUR ABSENCE!
BUT YOUR VISION IS CONTINUING TO FAIL...
I HAVE MORE ENERGY THAN ANYONE ELSE HERE!
I'LL ADMIT YOU'RE VERY ENER-GETIC...
You'll be 100 years old this year.
BUT I...
...HAVE LOST MY PURPOSE.
TOMOR-ROW MORN-ING...
...I WON'T BE ABLE TO...
...GO IN AND WAKE YOU TO FACE THE DAY.

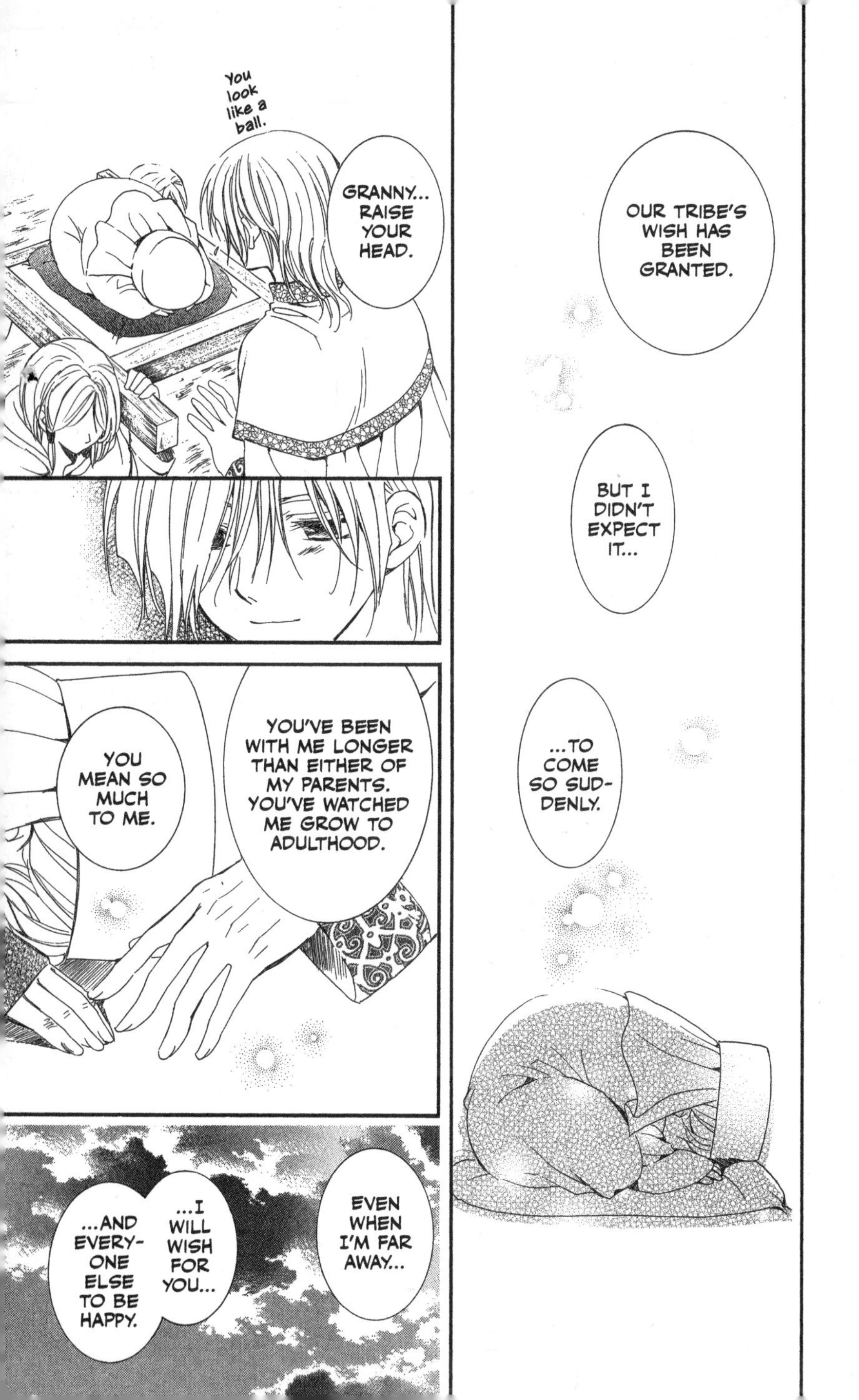

OUR TRIBE'S WISH HAS BEEN GRANTED.
BUT I DIDN'T EXPECT IT...
...TO COME SO SUD-DENLY.
GRANNY... RAISE YOUR HEAD.
You look like a ball.
YOU'VE BEEN WITH ME LONGER THAN EITHER OF MY PARENTS. YOU'VE WATCHED ME GROW TO ADULTHOOD.
YOU MEAN SO MUCH TO ME.
EVEN WHEN I'M FAR AWAY...
...I WILL WISH FOR YOU...
...AND EVERY-ONE ELSE TO BE HAPPY.

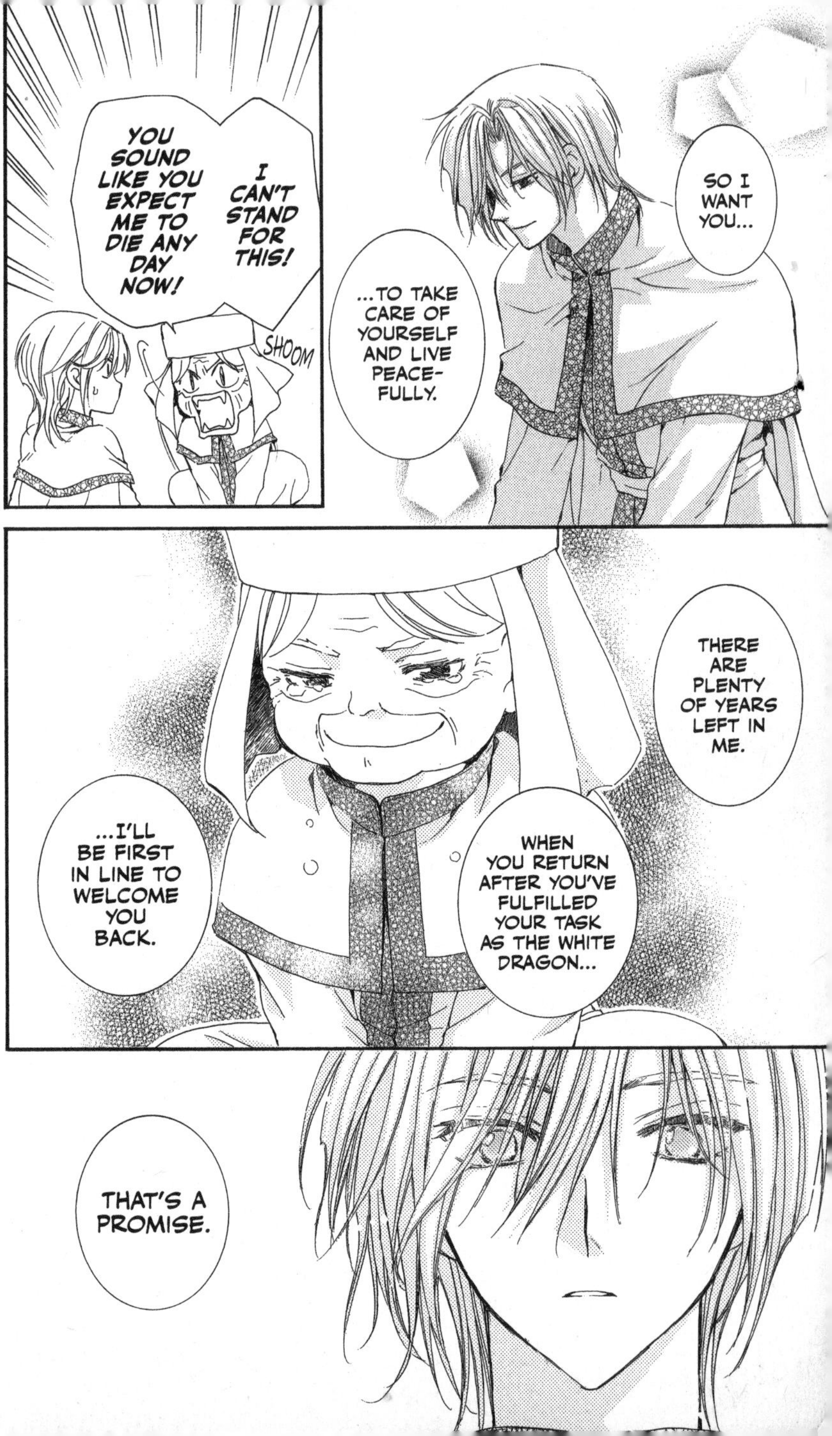
SO I WANT YOU...
...TO TAKE CARE OF YOURSELF AND LIVE PEACE-FULLY.
I CAN'T STAND FOR THIS!
YOU SOUND LIKE YOU EXPECT ME TO DIE ANY DAY NOW!
SHOOM
THERE ARE PLENTY OF YEARS LEFT IN ME.
WHEN YOU RETURN AFTER YOU'VE FULFILLED YOUR TASK AS THE WHITE DRAGON...
...I'LL BE FIRST IN LINE TO WELCOME YOU BACK.
THAT'S A PROMISE.

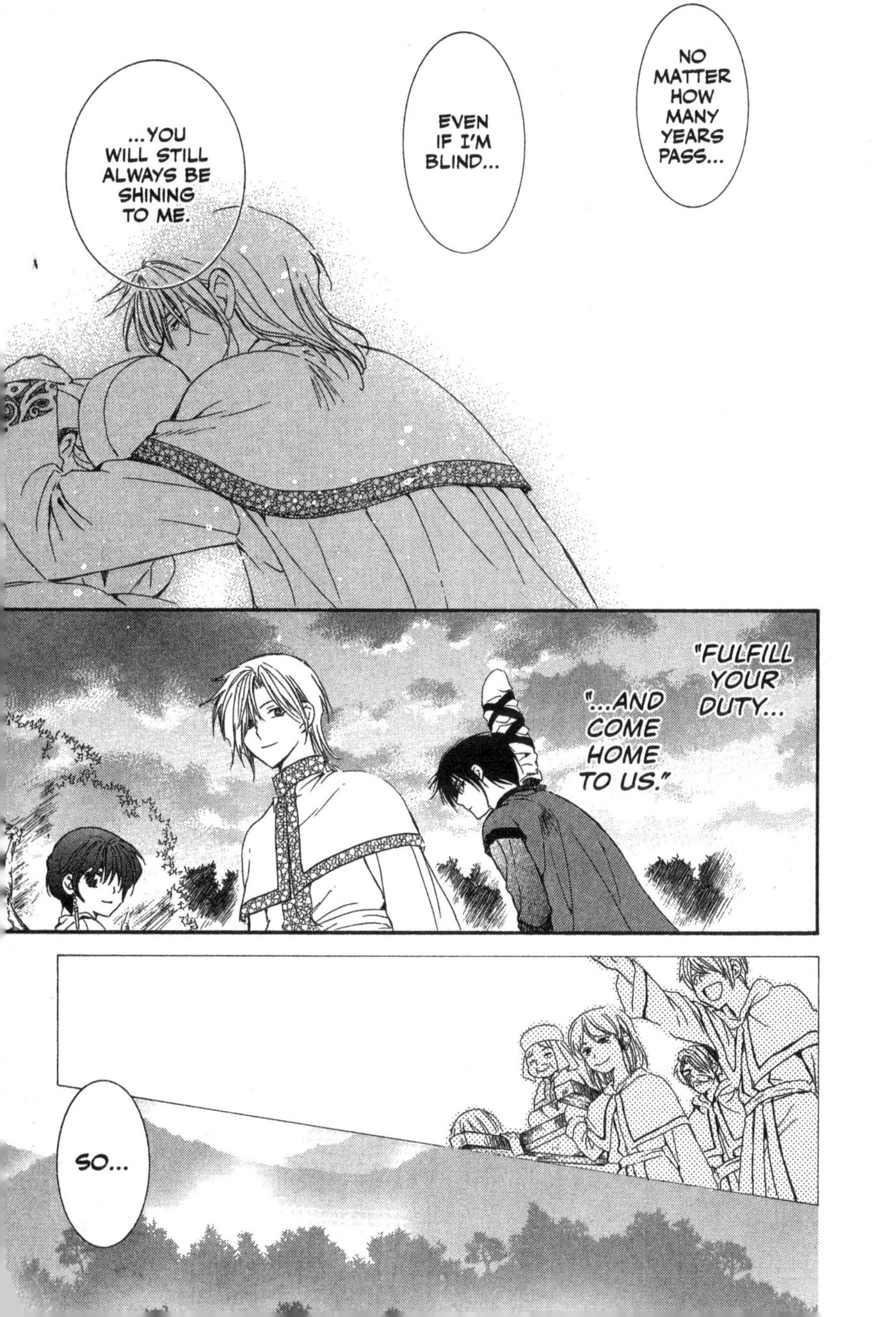
NO MATTER HOW MANY YEARS PASS...
EVEN IF I'M BLIND...
...YOU WILL STILL ALWAYS BE SHINING TO ME.
"FULFILL YOUR DUTY...
"...AND COME HOME TO US."
SO...

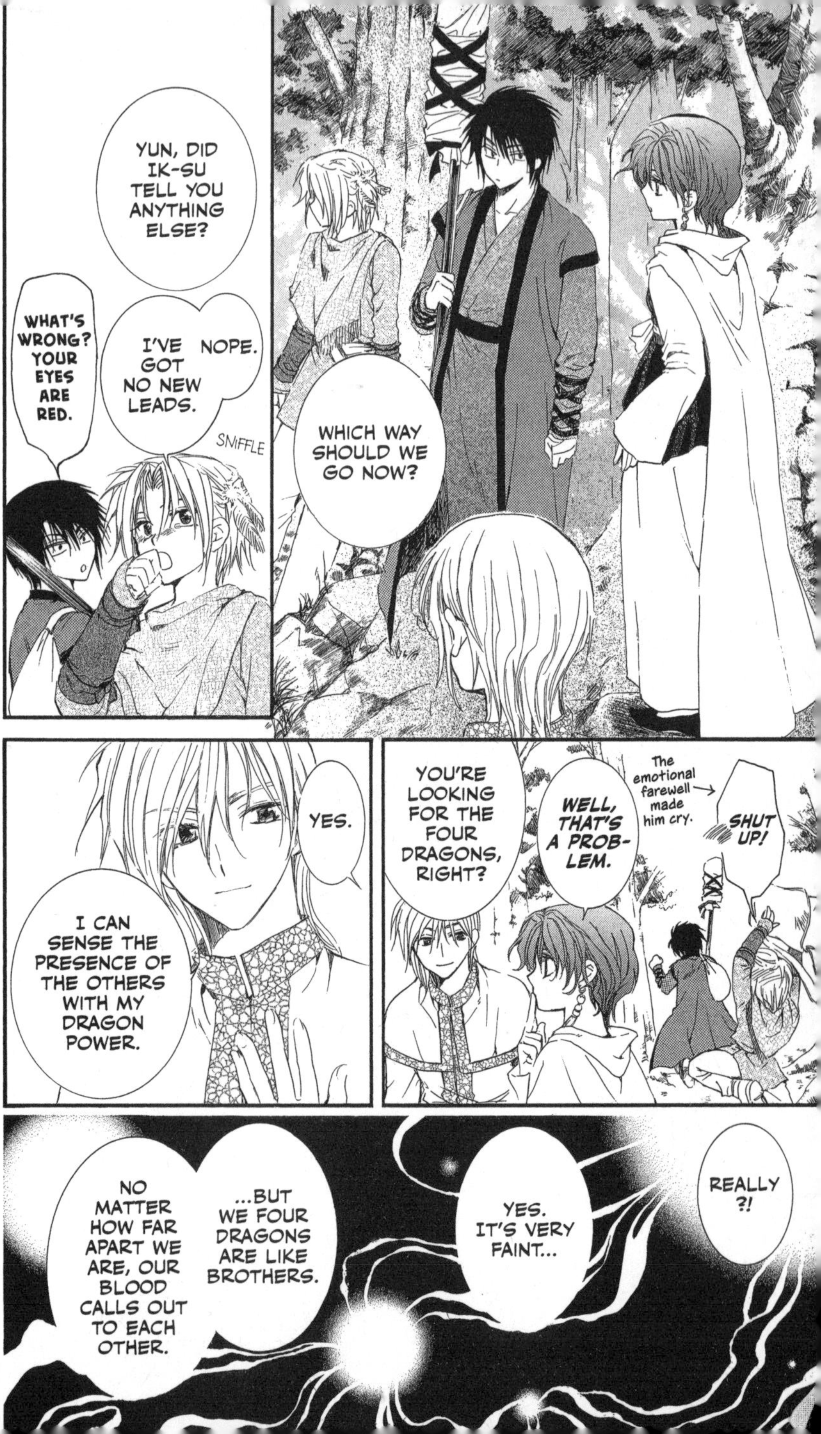
WHICH WAY SHOULD WE GO NOW?
YUN, DID IK-SU TELL YOU ANYTHING ELSE?
NOPE. I'VE GOT NO NEW LEADS.
SNIFFLE
WHAT'S WRONG? YOUR EYES ARE RED.
The emotional farewell made him cry.
SHUT UP!
WELL, THAT'S A PROB-LEM.
YOU'RE LOOKING FOR THE FOUR DRAGONS, RIGHT?
YES.
I CAN SENSE THE PRESENCE OF THE OTHERS WITH MY DRAGON POWER.
REALLY?!
YES. IT'S VERY FAINT...
...BUT WE FOUR DRAGONS ARE LIKE BROTHERS.
NO MATTER HOW FAR APART WE ARE, OUR BLOOD CALLS OUT TO EACH OTHER.

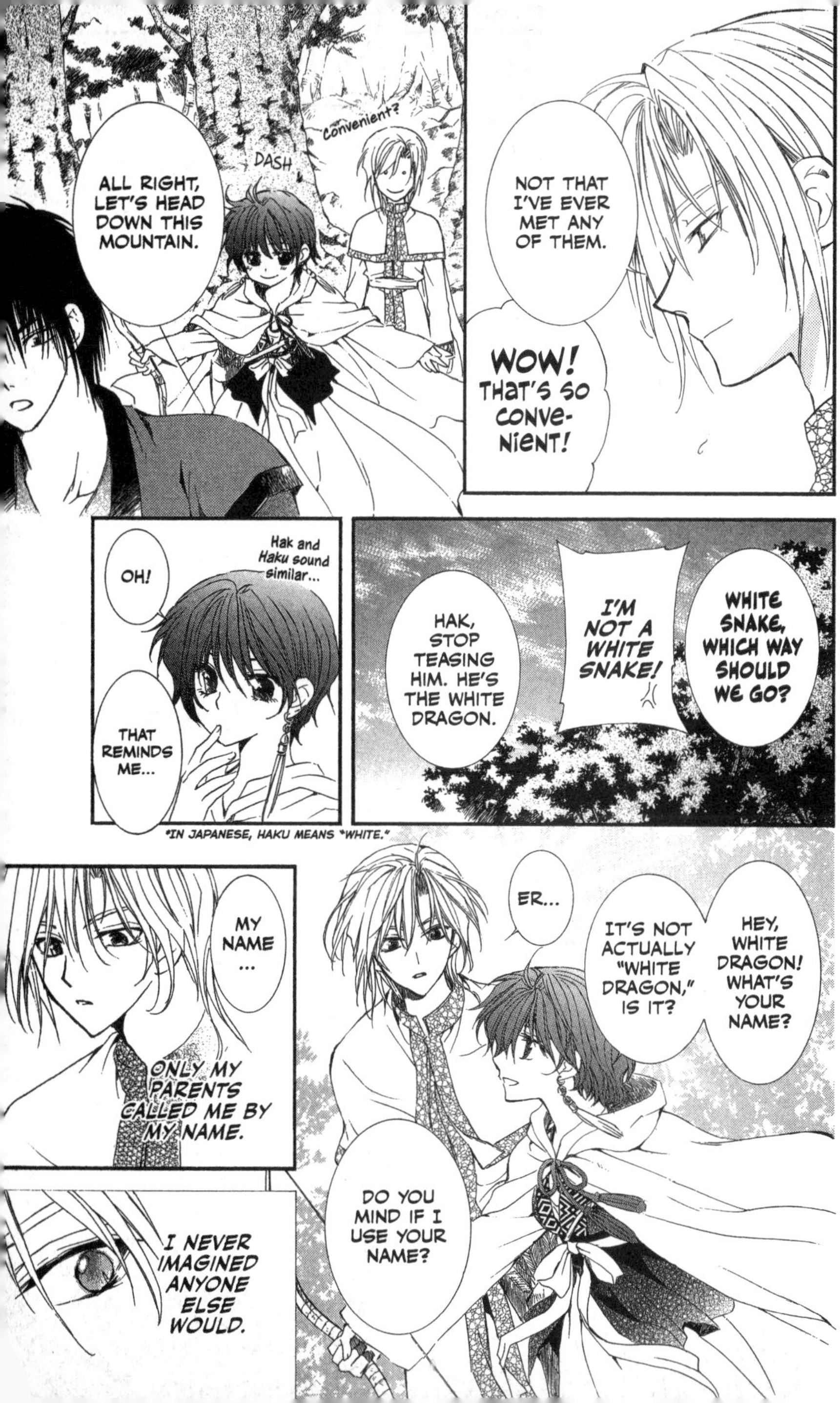
NOT THAT I'VE EVER MET ANY OF THEM.
WOW! THAT'S SO CONVE-NIENT!
ALL RIGHT, LET'S HEAD DOWN THIS MOUNTAIN.
DASH
Convenient?
WHITE SNAKE, WHICH WAY SHOULD WE GO?
I'M NOT A WHITE SNAKE!
HAK, STOP TEASING HIM. HE'S THE WHITE DRAGON.
OH!
Hak and Haku sound similar...
THAT REMINDS ME...
*IN JAPANESE, HAKU MEANS "WHITE."
HEY, WHITE DRAGON! WHAT'S YOUR NAME?
IT'S NOT ACTUALLY "WHITE DRAGON," IS IT?
ER...
DO YOU MIND IF I USE YOUR NAME?
MY NAME...
ONLY MY PARENTS CALLED ME BY MY NAME.
I NEVER IMAGINED ANYONE ELSE WOULD.

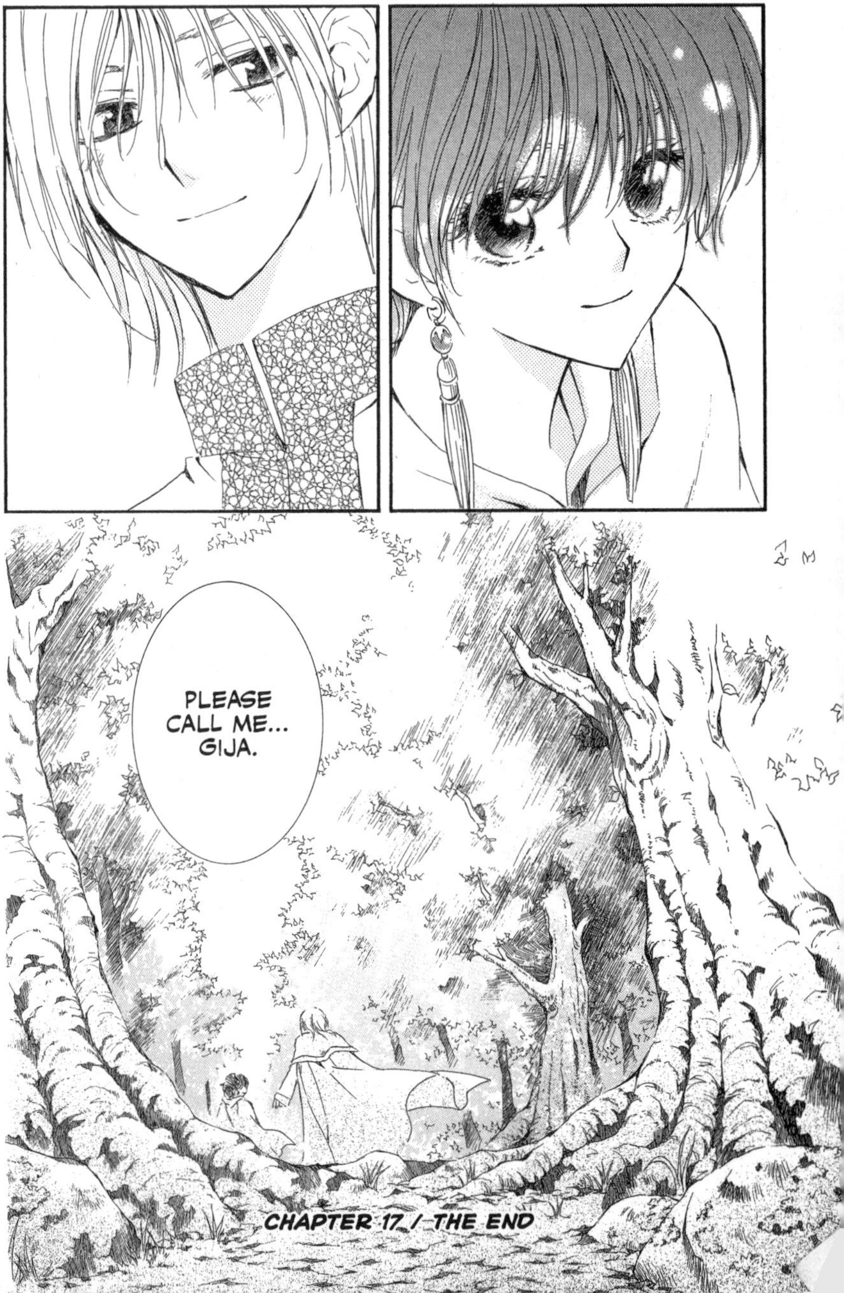
PLEASE CALL ME... GIJA.
CHAPTER 17 / THE END

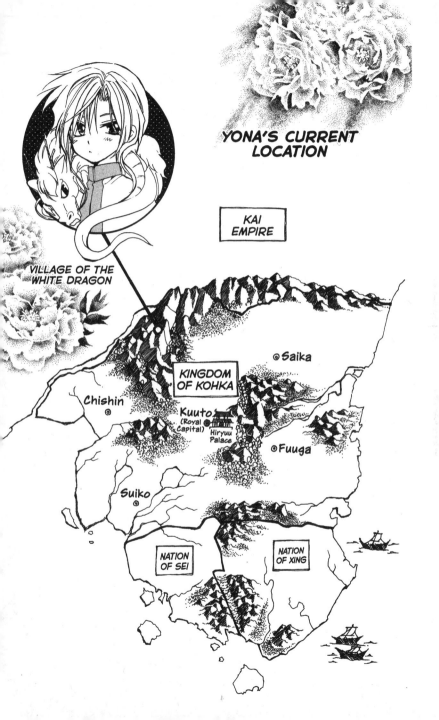

YONA'S CURRENT LOCATION

KAI EMPIRE

VILLAGE OF THE WHITE DRAGON

⊙ Saika

KINGDOM OF KOHKA

Chishin ⊙

Kuuto (Royal Capital) ⊙ Hiryuu Palace

⊙ Fuuga

Suiko ⊙

NATION OF SEI

NATION OF XING

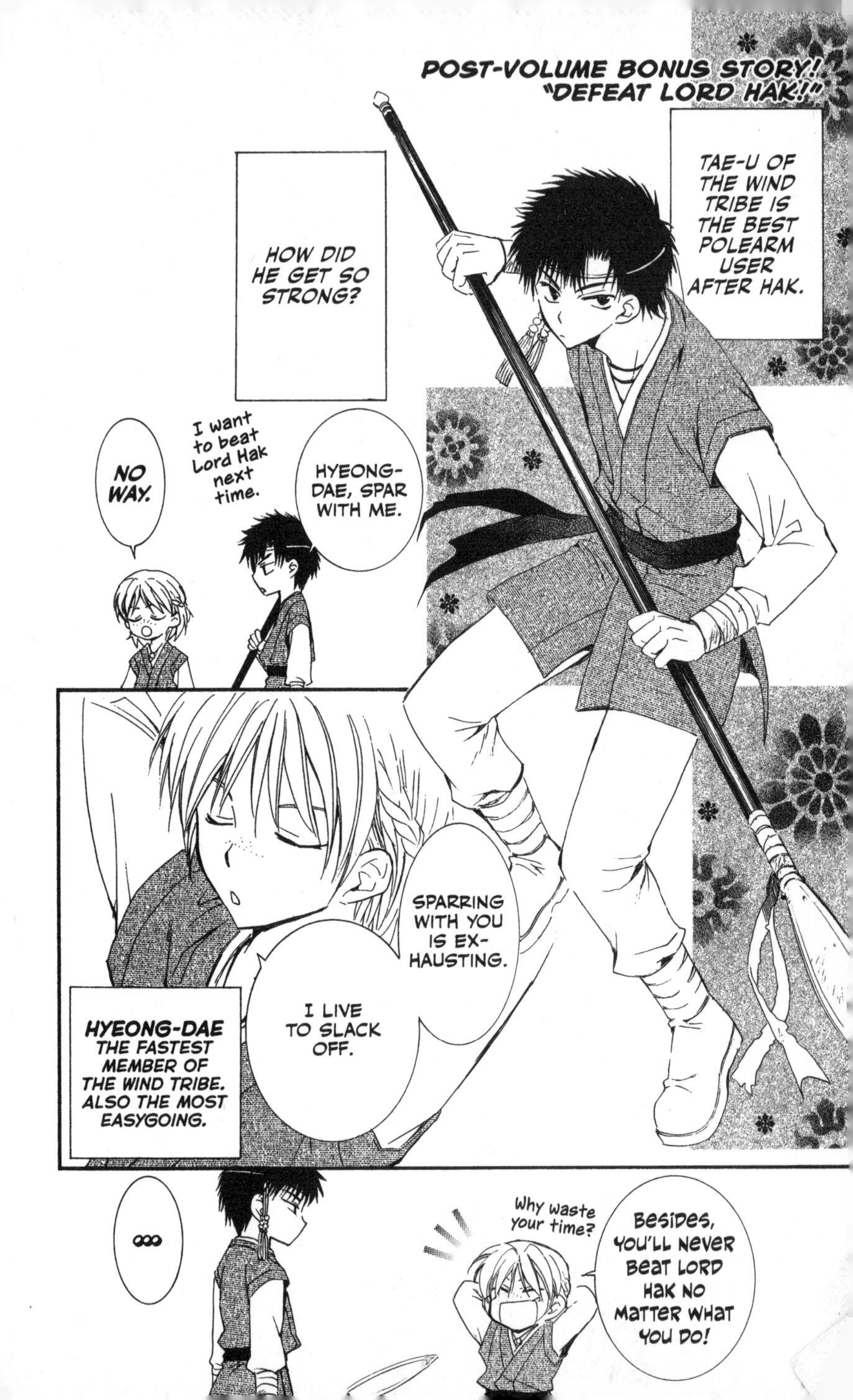
POST-VOLUME BONUS STORY! "DEFEAT LORD HAK!"
TAE-U OF THE WIND TRIBE IS THE BEST POLEARM USER AFTER HAK.
HOW DID HE GET SO STRONG?
HYEONG-DAE, SPAR WITH ME.
I want to beat Lord Hak next time.
NO WAY.
SPARRING WITH YOU IS EX-HAUSTING.
I LIVE TO SLACK OFF.
HYEONG-DAE THE FASTEST MEMBER OF THE WIND TRIBE. ALSO THE MOST EASYGOING.
Besides, you'll never beat Lord Hak no matter what you do!
Why waste your time?
...

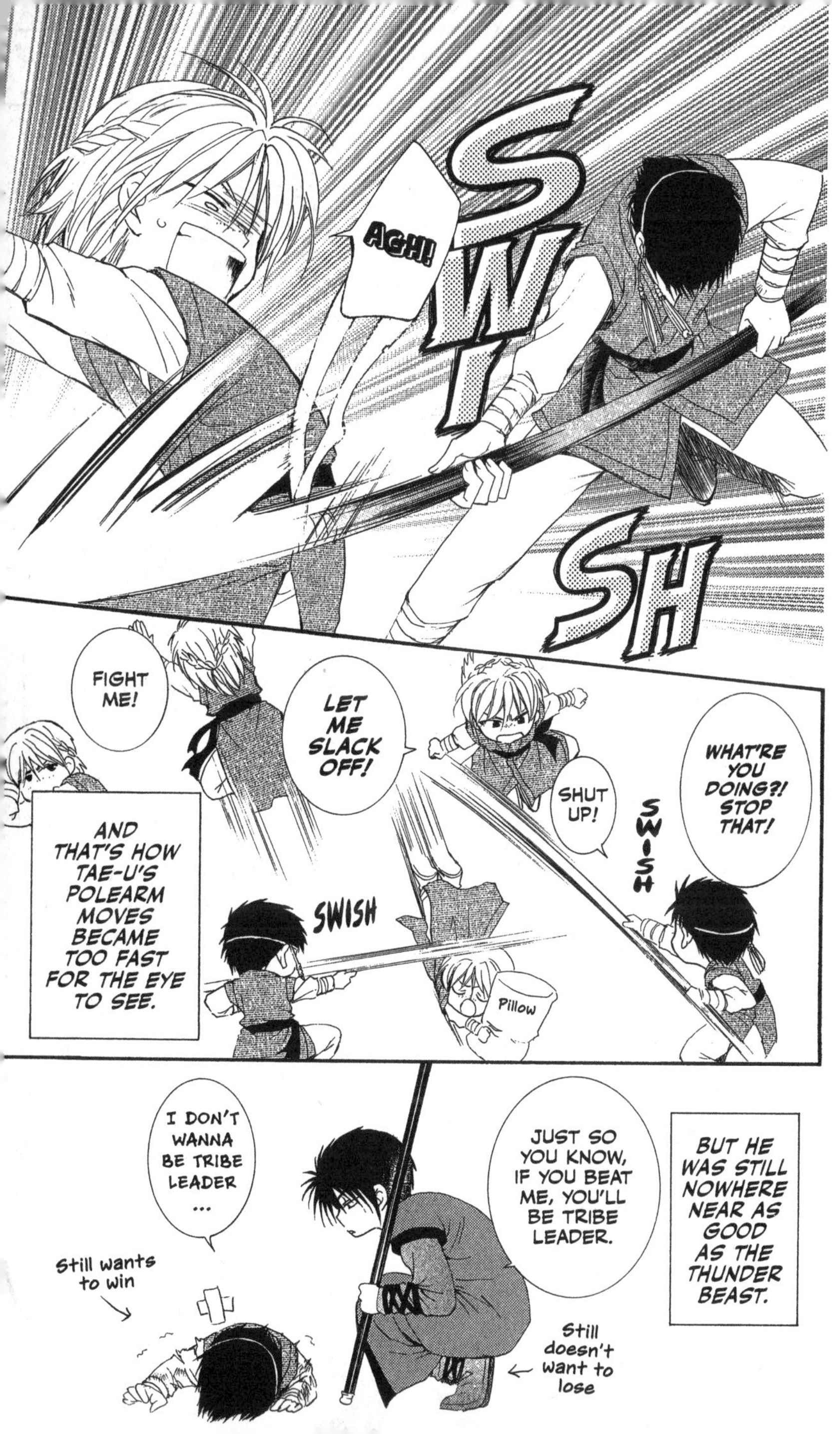
AGH!
SWISH
WHAT'RE YOU DOING?! STOP THAT!
SWISH
SHUT UP!
LET ME SLACK OFF!
FIGHT ME!
SWISH
Pillow
AND THAT'S HOW TAE-U'S POLEARM MOVES BECAME TOO FAST FOR THE EYE TO SEE.
BUT HE WAS STILL NOWHERE NEAR AS GOOD AS THE THUNDER BEAST.
JUST SO YOU KNOW, IF YOU BEAT ME, YOU'LL BE TRIBE LEADER.
I DON'T WANNA BE TRIBE LEADER ...
Still doesn't want to lose
Still wants to win

I hope to see you in volume 4.

Ik-su, age 26
Yun, age 8

Born on February 3 in Kumamoto
Prefecture in Japan, Mizuho Kusanagi
began her professional manga
career with *Yoiko no Kokoroe* (The
Rules of a Good Child) in 2003. Her
other works include *NG Life*, which
was serialized in *Hana to Yume* and
The Hana to Yume magazines and
published by Hakusensha in Japan.
Yona of the Dawn was adapted into an
anime in 2014.

YONA OF THE DAWN
VOL.3
Shojo Beat Edition

STORY AND ART BY
MIZUHO KUSANAGI

English Adaptation/Ysabet Reinhardt MacFarlane
Translation/JN Productions
Touch-Up Art & Lettering/Lys Blakeslee
Design/Yukiko Whitley
Editor/Amy Yu

Akatsuki no Yona by Mizuho Kusanagi
© Mizuho Kusanagi 2010
All rights reserved.
First published in Japan in 2010 by HAKUSENSHA, Inc., Tokyo.
English language translation rights arranged with
HAKUSENSHA, Inc., Tokyo.

Printed in the U.S.A.

Published by VIZ Media, LLC
P.O. Box 77010
San Francisco, CA 94107

10 9 8 7 6 5 4 3 2 1
First printing, December 2016

www.viz.com   www.shojobeat.com

Behind the Scenes!!

STORY AND ART BY **BISCO HATORI**

Ranmaru Kurisu comes from a family of hardy, rough-and-tumble fisherfolk and he sticks out at home like a delicate, artistic sore thumb. It's given him a raging inferiority complex and a permanently pessimistic outlook. Now that he's in college, he's hoping to find a sense of belonging. But after a whole life of being left out, does he even know how to fit in?!

This is the last page.

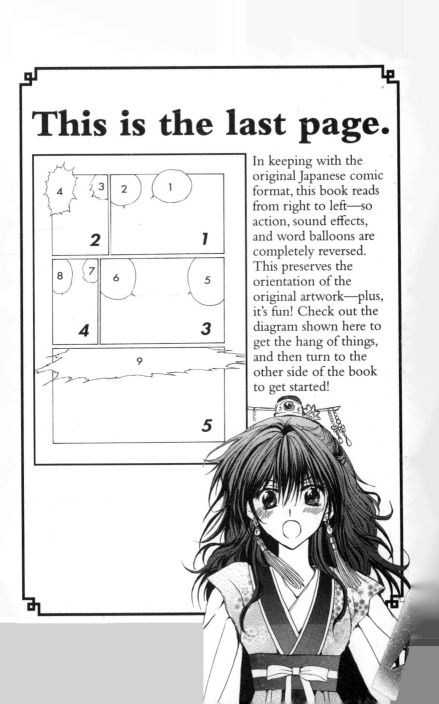

In keeping with the original Japanese comic format, this book reads from right to left—so action, sound effects, and word balloons are completely reversed. This preserves the orientation of the original artwork—plus, it's fun! Check out the diagram shown here to get the hang of things, and then turn to the other side of the book to get started!